46 STEP-BY-STEP
WOODEN TOY
PROJECTS

BY LEWIS H. HODGES

D1307293

L-28-2

Other TAB Books by the Author

No. 1315 *The Master Craftsman's Illustrated Woodworking Manual—with projects*
No. 1655 *The Woodturning Handbook, with Projects*

FIRST EDITION

FIRST PRINTING

Copyright © 1984 by TAB BOOKS Inc.
Printed in the United States of America

Library of Congress Cataloging in Publication Data

Hodges, Lewis H.
46 step-by-step wooden toy projects.

Includes index.
1. Wooden toy making. I. Title. II. Title: Forty-
six step-by-step wooden toy projects.
TT174.5.W6H63   1984   745.592   83-24384
ISBN 0-8306-0675-0
ISBN 0-8306-1675-6 (pbk.)

Cover photograph by the Ziegler photography studio.
Cover illustration by Larry Selman.

Contents

Acknowledgments

Many of the following suppliers/manufacturers have provided invaluable assistance to me by supplying catalogs, patterns, plans, kits, instructions, and valuable hints for making wooden toys. I owe them a debt of gratitude. Addresses for these companies can be found in Appendix A.

Amor Products
Craftsman Wood Service Co.
J. Lewman, Toymaker
L.L. Enterprizes
Love-Built Toys and Crafts
Makin' Things
Mayco Sales
Small World Toys
Week End Enterprises
Woodcraft Supply Co.
The Wooden Toy
Woodworks

The following companies granted me permission to reproduce some or all of their projects in this book. Due to space limitations, however, not all of their projects are included.

Cherry Tree Toys
Craft Value Center
Criss-Cross Creations
Design Group
Hayes Patterns
Sleepy's Toys
Stanley Tools
Toys by Leroy
Toy Designs
Uncle Andy's Scrapwood Toys

Introduction

Why wooden toys? Because wood is more durable and more pleasant to the touch than are metal, plastics, and other materials. Wood is warm to the touch, not cold like metal. If wooden toys are homemade, they are far less expensive than other materials. Furthermore, because wood is durable, wooden toys often become heirlooms.

Commercial toy packaging is often more expensive than the toy itself. Much of the detail, decorations, bright paint, and advertising is intended to appeal to the adult who makes the purchase, not the child who will play with it. Most children do not care about these elements. Witness how they play with simple blocks of scrap wood with no decoration whatsoever. The imagination of children is endless; simplicity is the watchword. When an outline or decoration is considered necessary, however, it is better to use a wood-burning tool than paint.

Safety is of paramount importance, both in the use of tools and in the use of the toy. All sharp edges of the toy should be rolled or rounded off. All metal parts, such as nails and screws, should be kept to a minimum. Be sure that the finish applied is non-toxic.

Subdued earth colors seem to have more lasting appeal to youngsters than the glaringly bright colors that often attract adults. Combinations of differently colored woods will achieve this objective. Only transparent finishes should be used on such combinations as maple, cherry, walnut, mahogany, and the exotic woods, such as teak, zebrawood, bubinga, ebony, padauk, rosewood, and purpleheart. Many penetrating finishes can be used with safety, but only after complete *polymerization,* or stabilization of chemicals, has taken place, which may take as long as six weeks. Probably clear spray Deft is one of the safest finishes in that the toy can be used after only a few hours of drying. Toys that are apt to go into a child's mouth, such as a rattle, should be treated with several coats of mineral oil. If colors are to be used on toys, let the child be the selector and judge of the colors. Even when opaque colors are used, it is a good idea to leave the natural wood show in some areas.

The adult benefits should not be overlooked in

toymaking. Often the adult derives more pleasure from the making of a toy than the child does in playing with it.

Although there are a multitude of patterns, plans, ideas, and kits from which to choose, you will derive the greatest pleasure and satisfaction by using them as ideas for creating toys of your own.

The true test of a wooden toy is the length of time that a child uses and cherishes it.

You should make every effort to involve your child in the project. There are many operations, such as sanding, gluing, clamping, and assembling, that a child can perform. Working together will enhance your relationship. Keep in mind that no matter how poorly a toy turns out, a child will not only cherish it as a toy, but will also be constantly reminded of the time when you worked together, and thoroughly enjoyed yourselves in the process.

Keep in mind when designing toys that a full-size paper drawing will never appear quite as large as the real three-dimensional object. It is a good idea, therefore, to cut rough pieces out of scrap stock to ascertain the appearance before cutting the pieces of expensive lumber.

Another important aspect is the grip span of a child's hand. Toys that are too thick are difficult for a child to handle comfortably.

Generally animal toys are designed squattier, plumper, shorter, and with larger feet and paws, ears, and eyes than their real counterparts.

Toy parts should be temporarily assembled without glue to determine if there are some last minute adjustments that should be made. In some cases, it is possible to make changes after the glue is applied.

The maker of wooden toys should fully realize the difference between toymaking and miniature making. Miniatures are generally much smaller and are executed in great detail. Miniatures generally wind up in dollhouses or in a collection. Some miniatures are displayed in shadow boxes. At times they are moved about within the dollhouse and in this sense could be considered toys, but they are much too fragile to be roughly used on a daily basis.

1

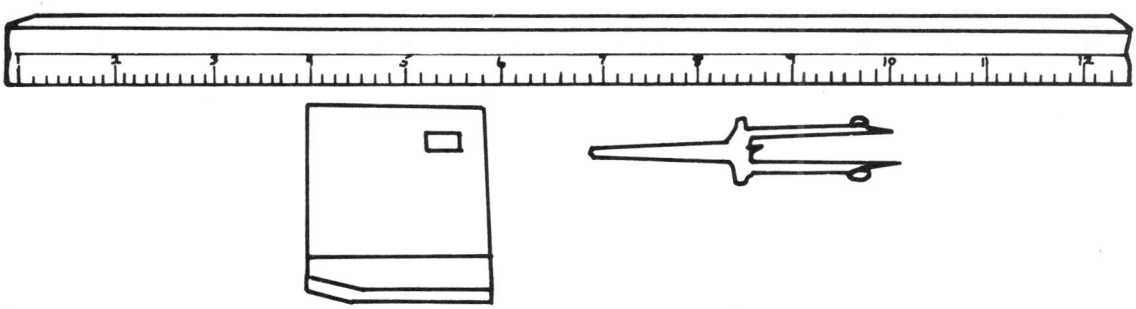

Tools, Materials, and Components

You do not need a multitude of tools to make wooden toys. Simple hand tools found around the home generally suffice, although a few power tools, such as a small electric hand drill and a saber saw or jigsaw, speed up construction.

As a maker of wooden toys you should, early in the process, determine to what extent you will construct the toys. The craftsman with a well-equipped power tool workshop can make practically everything required. Many components, such as wheels of various sizes and shapes, engine smokestacks, headlights, axles, and "people," are available at moderate prices for the craftsman with only a minimum number of hand tools.

HAND TOOLS

The two main categories of hammers most generally used in woodworking and carpentry are the claw hammer and the ripping, or straight claw, hammer.

The size of a claw hammer is indicated by weight, which ranges from 1 to 20 ounces. A 10-ounce hammer is about right for the wood toy-maker; a smaller one for backup, such as a 7-ounce claw hammer, tack hammer, or upholsterer's hammer will, however, come in handy at times.

Wooden or plastic mallets are used considerably for driving in dowels or forcing jointed parts together. Never use a metal hammer for this purpose since it will bruise the fibers of the wood.

A special type of mallet is the carving mallet. The small sizes that weigh 16 or 18 ounces are the best for the average craftsman. The best carving mallets are made of lignum vitae and beechwood.

The brad driver is not a true pounding tool, but it can be used like a hammer to drive brads and small finishing nails (Fig. 1-1).

Sawing Tools

Ripsaw. The teeth on a ripsaw are like little chisels. They take out large rectangular chunks of wood. The ripsaw is used to cut with the grain, never across it.

The channel or slit that is cut out by the teeth

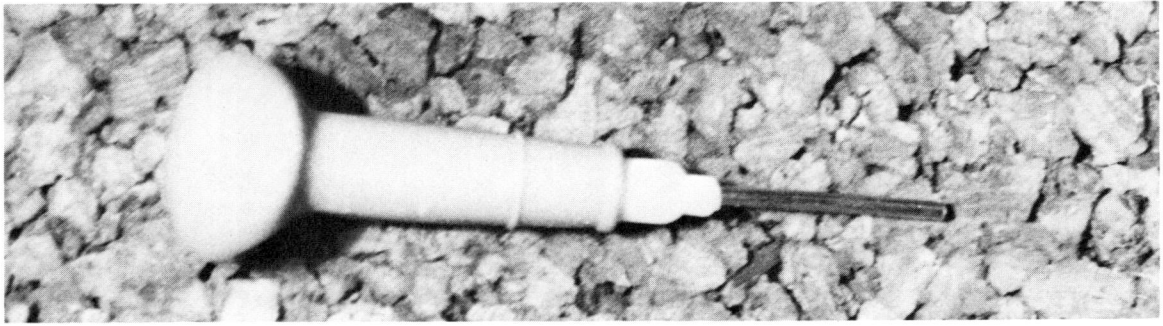

Fig. 1-1. Brad driver.

of any saw is called the *kerf*. Alternate teeth are pointed in opposite directions to prevent the saw from binding in the cut.

Ripsaws have larger teeth than other handsaws, and the number of points per inch is generally 5 1/2. There is one more point per inch than there are teeth. The recommended length of the ripsaw is 26 inches (Fig. 1-2).

Crosscut Saw. The crosscut saw, sometimes called a *panel saw,* is used to cut across the grain. The teeth are knife- or wedge-shaped, and the points are very sharp and pointed.

The crosscut saw has many more points per inch than the ripsaw. They range from 8 to 12 points per inch (Fig. 1-3). The 10-point saw is probably the most often used. In length, the crosscut saw runs from 20 to 26 inches.

From time to time the saw blade should be checked with a try square to see if the blade is sawing perpendicular to the wood.

Sawing should always be on the waste or surplus side of the line. The first and last strokes should be short; otherwise you should use long, easy strokes. Keep moderate, not excessive pressure on the saw. Short strokes at the end will prevent splintering off before the sawing is completed. Be sure to hold the surplus stock as you near the end of sawing; if you don't, the weight of the piece will cause splintering near the end of the cut.

Backsaw. The backsaw is used for fine, accurate cabinetwork. It is called a backsaw because it features a steel stiffener along its back opposite the teeth. The blade is very thin, and the teeth are smaller than the teeth on a crosscut saw. The length

of the saw is generally 12 or 14 inches.

Dovetail Saw. The dovetail saw is specially designed to make fine cuts (Fig. 1-4). It is extensively used for handmade dovetail joints. It can cut both with and across the grain. The dovetail saw has

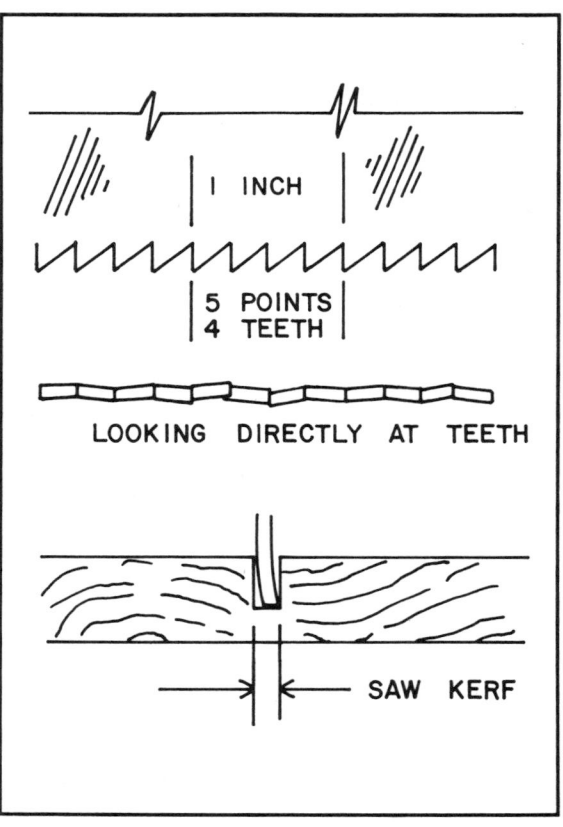

Fig. 1-2. Measurement of ripsaw teeth is shown, as well as the kerf made by the teeth.

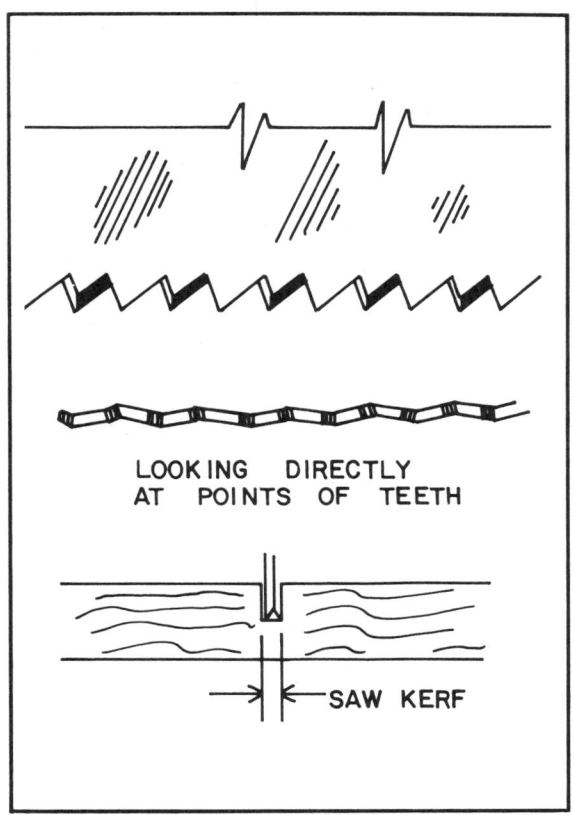

LOOKING DIRECTLY
AT POINTS OF TEETH

SAW KERF

Fig. 1-3. Measurement of crosscut saw teeth is shown, as well as the kerf made by the teeth.

smaller teeth and a thinner blade than the backsaw. The handle on a dovetail saw is similar to a file or chisel handle; the handle on a backsaw is identical with the handle on a ripsaw or crosscut saw.

Razor Saw. The razor saw is especially useful in making small toys and miniatures (Fig. 1-5). X-Acto manufactures a number of fine-tooth saw blades ranging in width from 3/4 to 1 1/4 inches and with teeth numbering up to 70 per inch. An angled shank on the blade fits into a collet on a plastic handle.

Starting cuts with this saw are best made toward the user—that is, on the backward stroke.

Small strips, moldings, and dowels are held in a miter box for sawing to length with the razor saw. The long pieces should be held against the side of the miter box next to the user.

Compass Saw. The compass saw is designed to cut interior holes after the blade is inserted through a drilled or bored hole. It will cut interior curves of large radii, but the coping saw or saber is best adapted for that purpose. The compass saw is able to cut exterior curves, but certainly not with the efficiency of the band saw.

Keyhole Saw. The keyhole saw has a shorter blade and a sharper point at the end than the compass saw. Obviously, the saw was designed to make keyholes. Some keyhole saws have a pistol grip, while others have a handle similar to a file or chisel handle.

Coping Saw. You can use a coping saw to cut short radii and exterior and interior curves by inserting the blade through a drilled hole (Figs. 1-6 and 1-7). The coping saw has considerable trouble sawing stock over 1/2-inch thick, however. The blade in a coping saw may be turned from one side to the other, without turning the handle. The home craftsman uses the coping saw with the teeth pointed toward the handle. The work is held in a horizontal position on a V block sawing bracket, and the sawing is done near the point of the V.

The carpenter uses the coping saw with the teeth pointed away from the handle in coping mold-

Fig. 1-4. Dovetail saw.

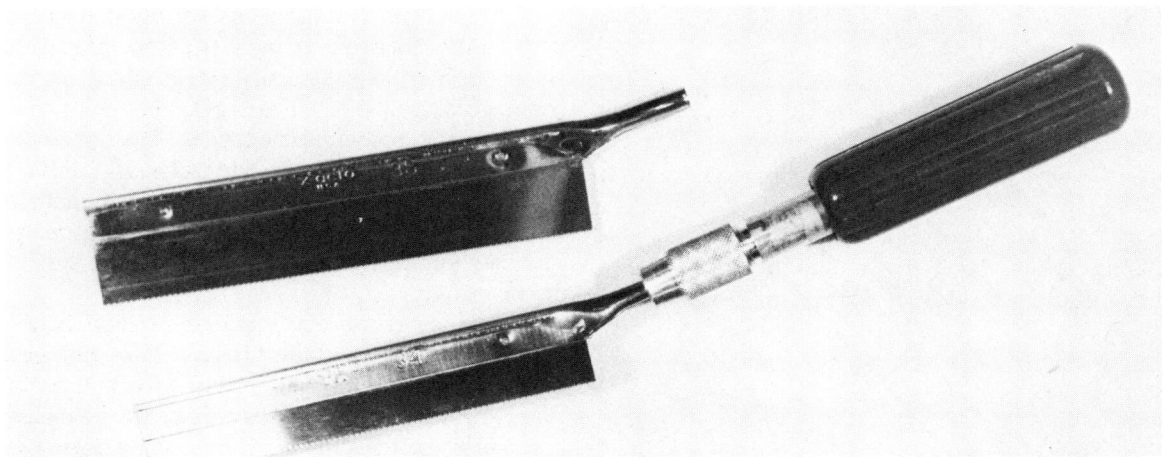

Fig. 1-5. Razor saw.

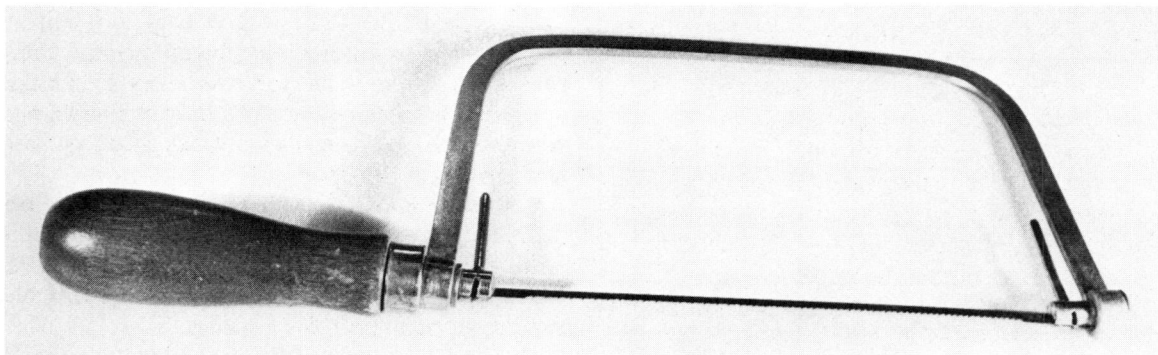

Fig. 1-6. Coping saw.

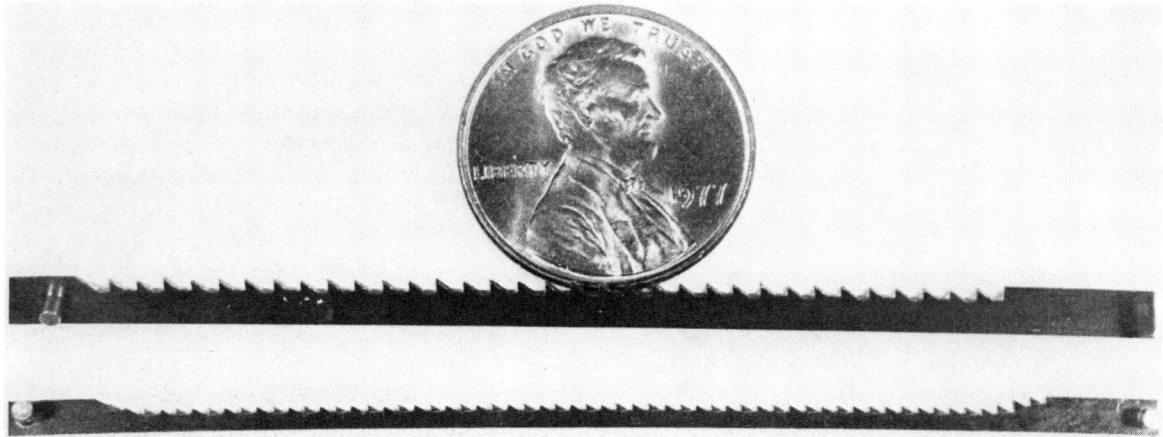

Fig. 1-7. Coping saw and jigsaw blades.

ings which are placed in the corners of ceilings or floors in a building.

Planing Tools

No matter which plane is used to plane end grain, certain precautions should be taken to prevent the splitting of the wood.

☐ Plane toward the center of the board from both ways.

☐ Cut a small 45-degree chamfer in the waste stock.

☐ Put a piece of scrap stock behind the piece to be planed and secure both pieces at the same height in a vise. In this way the splitting will take place on the scrap piece.

Block Plane. The block plane differs from other planes in several aspects. It is designed to be used in one hand; there are very few parts in this small plane, and the plane, or cutting, iron is set much lower than others. The bevel of the cutting edge is turned up instead of down, and the block plane is used to plane end grain.

Jack Plane. The jack plane is an all-purpose plane that can be used for many purposes. You might call it the "jack-of-all-trades" plane. If you can only afford one plane, this is the one to purchase.

The jack plane is usually 14 inches long with a 2-inch-wide blade. There are 18 parts to a jack plane compared to only 3 for the block plane. The plane iron can be easily shifted so that it will not cut too deeply on either cutting corner.

Fore Plane. The fore plane is generally 18 inches long with a plane iron somewhat wider than that found on a standard jack plane. Boards are often jointed on the edge with the fore plane before being glued together. It is used to some extent on the face of large stock.

Jointer Plane. As its name suggests, the jonter plane is used almost exclusively for jointing edges of boards. Lengths of jointer planes run from 22 inches upward to nearly 3 feet.

Smoothing Plane. The smoothing plane looks like a chopped off jack plane. The bed is much shorter and extends only to the back of the handle. Smoothing planes are 8 to 9 inches long and are used for smoothing surfaces.

This plane is especially useful on small pieces. it should be kept very sharp, with the plane iron very close to the plane-iron cap to produce a small, silky shaving almost of the same quality as that produced by a well-sharpened scraper.

Router Plane. The router plane differs radically from all of the previous planes. It has two round, identical handles and an oblong base with a narrow, adjustable knife extending through the base between the handles.

The router plane is used to smooth the bottom of rabbets, grooves, and dadoes. You will have limited use for this tool in making wooden toys.

Rabbet Planes. There are a number of planes for cutting rabbets. One plane can be used with either the left or right hand. On the bullnose rabbet plane, the plane iron is near the front and extends across the whole plane.

A combination plane can be used both for regular and bullnose planing. *Bullnosing* is the process of smoothing the bottom of a cut, such as a rabbet, dado, or groove, that does not extend all the way across a piece of stock.

Spokeshave. The spokeshave was originally used to make spokes for a wheel. You can use it effectively for rounding corners of stock and for cutting chamfers. It can also get into places that would be impossible for a plane.

The spokeshave has two winglike handles and a plane iron which cuts in the same fashion as a plane.

Universal Plane. The universal plane is designed to do all kinds of planing jobs, including making moldings. A universal plane is a rather expensive tool and one that is hard to keep sharpened and adjusted. The biggest objection, however, is that it is rather difficult to use. Money spent on this tool might better be spent on a power router which will do the same job faster and better.

Circular Plane. The circular plane has a flexible, steel spring bed and is designed to plane both convex and concave curves to many sizes.

Drilling and Boring Tools

Auger Bits. Auger bits are used for boring holes in wood. They are available in sizes from 1/4 to 1 1/4 inches in diameter. Sizes are indicated by a number indented on the *tang*—the square part of the bit which fits into the brace. This number designates the size in 1/16 inch. A number 6 on the tang identifies a 3/8- or 6/16-inch bit.

A small tapered screw, called a *feed screw*, on the tip of the bit pulls the bit into the wood so that the *spurs*, or knifelike projections, can cut the outline of the circle. The cutting edges cut away the remainder of the hole, the pieces of which follow up the twist of the bit.

Auger bits are of two kinds: *single twist* and *double twist*. The double twist is considered the best for boring easily and for making smooth, clean holes.

The depth of the hole can be roughly estimated by counting the number of turns that the bit makes. Each turn of the bit will pull the bit into the wood approximately 1/16 inch.

Drill Bits. Drill bits are used for drilling both metal and wood. They are available in fractional and letter sizes. Fractional sizes run from 1/32 to 1/2 inch in increments of 1/64 inches. Letter sizes are available in sizes from 1/4 to 1/2 inch where fractional sizes are not applicable. Fractional sizes, however, are usually adequate for all wood drilling.

Bits used exclusively for wood drilling have sharper points than bits used exclusively for metal drilling.

Spade Bits. Spade bits are used for boring wood. The flat, spade-shaped bits are available in sizes from 1/4 to 1 inch in increments of 1/16 inches. The shanks of all spade bits are round and 1/4 inch in diameter; so they can be used in portable electric drills. Spade bits bore faster and cleaner than many other bits. They are ideal for the home craftsman.

Expansion Bits. Expansion bits are available in two sizes: those that bore holes from 5/8 to 1 3/4 inches and those that bore holes from 7/8 to 3 inches in diameter. One type of expansion bit has a micrometer dial that gives precision boring to 1/1000 inch. It also has a depth gauge which instantly shows how deeply the hole has been bored.

The expansion bit is more difficult to use than the spade bit because it has a square tang which

allows it to be used only in a brace. When boring larger holes of 2 to 3 inches, it is almost impossible to turn the brace.

The expansion bit is not a good purchase for the home craftsman.

Multispur Bits. The multispur bit has a 1/4-inch round shank; so it may be used in a portable electric drill. It is a very fast, clean-boring bit. It will bore a portion of a circle on the edge of a piece of wood, something other bits cannot do. In addition, it will bore at an angle, overlapping, or on close centers without splitting the wood. It also works very well on veneer stock without tearing.

Multispur bits are available in sizes from 1/2- to 1-inch increments of 1/16 inches, and in sizes from 1 to 1 1/4 inches in increments of 1/8 inches.

Forstner Bits. Forstner bits are available in sizes from 3/8 to 1 inch in increments of 1/16 inches. Sizes stamped on the shank are the same as those stamped on auger bits. There are also Forstner bits available in sizes from 1 1/4 to 2 inches in increments of 1/4 inches.

Forstner bits are used for counterboring and, like the multispur, will bore a hole close to or on the edge of stock without tearing. It will bore nearly through wood without the spurs or feed screw coming through and puncturing the reverse side of the stock.

Dowel Bits. The dowel bit is simply a shortened auger bit for boring dowel holes and is much easier to hold perpendicular to the work. A dowel bit is also advantageous to use whenever a shorter bit would do the job better than the standard auger bit.

Router Drill Bits. The router drill bit can be used in a fashion similar to the saber. It cuts its own hole and can move from there in any direction. A router drill bit is ideal for making small, irregularly shaped holes.

Combination Wood Drill and Countersink. The combination wood drill and countersink performs three operations at one time: it drills a pilot hole for the spiral part of a wood screw; it drills a shank hole, and it countersinks so that the top of a flathead screw will fit flush with the wood. It is especially helpful where speed and mass production are needed. It would be a luxury and not a necessity for the average home craftsman. It comes in various sizes, from 3/4-inch No. 6 to 2-inch No. 12. (The first number indicates the length of the screw, and the second number gives the wire size of the shank.)

Plug Cutter. The plug cutter is a short, hollow bit which cuts short dowels to cover the heads of counterbored screws. It is available in 3/8-, 1/2- and 5/8-inch diameter sizes. With a plug cutter you can make short dowels of the same wood as the project, rather than needing to reply on the standard commercial birch dowel.

Countersink Bits. The most commonly used countersink is sometimes called the rose countersink because it has many flutes around the conical point which bores a recess for the screw heads.

This bit has two types of shanks: one with a square shank to use in a brace, the other with a round shank to use with a hand drill, portable electric drill, or drill press.

Circle-Cutter Bits or Fly Cutters. The circle cutter or fly cutter is a tool for cutting holes in thin metal, plastic, or wood up to 8 inches in diameter. It can be used for making wheels for wooden toys. A small drill bit starts the hole and a cutter on an adjustable arm cuts the outside circumference. The circle cutter is available with either a square or round shank.

Hole Saw. The hole saw is used in a similar fashion to the circle-cutter bit. It is ideal for making wheels for wooden toys. Blade segments of different sizes fit into grooves in the head and are held in place by set screws (Fig. 1-8). The center drill, which is 1/4 inch in diameter, is the same size as most axles used with wheels on toys. After the blank wheels are cut out with the hole saw, they are placed on a lathe faceplate jig.

The jig is constructed of a circular piece of wood and fastened to the faceplate with flathead screws (Fig. 1-9). A 1/4-inch drill bit is then placed in a Jacobs chuck, and the Morris tapered end is placed in the tailstock. With the lathe running, the drill bit is advanced into the wood faceplate. A hole is drilled completely through the wood faceplate. A 1/4-inch birch dowel about 1 3/8 inches long is glued into the wood faceplate, and the point is tapered to a blunt, round point with coarse sandpaper while the lathe is running. Three or four small brads are then driven into the wood faceplate about 3/4 inch from the dowel. The heads of the brads are snipped off and given a sharp point with a file. When the wheel blank is driven onto the jig with a mallet, the sharp points engage the wheel blank. The wheel can then be shaped to any desirable form with the lathe-cutting tools with no danger of the wheel sliding around on the dowel.

Auger Bit Brace. Auger bit braces can be used with a boring or drilling bit that has a square tang. Sizes available are 8, 10, and 12 inches—the

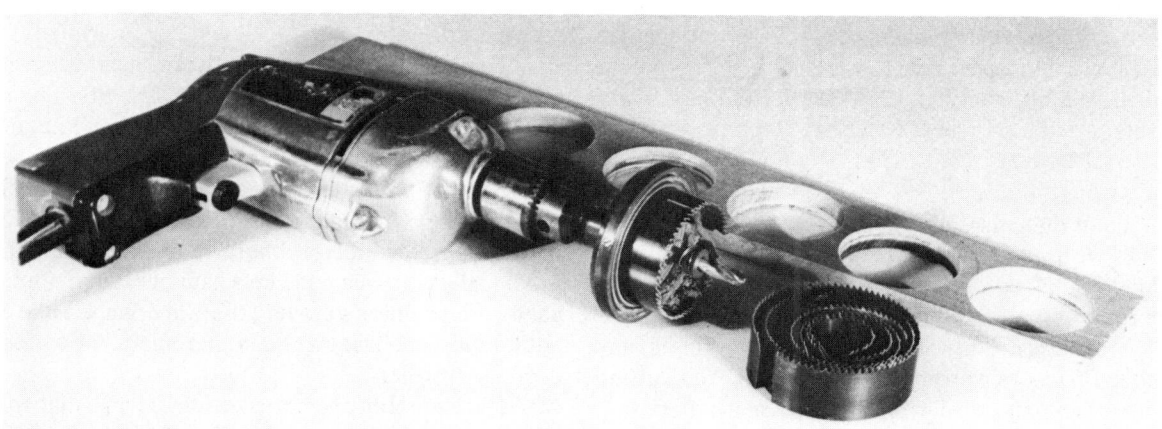

Fig. 1-8. Hole saw.

Fig. 1-9. A faceplate wheel shaping jig is shown. One-half inch fir plywood was used.

diameter of the circle made by turning the handle. Present-day braces are equipped with a ratchet which allows them to be used in cramped areas.

Hand Drill. The hand drill is built to handle round shank drill bits 1/4 inch in diameter and less. It is an indispensable tool to the home craftsman, particularly if a portable electric drill is not available.

Breast Drill. The breast drill is an oversized hand drill that can use bits up to 1/2 inch in diameter. It has a breast plate for the operator to lean on to apply more pressure to the drill bit. The breast drill is a necessity where electricity is not available.

Chiseling Tools

Each of the chisel blades below is used in conjunction with a specialized task. The thickness of the blade depends on the chore it is required to perform.

Firmer Chisel. The firmer chisel is any chisel that has a straight cutting edge. The cutting edge face on a firmer chisel is perfectly flat.

Gouge. The gouge is any chisel with a round or U-shaped cross section. Hand gouges are inside or outside ground and are straight across the cutting edge. Lathe-turning gouges are outside ground only, and the cutting edge is rounded.

Bevel-Edge Chisel. The bevel-edge chisel blade is easier to use because of the visibility it provides. It also is lighter in weight. Most firmer chisels have bevel edges.

Straight-Edge Chisel. Straight-edge chisels are used where great strength is required. The mortise chisel is a good example of a type of straight-edge chisel.

Tang Handle. Chisels with tang handles have a long, sharply pointed projection that fits into a handle with a metal ferrule. Mallets should never be used with tang-handle chisels or gouges.

Socket Handle. The socket-handle chisel will withstand considerable abuse and is often used with wood, rawhide, rubber, or plastic mallets. Most mallets are shaped like a hammer, but mallets used with sculptor's carving tools are shaped like a potato masher. The steel hammer should never be used as a mallet.

Pocket Handle. Pocket-handle chisels are built for extremely hard usage. The blade and shank are forged in one piece which extends through the

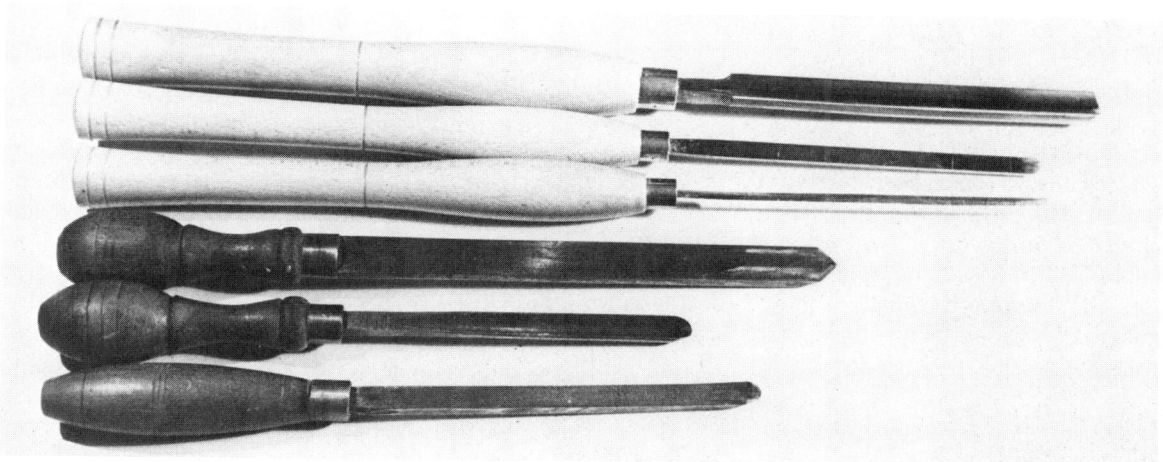

Fig. 1-10. Lathe, or turning, chisels.

handle to a steel cap on the noncutting end.

Butt Chisel. The butt chisel is a firmer chisel with a short blade. It is a general purpose chisel with both tang and socket handles. Most butt chisels have bevel edges.

Mortise Chisel. The mortise chisel is a socket-handled, narrow, straight-edge, long, thick-bladed chisel used for cutting mortises.

Turning Chisel. The lathe-turning tools are quite different from other chisels (Fig. 1-10). The handles are much longer and somewhat smaller in diameter. All turning chisels and gouges have tang

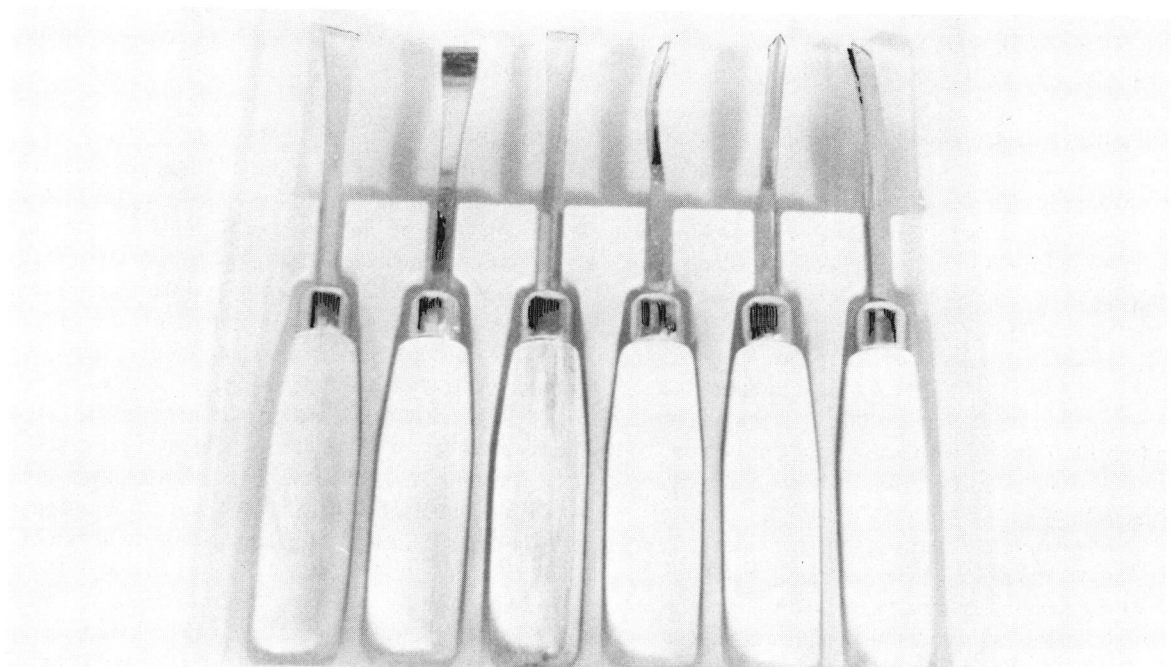

Fig. 1-11. X-Acto beginner's wood-carving chisels.

handles, and the tang fits into a ferruled handle.

Chisels used for turning are: the full skew, full and half roundnose, diamond point, parting tool, and gouge.

Carving Chisel. Carving tools are used for surface decoration and sculpturing (Fig. 1-11). The tools include: the skew, the parting tool, the fishtail chisel, the firmer chisel, the corner chisel, the front bent chisel, the veining tools, the straight gouge, the "U" gouge, the medium gouge, the narrow gouge, the shallow gouge, the spoon gouge, and the wide swing gouge.

Scraping Tools

Hand Scraper. The hand scraper is a thin, rectangular piece of flexible steel varying in size from 2 1/2 × 5 inches to 3 × 6 inches.

Handle Scraper. The handle scraper is a highly advertised commercial product that is held in rather low esteem by cabinetmakers. When in use it has two hooked cutting edges that can be reversed to form two more cutting edges. Blades are usually 2 1/2 inches wide. It is difficult to keep sharpened.

Cabinet Scraper. The cabinet scraper looks like an enlarged spokeshave. The blade is usually 2 3/4 inches wide. It is the best scraper to use on flat surfaces. Because of its solid frame, handles, and established angle, more pressure can be put on the blade, providing faster cutting. It is a good investment for the serious home woodworker.

Scraper Plane. The scraper plane has great stability because of its large bed. The blade can be adjusted for different angles. It is a good scraper for heavy work.

Hoe-Type Scraper. The hoe-type scraper has a long handle like the handles on lathe tools. It has a swivel head, and the blade can be adjusted to different angles. The blade sticks out in front so it can be used in corners that other scrapers cannot reach.

Swanneck Scraper. The swanneck scraper has many curves of different radii, similar to the French curve used in mechanical drawing. It can be used to scrape moldings or concave surfaces, such as the bottom of a bowl or tray.

Abrasives

Abrasives are not true tools, but functionally they must be considered in the same category. They are used to remove materials by shaping and smoothing surfaces. Abrasives are important to the maker of wooden toys because of their dual function. Abrasives are used to smooth the surface of wood and other materials and also to smooth finishes such as varnish, shellac, lacquer, enamel, Deft, and polyurethane.

Toymakers have little use for very coarse sandpaper, except on motorized sanding equipment. Aluminum oxide and garnet paper are the best sandpaper, and in the long run they are the least expensive. They last much longer than the cheaper flint sandpaper. For a starter, the craftsman should acquire a few sheets of each of the following grades:

Medium Grade	100-2/0
Fine Grade	150-4/0
Very Fine Grade	220-6/0
Extra Fine Grade	320-9/0

Medium grades are used to eliminate planer marks or other tool marks. Extra fine grades are used on finishes.

Screwdrivers

Phillips Screwdriver. The Phillips screw has a recessed indentation in its head, and Phillips screwdrivers are designed to fit that indentation.

The point size of Phillips screwdrivers range from No. 4 (the largest), to No. 0 (the smallest). Sizes 1, 2, and 3 are the most commonly used. The Phillips screwdriver is less apt to slip than the standard screwdriver, particularly on small screws.

Conventional Straight Blade Screwdriver. A set of small screwdrivers of good steel are very important tools. Lucky is the man who has a set of gunsmith screwdrivers with conventional straight blades. They are made of high quality steel, and the tips are parallel ground. The variety of sizes provides a better chance of getting the exact size needed, which prevents marring and ruining screws.

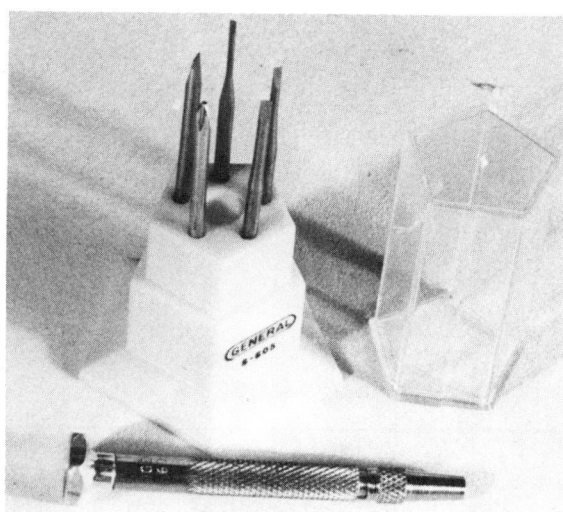
Fig. 1-12. Jeweler's screwdrivers.

Jeweler's and Miniature Screwdrivers. A few professional miniaturists use very small screws and screwdrivers to assemble their miniatures (Fig. 1-12). They use screws of the size used in eye glasses, cameras, and other precision instruments. Usually the screws are sharpened to a point when used in wood objects.

Measuring and Marking Tools

Folding Rules. The folding rule was the favorite measuring device of home woodworkers and carpenters until the steel tape rule came into use. The 3- or 6-foot folding rule is small enough to slip into the pocket. Usually one side of the folding rule is divided into 1/8 inches, and the other side is divided into 1/16 inches. Folding rules are made of hardwood or aluminum (Fig. 1-13).

Steel Rules and Tapes. Steel rules vary in length from 6 feet to 12 feet in increments of 2 feet. Steel tapes, used extensively by builders and carpenters, are seldom used by the home craftsman. Steel tapes are generally 50 or 100 feet in length.

Some steel rules have a square corner to conveniently make inside measurements. Some have a push-button rewind and a blade that can be stopped in any position.

Hook Rule. The hook rule is a good rule to use when you cannot see the edge of the wood you are measuring. It is 6 feet long, and the hook can be folded out of the way, or if necessary, it can be removed.

Bench Rules. Bench rules are probably the most extensively used tools in the home workshop. They come in both 1-foot and 2-foot lengths. They are made of wood or steel. Wood bench rules are usually marked in both 1/8 and 1/16 inches, while steel rules are graduated in 1/16 inches only. Some bench rules read from both left and right.

Steel Scales. Steel scales or rules are 6 to 12 inches long. The 6-inch length is the most popular because it can be carried in an apron pocket. The main advantage of steel scales is that many are graduated in 1/64 inches for accurate measuring. Some scales come with a leather case with a clip to hold to the edge of a pocket.

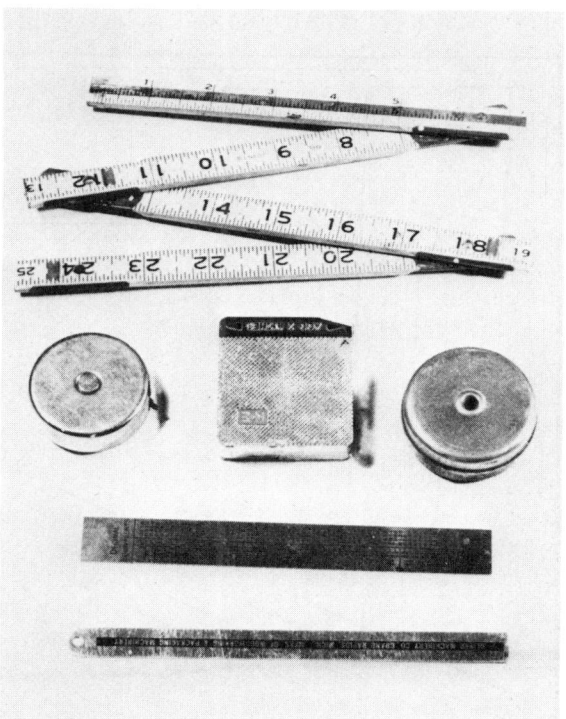
Fig. 1-13. Folding rules, measuring tapes, and 6-inch scales are shown.

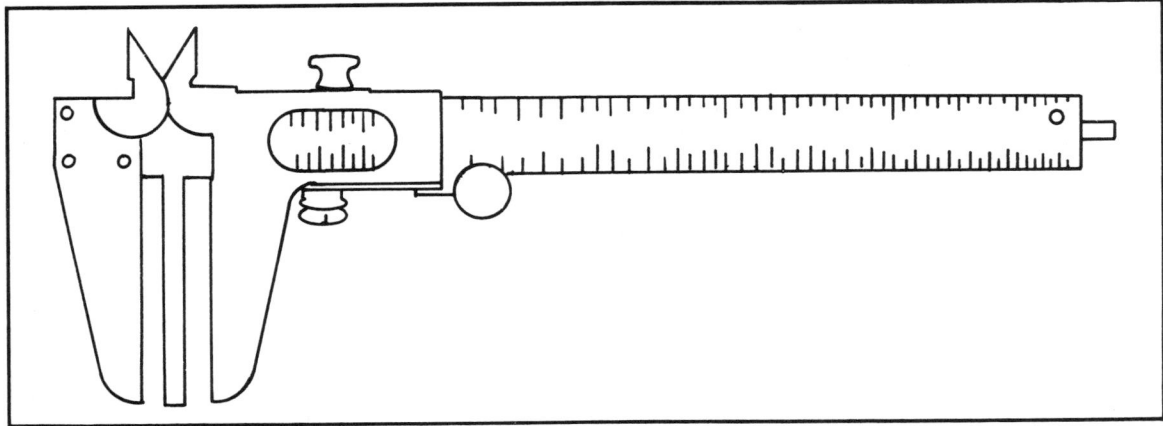

Fig. 1-14. Vernier slide calipers.

Vernier Slide Calipers. A useful, but optional, tool is the vernier slide calipers with inside and outside jaws, 5-inch capacity depth gauge, and graduations of 1/16 and 1/32 inches with vernier readings to 1/128 inch (Fig. 1-14).

Protractor. A protractor lays down and measures angles. It comes in handy at times to the home craftsman.

Framing Square. The framing square is used by the home craftsman to square wide lumber and to

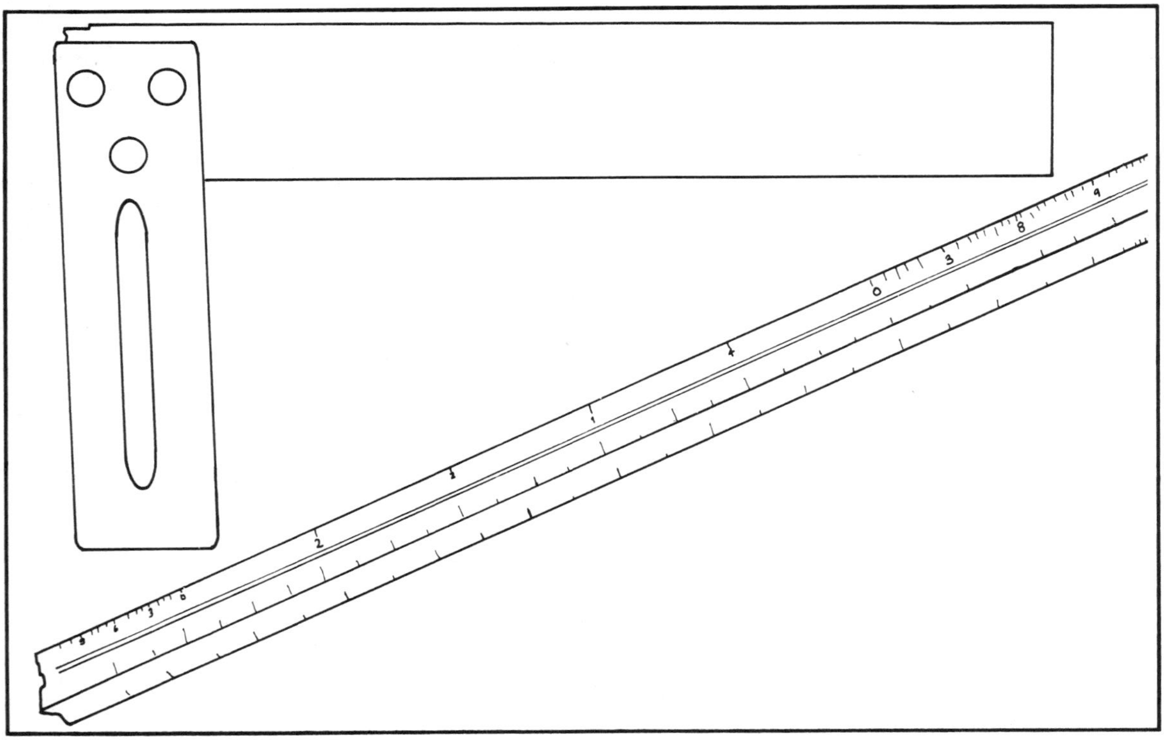

Fig. 1-15. Try square and architectural scale.

Fig. 1-16. Combination or bevel square.

test projects for squareness.

For the carpenter, the framing square is an indispensable tool used for a multiple of purposes, and next to the hammer and saw it is probably the most used tool. The carpenter uses the framing square to figure rafter lengths and angles, to measure braces, and to figure board feet.

Try Square. The home craftsman relies more on the try square than the framing square, mainly because the size of the framing square adds to the difficulty of handling.

Try squares are available with blades from 6 to 12 inches in increments of 2 inches. The smaller sizes are the most popular. The blades are made of steel; the handles, or cross members, are made of rosewood or cast iron (Fig. 1-15).

T-Bevel Square. The T-bevel square is not really a true square for laying out 90-degree angles. It can be set for any angle and locked into position with a thumbscrew on the end of the handle. It is used extensively to test, duplicate, and check chamfers and bevels. Sizes generally run 6, 8, and 10 inches long. It is available with either an iron or rosewood handle.

Combination or Bevel Square. The blade of a combination square is slotted. A head which measures both 45 degrees and 90 degrees slides along the slotted blade (Fig. 1-16). The head also contains a level glass. The length of the blade can be read from left to right or from right to left. The combination square can be used in situations where it would be difficult to use the try square.

Marking Gauge. The marking gauge is used to mark parallel scribed lines to an edge of a piece of straight wood. Marking gauges are made of both steel and wood and can mark lines up to 6 inches from the starting edge. The beam, head, and spur are the main parts (Fig. 1-17). A thumbscrew holds

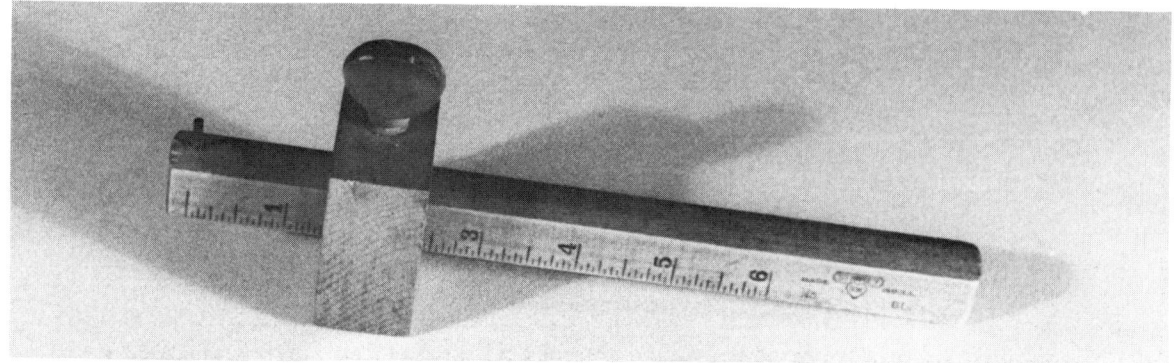

Fig. 1-17. Wooden marking gauge.

the head in position on the beam. Sometimes a short pencil is used in place of the steel spur where the inscribed line would be objectionable.

Mortise Gauge. The mortise gauge is essentially the same as the marking gauge except that the mortise gauge has two spurs which are adjustable for distance apart from the end of the beam. It also insures that all mortises are laid out with exact widths.

Panel Gauge. The panel gauge is simply a large marking gauge. It is particularly useful in laying our panels for doors.

Dividers. Dividers are sometimes called wing dividers. Some dividers are equipped with a fine adjustment screw to insure accurate settings. Others have one removable leg which can be replaced with a pencil so that it can be used as a compass. Dividers are used to scribe circles and arcs and to transfer measurements.

A pair of dividers are indispensable in laying out small, accurate distances, especially if those distances are repeated. This tool will probably be used more than any other tool for layout work. Of course, if the craftsman has a set of drafting instruments, a pair of small dividers will be included with many other tools.

Trammel Points. Large arcs and circles are scribed with trammel points. Trammel points are attached to a hardwood bar 3/8-inch thick and 3/4-inch wide. The maximum size of the circle or arc is determined by the length of the bar.

Scratch Awl. The scratch awl looks somewhat like an ice pick and comes in a variety of point lengths. The shorter, but more pointed, awl is used

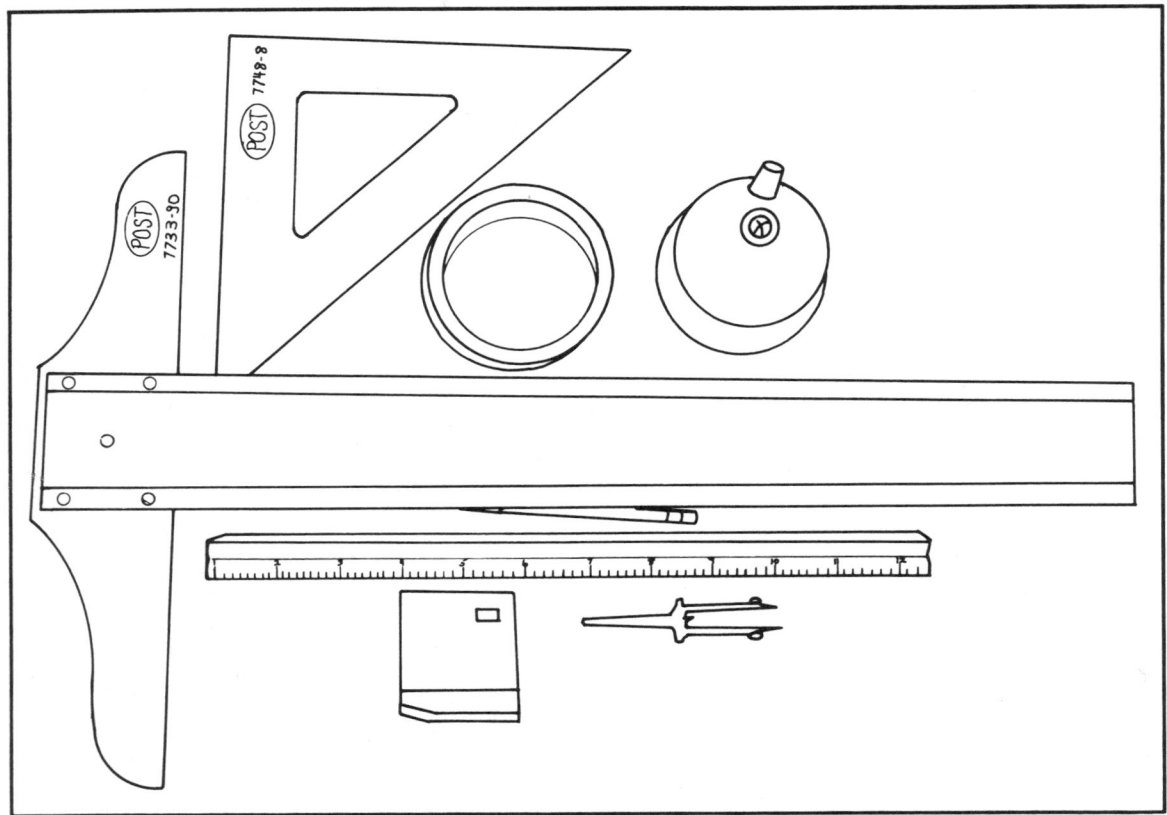

Fig. 1-18. Layout and drawing tools are shown, including a T-square, architectural scale, tape measure, dividers, masking tape, and pencil pointer.

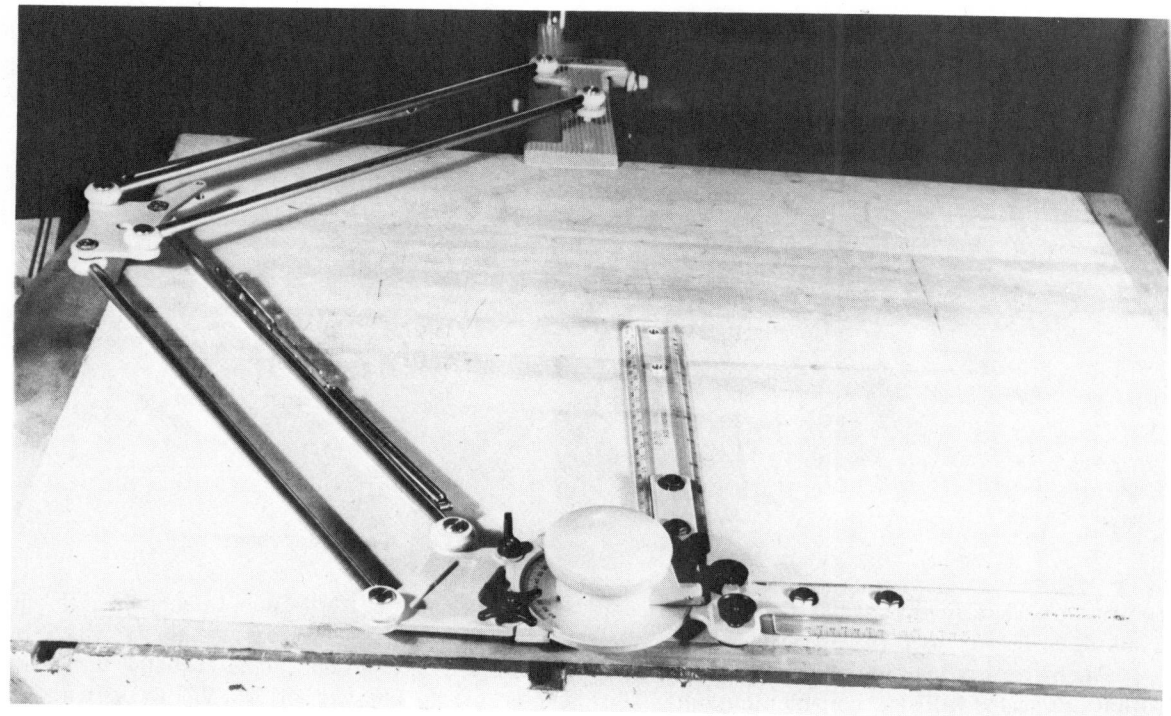

Fig. 1-19. Universal drafting machine.

for piercing leather. The longer awl, ordinarily used in woodshops, is about 6 inches long. It is used primarily for indenting locations for holes which are to be drilled or bored. The drill automatically centers itself in the depression made by the awl. This inexpensive tool should be an integral part of every woodshop.

Sloyd Knife. Sloyd knives are sturdy and short bladed. They will stand a lot of punishment and resharpening. The knife blades vary in length from 1 7/8 inches to 3 1/8 inches.

Sloyd knives were first used in Scandinavian countries to teach whittling methods. They were later used in the United States in the early days of manual training for the same purpose.

Sloyd knives are still used a great deal today for layout and marking operations.

Lead Pencil. A hard lead pencil with a chisel point is used a great deal for layout purposes, particularly where scribed lines would be objectionable and hard to remove.

Layout and Drawing Tools
Drawing Board. A drawing board, at least 11 inches by 15 inches, is a good investment. You can make your own from 3/8- or 1/2-inch basswood plywood.

T-Square. A T-square at least 1 inch longer than the long dimension of the drawing board is a must. You can make your own out of hardwood, but commercial T-squares come with plastic transparent edges, which have certain advantages (Fig. 1-18).

Triangles. An 8-inch, 45-degree and an 8-inch, 30-60-degree triangle will be useful in scribing lines in multiples of 15 degrees.

Universal Drafting Machine. The more affluent craftsman who does considerable drafting and layout work, may want to invest in a universal drafting machine. They are built for speed and accuracy and eliminate the need for T-squares, triangles, protractors, etc. Some drafting machines have an additional feature which makes closely

15

Fig. 1-20. Circular saw.

controlled parallel lines possible. Prices range from $120.00 upward (Fig. 1-19).

Architectural Scale. The architectural scale with its 12 scales will save considerable time. The outstanding characteristic of this tool is that each graduation is deep enough so that the dividers naturally fall into these recesses when the correct dimension is reached. The architectural scale should never be used as a drawing tool because the sharp corners will be worn down and the scale will lose its accuracy.

Additional tools and accessories used for layout and drawing include a pencil sharpener or pointer, drawing and graph paper, assorted grades of pencils, masking tape, and erasers.

POWER TOOLS

Circular Saw. The stationary circular saw is also known as the *variety saw* and the *universal saw* (Figs. 1-20 and 1-21). Circular saw blades are of many sizes and types; the most common are the crosscut or cutoff, rip, and combination.

Combination blades are either flat-ground or hollow-ground planer blades. The hollow-ground planer combination blade is probably the best all-around blade to use in the circular saw to avoid the need to change blades. It rips and crosscuts with

equal ease, and the cut is smooth enough so that it needs little or no sanding. The only drawback in using the hollow-ground blade is that it is nearly impossible to cut wet or warped wood without burning the blade.

Some blades have a nonstick coating for easier running and longer life. Some are available with carbide tips and seldom need sharpening. There are also combination blades that practically eliminate any chance of dangerous "kickback."

Circular saw operations involve ripping, crosscutting, rabbeting, dadoing, grooving, beveling, chamfering, mitering, and molding. Each task involves special precautions, and some require the use of attachments.

If the home carftsman were to buy only one power, straight-line, cutting saw, the circular saw would be the best choice.

Radial Saw. Practically all the operations done on the circular saw may be duplicated on the radial saw. Builders, carpenters, and lumber companies use it a great deal because most operations allow the stock to remain stationary while the saw moves.

Many school shops use the radial saw as a cutoff saw for long boards. They use the circular saw for all other operations.

16

Portable Electric Circular Saw. The portable electric circular saw is an indispensable tool for the builder and carpenter. In the home workshop its use is very limited; however with a special table and with the saw turned upside down under the tabletop it can be used as a circular saw. The saw blade extends through a slot in the tabletop.

Automatic Drill Bit. The automatic drill bit is an accessory of the automatic drill that works on the same principle as the Yankee screwdriver. It drills a hole only on the forward or downward stroke of the automatic drill. Drill bits are available in sizes from 1/16 to 11/64 inch in increments of 1/64 inch. All automatic drill bits have notched shanks. The automatic drill is a hard drill to use and has no useful purpose except in very close quarters. The hand drill is much easier to use.

Power Planing Tools

Planer or Surfacer. The terms planer and surfacer are used interchangeably. The smaller planers take stock up to 12 inches wide and 4 inches thick.

You should be at the back of the planer to catch long pieces as they come through. If you are not, the end of the board coming through last is apt to be thinner than the rest.

The grain direction should be checked before you insert stock into the planer, or the surface may be badly checked and rough.

Short pieces of stock should be pushed through the planer, one piece behind the other. Generally, slightly angled pieces will go through the planer easier.

Jointer. A power jointer can do many more operations than the planer, and from the home woodworker's standpoint, it is much less expensive.

The power jointer is especially valuable when you need to rip a large number of long pieces. All stock must be jointed on one edge before ripping can be done safely.

When working with stock that is as wide as or narrower than the jointer, the jointer can do a good job of surfacing. By pushing the stock at a slow speed, a very smooth surface can be achieved.

The jointer is an excellent tool for tapering items such as table legs. A mark is made on the leg where the taper begins. The leg is placed across the top of the jointer blade, and the mark is lined up with the front edge of the back bed or outfeed table. For instance, if the taper starts at zero and ends at 1/4

Fig. 1-21. Circular saw "throats."

inch, four cuts of 1/16 inch each would be made.

When thin, narrow strips are being jointed or cut it is best to use a *feather board,* a board with a number of saw kerfs close together in one end to form a spring-type pressure against the fence. It is clamped to the infeed table to push the stock up against the fence and to prevent possible injury to the operator.

Router. The portable, motorized router is a highly versatile tool (Fig. 1-22). Its fast-turning motor, with revolutions per minute up to 27,000, produces cuts that need no sanding. Motors are rated from 1/4 horsepower to 2 1/4 horsepower. Cutters are designed to make a variety of cuts, including rabbets, chamfers, round corners, beads,

coves, ogees, flutes, "V" grooves, and veins. In addition there are cutters for making dovetail joints.

A router should always be moved from left to right since the cutter moves in a clockwise direction in normal operation. The router should be moved at a consistent speed because too slow a movement will cause the wood to burn. Work should be securely clamped to the bench top or held in a vise so that the router can be held with two hands. If a deep cut is to be made, it is best to take two or three passes over it, otherwise the motor will slow down with the increased load and will not operate effectively.

Electric Plane. The electric plane is, in es-

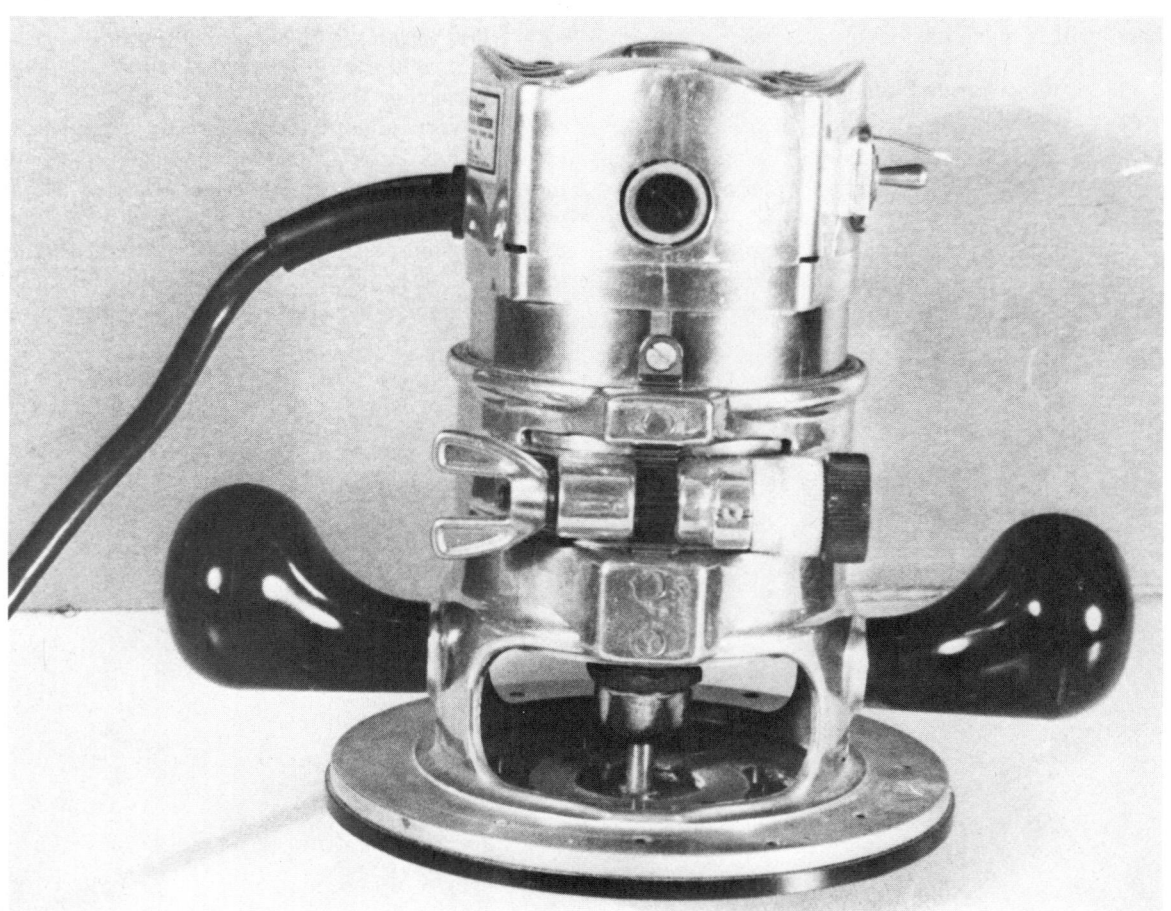

Fig. 1-22. Power router.

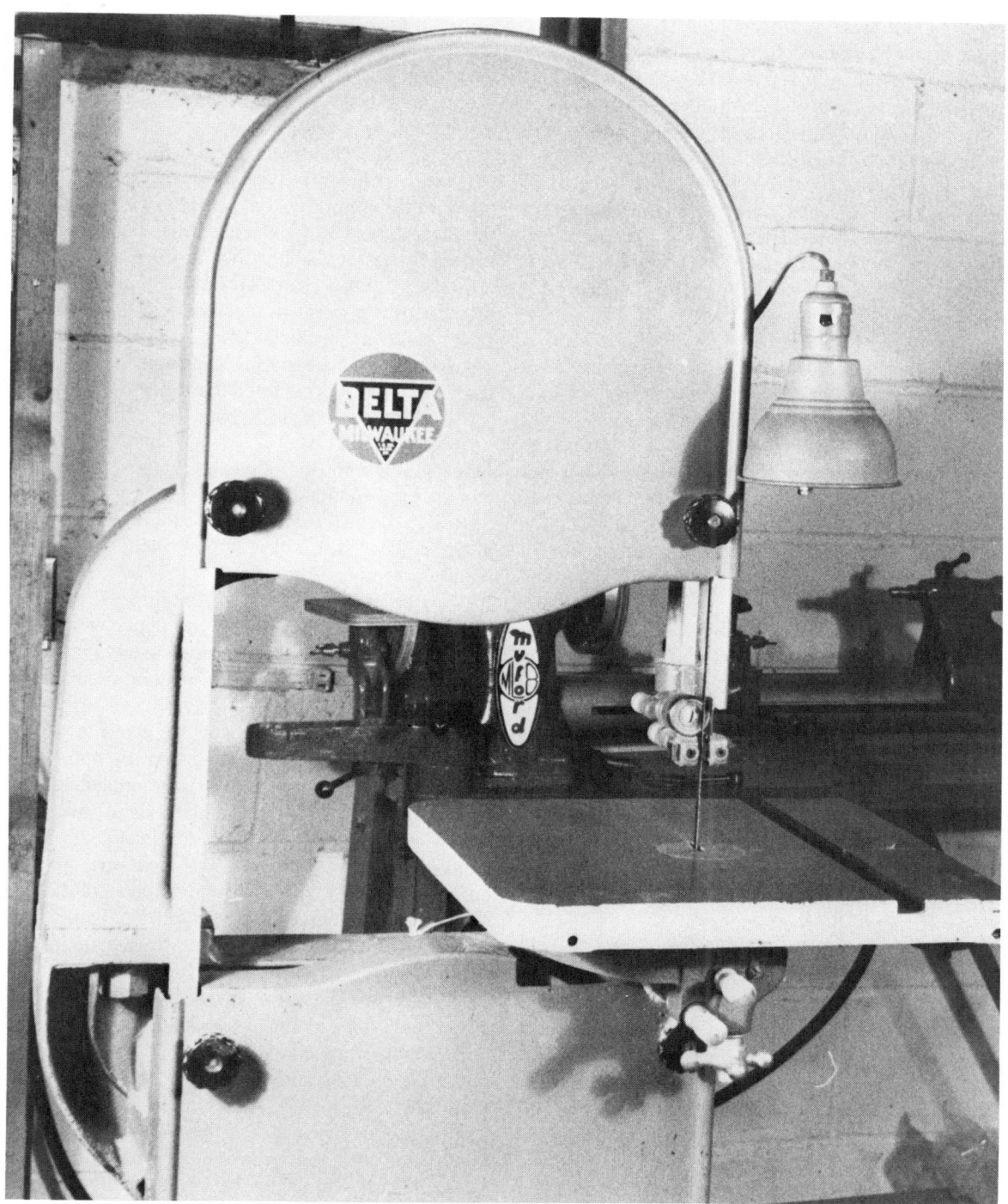

Fig. 1-23. A band saw is shown, with a Myford lathe in the background.

sence, a motorized router mounted on a plane bed. It can do both edge and surface planing. It can make cuts up to 1/8 inch in depth and 3 inches wide. The electric plane is like a miniature, upside down jointer in that it has both adjustable infeed and outfeed tables. It also possesses a fence.

The electric plane comes in handy when you are working on large pieces. When using this machine you have a distinct advantage—you can take this highly portable tool to the work instead of vice versa.

Power Curve-Cutting Tools

Band Saw. Band saws (Fig. 1-23) vary in size from the 10- and 12-inch wheel diameters with a 1/8-inch blade that create fine scroll work to huge 75 feet long blades with 16-inch wide blades. These huge saws have teeth on both edges of the blade for sawing giant logs in both the forward and backward passes of the carriage.

The 14-inch band saw is the most popular in home workshops as well as in pattern shops, small school shops, cabinet shops, maintenance shops, and small furniture shops. In vocational schools, technical institutes, and large furniture plants, band saws vary from 36 inches to 42 inches in wheel diameter. The blades most commonly used are 3/8-inch to 3/4-inch wide.

The gauge thickness of band saw blades varies according to wheel diameter. The thinner blades are used on the smaller band saws. The skip-tooth blade is used to saw faster in certain kinds of wood, and because of its hardness will last longer. When it does get dull, however, the blade must be thrown away; it cannot be resharpened.

The band saw is safer to use than the circular saw because there is no chance of a kick-back. There are certain precautions, however, that must be taken. Round stock must never be cut unless it is securely clamped to a V block. Irregular surfaces that rock on the band saw table should be avoided. Watch both hands at all times. The distance between the top surface of the work and the top guide should never be over 3/8 inch.

One of the first things that a craftsman must learn is how to fold a band saw's blade. Many methods may be used, but they all arrive at the same result—a three-loop circle that can easily hang over dowel pegs when not in use. The best way to learn how to fold a band saw is from another craftsman.

The major function of the band saw is to cut outside, irregular curves. There are, however, many other operations that a band saw can perform, the most important of which is resawing. *Resawing* is the process of placing stock on edge and pushing it through the band saw. This method provides two or more thin boards in place of one thick one. A wider blade and a special fence are used for resawing. In a pinch, the band saw can be used for ripping if a special fence is clamped to the top of the table.

Before sawing on a band saw, turn on the switch and stand back a few seconds. Watch and listen for any unusual signs or sounds. Are there any clicking sounds that indicate a saw is about to break? Is the saw *wandering* or running erratically, in the guides? If it is, the upper wheel may not be tilted correctly.

When properly adjusted, the blade should run close to the guide wheels in the upper and lower guides at idle, but when the pressure of cutting is put on the blade, the guide wheels should spin rapidly.

Jigsaw or Scroll Saw. The jigsaw is essentially a motorized coping saw, and for most purposes it uses the same type and size of blades. The jigsaw cuts much slower than the band saw. The jigsaw cuts only on the downward stroke while the band saw cuts continuously. The band saw will also cut much heavier stock. The advantages of the jigsaw are the ability to cut curves with small radii, the ability to cut fine lines, and the ability to cut interior curves as well as exterior curves.

The teeth of a jigsaw should point downward to assist in holding the work against the table. The spring hold-down should be able to hold the work against the table under ordinary conditions. The work should be pushed slowly into the blade. If the work starts to chatter, ease up on the rate of speed you are pushing the work into the blade.

One of the most popular of the smaller jigsaws is the Dremel Moto-Shop jigsaw (Fig. 1-24). The

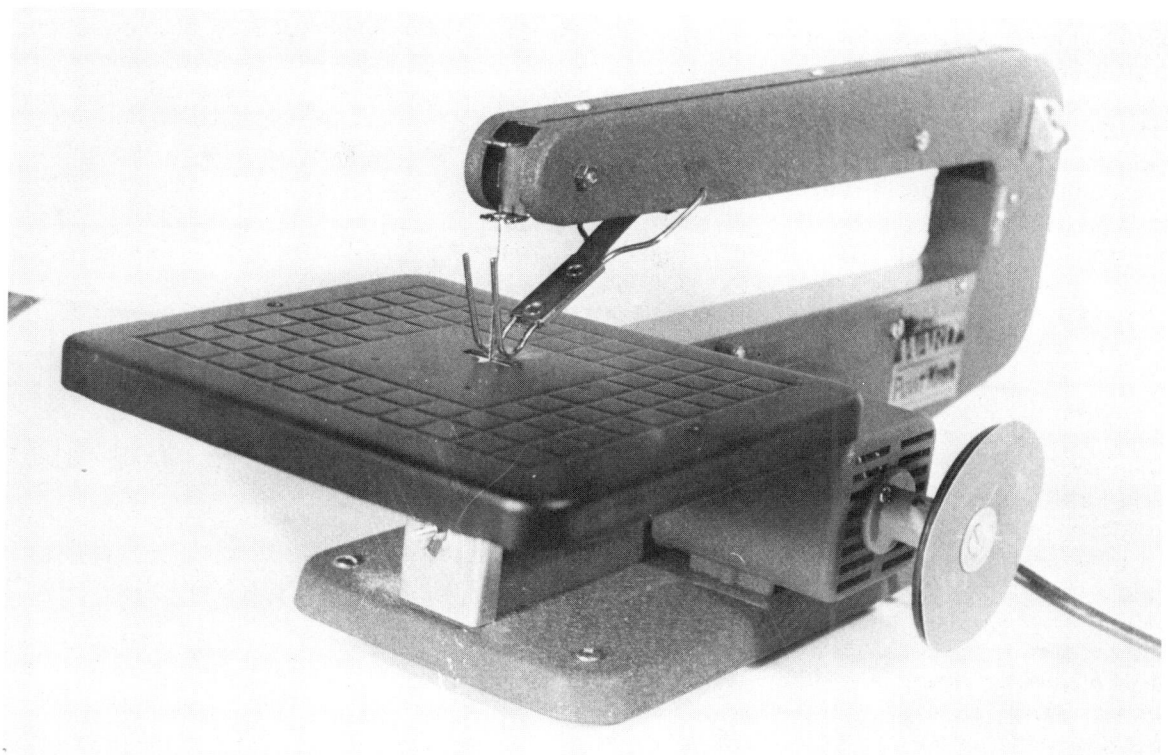

Fig. 1-24. Dremel Moto-Shop tool.

15-inch jigsaw has a disc sander attached to it which increases its versatility. A flexible shaft and accessories are also available at extra cost. Drilling, routing, deburring, sharpening, and carving are possible with the added attachments.

This multipurpose jigsaw will cut softwood stock up to 1 3/4 inches thick and hardwood stock up to 1/2-inch thick. When cutting thick stock it sometimes becomes necessary to remove the blade guard and pressure foot. Reinsert them to cut thin wood.

The table raises and lowers to utilize the full length of the blade, and it also tilts to 45 degrees both left and right of the perpendicular. The saw will cut to the center of a 30-inch circle.

Jigsaw blades for the Dremel jigsaw have a pin in each end. The distance between pin centers is 2 3/4 inches. Blades are generally available in fine, medium, and coarse grades. The coarse blade is wider than the others and has 16 teeth per inch. It

should be used only for straight cuts and curves with large radii. Although the blades seldom break, they should be discarded when they become dull. It is false economy and a waste of time and effort to work with a dull blade when the cost of a sharp one is so little.

The Dremel Moto-Shop jigsaw is a satisfactory compromise between the tiny, vibrating, magnetic jigsaw and the large, heavy, industrial jigsaw which has a separate motor and is belt driven. It is enjoyable to use and takes most of the drudgery out of cutting curves.

Saber Saw. The saber saw is like a miniature, upside down, portable jigsaw with only one chuck fastened to the motor. Because of this feature, the blades must be much stiffer than coping saw blades.

There are many types and sizes of blades available for the saber saw. Many of the blades cut materials other than wood. The number of teeth per inch varies from 6 for wood to 32 for metal. When purchasing saw blades be certain to get ones that will fit the machine.

If you do not have any power curve-cutting equipment, you should consider buying only the best quality saber saw, which generally has the greatest versatility. Quality saws will have a tilting base for angled cuts, a variable speed motor, and enough power to saw through a 2-×-4.

One distinct advantage of the saber is that it will saw internal or inside, cuts without drilling or boring holes. This feature makes working with paneling much easier. This type of sawing is called *plunge* sawing. The saw is tilted up on the front end, and the saw blade is slowly lowered into the work, thus cutting its own hole. It is best to try this procedure on waste stock first since it takes some practice.

Bayonet Saw. The bayonet saw is the "big brother" of the saber saw. It is heavier, more powerful, and must be operated with two hands. The most expensive models have two speeds and also a switch for selecting either orbital or reciprocating blade motion. The blade of the bayonet saw sticks out in front of the motor, while the blade of the saber saw points downward.

Power Drilling and Boring Tools

Portable Electric Drill. You can buy portable electric hand drills that drill from 1/4 inch to 2 inches in diameter in wood, and up to 1 inch in steel. The larger models are controlled with both hands. The 1/4-inch, pistol grip, one-handle model is the most popular for the home workshop. Smaller drills operate at higher speeds than larger ones.

Drill Press. Drill presses come in bench and floor models. Most drill presses have from three to six speeds made possible by pulleys of different sizes. Six speed drill presses operate at speeds from 350 to 5,600 revolutions per minute. One model has a variable speed motor, and any speed between 450 and 4,800 revolutions per minute may be obtained by simply turning a dial, eliminating the dirty and time-consuming job of changing belts on cone pulleys.

Slow speeds are used when boring or drilling holes with large-diameter bits. High speeds are necessary for drilling small holes, shaping, routing, and mortising. Auger bits may be used in the drill press if the square tang is cut off and the threads on the feed screw are filed off.

The 15-inch drill press is the most popular for small industries, schools, and home workshops.

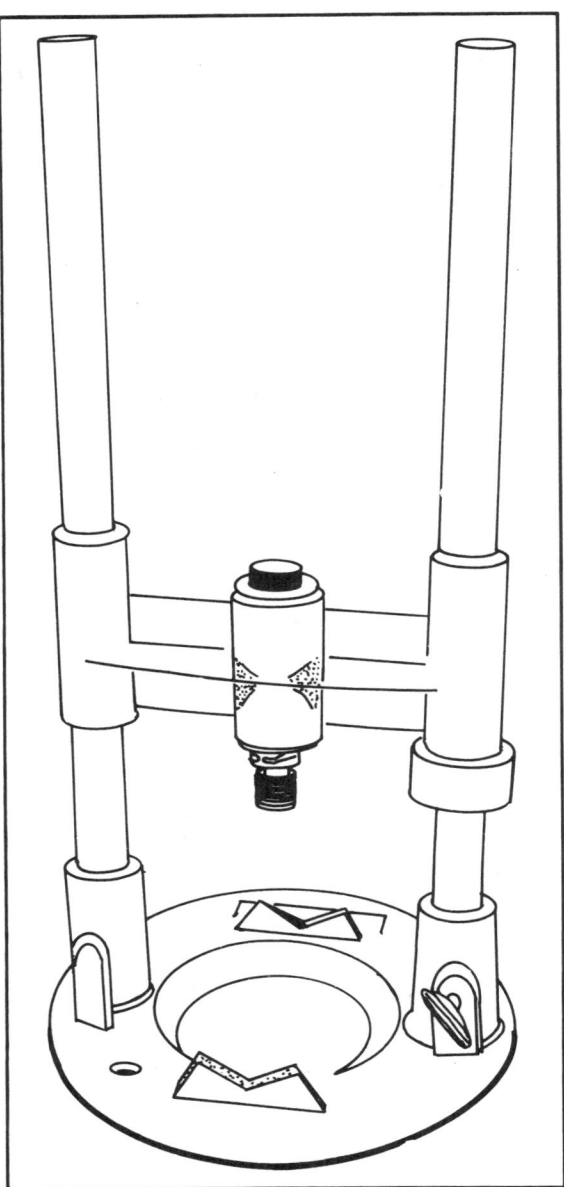

Fig. 1-25. Portalign.

A portable electric drill can be converted into a small drill press by attaching it to a Portalign. See Fig. 1-25.

Power Turning on a Lathe

A lathe is used to perform two basic operations: faceplate turning as for a salad bowl, and turning between centers as for a baseball bat (Fig. 1-26). The common turning chisels are the gouge, skew, roundnose, diamond point, and parting tool.

A pair of outside calipers and a steel rule or scale are necessary accessories to turning wood. Calipers are never used on turning stock until it has been turned perfectly round. Calipers caught by turning stock may cause serious injury.

There are two basic turning techniques: the turning method and the scraping method. The turning method is very difficult and takes a long time to learn. The professional turner does most of his turning by this method. It looks easy, but it certainly is not. Home craftsmen should stick to the scraping method.

To use the scraping method for turning between centers, each end of squared stock should be marked diagonally across the corners. On one end, saw two kerfs about 1/8-inch deep. This end will be driven by the spurs on the live center in the headstock. Where the two lines cross on the other end, drill a small hole for the dead center. Then take the two centers out of the lathe, place them over their corresponding ends on the stock, and tap the butt end of each center sharply with a mallet (Fig. 1-27).

Place the stock in the lathe after the centers have been reinserted. Cut off the corners of the squared stock with a drawshave to form a rough octagon in the cross section. Check to see if the tailstock is locked and force the dead center into the

Fig. 1-26. Turning between centers on the Myford lathe.

Fig. 1-27. Driving lathe centers into stock.

gouge. A shearing cut should be used, moving to the right with the right corner of the gouge and to the left with the left corner.

When the stock is still oversize, measure the lengths between the square parts and round parts, as well as between beads, Vs, and other parts. It is best to mark the distances on a piece of scrap wood or marking template. A V-shaped knife cut should be made at each mark on the template so that the lead of a pencil automatically centers the mark. Hold the template about 1/8 inch from the revolving stock and mark (Fig. 1-28). Never hold a steel scale against a revolving piece of stock.

At or near the inscribed lines, establish diameters with calipers and a narrow parting tool. Hold the calipers set at the right diameter in your right hand and the parting tool in your left hand. The handle of the parting tool should extend along your forearm (Fig. 1-29). Use the parting tool and calipers alternatively until the correct diameter is reached. Never force the calipers, or you will get a false measurement.

Remove all excess waste stock with the gouge. Make the necessary tapers, coves, beads, concave and convex cuts, flats, and V-shaped portions with the appropriate tool.

Myford Lathe. The Myford ML8 woodturning, English-built lathe has been a traditional favorite of British turners and is rapidly becoming popular in this country.

The Myford lathe is cleverly designed and solidly built with fine castings and precision-machined parts. It is simple to operate, and versatile, and an extensive variety of accessories is available.

There are three sizes: 30, 36, and 42 inches between centers. In addition to an inboard faceplate, it has an outboard one which turns faceplate turnings up to 16 inches in diameter.

Attachments convert the Myford lathe into a circular saw, band saw, mortiser, grinder, and disc sander.

Dremel Lathe. Another lathe is the Dremel lathe. See Figs. 1-30 and 1-31. As with the Myford lathe, the Dremel can use a disc sander as an attachment (Fig. 1-32).

wood with the crank on the tailstock until it is firmly seated. Turn the stock over by hand.

Check the speed setting, stand to one side, and turn on the switch. If the lathe starts to vibrate, turn off the lathe immediately and set it on a lower speed.

The stock is turned to the round with a large

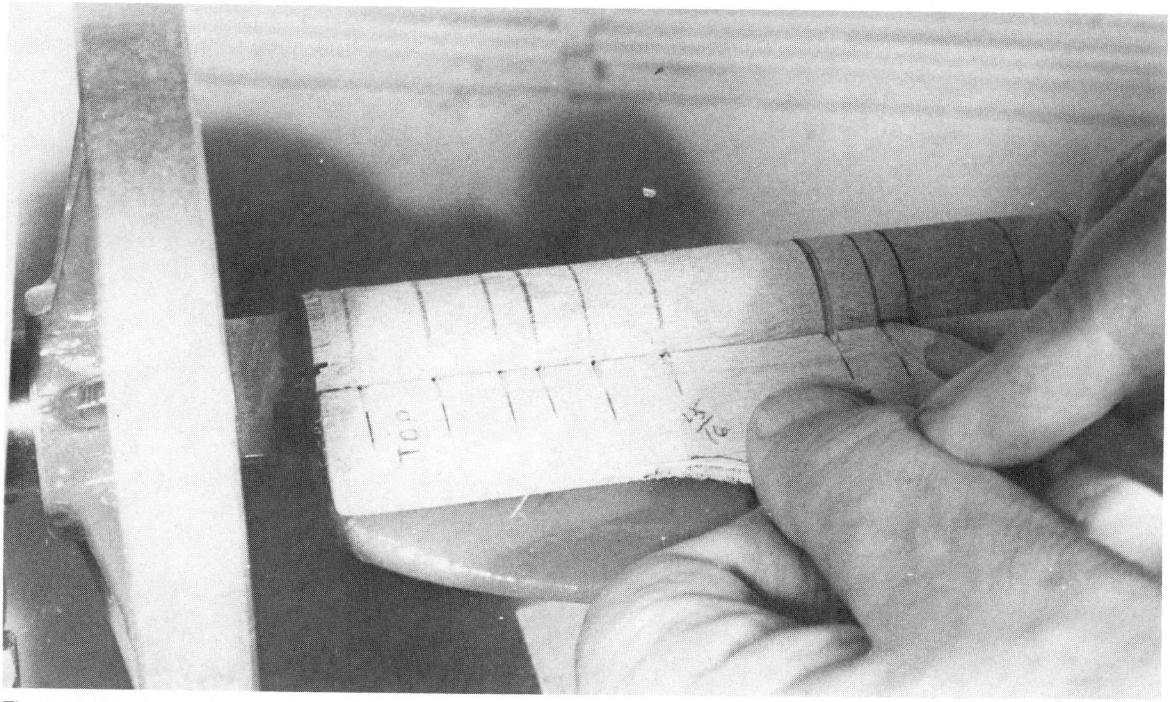

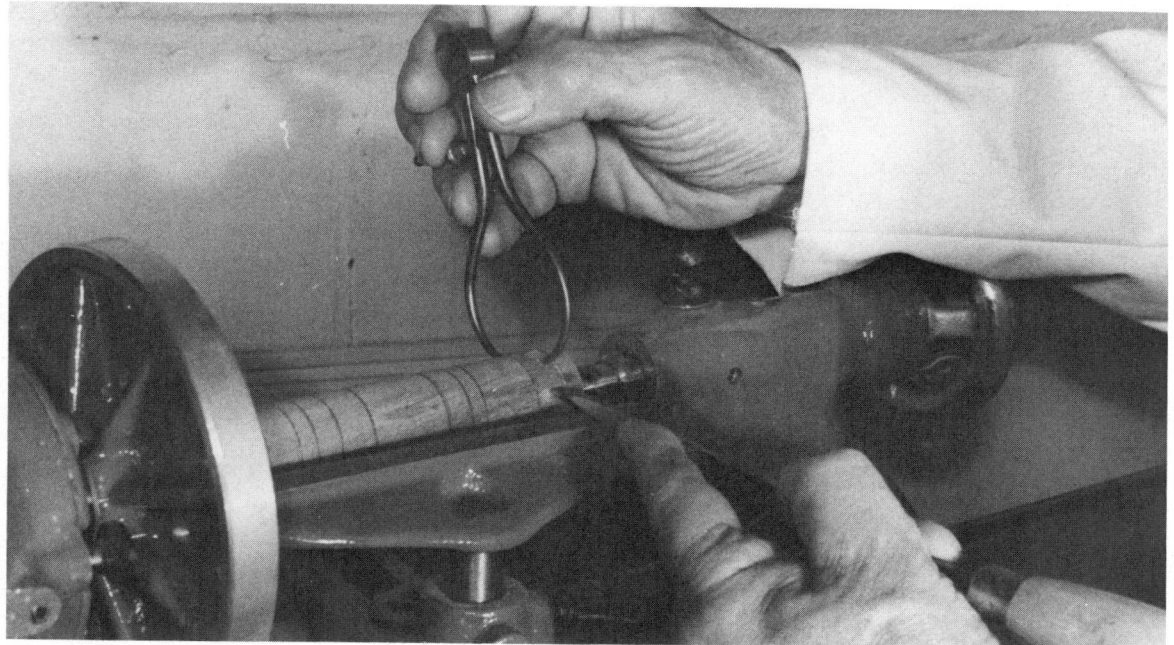

Fig. 1-28. Marking stock with a template.

Fig. 1-29. The positions of the calipers and parting tool are shown.

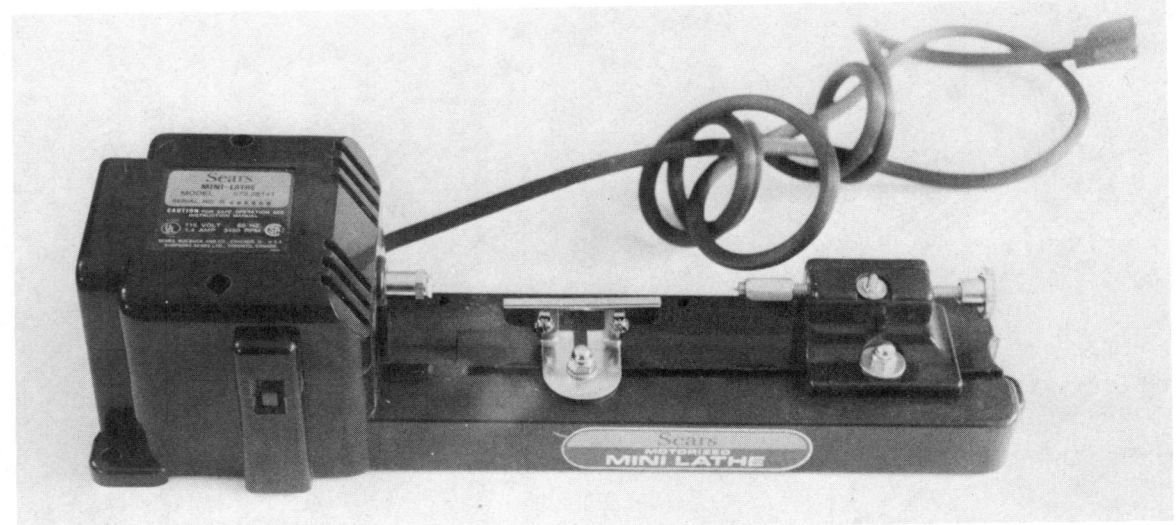

Fig. 1-30. Dremel lathe.

Fig. 1-31. Dremel lathe with turning between centers.

Fig. 1-32. Homemade disc sanders for the Dremel lathe.

Upside Down Belt Sander. There are a number of power sanders, but the one with the greatest practical use for the toymaker is the portable belt sander turned upside down. Small pieces can be sanded with greater control with this tool than with any other method.

WOOD

Natural woods should be used whenever possible when you are making wooden toys. Adults are attracted to toys with bright, flashy, and gaudy colors, but children seem to go for the more subdued and earth colors.

There are a number of natural woods with color tones to give emphasis and life to wooden toys. The high quality wooden toy is usually a combination of naturally colored woods with a minimum of enamel and paint. If it is necessary to outline certain sections of a toy, a burning tool should be used.

Hardwoods

Hardwoods and softwoods are classified botanically as broad-leaved and needle-bearing trees respectively. This classification is misleading, however. For example, basswood, which is classified as a hardwood, is actually softer than yellow pine, which is classified as a softwood.

The following list gives the color and uses of various hardwoods. You can use the list as a guide in selecting woods for making toys.

Apple. Pinkish-brown in color, apple wood is a strong, hard, tough wood. It is generally available in small pieces only and therefore should be used sparingly in making wooden toys. Traditionally apple wood has been used for tool handles.

Ash. Black ash is a dark grayish-brown wood. Oregon and white ash are grayish-brown, but they sometimes have a reddish tinge.

Balsa. Balsa is a very lightweight wood, and it is not very strong. It is used to a great extent in building model airplanes, but it has very limited use in building wooden toys which are exposed to rough handling.

Basswood. Basswood is creamy white to creamy brown in color, with an occasional reddish tinge. It is a very good wood to use for larger wooden toys. Generally uniform in color with little distinguishable grain, basswood is an excellent wood for carving and sculpturing.

Beech. Beech is white with a reddish to a reddish-brown tinge. When quartersawed, the rays appear as small, dark brown flecks. Beech is apt to be unstable, but it is an excellent wood to use when the part calls for steam bending.

Birch. Birch is an excellent wood for toy construction and is readily available. The color varies from a light brown to a dark reddish-brown. It is heavy, hard, and dense, making it ideal for toys which are apt to get a considerable amount of abuse.

Boxwood. Boxwood, a fine-textured wood, yellow in color, is extremely heavy. It is an excellent wood for turning and carving, but it is generally available in small pieces only.

Brazilwood. Brazilwood is a dark red wood of fine texture. It is quite hard and heavy, although it can be worked fairly easily with sharp tools. Originally this wood was highly valued as a source of red dye.

Bubinga. Bubinga is a reddish-brown hardwood from West Africa.

Butternut. Butternut, sometimes called white walnut, can be used as a substitute for black walnut for toy construction, but it does not have the hardness, strength, and beauty of black walnut.

Cherry. Cherry, a rather heavy, dense, close-grained wood, varies in color from light red to dark reddish-brown. Sometimes known as wild cherry, black cherry, or choke cherry, it is one of the best woods to use for making toys.

Chestnut. The heartwood of chestnut is grayish-brown or brown and becomes darker as it ages. Clear chestnut is hard to find today. Most available chestnut today is "wormy chestnut" and is used mostly for paneling. It has limited uses for making toys.

Cottonwood. Cottonwood or poplar, a grayish-white to light-brown wood, can be used in place of basswood or white pine.

Cocobolo. Cocobolo is a heavy, dense wood that is basically orange-red, but streaked with darker stripes. It can be used as decorative accent pieces on toys.

Ebony. A very heavy, hardwood, ebony is generally a dense black, but it may be a medium to dark brown according to species. It tends to be very brittle and must be worked with considerable care.

Elm. There are six species of elm grown in the United States: American elm, slippery elm, rock elm, winged elm, cedar elm, and September elm. The heartwood is generally a light brown with traces of red. Elm can be steam bent with ease, but otherwise it is not a very good wood to use in making toys.

Hickory. Hickory varies from white, in its sapwood, to a reddish color, in its heartwood. It is a very tough, heavy, hard, strong, flexible wood, and it is an excellent wood for toy parts that are small in cross section. It makes excellent handles for toys and will take severe, rough handling and abuse.

Holly. See Boxwood.

Magnolia. Magnolia is a straight-grained wood of close, uniform texture. The sapwood varies from yellowish-white to dark brown tinted with yellow or green. It is similar in characteristics to yellow poplar.

Mahogany. Mahogany, a stable wood, is generally a pink to reddish-brown in color, is fairly easy to fashion, and takes an excellent finish. There are many species, including African, American, Cuban, and Philippine. With the exception of Philippine mahogany, mahoganys are well suited to toy construction.

Maple. Maple and birch are probably the two best light-colored hardwoods for toy construction. Maple is a creamy white and will remain so with age. It is quite readily available.

Oak. The two large categories of oak are red oak and white oak. Red oak is probably better to use in toy construction because of its color and highly conspicuous broad rays when the lumber is quartersawed.

Padauk. Padauk in most species is a brilliant red, and in that respect resembles Brazilwood. This beautiful wood is ideal for color accents on toys. Considering its weight and hardness, it is not a difficult wood to fashion with standard woodworking tools.

Pear. Pear wood is strong, heavy, and tough.

It is very stable when dry and for that reason is many times used in making drawing instruments and rulers. It is also a fine wood for carving and making toys. The color is a pinkish-brown.

Poplar. See Cottonwood.

Purple Wood. This distinct wood, as you would assume, is purple and comes from Dutch Guiana. It is tough, dense, and strong. If you possess carbide-tipped tools, you should consider purple wood for your toy parts, but the wood would dull the edges of standard cutters very rapidly.

Rosewood. Rosewood from South America is reddish-brown with dark streaks running through it. Rosewood from the East Indies is a deep red or purple. It is very heavy and extremely hard; so it is difficult to work with it. It adapts readily to toymaking, particularly for the larger pieces where the distinctive grain and color shows to advantage.

Sassafras. Sassafras, a wood at one time used by Indians to make dugout canoes, is a moderately heavy wood often confused with black ash. The heartwood varies from a dull grayish-brown to a dark brown. It does not have a high priority as a toymaking material.

Sweet Gum. Sweet gum, often used as a substitute for walnut in furniture construction, has a reddish-brown heartwood and would contribute to the overall attractiveness of any wood toy.

Satinwood. Satinwood, often used for inlays and furniture parts, comes from Ceylon and is light yellow in color.

Sycamore. Sycamore is a fine-textured wood, and is reddish-brown in color. Figured sycamore is highly prized as a wood for use on the backs of violins, and for that reason is sometimes called "fiddle back sycamore." Figured sycamore adds a great deal to the quality of wooden toys.

Teak. Teak is almost a universal wood. It varies from light brown to dark brown and comes from Thailand and Burma. It is a very heavy wood and will sink in water when it is green. It is difficult to use because of its abrasive nature. It is used extensively for shipbuilding and furniture construction. You should have considerable patience when working with this wood.

Walnut. American black walnut has long been cherished as a furniture and architectural wood. This beautiful, rich dark brown wood is strong, hard, and heavy but works well with the standard woodworking tools. Toys made partially or entirely of walnut have an instant appeal both to children and adults.

Zebrawood. A distinctive wood from Western Africa, zebrawood is identified by alternate stripes of light tan and dark brown or black, and it gets its name from this feature. It is an excellent toymaking wood, and it makes a wonderful substitute for upholstery in toys.

Softwoods

Softwoods have limited use in toy construction. They should be used only for large parts with sufficient cross sections to alleviate the possibility of breakage. Softwoods should not be used where nicks, bruises, and scratches would be objectionable.

White pine, basswood, poplar, and spruce are softwoods that are readily available and adaptable to toymaking.

Cedar. There are many kinds of cedar: Alaska, incense, Eastern red, Southern red, Western red, and white.

Eastern and Southern cedar are the best woods for toys. These woods are used extensively for making pencils, novelties, small boats, scientific instruments, and chests.

Douglas Fir. Douglas fir, grown in the western part of the United States, varies widely in weight and strength. Whenever a wood is needed with contrast between spring and summer growth, you might try Douglas fir.

Hemlock. Western hemlock has limited use as a toy material, but it can be used in "sandwich" construction when protected by harder lumber. This wood often contains small, black knots that do not necessarily detract from its use.

Redwood. Redwood from the large sequoia varies from a light brown to a dark mahogany color. It is easy to work with straight-grained wood. Its pleasing color is suitable for toy parts with large cross sections. It is particularly valuable as a material for making outdoor toys because of its durability and resistance to decay.

White Pine. White pine is probably the ultimate softwood choice for toymaking. Eastern white pine and sugar pine are the best selections for toy construction, because of their straight-grained, uniform texture. This wood has a creamy-pinkish color which turns a light orange-red with age. It is readily available and is easy to work with ordinary woodworking tools.

FASTENERS AND HARDWARE

Originally nails were identified by the term "penny," abbreviated to "d." The penny size indicated the weight of 1,000 nails. For example, a 6d nail weighed 6 pounds per thousand.

Currently the penny size indicates the length of nails. A 2d nail is 1 inch long; a 6d nail is 2 inches long; a 10d nail is 3 inches long, and a 20d nail is 4 inches long. Common nails over 20d are referred to as spikes, and sizes run to 60d, or 6 inches long.

The three broad groups of nails are brads, nails, and spikes. The brad is a small finishing nail.

There are six kinds of nails: box, common, finishing, brad, casing, and square cut. The brad is probably the only one used extensively for toymaking. Any kind of nail should be avoided if possible. Dowels and glue are the major methods of fastening toy parts together.

Box Nail. The box nail differs from the common nail in that it is smaller in diameter and has a thinner head than the same penny-sized common nail.

Common Nail. The common nail is used in general wood construction where the visible head is not objectionable. It is made in a wide variety of sizes.

Finishing Nail. Finishing nails are generally used for interior trim where a visible head would be unsightly. The head is small and should be sunk below the surface of the wood with a nail set. The resulting hole should be filled with putty, plastic wood, or other suitable material.

Brads. Brads are small finishing nails from 1/2 to 1 1/2 inches long. The smaller brads should be driven in with a brad driver.

Casing Nail. Casing nails are similar to finishing nails except that they have a larger conical head which provides more holding power.

Square-Cut Nail. Square-cut nails are used primarily on rough construction, as in barns, outbuildings, etc., for nailing large hinges in place. When the nails are clinched they have more holding power than other nails. The cut nail is sometimes used in antique reconstruction and antique furniture reproduction.

Tacks. Common tacks, upholsterer's tacks, gimp tacks, and decorative tacks are a few of the many varieties. Decorative tacks and gimp tacks are sometimes used to decorate wooden toys (Fig. 1-33).

Escutcheon Pins. Escutcheon pins are small brass nails with round heads. Normally they are used to fasten draw pulls and escutcheon key plates to the fronts of drawers, but in some cases they lend themselves well for decorative accents on wooden toys.

Staples. Staples are double-pointed tacks. Their use is limited on wooden toys.

Screws. There are many types of screws: flathead, ovalhead, roundhead, Phillips head, sheet metal, and self-drilling.

Sometimes roundhead screws are used for wheel axles as a substitute for wooden axles on cars, trucks, and vans. The size of screw usually used for the front axle is a 2-inch No. 10, 11, or 12, and a 2 1/2-inch No. 12 or 14 is used for the rear axle. Whenever flathead screws, commonly called flathead brights, are used on toys the screws should be counterbored, not countersunk, and a piece of dowel or screw hole button should be used to cover the head of the screw.

Round Steel Rod. Round steel rods, 1/4 or 3/8 inch in diameter, are sometimes used instead of wooden axles for wheel bearings. When they are, the proper size Palnuts or push nuts should be placed on the ends of the rod axles to give a finished hubcap appearance to the wheel (Fig. 1-33).

Rubber Glides. Rubber cushion glides (15/16 to 1 1/4 inch in diameter), rubber screw bumpers (7/8 inch in diameter), rubber tack bumpers (1/2, 5/8 and 3/4 inch in diameter), and steel glides may be used as headlights on toy cars,

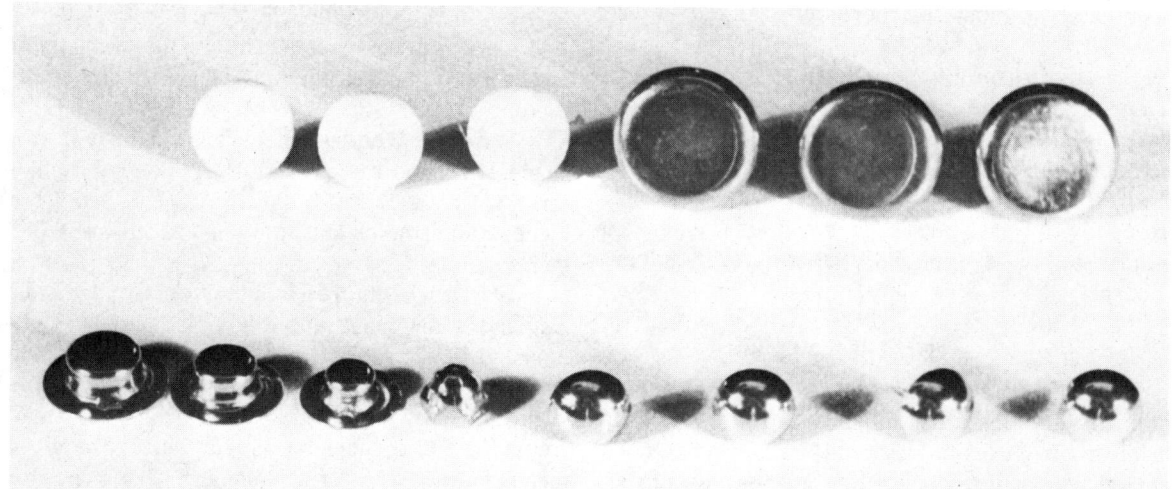

Fig. 1-33. Components. Back row: Tack bumpers and furniture glides. Front row: Pushnuts, or palnuts, and nickel upholstery nails.

trucks, and vans (Fig. 1-33).

Ferrules. Ferrules, or tubelike sleeves, may be fitted over wheel axles whenever it is necessary to extend the wheels away from the body of a toy car. It may be made of copper tubing.

Natural Glue

Animal Glue. Animal glue is a gelatinlike substance made from hide trimmings and other portions of animals. Cattle hide makes the best quality animal glue. Animal glue works best when it is hot and the wood is warm. Animal glue is prepared in a double boiler or an electric glue pot.

Casein Glue. Casein glue is a water-resistant glue that is made from the protein, or curd, of milk. It is mixed with water and stirred. An electric mixer works fine.

Fish Glue. Fish glue is made of fish scraps and kept in a liquid state by adding acid. Many liquid glues are fish glue. They generally come in a tube.

Synthetic Glues

Contact Cement. Contact cement remains somewhat elastic after it cures. It must be applied to both surfaces before bonding, and it is used primarily with plastic laminates. Care must be taken in gluing parts together because there is an immediate, strong bond upon contact between the pieces.

Polyvinyl Acetate. Probably the best by far for making toys of wood, polyvinyl acetate is white in color and ready to use in a liquid form. It is used a great deal in furniture construction because of its strength and rapid setting action at room temperatures. Elmer's glue is one of the best-known white glues. Sobo glue is another white glue that is particularly effective in gluing miniatures. These glues are generally packaged in a squeeze bottle or tube.

Urea Resin. Urea resin glue is made of synthetic urea crystals and formaldehyde. It usually comes in powdered form and is used a great deal in gluing layers of veneers to form plywood.

Phenolic Glue. Phenolic glue is used to glue exterior plywood and is used extensively in boat construction.

Resorcinol Resin. Resorcinol resin glue is a dark reddish liquid. It will withstand high humidity for long periods of time.

Epoxy Resin. Epoxy resin glue is probably the strongest of any of the adhesives and will bond together almost any materials including metals. It does not require very high pressure to bond well, and it is water resistant. The resin and the catalyst come in the same size of packages or tubes, making them very convenient to use. Equal parts of resin

31

and catalyst must be thoroughly mixed before using.

Epoxy resin glue is a very practical and efficient glue for the wooden toy craftsman, particularly whenever small and delicate parts must be joined.

Polyester Resin. Polyester resin is similar to epoxy, but it is not as strong. It also requires a catalyst and is especially useful for adhering fiberglass.

FINISHES

Spray Deft, spray lacquer, and spray polyurethane are all very fine clear finishes and are generally available in aerosol spray cans. Polyurethane goes on much heavier than the other finishes, and for that reason it does not require as many coats. It does have the disadvantage, however, of drying much slower. Each coat should be sanded with fine sandpaper (220-6/0 or finer) between coats. Use steel wool (0000) on parts that are hard to sand. Make sure that the finish is thoroughly dry before sanding. Make sure, also, that all finishes are nontoxic before applying.

COMPONENTS

Addresses for companies who supply component parts can be found under Appendix A: Suppliers at the end of the book.

Wheels. Wooden wheels are available in two shapes: flat and round, with the following diameters; 3/4, 7/8, 1, 1 1/4, 1 1/2, 2, 2 1/4, and 2 1/2 inches. Their holes and axle pegs are 1/4 and 3/8 inch.

Plastic wheels are available from Goffton Ltd., England. Plastic and rubber wheels, made by Hobbies and Handicrafts (Dereham) Ltd., are available from Woodcraft Supply Corp. They are available with the following diameters: 2 inches, for small trucks, 3 3/8 inches, for medium-size wheels, 4 inches for large tractor wheels, and 4 1/4 inches for large-spoke wheels. An assortment of wheels are illustrated in Figs. 1-34 and 1-35.

Steam Engine and Locomotive Smokestacks. Smokestacks are made in a number of sizes and designs. Sometimes items such as wooden knobs and Shaker clothe pegs may be used for smokestacks. (See Fig. 1-35.)

People. "People," sometimes called "little

Fig. 1-34. Plastic/rubber wheels made by Hobbies and Handicrafts Ltd.

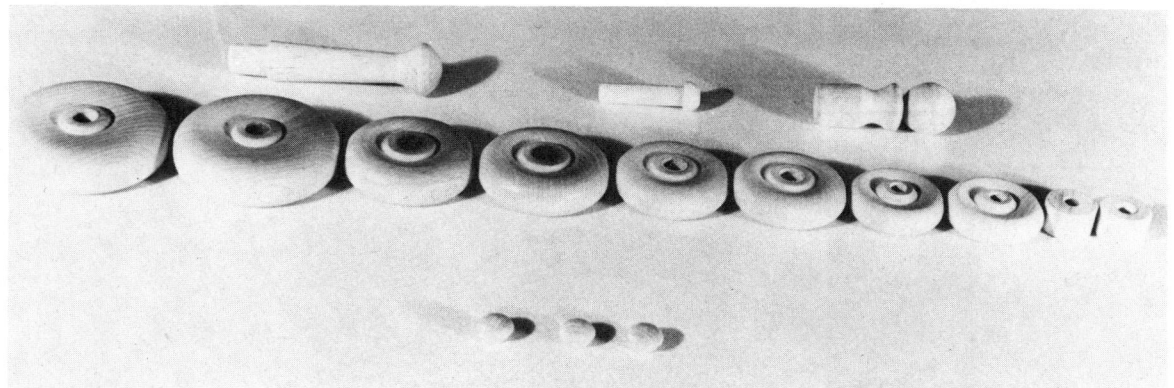

Fig. 1-35. Components. Back row: Steam engine smokestack, axle rod, and "people." Middle row: Different sizes of wheels. Front row: Screwhole buttons sometimes used as headlights on small cars, vans, trucks, and other vehicles.

people," are turned items that simulate the human body.

Screwhole Plugs and Screwhole Buttons. Screwhole plugs, sometimes known as furniture plugs, are used to cover flathead screws that have been counterbored. Some plugs are slightly rounded on the top while others are flat. The sides of these plugs are slightly tapered.

Screwhole buttons have a buttonlike top which is larger in diameter than the part that fills the hole (Fig. 1-35).

Screwhole plugs and screwhole buttons with rounded tops are often used as headlights on toy cars, trucks, and vans.

Plugs and buttons are made in 3/8- and 1/2-inch diameter holes. Plugs and buttons are available in many species of wood, such as beech, birch, maple, cherry, oak, and walnut.

Trolley Car Wheels. Trolley car wheels and track are available from Criss-Cross Creations.

2

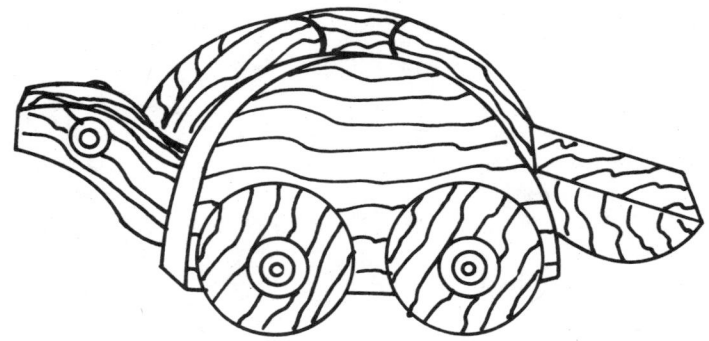

Animal Toys

This chapter contains step-by-step directions for making 12 animal toys. Also included are tables of materials and illustrations to help you create these projects.

KANGAROOS

This whimsical Mother Kangaroo and her adorable Baby Kangaroo by Design Group are irresistible to children (Fig. 2-1). Use 1/4-inch birch plywood for the hind legs to provide more strength. Redwood wheels are used for accent.

Preparation

☐ Make patterns for the mother's body, head, hind legs, ears and front legs. Also make patterns for baby's head and ears. Be sure to enlarge patterns to 1/2-inch squares (Figs. 2-2 and 2-3).

☐ Transfer the enlarged pattern outlines to the appropriate thickness of stock (Table 2-1). Cut out the wood pieces with a band saw, jigsaw, saber saw, or other curve-cutting tool.

☐ Sand the edges with different sizes of drum

sanders or homemade cylindrical sanders used between lathe centers.

Assembly

☐ Drill a 1/4-inch hole in the mother's body for the baby's head support. Also drill the same-sized hole in the baby's head.

☐ Cut the head support and glue the dowel into both parts.

☐ Glue on the mother's ears, and front legs and the baby's ears.

☐ Bore a 1/4-inch hole in the front part of the mother's hind legs, and a 17/64-inch hole in the rear part of the mother's hind legs.

☐ Glue the mother's hind legs to her body.

☐ After the glue has set, drill a 17/64-inch hole through the mother's body using the holes in the hind legs as a guide.

☐ Cut the three wheels with a hole saw. Enlarge the 1/4-inch hole in the front wheel to 17/64 inch.

☐ Cut the rear and front axle rods.

Fig. 2-1. Kangaroo. Courtesy of Design Group.

☐ Glue the end of the rear axle into one end of the rear wheels.

☐ Insert the rear axle into the holes in the mother's hind legs and body. Glue on the other rear wheel.

☐ Insert the front axle through the front wheel. Glue the ends into the front part of the mother's hind leg.

Finishing

☐ Finish with clear spray Deft or poly-urethane.

☐ Paint or enamel the eyes on both the mother and baby with a nontoxic finish. Figure 2-4 shows the finished project.

FIGHTING ROOSTERS

The roosters can be pecking at each other or tugging on a worm (red rubberband). If the worm is to be used, a 1/32-inch hole must be drilled through the beak of each rooster as indicated by the dot to hold the rubberband. Because of the delicate nature

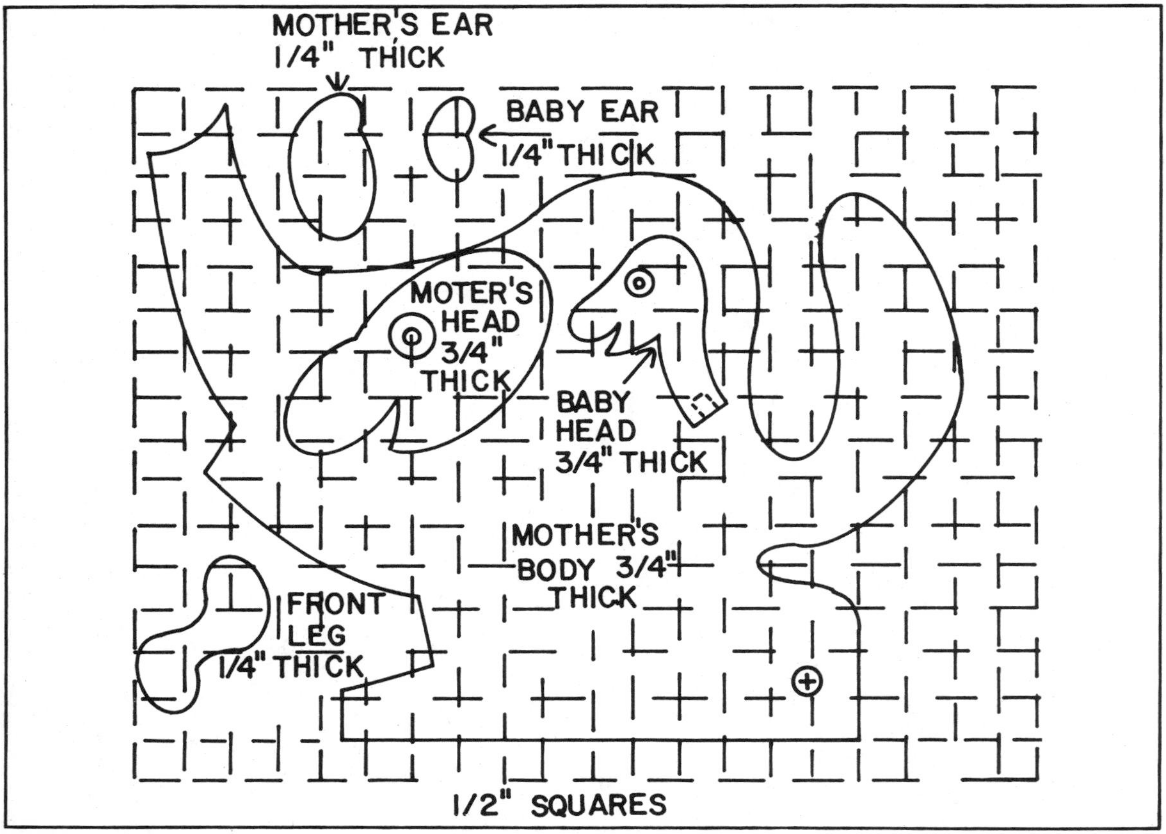

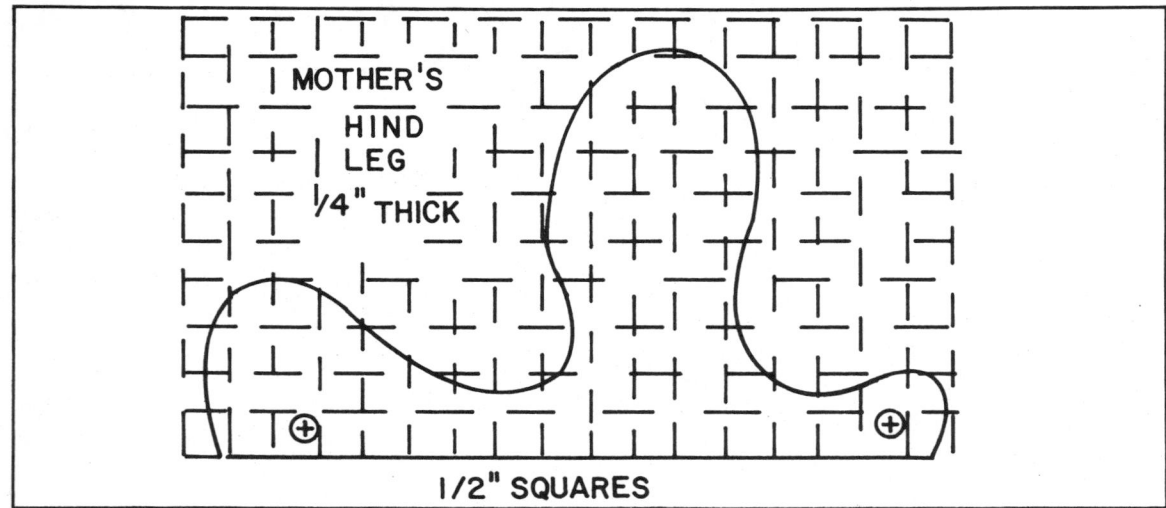

Fig. 2-2. Pattern for Kangaroo body, head, leg, and baby parts is shown. Courtesy of Design Group.

Fig. 2-3. Pattern for Kangaroo mother's hind leg is shown. Courtesy of Design Group.

Table 2-1. Materials for the Kangaroo Project Are Listed.

NUMBER OF PIECES	PART	SIZE	MATERIAL
1	mother's body	3/4" x 7 1/4" x 9"	pine, maple, or birch
1	mother's head	3/4" x 2" x 3 1/2"	pine, maple, or birch
2	mother's hind legs	1/4" x 4 3/4" x 8 1/4"	birch plywood
2	mother's ears	1/4" x 1 1/4" x 1 3/4"	birch plywood
2	mother's front legs	1/4" x 1" x 1 3/4"	birch plywood
1	baby's head	3/4" x 1 3/4" x 2"	pine, maple, or birch
1	baby's head support	3/4" length	1/2" birch dowel
2	baby's ears	1/4" x 5/8" x 7/8"	birch plywood
2	rear wheels	3/4" x 2" diam.	redwood
1	front wheel	3/4" x 1 3/4"	redwood
1	rear axle	3" length	1/4" birch dowel
1	front axle	1 3/8" length	1/4" birch dowel

of the beak, these holes should be drilled before the outline of the roosters is sawed.

Preparation

☐ Cut stock for the roosters from any 1/2-inch thick straight-grained wood. You can use white pine for one rooster and redwood for the darker one (Table 2-2).

☐ Enlarge the pattern in Fig. 2-5 to 1-inch squares.

☐ Trace the outline of the roosters on the stock and cut out the pieces.

Assembly

☐ Drill the two 1/4-inch holes in each of the roosters.

☐ Saw the outline of the roosters with a cop-ing saw, jigsaw, or band saw.

☐ Saw the 1/2-inch square rooster control sticks 12 inches long. You can use black walnut for these sticks.

☐ Secure the roosters to the control sticks with 1-inch #8 roundhead screws.

☐ Separate the roosters from the control sticks by thin metal washers with an outside diameter of 1/4 inch and a 5/32-inch hole at each of the four connections. The four crosses on the control stick drawing indicate the position of the screw holes.

Finishing

☐ The combs and waddles may be painted or enameled red, or you can make them of appliqued padauk, of a brilliant red, 1/32-inch thick.

☐ The beaks and eyes are enameled yellow.

Fig. 2-4. Completed Kangaroo project. Courtesy of Design Group.

Table 2-2. Materials for the Fighting Roosters Project Are Given.

NUMBER OF PIECES	PART	SIZE	MATERIAL
2	roosters	6" x 6" x 1/2"	straight - grained wood
2	control sticks	2 1/2" x 12" x 2 1/2"	black walnut
1	worm (optional)		rubberband

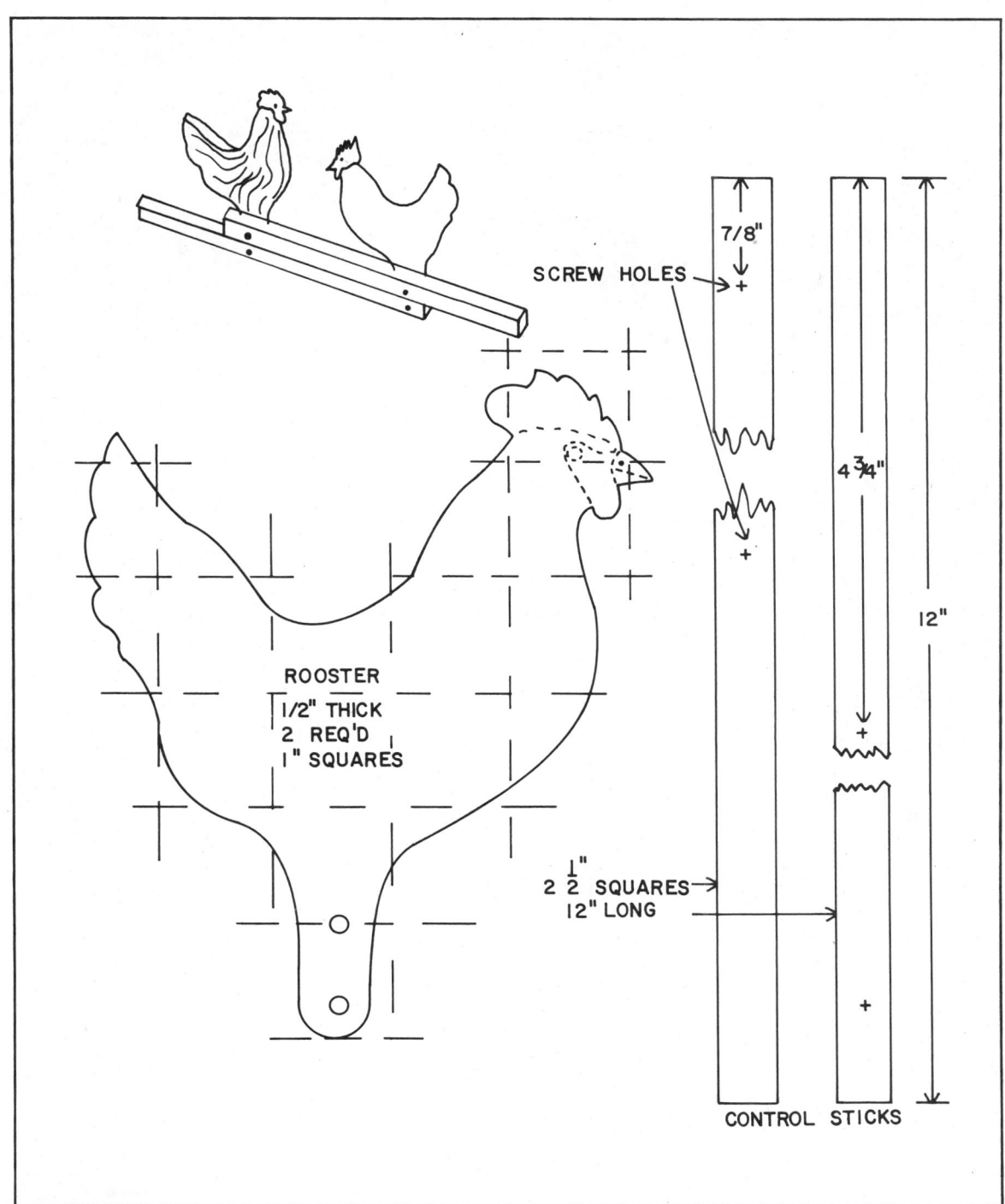

SCREW HOLES

7/8"

4 3/4"

12"

ROOSTER
1/2" THICK
2 REQ'D
1" SQUARES

2 1/2" SQUARES
12" LONG

CONTROL STICKS

Fig. 2-5. Fighting Roosters pattern and sizes. Courtesy of Stanley Tools.

Fig. 2-6. Completed Fighting Roosters project. Courtesy of Stanley Tools.

Figure 2-6 shows the finished project.

ANIMATED ALLIGATOR

Michael Murphy of Cherry Tree Toys has designed a unique collection of animated toys. He has given me permission to use plans of some of these toys in this book.

The alligator is rather easy to make and can be completed in three or four hours. The band saw is the best tool for cutting out the parts; however, you could use any other curve-cutting tool.

I used white pine for the project, but almost any straight-grained lumber may be used.

Preparation

☐ Make a pattern for the body which includes

Table 2-3. Animated Alligator Materials Are Listed.

NUMBER OF PIECES	CODE	PART	SIZE	MATERIAL
1	F	body	1 1/4" x 2 7/8" x 18 1/4"	any suitable material
2	G	jaws	5/16" x 2 3/8" x 5 7/8"	any suitable material
4	B	wheels	3/4" thick x 2 1/4" diam. with 3/8" hole	any suitable material
2	A	pins	head 1/2" diam. x 3/8" pin diam. 1/4" x 1/2"	from Cherry Tree Toys
2	C	axles	1 1/16" length	1/4" birch dowel
1	D	axle	2 13/16" length	3/8" birch dowel
1	E	axle	3 7/16" length	3/8" birch dowel

40

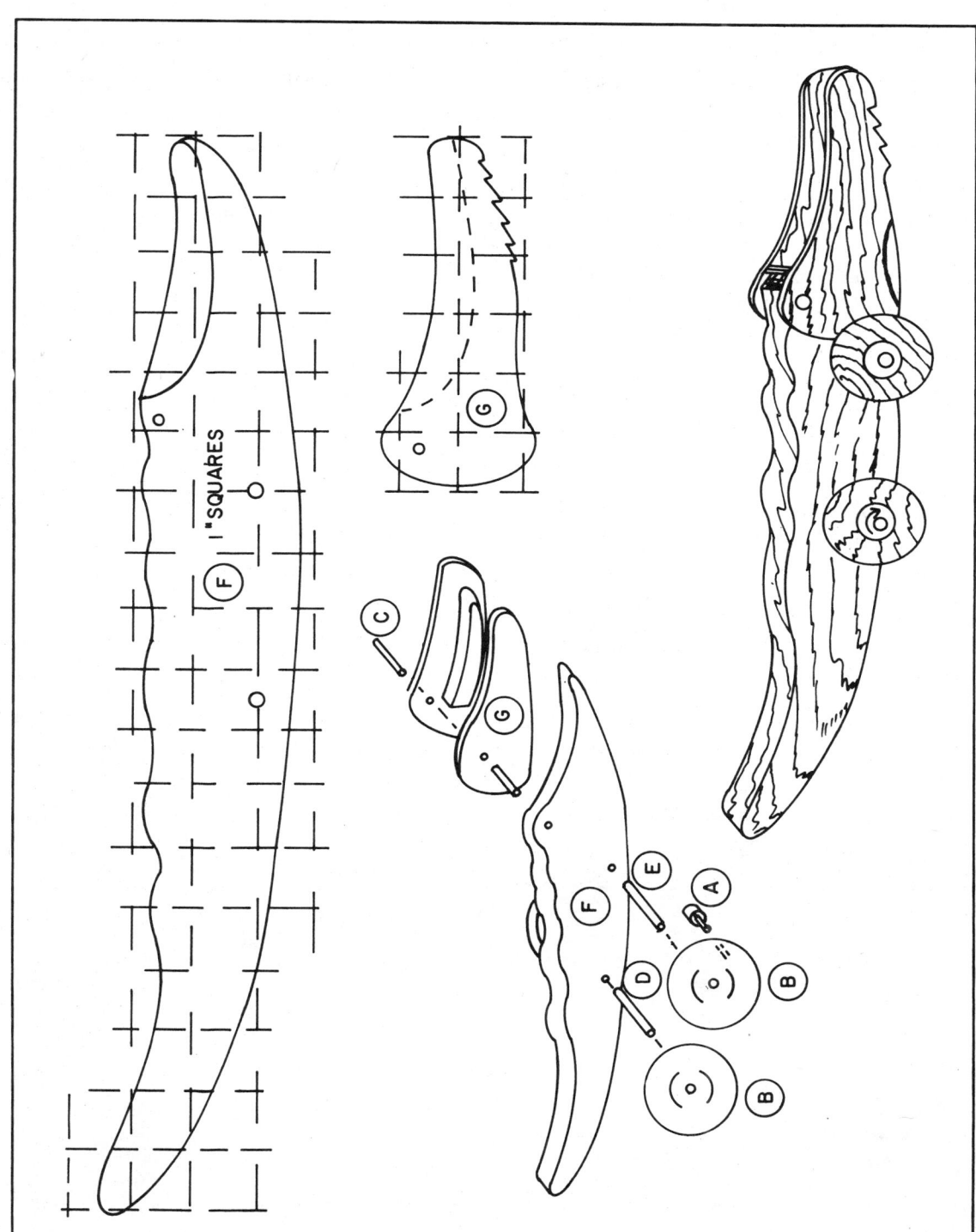

1" SQUARES

Fig. 2-7. Alligator patterns and assembly. Courtesy of Cherry Tree Toys.

the nose portion that is glued between the two jaw pieces (Table 2-3). Be sure to enlarge the pattern to 1-inch squares (Fig. 2-7).

☐ Mark the design on 1 1/4-inch stock.

☐ Saw the outline of body and nose portion with a band saw or other curve-cutting tool.

☐ Plane down the body so that it is about 1/16-inch thinner than the nose portion to prevent the binding of the jaws against the body when the jaws are activated.

Assembly

☐ Bore the two 7/16-inch holes in the lower part of the body.

☐ Make the pattern for the jaws. Be sure to enlarge it to 1-inch squares.

☐ Mark the design on 5/16-inch stock.

☐ Cut the outline with a curve-cutting tool.

☐ Sand the edges of the body and the jaws with a drum sander or cylindrical sander in the lathe.

☐ Glue the nose portion between the two jaw pieces.

☐ Clamp the nose and jaws assembly against the body and bore the 1/4-inch hole that simulates the eye of the alligator.

☐ Remove the nose and jaws assembly. Rebore the 1/4-inch hole in the body to 17/64-inch diameter to permit the axle to turn freely. Insert 1/4-inch dowels.

☐ Bore a 1/4-inch hole on the flat side of two of the wheels. The center of the hole should be approximately 3/4 inch from the center of the 3/8-inch axle hole.

☐ Drive the pins into the two front wheels.

☐ Drive the 3/8-inch axle into one of the front wheels with the pin.

☐ Run the axle through the front hole of the body. Repeat the procedure for the back wheels.

☐ Attach the other wheel with a pin to the axle so that the heads of pins are 180 degrees to each other. This attachment provides a more frequent clacking of the jaws when the toy is rolled on the floor (Fig. 2-8).

Finishing

☐ Sand the entire piece with #220 sandpaper.

☐ Apply three or four coats of clear spray Deft or polyurethane.

☐ When the finish is dry, rub with #1000 steel wool, wax, and polish.

TANTALIZING TURTLE

This Tantalizing Turtle designed by Michael Murphy is another creation of Cherry Tree Toys. The up-and-down movement of the head and tail is a source of amazement to many youngsters.

This sturdy and substantial toy may be made of most any softwood or hardwood, but I chose to use

Fig. 2-8. Alligator project is shown with mouth open. Courtesy of Cherry Tree Toys.

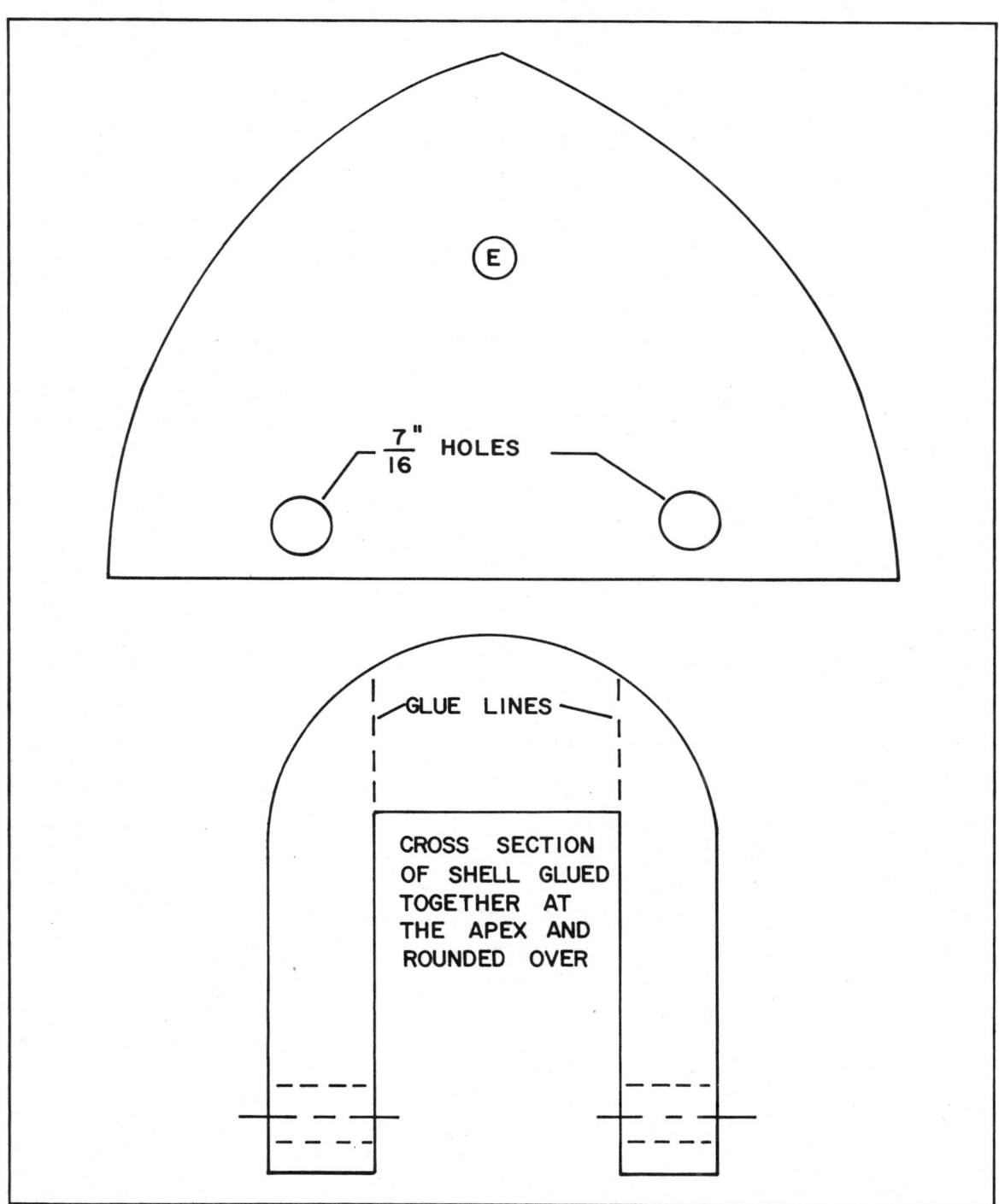

E

$\frac{7}{16}$" HOLES

GLUE LINES

CROSS SECTION
OF SHELL GLUED
TOGETHER AT
THE APEX AND
ROUNDED OVER

Fig. 2-9. Turtle shell parts. Courtesy of Cherry Tree Toys.

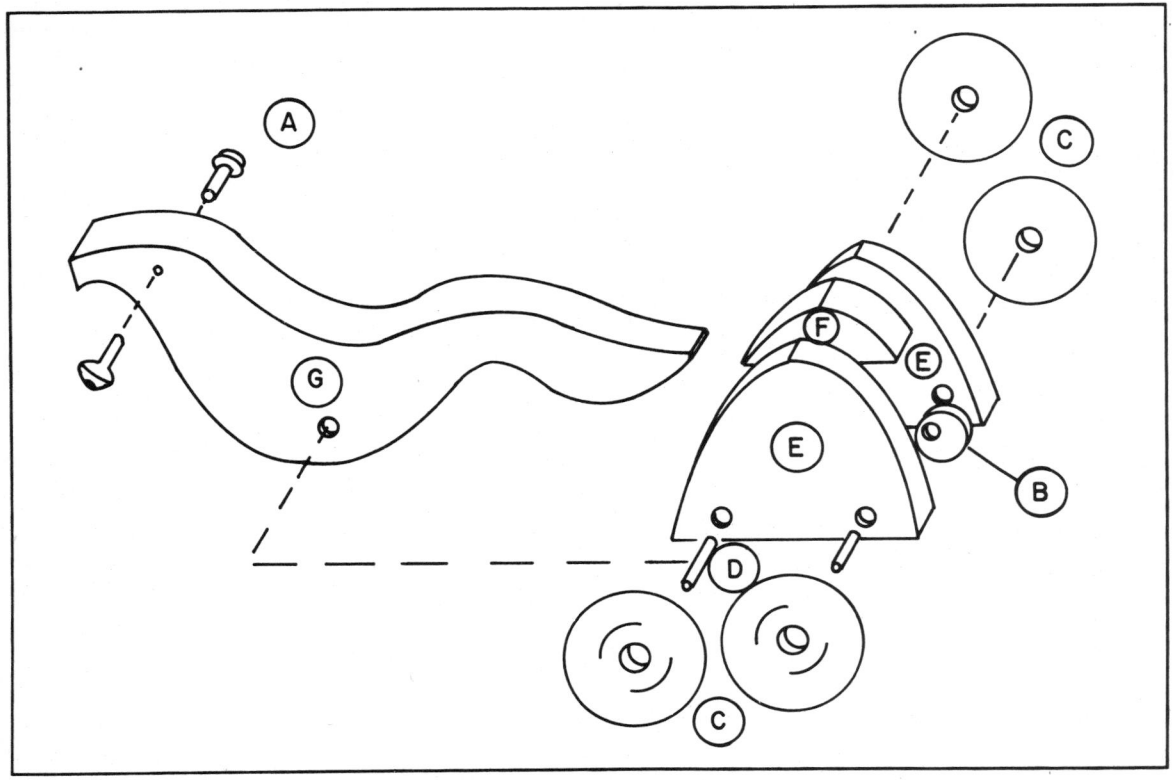

Fig. 2-10. Turtle assembly is shown. Courtesy of Cherry Tree Toys.

Table 2-4. The Tantalizing Turtle Can Be Made with the Materials Listed.

NUMBER OF PIECES	CODE	PART	SIZE	MATERIAL
2	A	eyes	1/4" diam.	from Cherry Tree Toys
1	B	offset wheel	5/8" x 1 1/4" diam. 3/8" hole	from Cherry Tree Toys
4	C	wheels	3/4" x 2 1/4" diam. 3/8" hole	from Cherry Tree Toys
2	D	axles	5" length	3/8" birch dowel
2	E	shell sides	3/4" x 4" x 5 $\frac{7}{8}$"	any appropriate wood
1	F	shell filler piece	1 $\frac{3}{4}$" x 1 $\frac{1}{2}$" x 4"	same as shell sides
1	G	head/tail	1 $\frac{3}{4}$" x 2 $\frac{13}{16}$" x 9 $\frac{15}{16}$"	any appropriate wood

maple for the head/tail unit and black walnut for the three-piece shell to achieve a pleasant contrast of colors. This toy, thus made of hardwood, could well become an heirloom.

Preparation

☐ Make patterns for the shell sides, shell filler piece, and head/tail, or transfer the outline to the stock of the correct thickness (Table 2-4). Enlarge to the proportions shown on Figs. 2-9 through 2-11.

☐ Cut out the parts with a band saw or other curve-cutting tools. Sand the edges of the parts with a disc sander and cylindrical sander on the lathe.

☐ Bore the holes for the eyes and the axle in the head/tail unit and for the axles in the shell sides.

Assembly

☐ Glue the two shell sides to the shell filler piece. See Fig. 2-10.

☐ After the glue is set, round over the parts in the last step. See the cross-section drawing of the shell in Fig. 2-9. Use a drum sander, Surform, or rasp followed by a number of different grits of sandpaper.

☐ Attach the wheels to the front axle.

☐ Attach one wheel to the rear axle. Extend the axle through one of the shell sides, through the offset wheel, through the other shell side, and into the remaining wheel.

Finishing

☐ Sand the entire project with fine sandpaper.

☐ Apply three or four coats of clear spray Deft.

☐ Rub with #0000 steel wool, wax, and polish.

HIPPO

The Hippopotamus is still another of Michael Murphy's creations at Cherry Tree Toys. The anima-

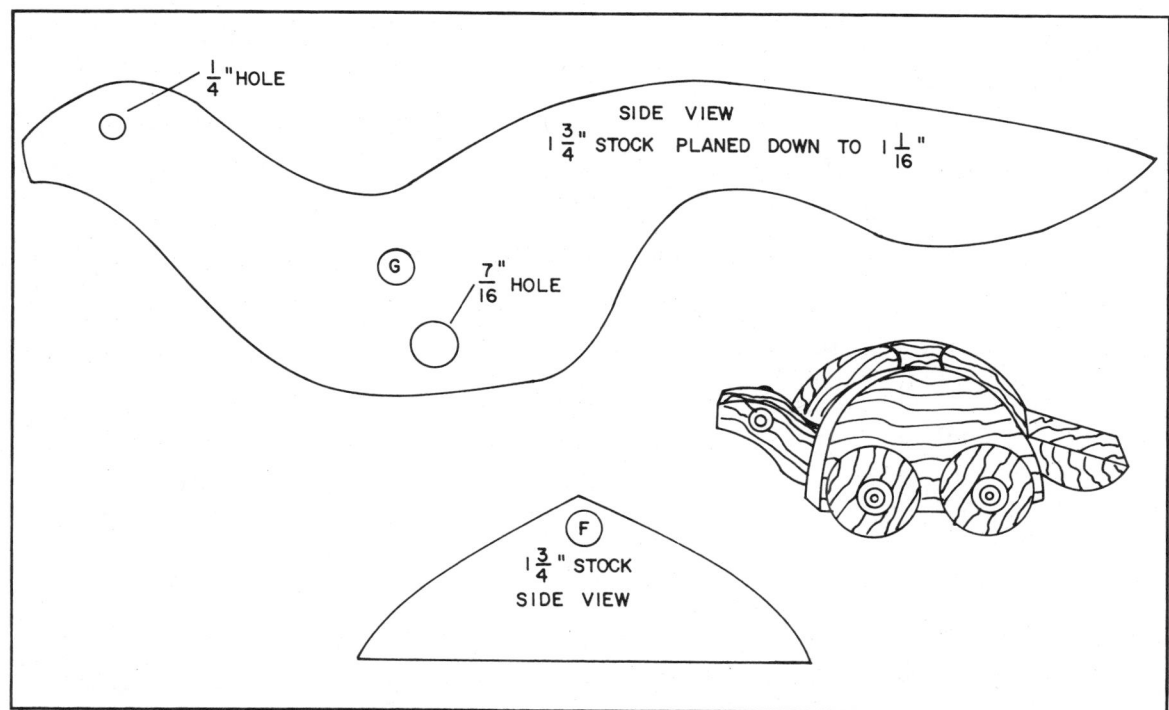

Fig. 2-11. Turtle patterns for head/tail and shell filler piece are shown, as well as a perspective view.

tion is accomplished by a method quite different than the techniques used in the other toys.

In this toy Mr. Murphy uses an offset wheel (the hole is off center) combined with a piston dowel that moves up and down pushing against the underside of the nose and upper jaw.

Almost any suitable wood may be used for this project. I chose mahogany because its natural color resembles a real hippopotamus.

Preparation

☐ Make the patterns for the nose/upper jaw, for the nose/upper jaw filler piece, and the body to the proportions shown in Fig. 2-12. The patterns were made from cardboard backs of tablets. This method proved more practical than trying to transfer the outline directly to the wood, because these patterns were used many times to help in the layout process and to verify size and shape.

☐ Trace outline of the body/nose parts on 1 3/4-inch stock (Table 2-5).

☐ Cut the outline with a band saw or saber saw.

☐ Sand the body/nose parts with a drum sander or cylindrical sander.

Assembly

☐ Bore the two 7/16-inch axle holes.

☐ Cut the 11/16-inch wide slot in the lower part of the body/nose part on the circular saw with a dado head.

☐ Bore the 17/32-inch piston hole.

☐ Trace the outline of the nose/upper jaw sides on 5/16-inch thick stock.

☐ Cut the outline on a jigsaw or band saw.

☐ Glue the two pieces to the body/nose piece (Fig. 2-13).

☐ When the glue is dry, sand the edges of the three pieces in the last step on a drum sander.

☐ Line up the 1/4-inch holes on the nose/upper jaw with the 17/64-inch hole on the body after

Table 2-5. Materials for the Hippo Are Listed.

NUMBER OF PIECES	CODE	PART	SIZE	MATERIAL
2	Ⓐ	"teeth" short pin	head 1/2" diam. x 3/8" pin 1/4" x 1/2"	from Cherry Tree Toys
2	Ⓑ	jaw hinge pin long pin	head 1/2" diam. x 3/8" pin 1/4" x 1 1/4"	from Cherry Tree Toys
1	Ⓒ	offset wheel	5/8" x 1 1/4" diam with 3/8" hole	from Cherry Tree Toys
4	Ⓓ	wheels	3/4" x 2 1/2" x 3/8" hole	from Cherry Tree Toys
2	Ⓔ	wheel axles	3 $\frac{5}{16}$" length	3/8" birch dowel
1	Ⓕ	"piston"	2 $\frac{5}{8}$" length	1/2" birch dowel
1	Ⓖ	body/nose	1 $\frac{3}{4}$" x 4 $\frac{7}{8}$" x 9 $\frac{1}{8}$"	suitable material
2	Ⓗ	nose/upper jaw sides	5/16" x 2 $\frac{1}{16}$" x 5 $\frac{3}{16}$"	suitable material

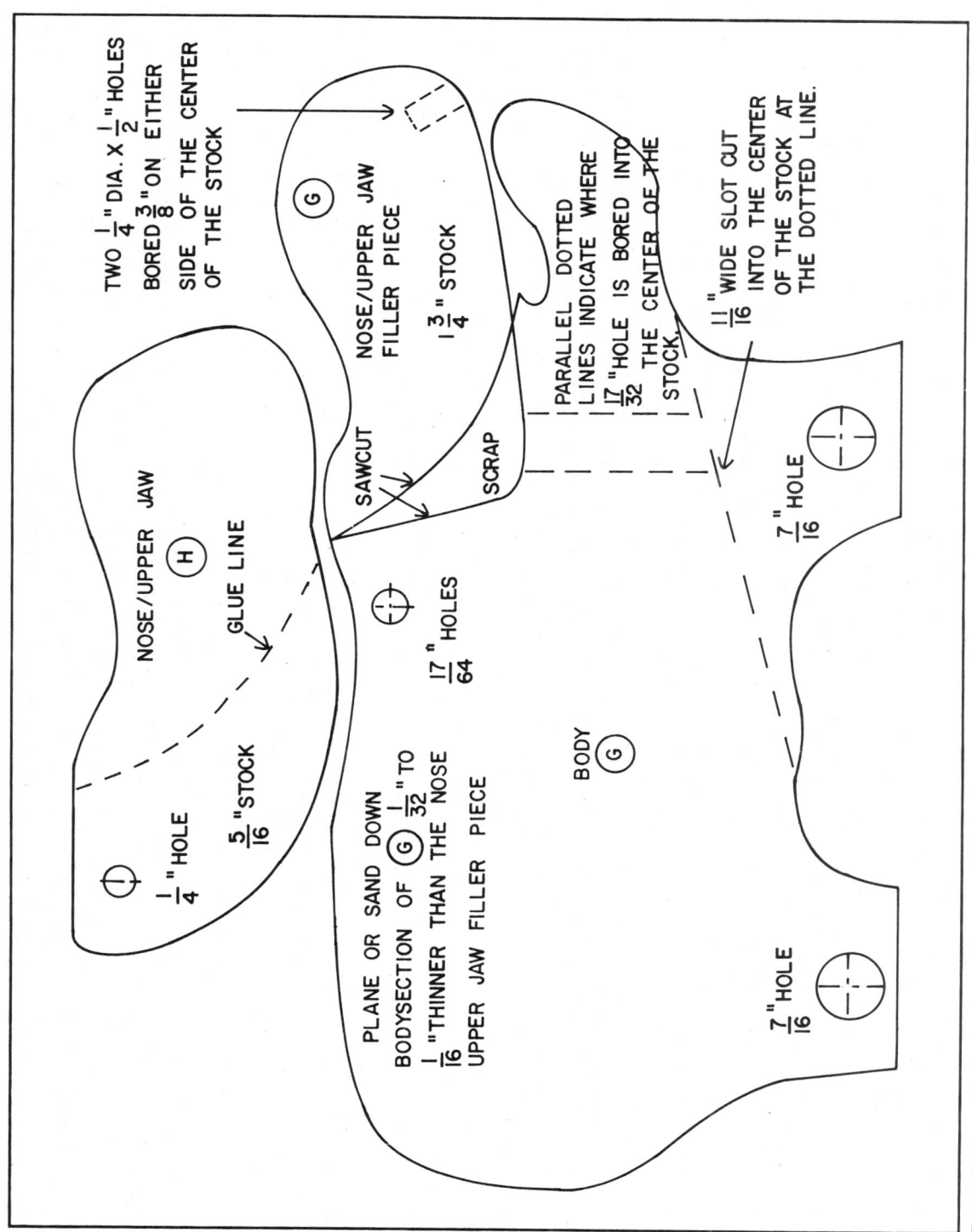

Fig. 2-12. Hippo details are shown. Courtesy of Cherry Tree Toys.

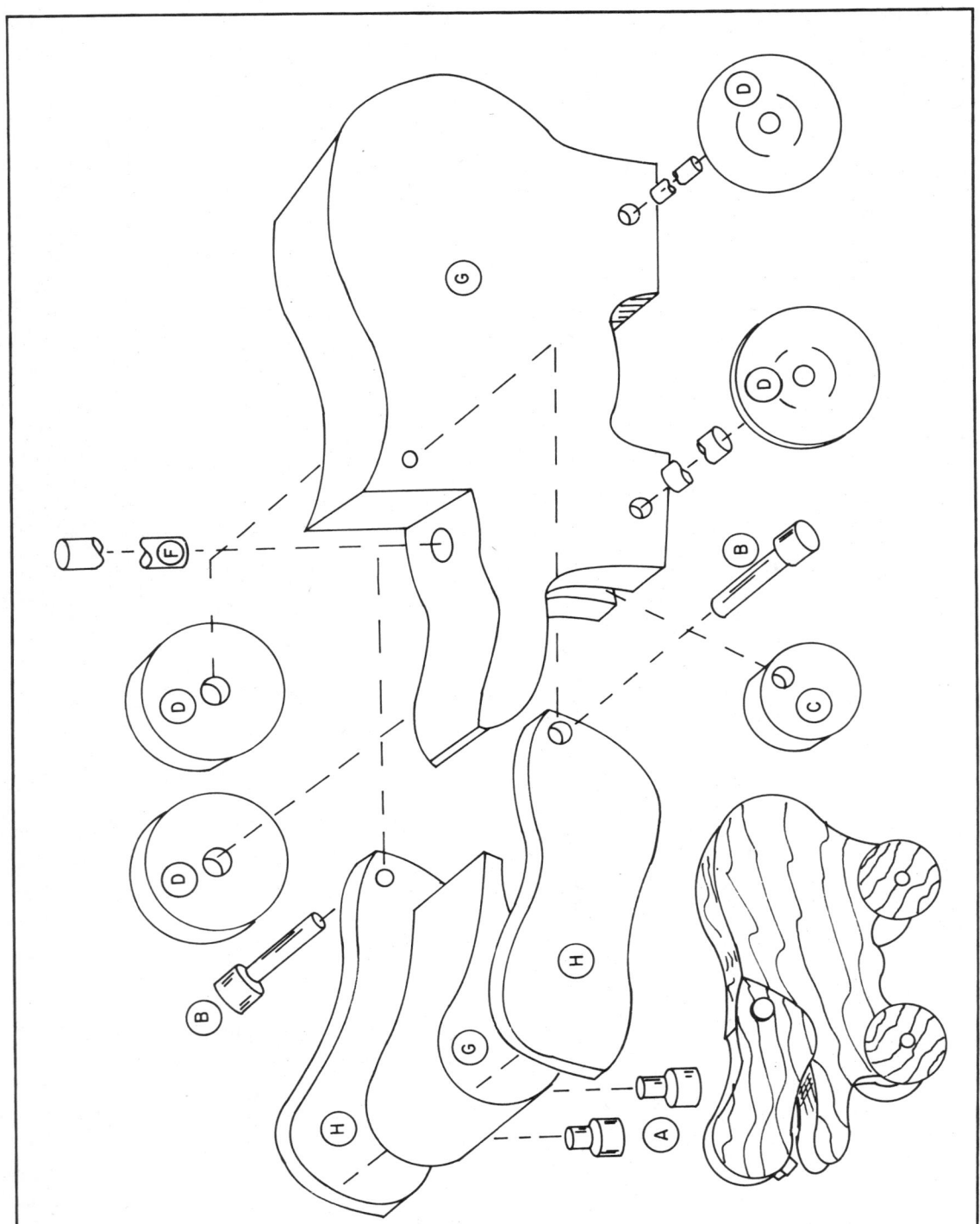

Fig. 2-13. Exploded view and perspective of the Hippo. Courtesy of Cherry Tree Toys.

Fig. 2-14. Completed Hippo project is shown, with mouth open. Courtesy of Cherry Tree Toys.

it has been planed or sanded down. See the note on Fig. 2-14.

☐ Clamp the three-piece assembly you have already glued to the body.

☐ Bore the 1/4-inch hole through the two nose/upper jaw parts and the body.

☐ Remove the nose/jaw assembly and rebore the 1/4-inch hole to 17/64 inch which will prevent the jaw hinge pins from binding.

☐ Sand the entire body and nose with fine sandpaper.

☐ Replace the three-piece nose assembly on the body and line up the three holes.

☐ Insert the jaw hinge pins into place, but only after the teeth holes are bored and the teeth inserted.

☐ Drive one wheel axle onto one wheel. Insert the axle half way through the front axle hole. Attach the offset wheel and the drive axle through the body and into the second wheel.

☐ Saw the "piston" to length. Insert it into the piston hole after the nose/jaw assembly is tipped back.

Finishing

☐ Try out the hippo by rolling the wheels on the floor. The nose/upper jaw should move up and down with a clattering sound (Figs. 2-14 and 2-15).

☐ Apply three or four coats of clear spray Deft. When dry rub with #0000 steel wool, wax, and polish.

HOPPIN' BUNNY PUSH TOY

The Hoppin' Bunny Push Toy is an adaptation of a similar design by Criss-Cross Creations. The shape is different; the body is much thicker; there are two thick wheels between the feet instead of four wheels on the outside of the feet; and a hinged handle has been added.

The hopping motion is accomplished by boring the axle dowel holes on the two wheels off center.

By rotating the wheels by half turns, the action can be changed from hopping on all fours at once to alternate hopping of the front and rear quarters. The hinged handle helps in the free and unrestricted motion of the rabbit.

Preparation

☐ Lay out the pattern of the body and transfer to 1 3/8-inch stock (Fig. 2-16 and Table 2-6).

☐ Cut the outline of the body on the band saw.

☐ Sand the outline with a drum sander, disc sander, and by hand.

☐ Make patterns for the front and rear legs.

☐ Transfer the outline to 1/2-inch birch plywood.

☐ Saw the outline of legs with a band saw or jigsaw. If the jigsaw is used it will save considerable sanding time.

Assembly

☐ Bore 1/4-inch axle rod holes in all four legs.

☐ Cut the two wheels with a hole saw. Be-

cause of the thickness, it will be necessary to cut from both sides of stock.

☐ Plug up the center holes with 1/4-inch dowels.

☐ Establish a center for a new hole 1/4 inch off center.

☐ Bore a hole 17/64 inch in diameter through the wheels using the new offset centers.

☐ Bore a 1/2-inch diameter hole in the top of the body 1/2-inch deep to accommodate the handle.

☐ Bore the 1/8-inch diameter hinge pin hole.

☐ Cut the handle to length from a 3/8-inch dowel (Fig. 2-17).

☐ Cut the two axle rods to length.

☐ Insert the axle rods through the legs and wheels.

☐ Glue the legs to the body. Make sure that the wheels do not rub on the body. It may be necessary to drive small brads into the legs and body to hold them in place while the legs are being clamped to the body.

☐ Make patterns for the ears and lay them out on 3/8-inch birch plywood.

Fig. 2-15. Completed Hippo with mouth closed. Courtesy of Cherry Tree Toys.

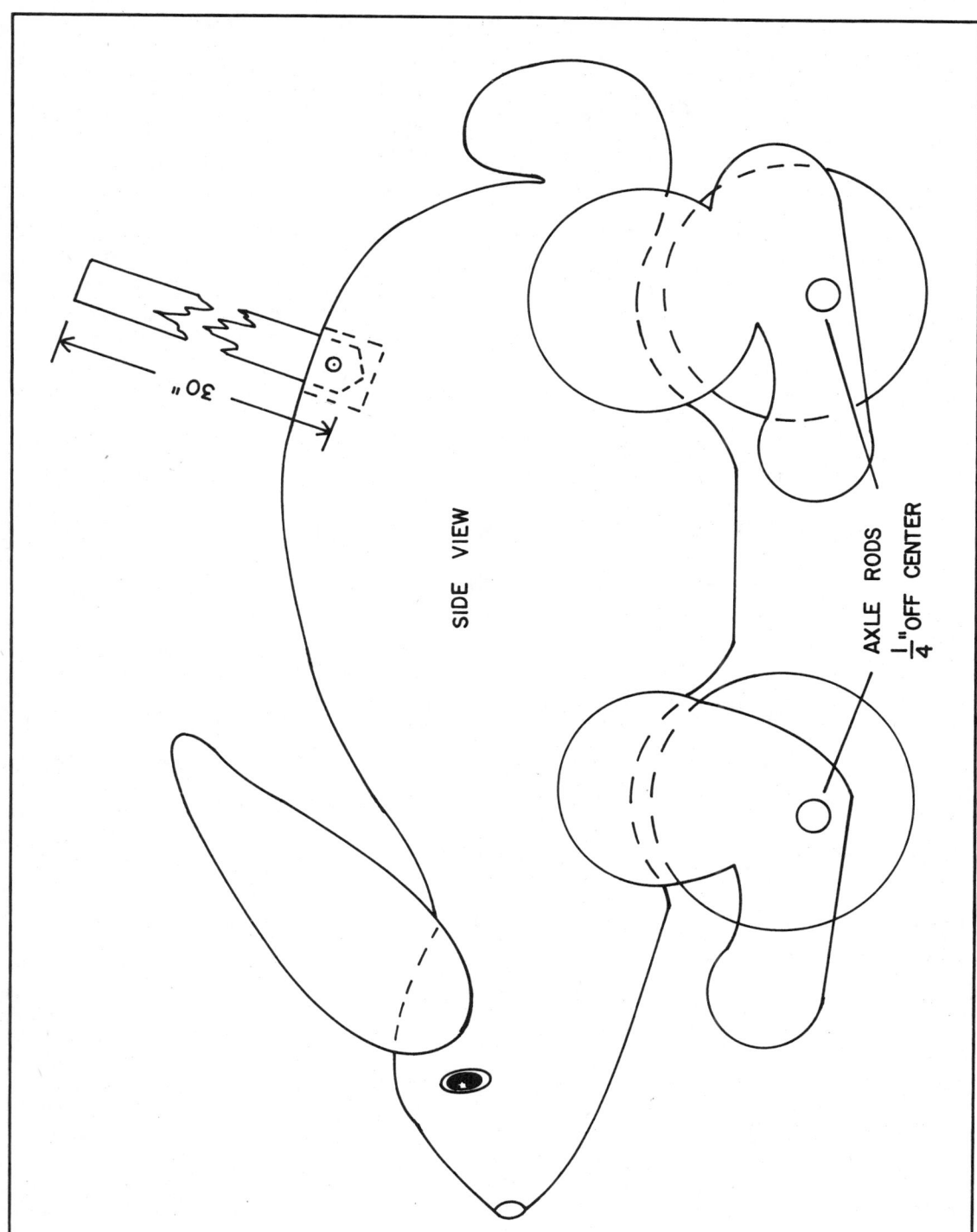

SIDE VIEW

30"

AXLE RODS
$\frac{1}{4}$" OFF CENTER

Fig. 2-16. Hoppin' Bunny side view is shown. Courtesy of Criss-Cross Creations.

NUMBER OF PIECES	PART	SIZE	MATERIAL
1	body	1 3/8"x 3 1/2"x 9 1/8"	maple or pine
2	wheels	2 1/8" diam.x 1 3/8"	maple or pine
2	front legs	1/2"x 2 1/4"x 2 3/4"	birch plywood
2	rear legs	1/2"x 2 1/2"x 2 7/8"	birch plywood
2	ears	3/8"x 1 1/8"x 3 1/8"	birch plywood
2	axle rods	2 3/8" length	1/4" birch dowel
1	handle	30"length	3/8" birch dowel
1	hinge pin	1 3/8" length	1/8" birch dowel

☐ Cut the ears with the jigsaw and sand the edges.

☐ Bore a 9/64-inch hole in the end of the handle.

☐ Cut a 1/8-inch diameter hinge pin to length and drive through the body and the end of the handle. This hinged handle allows the bunny to hop up and down without any restrictions.

Finishing

☐ Sand the entire project with fine sandpaper.
☐ Apply one or two coats of clear spray Deft.
☐ Paint the eyes and nose with black acrylic.

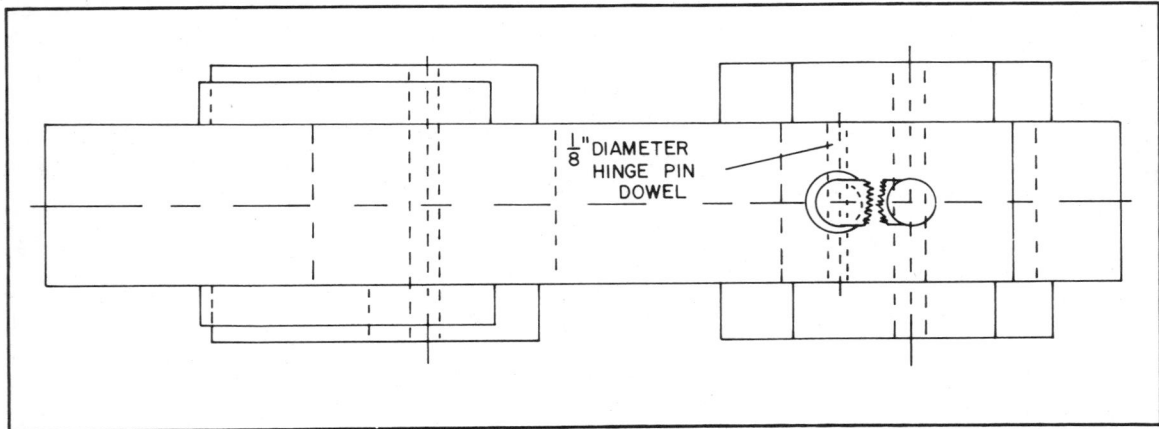

Fig. 2-17. Top view of Hoppin' Bunny is shown. Courtesy of Criss-Cross Creations.

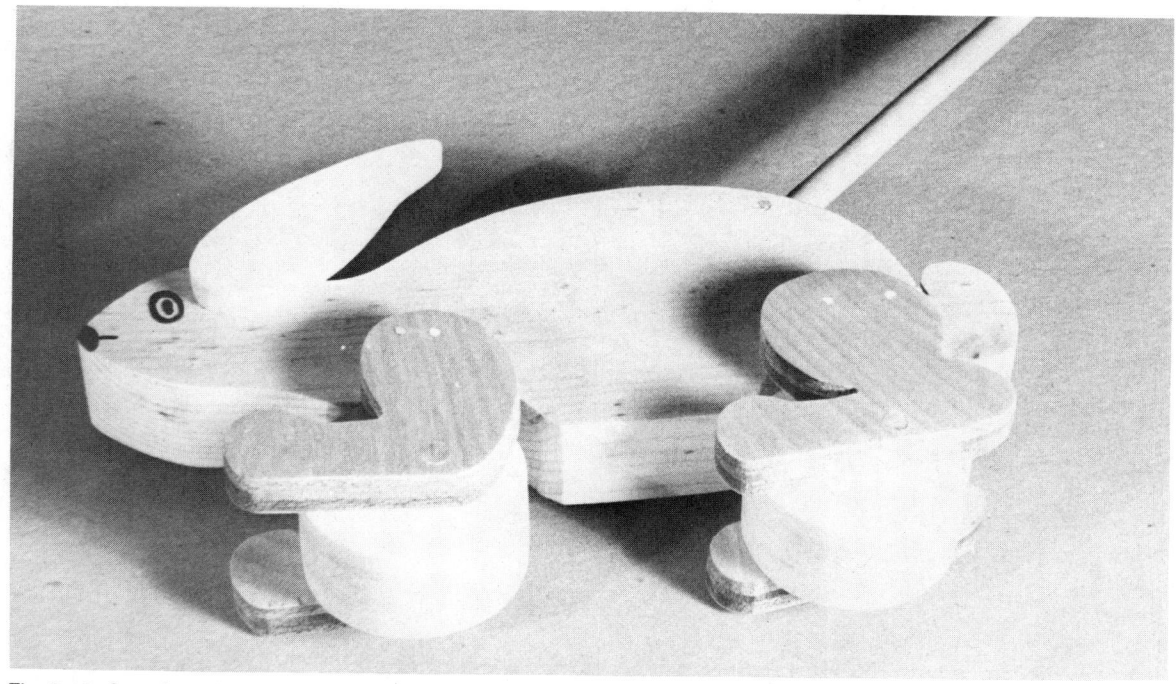

Fig. 2-18. Completed Hoppin' Bunny is shown. Courtesy of Criss-Cross Creations.

☐ Apply an additional coat or two of clear Deft.

☐ Rub the project with #0000 steel wool.

☐ Apply wax and polish. Figure 2-18 shows the finished project.

DIPLODOCUS OR DINOSAUR

The diplodocus, a herbivorous dinosaur, once roamed Wyoming and Colorado. This bizarre, whimsical, long-necked, and happy-looking creature is from the stables of Design Group.

Almost any wood can be used. It is best to use plywood for the legs because of the thinness of the elements.

The wheels can be cut by a hole saw, or commercial wheels can be used. I used white pine for the body and head and ¼-inch plywood for the legs and commercial wheels.

Preparation

☐ Make a full-size pattern of the body and head.

☐ Enlarge the pattern provided to 1-inch squares (Figs. 2-19 and 2-20).

☐ Transfer the outlines to 3/4-inch stock.

☐ Cut the outline with a band saw or other curve-cutting tool.

☐ Sand the edges on a drum sander and by hand.

☐ Make patterns for the front and hind legs.

☐ Transfer patterns to 1/4-inch plywood (Table 2-7).

Assembly

☐ Saw out legs on a jigsaw or band saw. Sawing with a jigsaw will lessen the amount of sanding.

☐ Saw out wheels with the hole saw, or purchase commercial wheels.

☐ Cut 1/4-inch dowels to the proper length for axles.

☐ Bore 17/64-inch holes in all the legs, and 1/4-inch holes in the body and head to accommodate dowels to allow the head to be turned.

☐ Insert the axles into the wheels after a

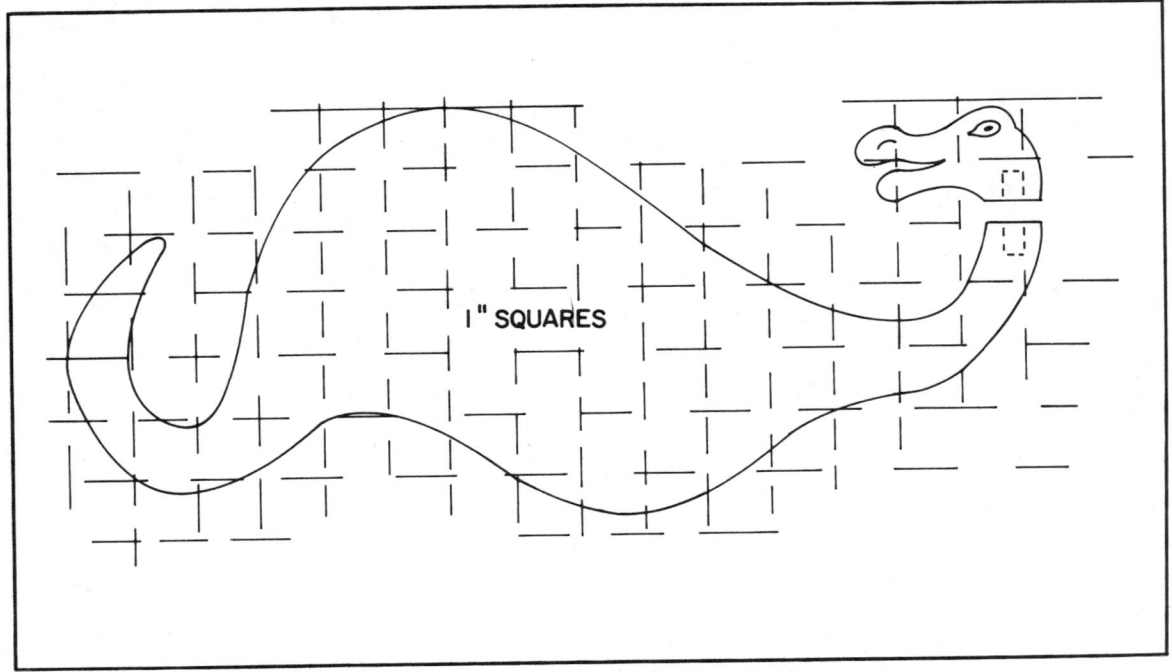

Fig. 2-19. Body and head pattern for the Diplodocus, or dinosaur, is shown. Courtesy of Design Group.

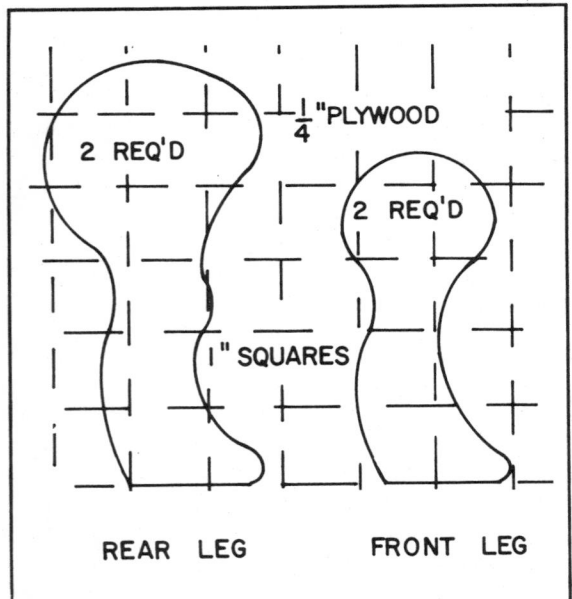

2 REQ'D

$\frac{1}{4}$"PLYWOOD

2 REQ'D

1" SQUARES

REAR LEG   FRONT LEG

Fig. 2-20. Pattern for the legs of the Diplodocus is shown. Courtesy of Design Group.

small amount of glue has been applied.
☐ Slip the axles through the holes in the legs.
☐ Glue on the other wheel.

Finishing

☐ Sand the entire project with fine sandpaper.
☐ Apply one coat of clear spray Deft. Paint the eye and nose with acrylic paint. Apply two more coats of Deft.
☐ Rub with #0000 steel wool, wax, and polish. Figure 2-22 shows the finished project.

DACHSHUND

This running Dachshund will bring a gleam of joy to the beholder and a broad smile to alert youngster.

These plans are my alterations of Criss-Cross Creations' designs. Compared with the original plans, the body is thicker, the ears are black walnut instead of brown felt, and the tongue is a brilliant red padauk instead of red felt.

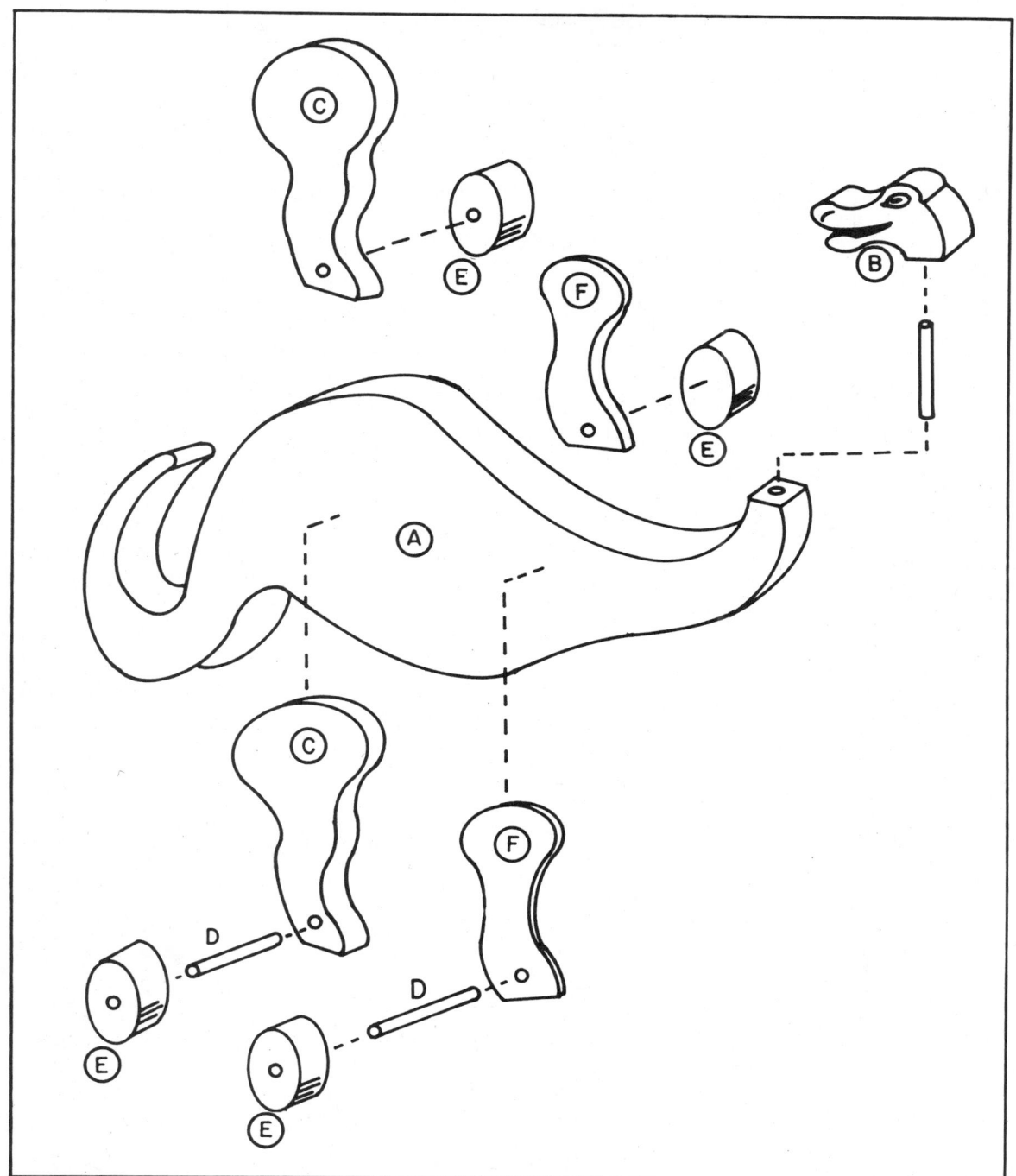

Fig. 2-21. Assembly of the Diplodocus. Courtesy of Design Group.

Table 2-7. The Diplodocus or Dinosaur Can Be Made with the Listed Materials.

NUMBER OF PIECES	CODE	PART	SIZE	MATERIAL
1	(A)	body	3/4"x 6 1/2"x 15	white pine , maple , or birch
1	(B)	head	3/4"x 1 5/8"x 2 7/8"	white pine, maple, or birch
2	(C)	hind legs	1/4"x 3"x 5 5/8"	birch plywood
2	(D)	axles	3" length	1/4" birch dowel
4	(E)	wheels	3/4"x 2" diam.	commercial or made by hand
2	(F)	front legs	1/4"x 2"x 4 1/2"	birch plywood

Preparation

☐ Make an enlarged pattern of the body and transfer to 1-inch stock (Fig. 2-23 and Table 2-8).

☐ Cut out the body with a band saw or saber saw.

☐ Bore the two 3/8-inch holes for the axles

☐ Mark and drill the four holes for the machine bolts that attach the upper legs to the body. The diameter of the holes should be slightly less than the diameter of the machine bolts.

☐ Cut the tongue, sand it, and glue it in the mouth.

☐ Sand the edges of the body with different sizes of drum sanders and sand the faces by hand.

Fig. 2-22. Perspective view of the Diplodocus. Courtesy of Design Group.

Table 2-8. Make the Dachshund with the Materials Given.

NUMBER OF PIECES	CODE	PART	SIZE	MATERIAL
1	(A)	body	1" x 6 1/4" 15 3/8"	redwood
4	(B)	upper leg	3/8"x 1 1/8"x 2 3/4"	birch or maple
4	(C)	lower leg	3/16"x 1 1/4"x 2 3/4"	birch or maple
4	(D)	wheels	1/4"x 2 3/8" diam.	cherry plywood
2	(E)	ears	1/8"x 1 3/16"x 2 3/4"	black walnut
1	(F)	tongue	1/4"x 1/2"x 1 3/4"	padauk
2		axles	1 5/8" length	3/8" birch dowel
2		flat washers	#10	
4		machine bolts	6-32x3/8"	
4		machine bolts	6-32x1/2"	
4		machine bolts	6-32x3/4"	

☐ Make a pattern for the ears and transfer to 1/8-inch thick black walnut.

☐ Saw the ears with a jigsaw and sand.

Assembly

☐ Glue the ears to the body.

☐ Make a pattern for the upper leg and trans-

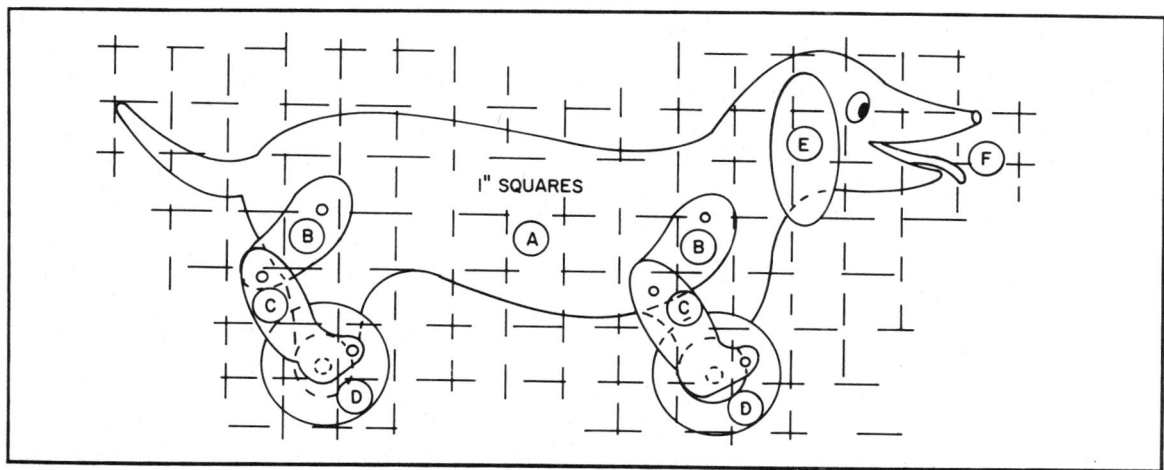

Fig. 2-23. Side view of the Dachshund. Courtesy of Criss-Cross Creations.

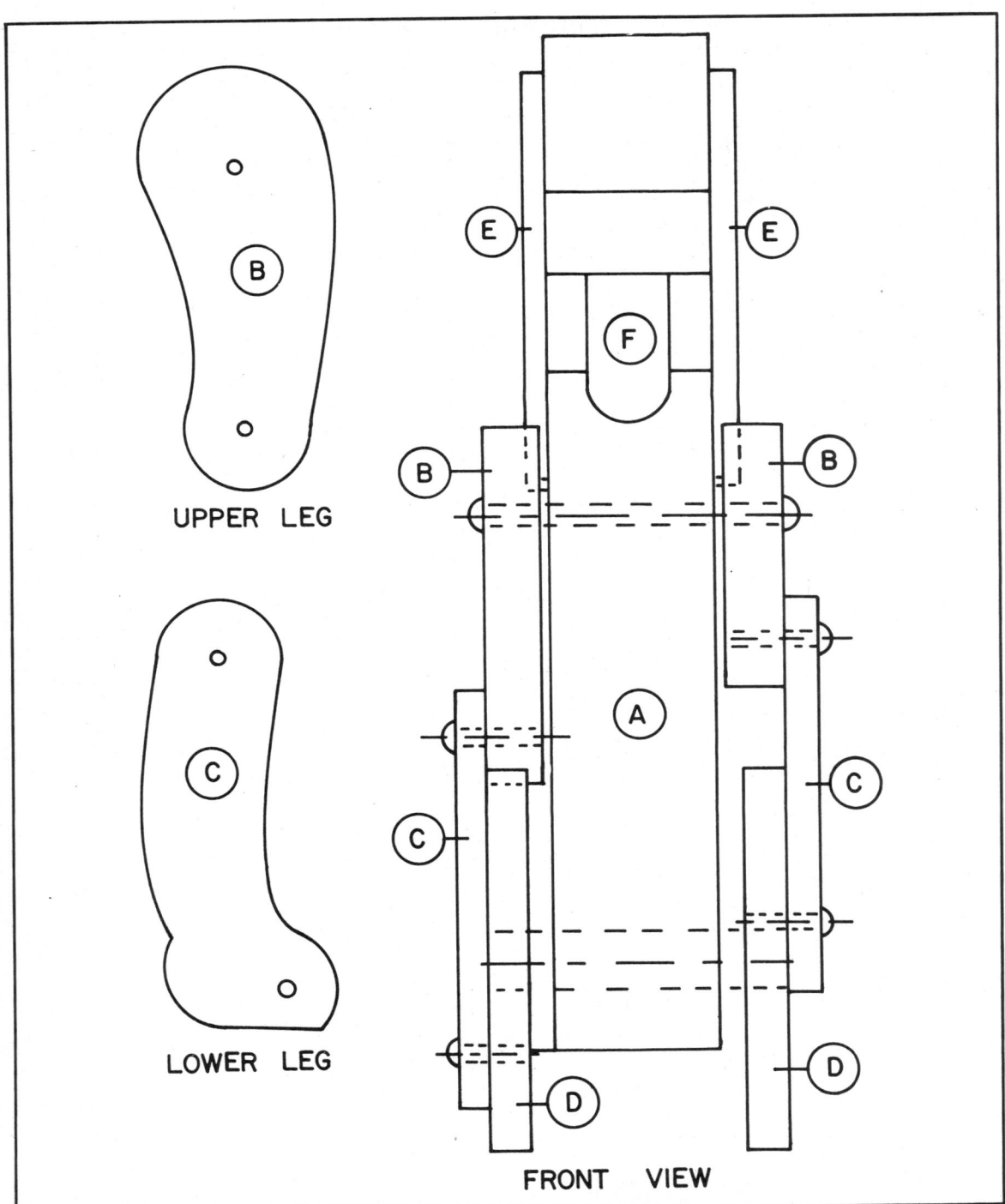

UPPER LEG

LOWER LEG

FRONT VIEW

Fig. 2-24. Front view and patterns for the Dachshund are shown. Courtesy of Criss-Cross Creations.

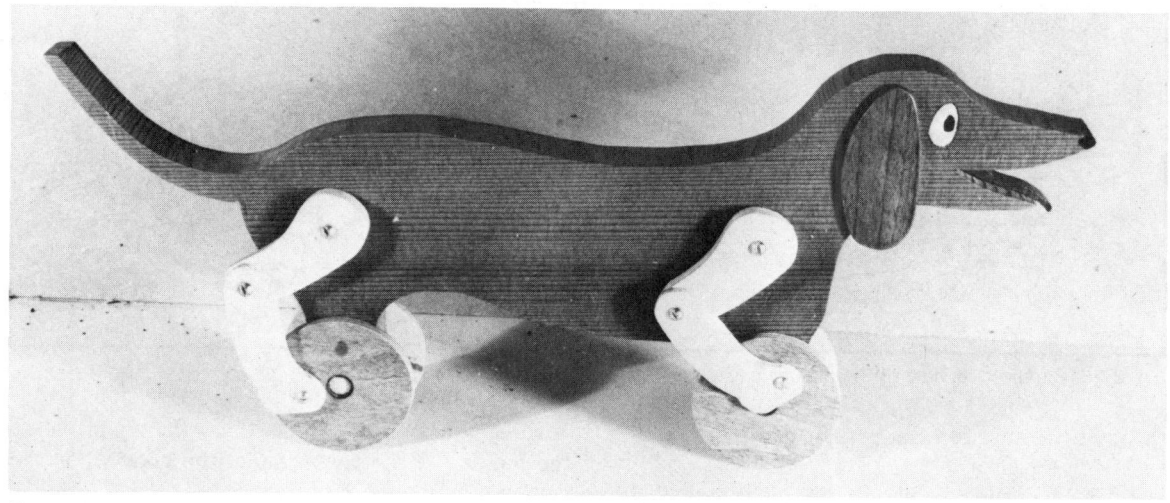
Fig. 2-25. Completed Dachshund project. Courtesy of Criss-Cross Creations.

fer four outlines to 3/8-inch stock (Fig. 2-24). Cut out the upper legs with a jigsaw.

☐ Make a pattern for the lower leg and transfer four outlines to 3/16-inch stock. Cut out the lower legs with a jigsaw.

☐ Cut the wheels from 1/4-inch stock with a hole saw. Enlarge the 1/4-inch center hole to 3/8-inch diameter.

☐ Drill the machine bolt holes in the four wheels slightly smaller than the diameter of the machine bolts.

☐ Drill the upper hole in the upper legs slightly larger than the machine bolts.

☐ Drill the lower hole in the upper legs slightly smaller than the machine bolts.

☐ Bore the holes in the lower legs slightly larger than the machine bolts.

☐ Cut the axles to length. Insert the axles through holes in the body and attach the wheels.

☐ Attach the upper legs to the body with six 32 × 3/4-inch machine bolts after inserting #10 washers between the upper legs and body.

☐ Attach the upper part of the lower legs to the lower part of the upper legs with six-32 × 1/2-inch machine bolts.

☐ Attach the lower part of the lower legs to the wheels with six 32 × 3/8-inch machine bolts. A small amount of epoxy glue should be applied to the

ends of the machine bolts before inserting in the holes.

Finishing

☐ Paint in the eyes. I used black-and-white acrylic paint.

☐ Apply three or four coats of clear spray Deft or polyurethane.

☐ When the finish is dry, rub with #0000 steel wool. Apply wax and polish. Figure 2-25 shows the finished project.

SHARKY JAWS

This interesting, animated Sharky Jaws will delight children, particularly if they have seen the movies and read the many stories concerning sharks (Fig. 2-26).

Sharky Jaws is rather easy to construct and can be completed in three or four hours. A band saw is the best tool for cutting out the parts; however, other curve-cutting tools may be used.

I selected white pine for the project, but almost any straight-grained lumber may be used.

Preparation

☐ Make a pattern for the body which includes the nose/upper jaw portion that is glued between

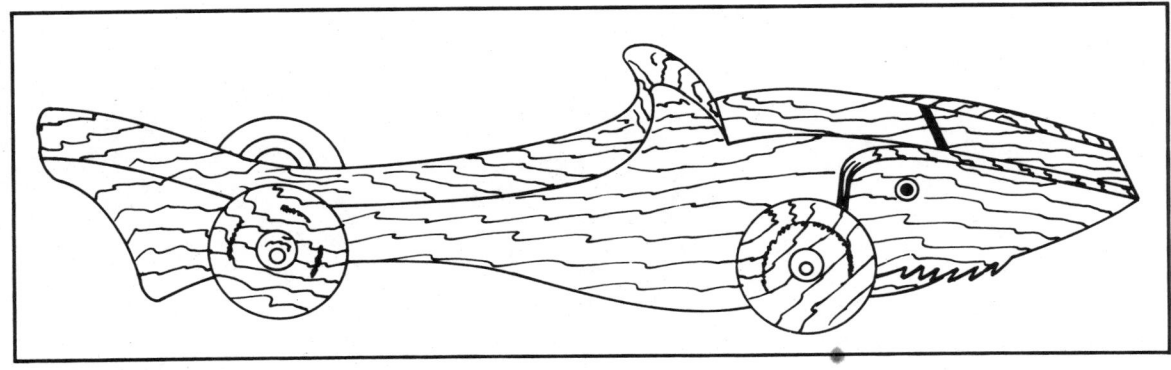

Fig. 2-26. Perspective view of Sharky Jaws.

the jaws. Be sure to enlarge the pattern in Fig. 2-27 to 1-inch squares.

□ Mark the design on 1 1/8-inch stock (Table 2-9).

□ Saw the outline of the body and nose/upper jaw portion with a band saw or other curve-cutting tool. See Figs. 2-27 and 2-28.

□ Plane down the portion of the body so that it is from 1/32 inch to 1/16 inch thinner than the nose/upper jaw filler piece. This planing prevents the binding of the jaws against the body when the jaws are activated.

□ Bore the two 13/32-inch axle holes in the lower part of the body.

□ Make the pattern for the jaws.

□ Mark the design on 5/16-inch stock.

□ Cut the outline with a jigsaw or other curve-cutting tool.

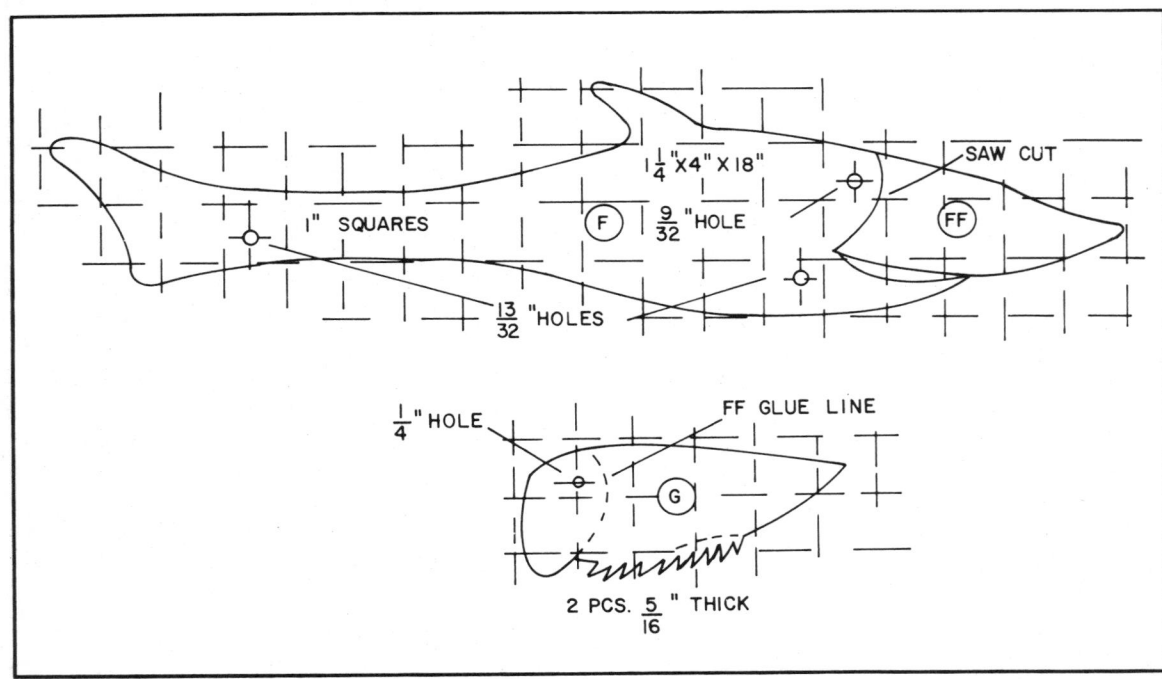

Fig. 2-27. Working plan for Sharky Jaws.

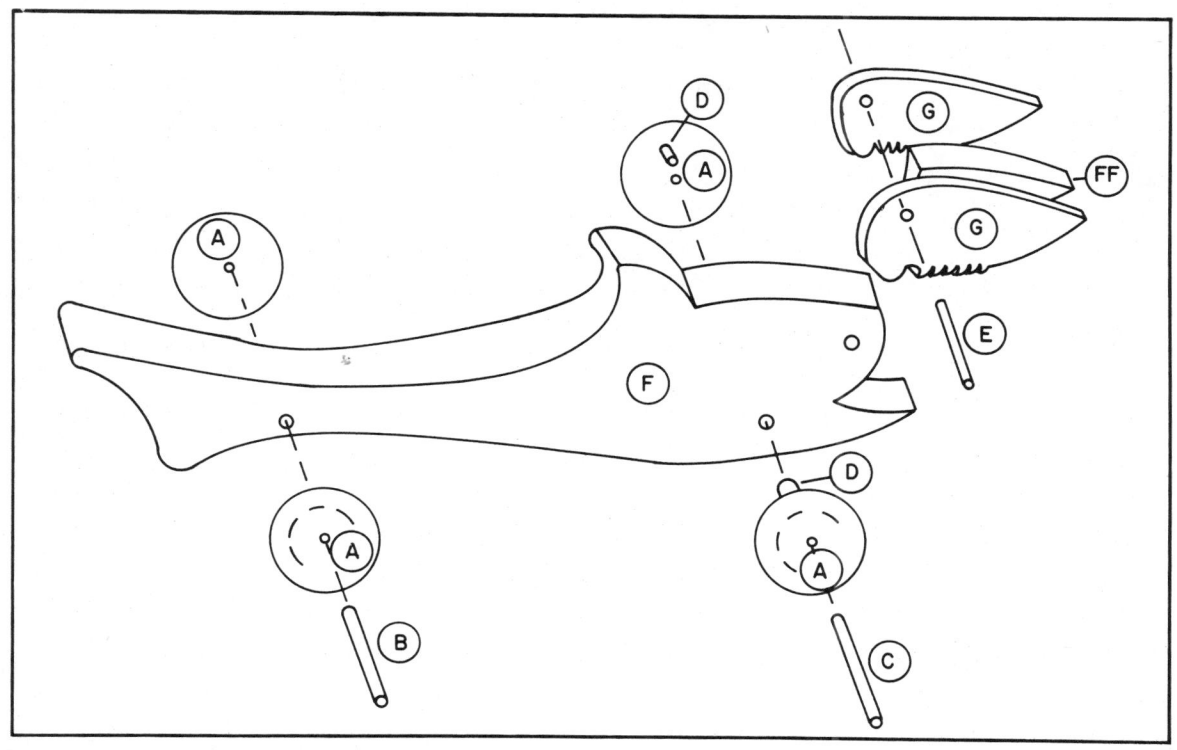

Fig. 2-28. Assembly of Sharky Jaws.

Table 2-9. Sharky Jaws Can Be Made from the Listed Materials.

NUMBER OF PIECES	CODE	PART	SIZE	MATERIAL
4	(A)	wheels	3/4" x 2 1/2"	birch
1	(B)	rear axle	2 1/2" length	3/8" birch dowel
1	(C)	front axle	3 1/4" length	3/8" birch dowel
1	(D)	activator pin	9/16" length	3/8" birch dowel
1	(E)	hinge pin	11 1/16" length	1/4" birch dowel
1	(F)(FF)	body	1 1/8" x 4" x 18"	white pine
1	(G)	jaws	5/16" x 2 3/8" x 5 3/8"	white pine

61

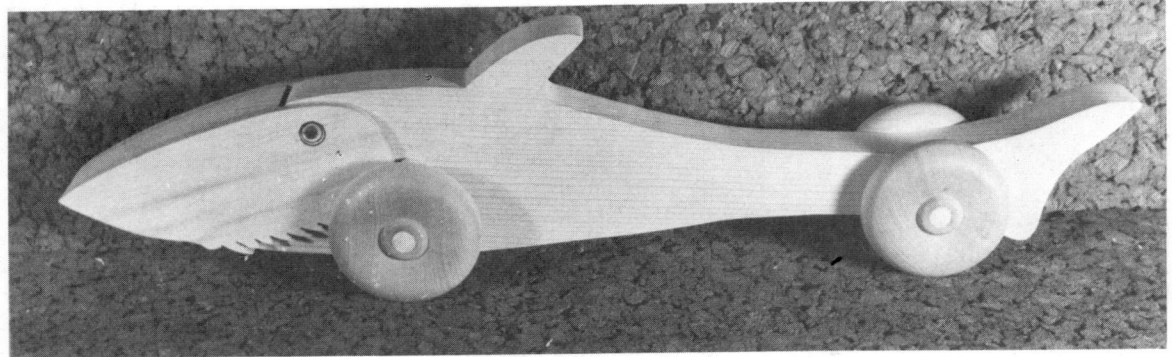

Fig. 2-29. The completed Sharky Jaws, with mouth closed.

☐ Sand the edges of the body and jaws with a drum sander.

Assembly

☐ Glue the nose portion between the two jaw pieces.

☐ Clamp the nose and jaws assembly against the body and bore the 1/2-inch hole for the hinge pin which simulates the eye of the shark.

☐ Remove the nose and jaws assembly and rebore the 1/4-inch hole in the body to 17/64 inch in diameter to permit the axle to turn freely. Insert the hinge pin.

☐ Bore a 3/8-inch hole on the flat side of two of the wheels near the circumference to the depth of

1/4 inch. The center of the hole should be approximately 7/8 inch from the center of the hole in the wheel.

☐ Cut the activator pin from a 3/8-inch dowel.

☐ Apply glue and drive the activator pins into the two wheels.

☐ Drive the front axle into one of the wheels.

☐ Run the front axle through the front hole of the body.

☐ Attach the other wheel with the activator pin to the axle so that the pins are 180 degrees from each other. This step provides more frequent clacking of the jaws when the toy is rolled on the floor. Repeat the procedure for the rear wheels. See Fig. 2-26.

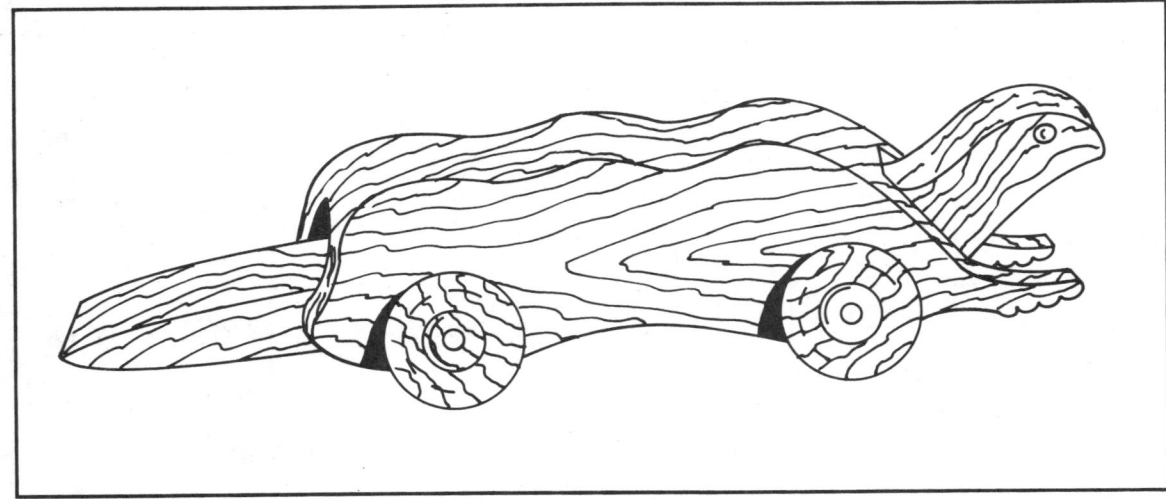

Fig. 2-30. Perspective view of the Undulating Otter.

Finishing

☐ Sand the entire piece with #220 sandpaper.

☐ Apply three or four coats of clear spray Deft or polyurethane.

☐ When the finish is dry, rub with #0000 steel wool, wax, and polish. Figure 2-29 shows the finished project.

UNDULATING OTTER

The Undulating Otter (Fig. 2-30), which I designed, has the same up-and-down movement of the head and tail that was incorporated into the Tantalizing Turtle.

This amazing toy may be made of any softwood or hardwood; however, I chose mahogany since its natural color is closer to the color of the otter.

The secret of the undulating movement is in the action of the offset, eccentric wheel with an off center axle hole.

Preparation

☐ Make a pattern of heavy paper or cardboard for the head/tail. Be sure to enlarge the pattern in Fig. 2-31 to 1-inch squares.

☐ Trace the outline on 1 5/8-inch stock (Table 2-10).

☐ Cut the outline with a band saw.

☐ Plane off about 1/32 inch of stock from the

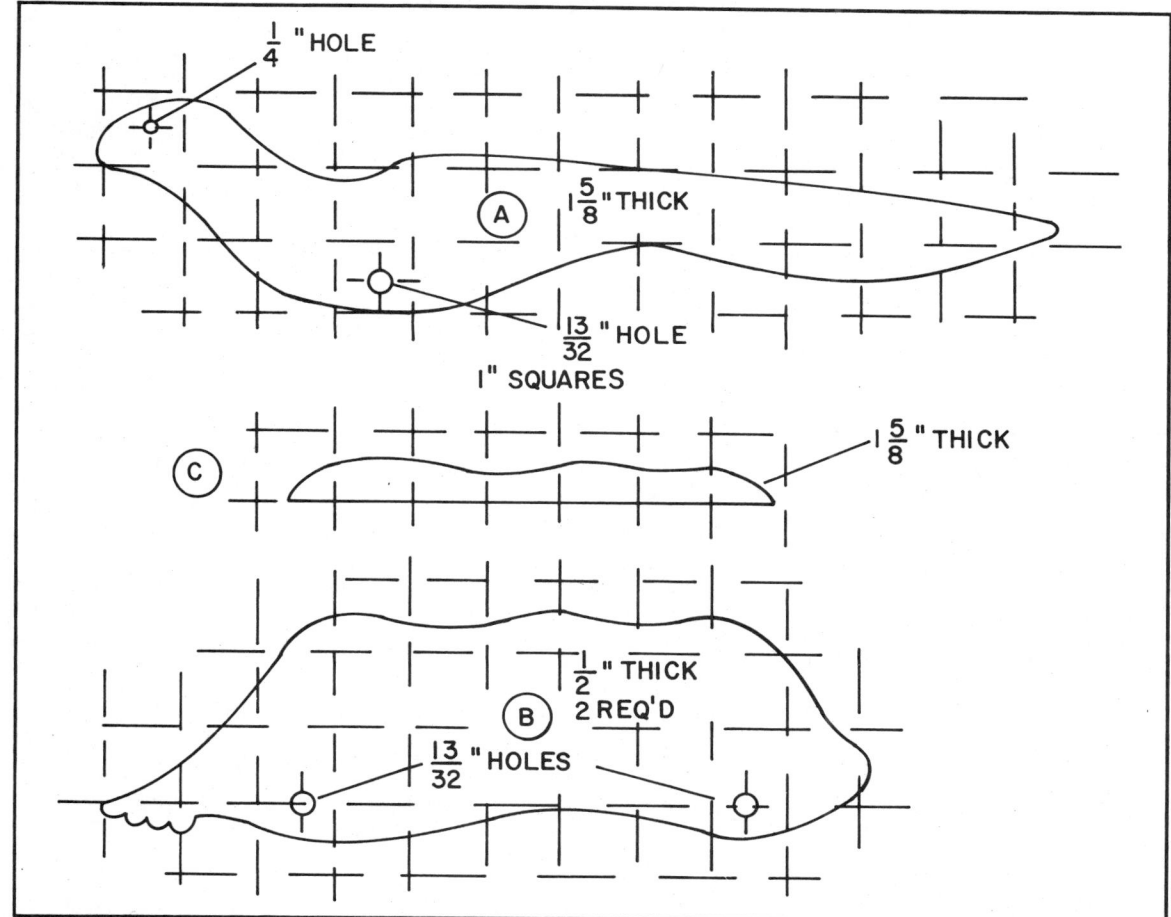

Fig. 2-31. Working plans for the Undulating Otter.

Table 2-10. Materials for the Undulating Otter Are Given.

NUMBER OF PIECES	CODE	PART	SIZE	MATERIAL
1	(A)	head/tail	1 5/8"x2 7/8"x12 3/4"	mahogany
2	(B)	sides	1/2"x3"x10 1/4"	mahogany
1	(C)	filler	1 5/8"x 3/4" x 6 1/2"	mahogany
4	(D)	wheels	5/8"x 2" diam. with a 3/8" hole	from Cherry Tree Toys
1	(E)	offset wheel	5/8"x 1 1/4" diam. with 3/8" hole, centered 3/8" from edge of hole	from Cherry Tree Toys
2	(F)	eyes	1/4" diameter	from Cherry Tree Toys
1	(G)	rear axle	3 7/8" length	3/8" birch dowel
1	(H)	front axle	3 7/8" length	3/8" birch dowel

head/tail so that it will not rub or bind between the sides. Sand the edges with a drum sander.

☐ Bore the 1/4-inch holes for the eyes and the 13/32-inch hole for the front axle. Insert the eyes into the holes with glue.

☐ Make a pattern for the sides.

☐ Trace the outline in 1/2-inch stock.

☐ Cut the outline with a jigsaw or band saw.

☐ Sand the edges with a drum sander.

☐ Bore the two 13/32-inch axle holes with the two sides clamped together.

☐ Make the pattern for the filler.

☐ Trace the pattern on 1 5/8-inch stock.

☐ Cut the outline with a band saw.

Assembly

☐ Glue the filler between the two sides. See Fig. 2-32.

☐ After the glue is set, round over the top edges of the sides and the filler to a 1/4- to 3/8-inch radius.

☐ Cut the front axle to length.

☐ Insert one end of the front axle into the flat side of one of the wheels. Push or drive the axle through so that the end is flush with the outside of the wheel.

☐ Push the axle through the front hole in one of the sides, through the front hole in the head/tail, and through the front hole in the other side piece. Drive the other wheel until the outside is flush with the axle end. See Fig. 2-32.

☐ Cut the rear axle.

☐ Insert the axle through one of the two sides.

☐ Force the rear axle through the hole in the offset wheel, then out through the hole in the other side.

☐ Drive the two remaining wheels on the rear axle.

Finishing

☐ Sand the entire project with fine sandpaper.

□ Finish with three or four coats of clear spray Deft or polyurethane. Rub with #0000 steel wool and wax. Figures 2-33 and 2-34 show the finished project.

RHINO

I designed the Rhino (Fig. 2-35) with the same animation devices as the Hippo. In this toy, the two principal activating items are an offset eccentric wheel and a piston or plunger activator. As the toy is pushed along the floor the nose and upper jaw bob up and down in a realistic manner.

Almost any suitable wood may be used for the Rhino. I chose American black walnut because its natural dark brown color resembles the color of a real rhino.

Preparation

□ Make a pattern of the combined body and nose. Be sure to enlarge the pattern in Fig. 2-36 to 1-inch squares.

□ Trace or transfer the pattern outline to 1 5/8-inch thick walnut (Table 2-11).

□ Cut the outline with a band saw. The ears

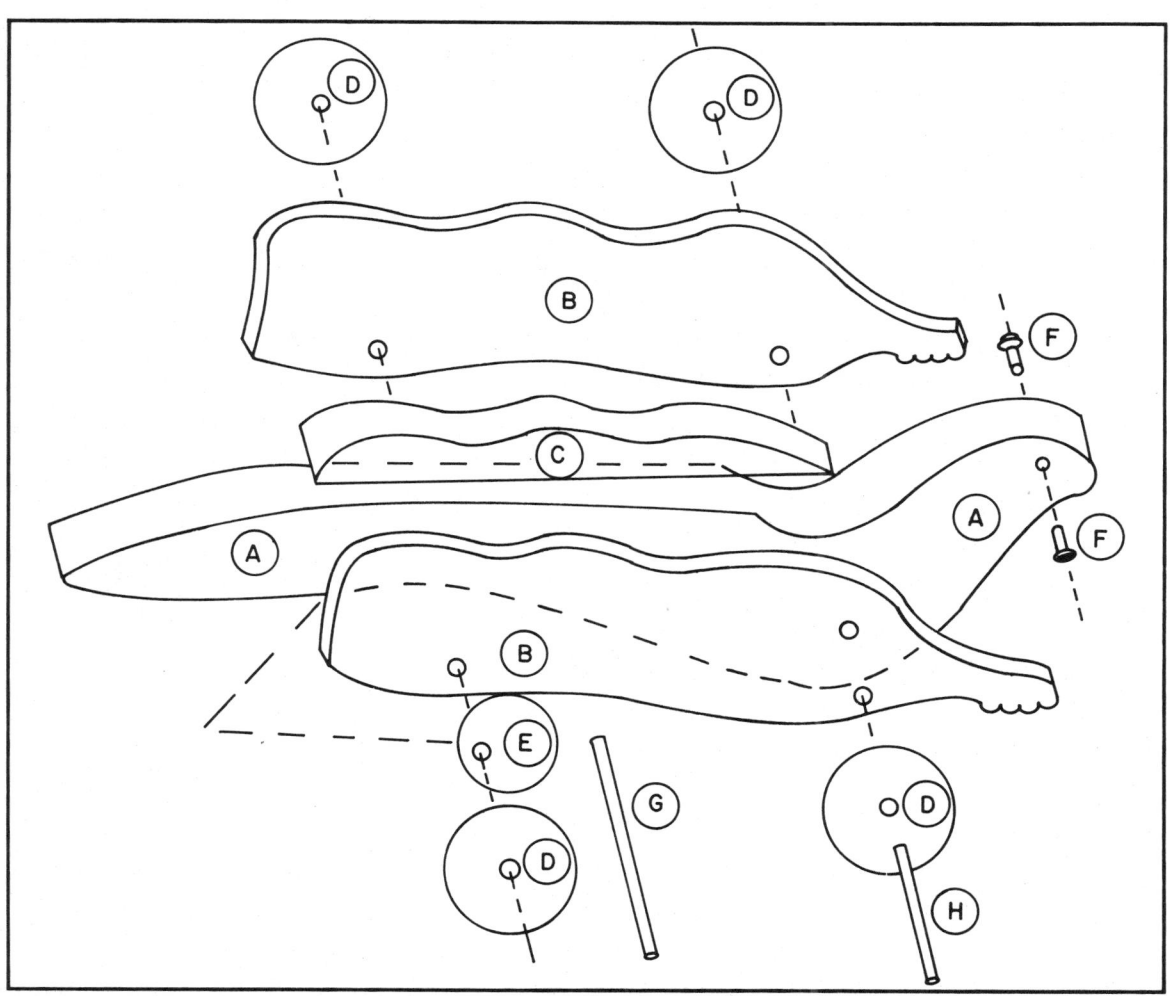

Fig. 2-32. Assembly of the Undulating Otter.

65

Fig. 2-33. Completed Undulating Otter.

Fig. 2-34. The underside of the Undulating Otter, with the offset wheel, is shown.

Fig. 2-35. Perspective view of the Rhino.

66

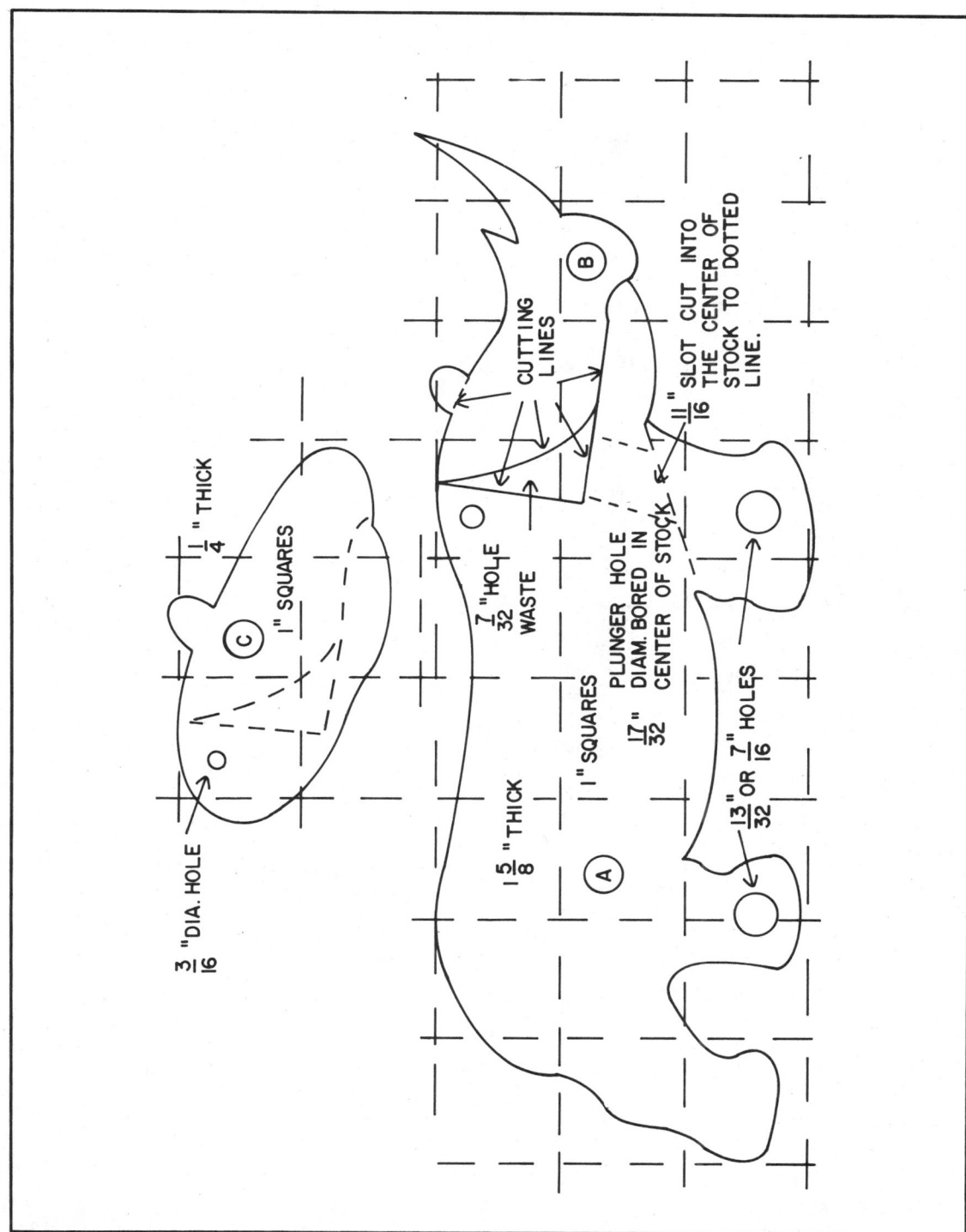

Fig. 2-36. Working plans for the Rhino.

67

Table 2-11. The Rhino Can Be Made Using the Materials Given.

NUMBER OF PIECES	CODE	PART	SIZE	MATERIAL
1	(A)	body 8	1 5/8"x3 1/4"x8 1/2"	walnut
	(B)	nose		
2	(C)	nose sides	1/4" x 1 3/4" x 3 1/4"	walnut
4	(D)	wheels	5/8"x2" diam.	commercial or homemade
1	(E)	offset eccentric wheel	5/8"x 1"diam. with 3/8" hole centered 3/8" from edge of wheel	maple or birch
1	(F)	plunger activator	1 3/8" length	1/2" birch dowel
1	(G)	hinge pin	2 1/4" length	3/16" birch dowel
2	(H)	axle rods	2 3/4" length	3/8" birch dowel

are cut off as they will appear on the nose sides.

☐ Cut the interior "cutting lines," which will result in a triangular waste piece, and separate the nose from the body.

☐ Plane down the body about 1/32 inch so that the nose sides will not bind on the body when the nose and nose sides move up and down.

☐ Bore the 7/32-inch hinge pin hole.

☐ Bore the two 13/32- or 7/16-inch axle holes.

☐ Set up a dado head on the circular saw and cut the 11/16-inch slot in the center of the stock in the front legs.

☐ Bore the plunger activator hole 11/32 inch in diameter in the center of stock. See Fig. 2-36.

☐ Sand the body and nose with 3/0-120 sandpaper. A drum sander can be used to advantage.

☐ Make an enlarged pattern for the nose sides. See Fig. 2-36.

☐ Trace or transfer the outline of the pattern to 1/4-inch thick walnut.

☐ Cut the outlines with a jigsaw.

☐ Bore the 3/16-inch diameter hinge pin hole.

☐ Sand the nose sides with 3/0-120 sandpaper.

Assembly

☐ Glue the nose sides to the nose aligning the edges carefully (Fig. 2-37).

☐ When the glue is dry, further align the nose sides with the nose with needle files, emery boards, and sandpaper.

☐ Align the hinge pin holes and insert the hinge pin.

☐ Turn the offset eccentric wheel and bore the 3/8-inch offset hole.

☐ Cut the plunger activator.

☐ Turn the Rhino upside down and insert the plunger activator. Leave the Rhino in this position until the front axle is inserted.

☐ Cut the axle rods to length.

☐ Insert one axle rod into the front legs. Insert an axle rod through the hole in the offset ec-

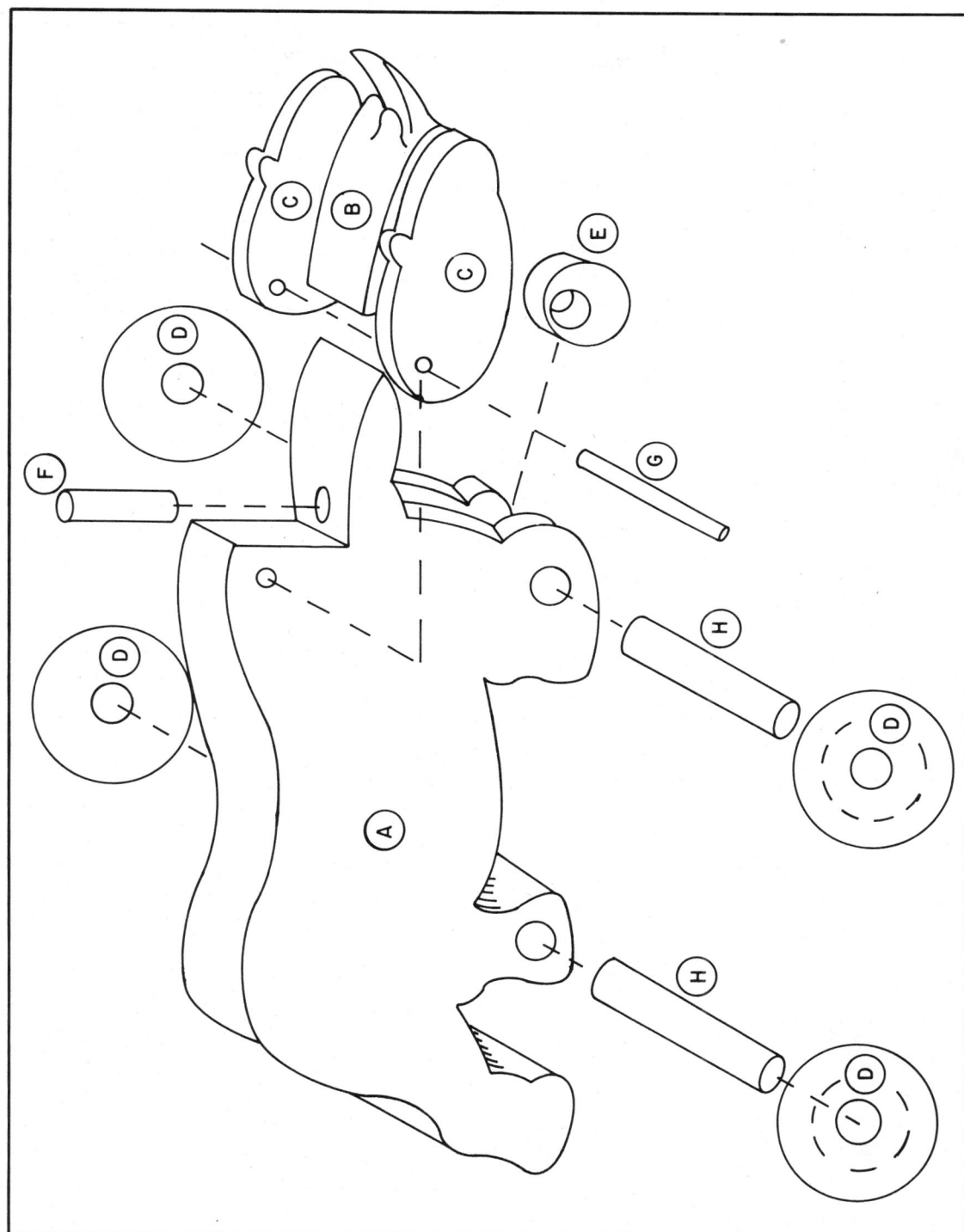

Fig. 2-37. Assembly of the Rhino.

69

Fig. 2-38. Completed Rhino, with mouth closed.

Fig. 2-39. Completed Rhino, with mouth open.

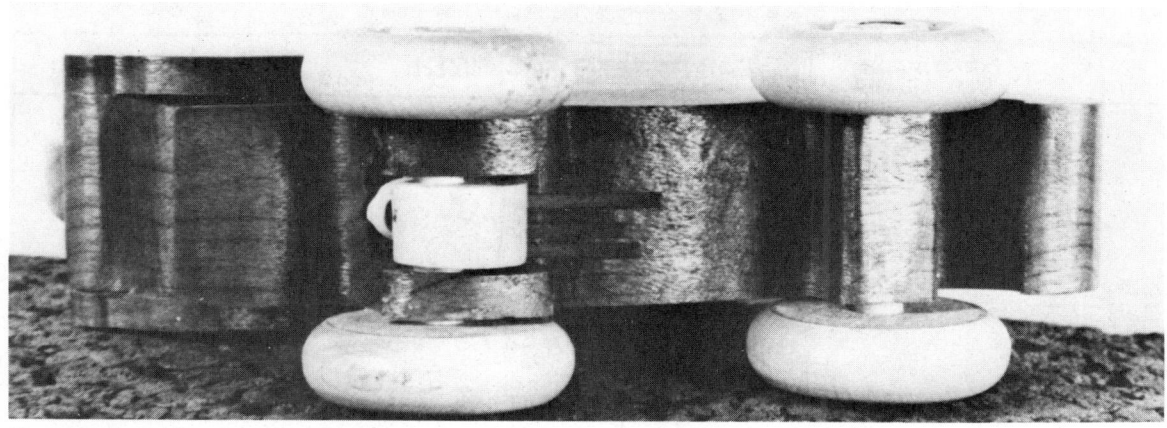

Fig. 2-40. Underside of the Rhino, showing the offset eccentric and the plunging activator.

centric wheel, and then on through the other front leg.

☐ Center the offset eccentric wheel on the axle. If the offset wheel has a tendency to turn on the axle, glue it in place or drive a small brad through the offset wheel into the axle.

☐ Drive on the two front wheels.

☐ Insert the rear axle rod through the rear axle hole and drive on the two remaining wheels.

Finishing

☐ Mix a few drops of animal glue in a cup of hot water.

☐ Sponge the entire project and let it dry overnight.

☐ Sand with 6/0-220 sandpaper.

☐ Spray on one coat of clear Deft.

☐ Paint on the eyes with black acrylic paint.

☐ Spray on two or three more coats of clear Deft.

☐ Sand with 9/0-320 sandpaper and rub with #0000 steel wool.

☐ Apply one or two coats of furniture wax and polish. A drop or two of water on the wax will increase the glossiness. Figures 2-38 through 2-40 show the finished project.

HOPPITY FROG

The happy Hoppity Frog is a delightful push toy for young children. The mechanism that causes the frog to hop is the same as in the Hoppin' Bunny Push Toy. The hopping motion is accomplished by boring the axle dowel holes off center.

By rotating the wheels by half turns, the action can be changed from hopping on all fours at once to alternate hopping on the front and rear quarters. The hinged handle helps in the free and unrestricted motion of the frog.

Almost any wood may be used; however, I chose white pine.

Preparation

☐ Make a pattern of the body. Be sure to enlarge the pattern in Fig. 2-41 to 1/4-inch squares.

☐ Trace or transfer the outline to 1 3/8-inch stock (Table 2-12).

☐ Cut out the body with a band saw.

☐ Sand the edges of the body with a drum sander and by hand.

☐ Lay out enlarged patterns for the front and rear legs.

☐ Trace or transfer the pattern to 3/8-inch stock.

Note: If the toy will be used roughly, it is better to use 3/8-inch plywood.

☐ Cut the outline of the legs with a jigsaw.

☐ Sand the edges of the legs with a small drum sander and by hand, and bore 1/4-inch axle holes.

☐ Lay out the wheels on 1 5/32-inch stock with a compass.

71

Table 2-12. Materials for the Hoppity Frog Project.

NUMBER OF PIECES	PART	SIZE	MATERIAL
1	body	1 3/8"x 4 3/8"x 6 3/4"	white pine
2	front legs	3/8"x 1 1/8"x 3 3/8"	white pine
2	rear legs	3/8"x 2 3/4"x 3 1/8"	white pine
2	wheels	1 5/32"x 2"diam.	white pine
1	handle	30" length	3/8" birch dowel
1	hinge pin	1 3/8" length	1/8"birch dowel
2	axle rods	2 1/8" length	1/4" birch dowel

☐ Bore a 1/4-inch hole through the centers.

☐ Cut the wheels, just outside the 2-inch diameter, with the band saw.

☐ Mount the wheels on a lathe faceplate mandrel, true up the circle, and sand while the wheels are turning in the lathe.

☐ Plug up the center hole with a 1/4-inch dowel.

☐ Mark a point 3/8 inch off center and bore a 1/4-inch offset hole in the wheels.

☐ Cut the two 1/4-inch axle rods 2 1/8 inches long.

☐ Ream out the 1/4-inch holes in the wheels to 17/64 inch to allow the wheels to turn, or sand down the two axle rods.

Assembly

☐ Insert the axle rods through the wheels and glue the legs in place on the ends of the axles.

☐ Clamp the wheel/leg assemblies to the body. It will be necessary to move the assemblies around until the wheels do not rub on the body. When the correct location is found, mark around the legs. The clamps are then removed, glue is applied, the assemblies replaced on the lines, and the clamps reapplied.

☐ When the glue is dry, bore a 1/2-inch diameter hole in the back of the body about 5/8-inch deep for the handle.

☐ Bore a 1/8-inch diameter hole through the body. The hole should go through the center of the handle hole and be located about 1/4 inch from the edge of the body. See Fig. 2-41.

☐ Cut the handle 30 inches long from a 3/8-inch diameter dowel.

☐ Bore a 1/8-inch hole about 1/4 inch from one end of the handle.

☐ Cut the 1/8-inch diameter hinge pin, 1 3/8 inches long, from a birch dowel.

☐ Place the handle in the hole in the body. Drive the hinge pin through the body and the end of the handle.

Finishing

☐ Sand the entire project with fine sandpaper.

☐ Spray on three or four coats of clear Deft or polyurethane.

☐ When dry, rub with #0000 steel wool, and apply furniture wax and polish. Figures 2-42 and 2-43 show the finished project.

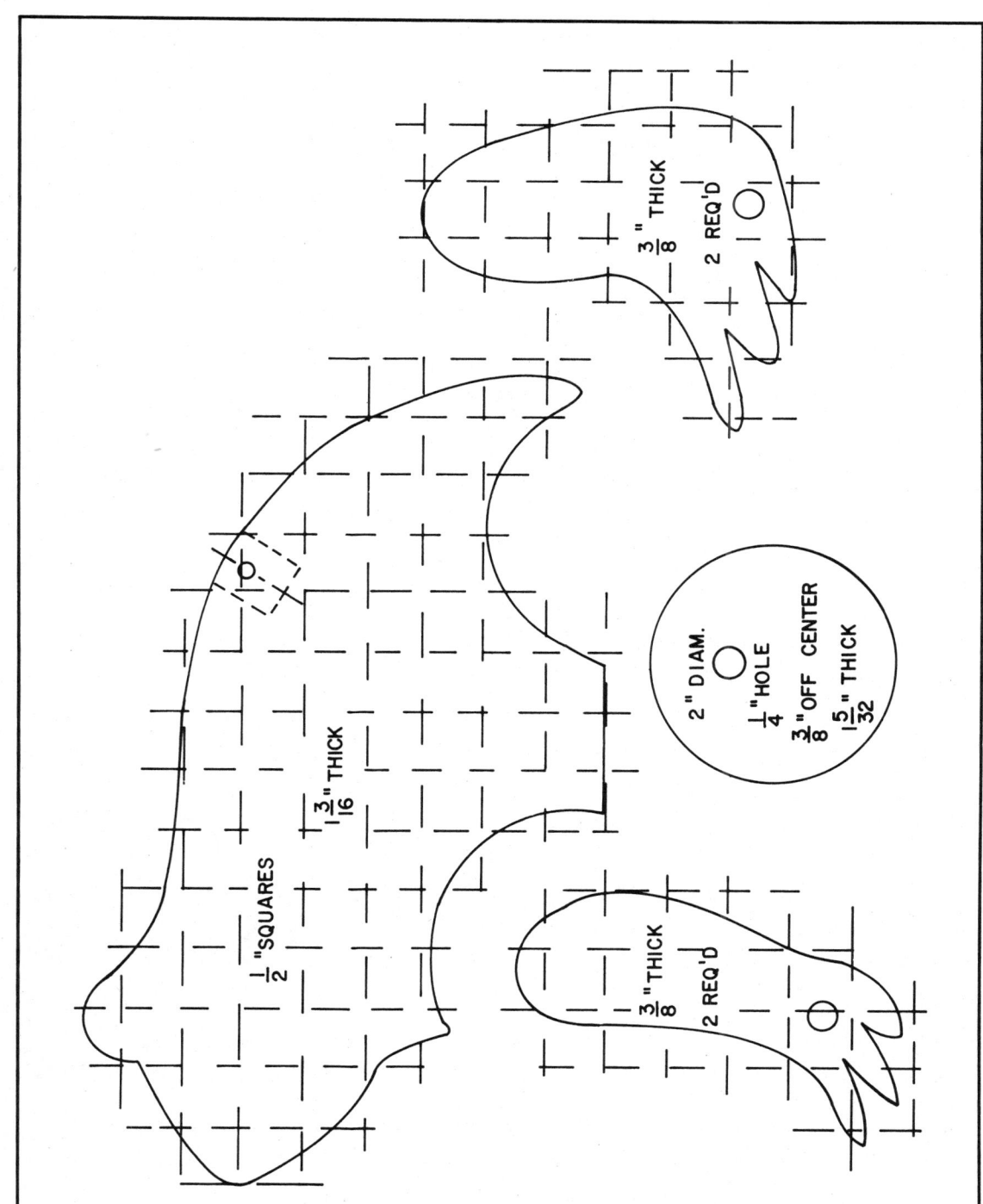

Fig. 2-41. Working plans for the Hoppity Frog.

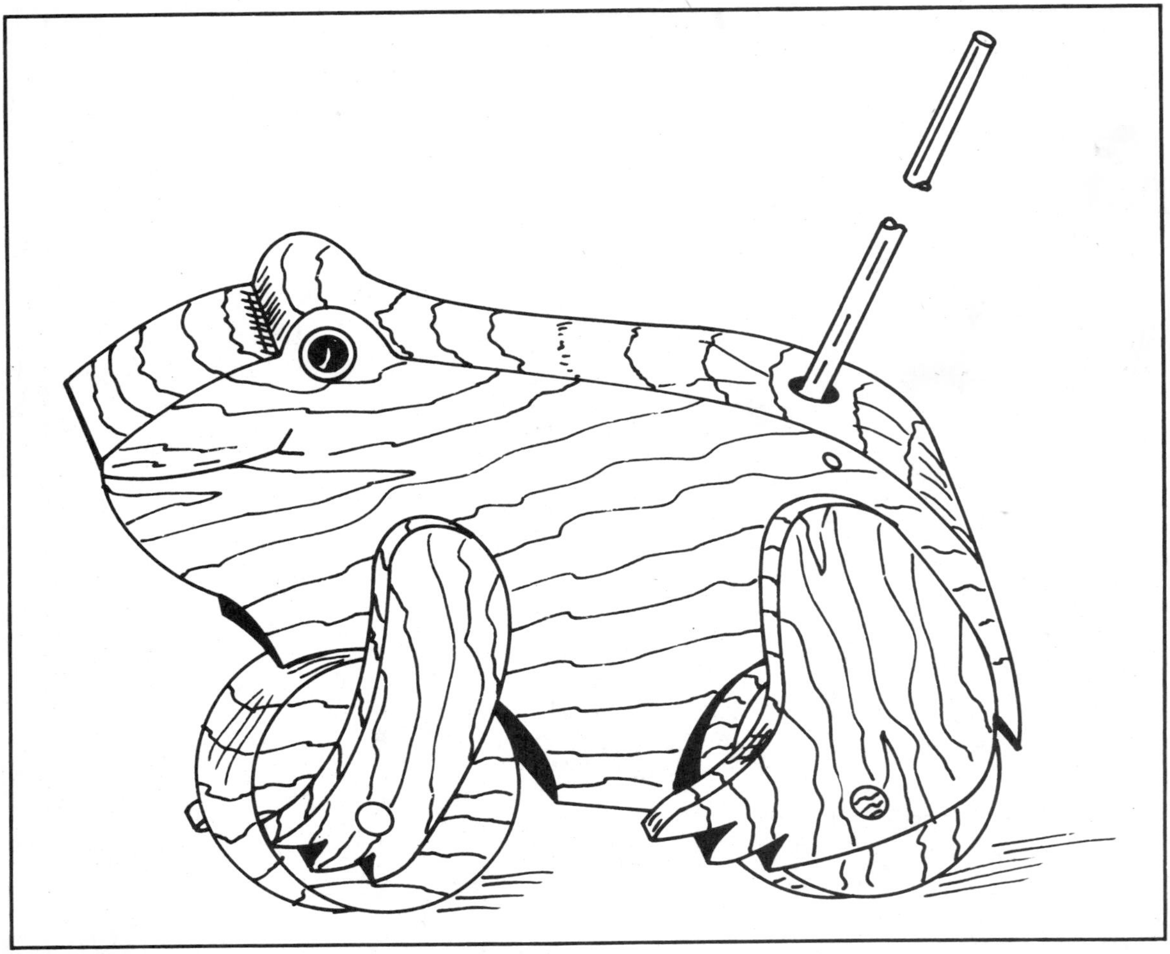

Fig. 2-42. A perspective view of the Hoppity Frog.

Fig. 2-43. The underside of the Hoppity Frog is shown.

3

Cars

This chapter contains step-by-step directions for making four toy cars. Illustrations and tables of materials are also provided to help you in the assembly of these cars.

SPORTS CAR

This classic sports car by Toy Designs is a favorite of youngsters because of its speedster design (Fig. 3-1). One adult described it this way: "It looks like it is going 80 miles per hour while it is standing still."

It is not cumbersome or heavy; it can be handled with ease. It is sturdily built and, with a minimum of care, might well become a family heirloom.

I decided to construct the body of maple in one piece rather than two pieces glued together. For contrast, the fenders were made of black walnut. As an added touch, I placed hubcaps over the ends of the wheel axles. These hubcaps are push nuts, sometimes called acorn nuts or Palnuts.

Preparation

☐ Make the patterns for the body and fenders. Be sure to enlarge the pattern in Fig. 3-2 to correct proportions.

☐ Glue up the stock for body if two pieces are going to be used.

☐ Cut the stock for the body (Table 3-1).

☐ Trace the enlarged pattern on the body stock.

☐ Cut the outline of the two ends only.

☐ Locate and bore a hole for "people."

☐ Cut out the cockpit with a band saw or other curve-cutting tool.

☐ Drill holes for the two running axles 17/64 inch in diameter.

☐ Drill a 1/4-inch hole for the spare tire axle.

☐ Drill a hole for the radiator cap.

☐ Cut the stock for the fenders.

☐ Trace enlarged patterns on the fender stock.

☐ Cut out fenders with a curve-cutting tool.

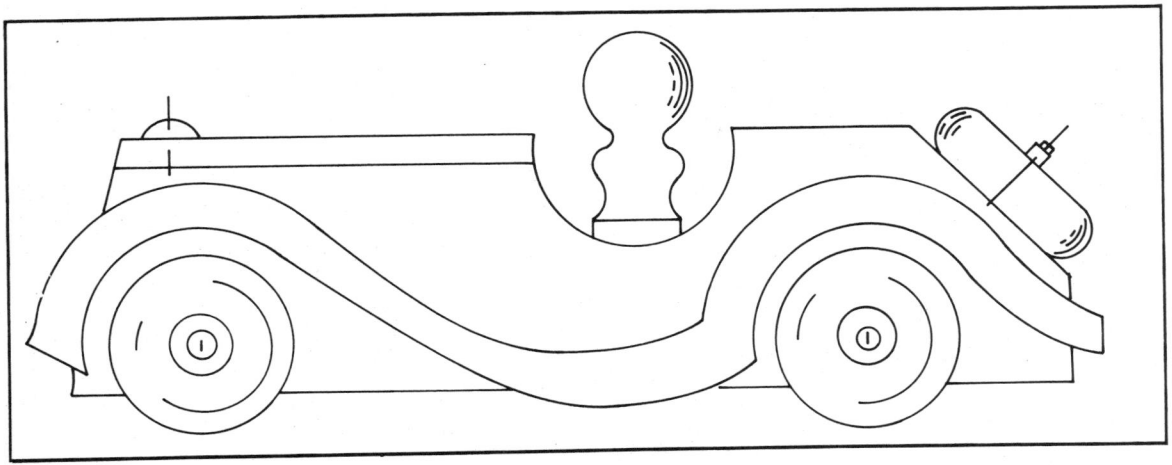

Fig. 3-1. Perspective view of the Sports Car. Courtesy of Toy Designs.

☐ Plane chamfers on the body; sand the fenders on the drum sander, and glue the fenders to the body.

Assembly

☐ Assemble and glue the spare tire and axle pin, glue the two wheels to the axle pins, and glue on the radiator cap.

☐ Insert the axles through holes in the body and attach the wheels.

☐ Attach push nuts for hubcaps.

Finishing

☐ Glue "people" in place.

Table 3-1. The Sports Car Uses the Materials Listed.

NUMBER OF PIECES	PART	SIZE	MATERIAL
1	body	1 1/2"x2"x 7 1/2"	any hardwood
2	fenders	3/4"x1 3/4"x 8 1/8"	any hardwood
1	"people"	3/4" base, 7/8" head	birch
5	wheels	1/2"x 1 1/2" diam.	birch
1	radiator cap	3/8" diam.	birch
2	wheel axles	2 3/4" length	1/4" birch dowel
1	spare tire axle	1 1/8" length	1/4" birch dowel
5	hub caps	1/4" diam.	push nuts

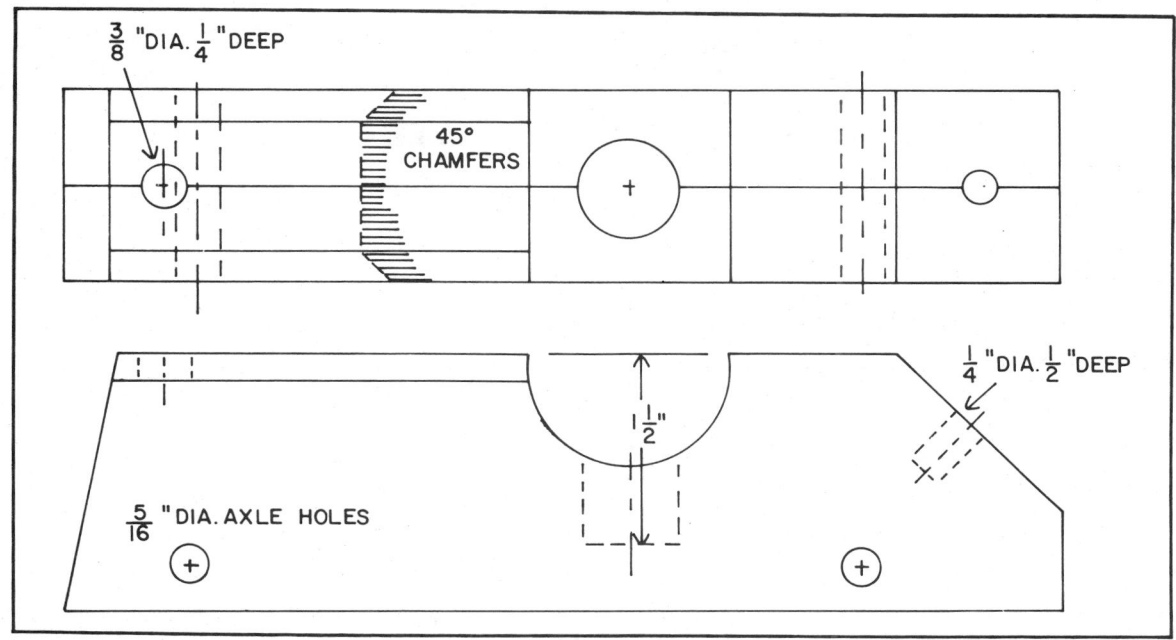

$\frac{3}{8}$ "DIA. $\frac{1}{4}$ "DEEP

45°
CHAMFERS

$\frac{1}{4}$ "DIA. $\frac{1}{2}$ "DEEP

$1\frac{1}{2}$"

$\frac{5}{16}$ "DIA. AXLE HOLES

Fig. 3-2. Pattern for the Sports Car body. Courtesy of Toy Designs.

☐ Finish with spray Deft.

☐ Paint on the hair and features on "people" with acrylic paint (Fig. 3-3).

RUMBLE SEAT RAMBLER

The Rumble Seat (Fig. 3-4), which I designed, has as much appeal to children as its full-size counterpart has to adults in the late 1920s and early 1930s. The fact that the seat can actually be positioned in an open or shut position makes it all the more attractive.

The use of zebrawood as an upholstery mate-

Fig. 3-3. Completed Sports Car. Courtesy of Toy Designs.

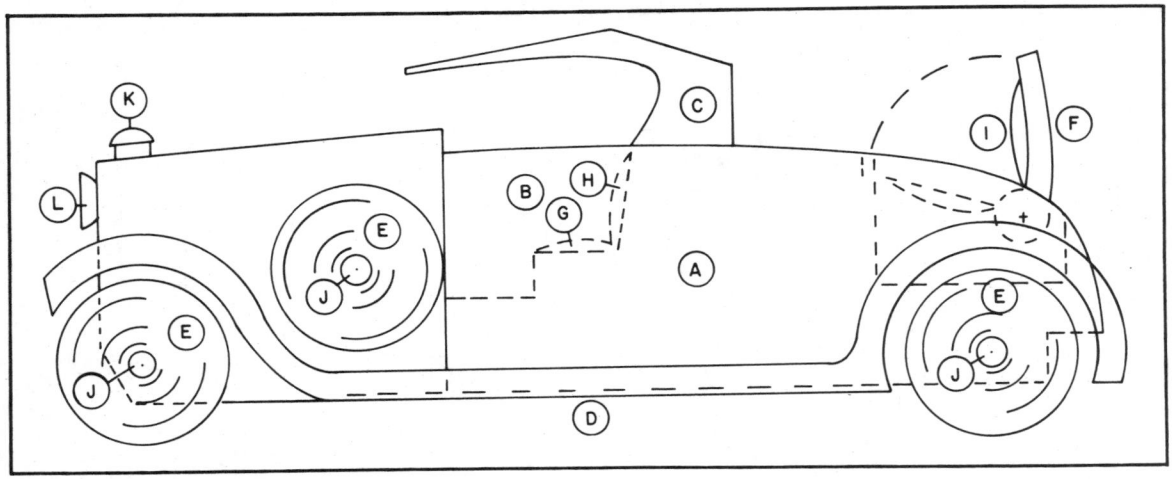

Fig. 3-4. Side view of the Rumble Seat Rambler.

Table 3-2. Materials for the Rumble Seat Rambler.

NUMBER OF PIECES	CODE	PART	SIZE	MATERIAL
1	A	body	1 3/4"x 2 1/2"x 8 3/4"	maple
2	B	side panels	3/16"x 2 1/4"x 5 3/4"	maple
1	C	top	1 1/8"x 1 11/16"x 2 7/8"	black walnut
2	D	running board	5/8"x 11/2"x 9 1/2"	cherry
6	E	wheels	1/2"x 1 1/2" diam.	commercial
1	F	rumble seat	5/8"x 15/16"x 1 3/4"	maple
1	G	bottom cushion	3/16"x 5/8"x 1 3/8"	zebrawood
1	H	back cushion	3/16"x 11/16"x 1 3/8"	zebrawood
1	I	rumble seat cushion	3/16"x 1"x 1 1/4"	zebrawood
3	J	axles	2 3/4" length	1/4" birch dowel
1	K	radiator cap	3/8" diam.	screw cover button
2	L	head lamps	5/8" diam.	bumper tacks

rial adds considerably to the attractiveness of this nostalgic mode of transportation. The use of contrasting woods, black walnut, maple, cherry, and zebrawood, not only adds to its beauty, but it also adds to the durability of this classic automobile (Table 3-2).

Preparation

☐ Make patterns of the body, side panels, top, and rumble seat. Enlarge the patterns in Fig. 3-5 to your specifications.

☐ Cut a rectangular piece of stock 1 3/4 inches by 2 1/2 inches by 8 3/4 inches.

☐ Mark and square a line around the piece that represents the distance from the radiator to the dashboard.

☐ Set the marking gauge at 3/16 inch, which is the thickness of the side panels, and mark the top

of the rear portion of body. With a hard-lead, chisel-edged pencil, darken in the marking gauge lines.

☐ Cut out the two 3/16-inch portions with a band saw. These cuts are very difficult to perform on the circular saw. Try to split the pencil line with the band saw's blade. Work slowly and carefully since it will save considerable time in smoothing the sides of the rear portion of the body.

☐ Mark out the outline of the body with the body pattern.

☐ Cut the outline of the body on the band saw. Place one of the 3/16-inch pieces under the rear portion of the body while using the band saw to prevent the pieces from tilting on the table.

☐ Mark the side panels on the 3/16-inch stock.

☐ Cut the side panels with a jigsaw.

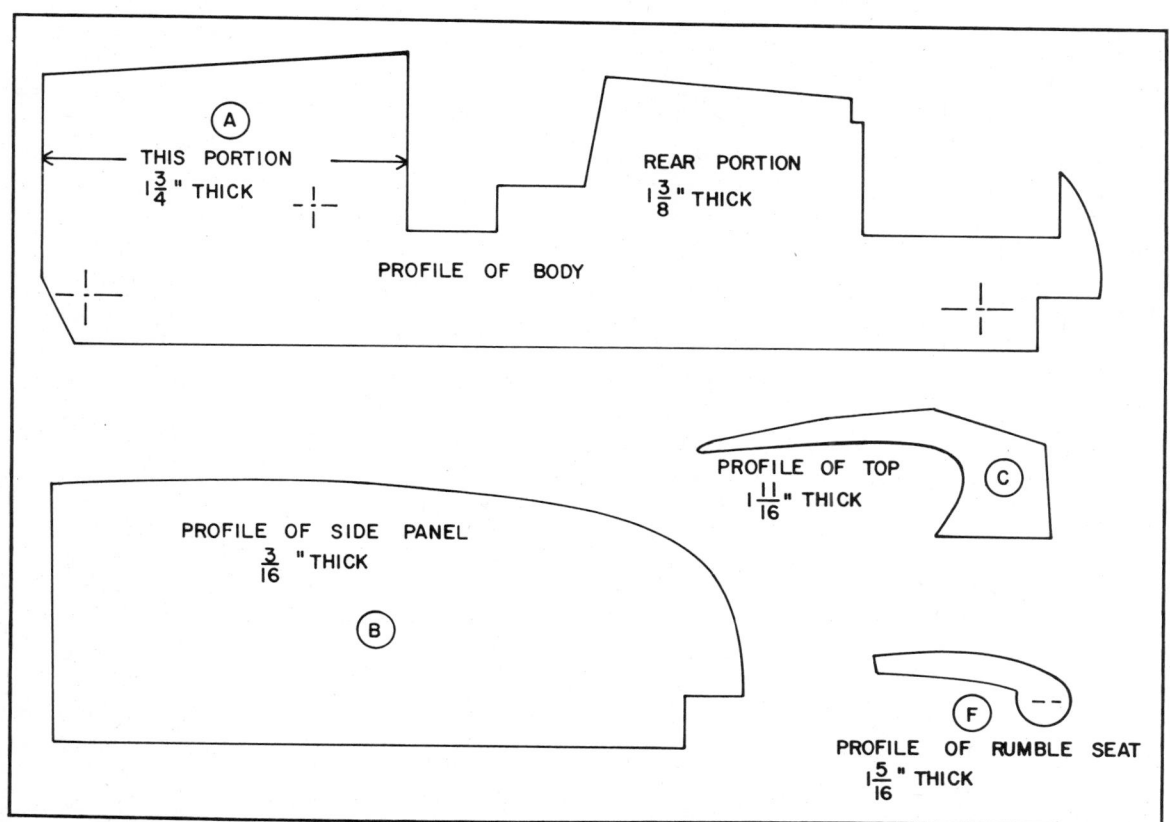

Fig. 3-5. Profile details of the Rumble Seat Rambler.

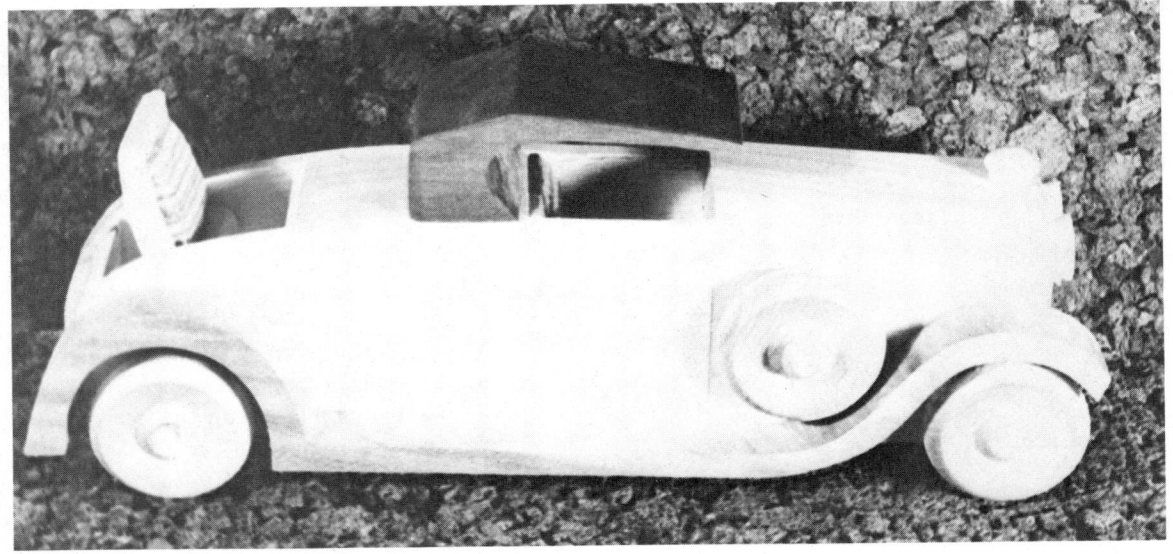

Fig. 3-6. Rumble Seat Rambler is shown, with the rumble seat up.

Assembly

☐ Glue the two side panels to the body and clamp.

☐ After the glue is dry, sand down the top of the body and side panels with a disc sander. Sand the sides of the body and panels with a belt, reciprocating, or orbital sander so that all surfaces are flush.

☐ Mark the rumble seat and saw with a band saw.

☐ Cut the cushion stock for rumble seat and glue in place.

☐ Tie a string around the rumble seat and lower it into the closed position.

☐ Drive hinge pins through the side panels into the rumble seat. See cross lines in Fig. 3-4. The brass points of the bumper tack headlights are just the right size and length. Be sure to protect your eyes when cutting off the points with side cutters or wire cutters.

☐ Lift up the rumble seat with the string and see if the seat works properly.

☐ Mark the top on 1 11/16-inch thick walnut and cut to shape with a band saw. Sand the inside curve with a small drum sander. The outside may be

sanded on a disc sander.

☐ Glue the top in place after the cushions have been made and glued in place.

☐ Lay out the running boards on 5/8-inch thick cherry.

☐ Cut the running boards with a band saw or jigsaw.

☐ Sand the bottom of running boards with a drum or cylindrical sander. The top may be sanded on a disc sander.

☐ Drill a 1/4-inch hole through the engine section for the two spare wheels and tires. Drive the axle through the hole and attach the two wheels.

☐ Drill two 17/64-inch holes for the other two axles and the four wheels. The extra 1/64 inch allows the 1/4-inch axles to turn easily. Drive the axles through and attach the wheels.

☐ Cut the points of the bumper tacks if you have not yet done so. Flatten the top to provide a gluing surface. Glue the headlamps to the front of the engine compartment with epoxy glue.

☐ Bore a 3/8-inch hole for the radiator cap about 1/8-inch deep. Place a spot of glue on the underside of the radiator cap and insert it in the hole.

Fig. 3-7. Rumble Seat Rambler, with the seat down.

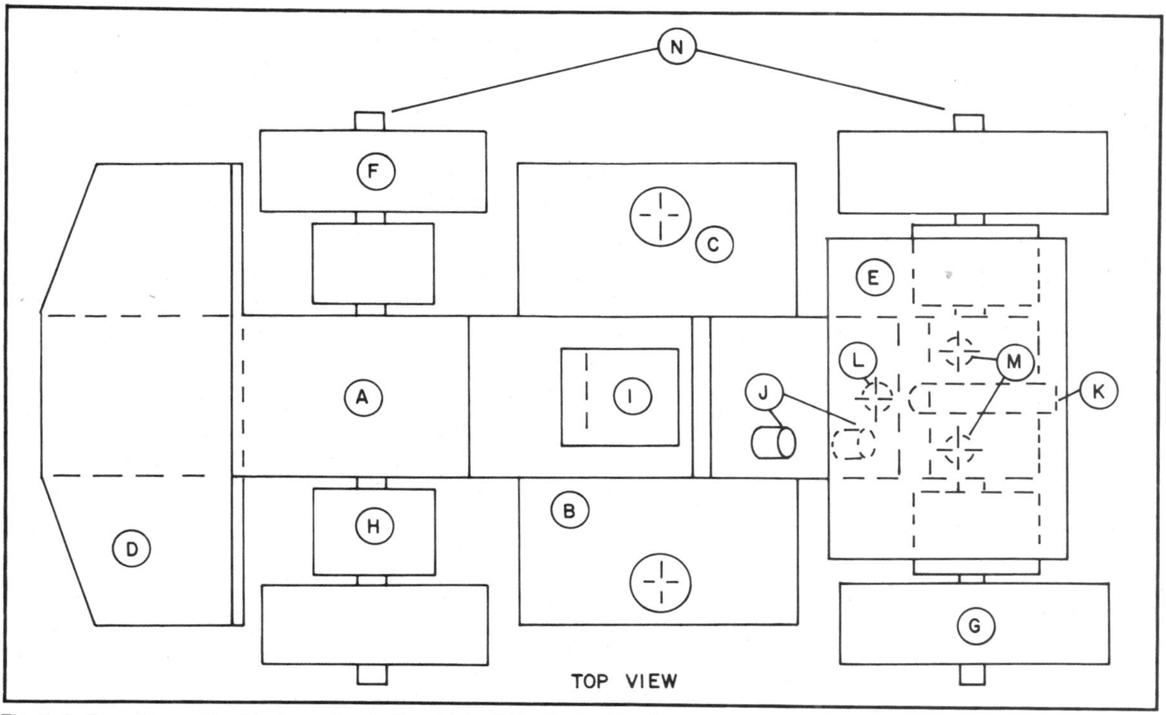

TOP VIEW

Fig. 3-8. Top view of the Modern Racer. Courtesy of Uncle Andy's Scrapwood Toys.

Finishing

☐ Sand the complete project with fine sandpaper. If there are small imperfections, dents, or scratches, sponge the entire car with a few drops of liquid animal glue added to a cup of hot water. Allow it to dry overnight and sand again.

☐ Finish with three or four coats of clear spray Deft or polyurethane.

☐ When dry, rub with #0000 steel wool, wax, and polish (Figs. 3-6 and 3-7).

MODERN RACER

The Modern Racer, by Uncle Andy's Scrapwood Toys, is a joy to behold, and is instantly admired by children. You can almost hear the throbbing of the powerful engine as it stands ready at the starting line. This speedy racer hugs the road, and air spoilers prevent the wingless airplane from taking off.

Preparation

☐ Make a pattern or transfer the outline of the body to 1 3/4-inch thick redwood. See Table 3-3 for sizes.

☐ Saw the outline with a band saw.

☐ Bore 17/64-inch axle holes.

☐ Bore 1/4-inch holes for the top exhausts.

☐ Bore a 1/4-inch hole for the rear exhaust.

Table 3-3. The Modern Racer Can Be Made from the Listed Materials.

NUMBER OF PIECES	CODE	PART	SIZE	MATERIAL
1	(A)	body	1 3/4"x1 3/4"x8 1/2"	redwood
2	(B)	gas tanks	3/4"x1 1/4"x2 1/4"	padauk
2	(C)	gas tank caps	3/16" length	1/2" birch dowel
1	(D)	front spoiler	3/8"x1 5/8"x4"	black walnut
1	(E)	rear spoiler	3/8"x2"x2 3/4"	black walnut
2	(F)	front wheels	3/4"x1 7/8" diam.	redwood
2	(G)	rear wheels	3/4"x2 1/4" diam.	redwood
4	(H)	wheel spacers	3/4"x1" diam.	redwood
1	(I)	driver	3/4"x1" diam.	birch
2	(J)	top exhausts	3" length	1/4" birch dowel
1	(K)	rear exhaust	1 5/8" length	1/4" birch dowel
1	(L)	front spoiler support	1 1/4" length	1/4" birch dowel
2	(M)	rear spoiler supports	1 3/4" length	1/4" birch dowel
2	(N)	axles	4 7/8" length	1/4" birch dowel

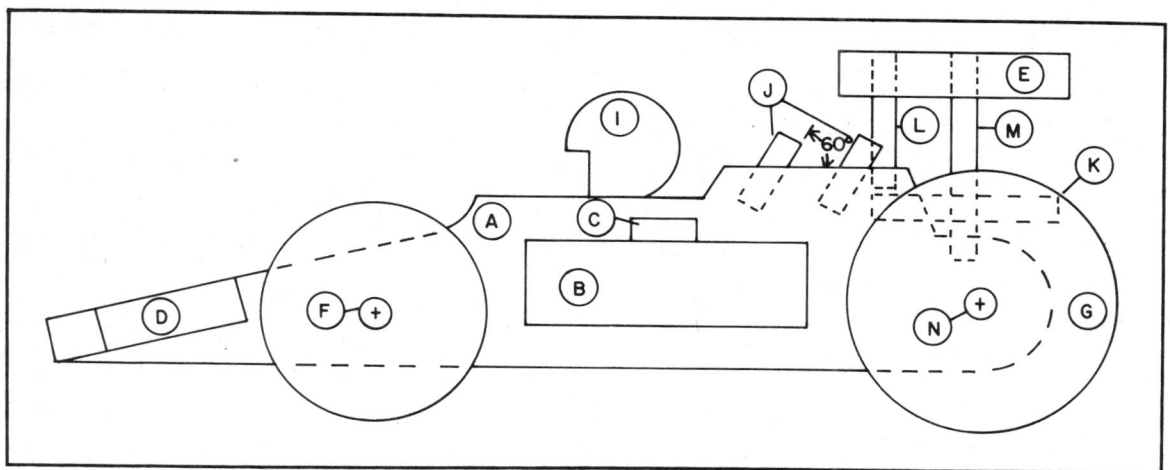

Fig. 3-9. Side view of the Modern Racer. Courtesy of Uncle Andy's Scrapwood Toys.

PERSPECTIVE VIEW

EXPLODED VIEW

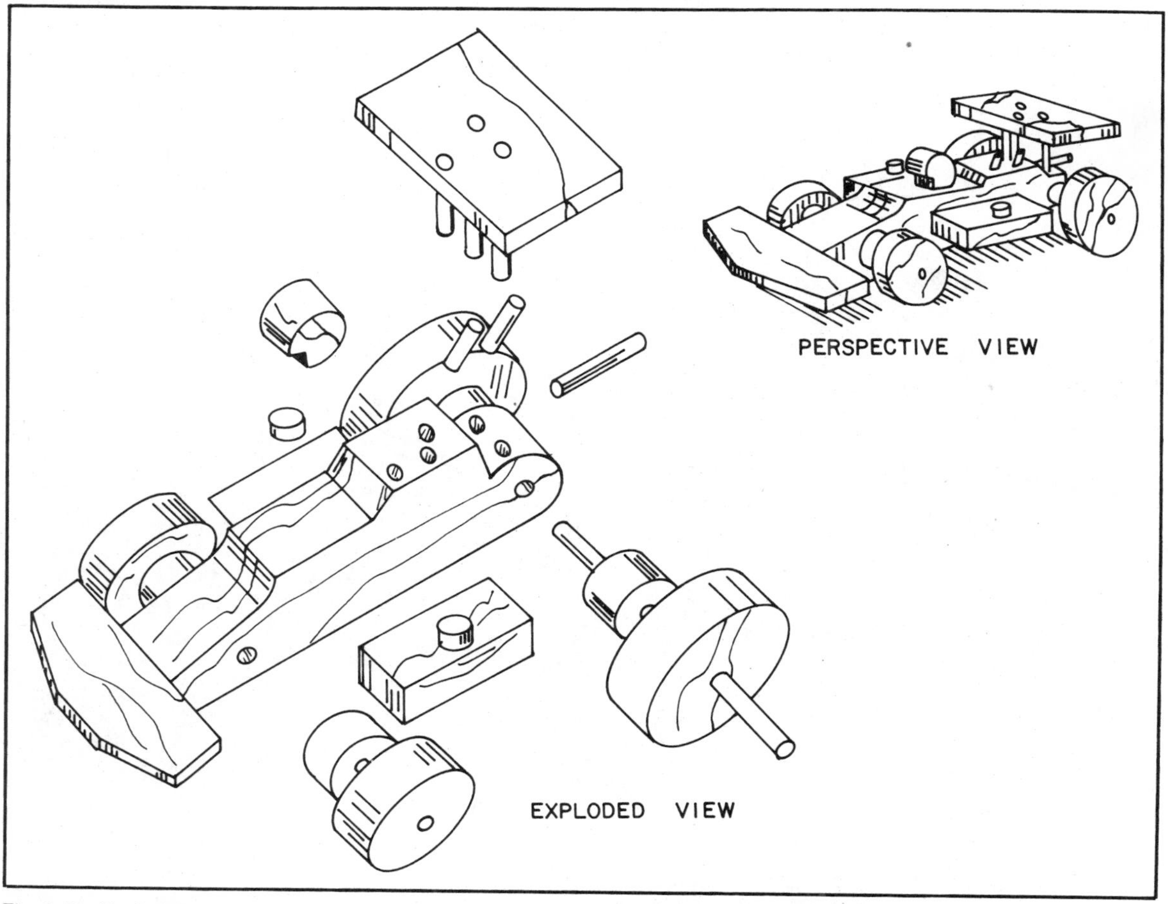

Fig. 3-10. Exploded and perspective views of the Modern Racer. Courtesy of Uncle Andy's Scrapwood Toys.

☐ Bore 1/4-inch holes for the spoiler supports.

☐ Sand the body.

Assembly

☐ Cut the front spoiler to size (Table 3-3) sand and glue it in place on the front of racer (Figs. 3-8 and 3-9).

☐ Cut the exhaust and glue it in place.

☐ Cut the rear spoiler to size. Bore holes in the rear spoiler for supports. Cut and glue both the front and rear spoiler supports, both in the body and spoilers.

☐ Cut the gas tanks to size.

☐ Cut the gas tank caps from dowel stock.

☐ Sand the tanks and caps and glue the caps in place.

☐ Glue the tanks with attached caps to the sides of the body.

☐ Cut the rear exhaust from dowel stock and insert it in the hole.

☐ Cut the driver from dowel stock. I cut the driver from 3/4-inch birch stock since I wanted a small visor attached to the helmet. Sand and glue the driver to the body.

☐ Cut the axle stock and attach the wheels and the wheel spacers.

Finishing

☐ Sand the entire project with fine sandpaper.

☐ Apply three or four coats of clear spray Deft.

☐ When dry, sand with #320 sandpaper and rub with #0000 steel wool.

☐ Wax and polish. Figures 3-10 and 3-11 show the finished project.

EARLY RACER

This Early Racer is characteristic of autos raced at county fairs and small dirt raceways during the 1920s and 1930s and at the early Indianapolis races. The plans were supplied by Uncle Andy's Scrapwood Toys. The toy fits neatly in the hand of a child.

Preparation

☐ Make a pattern or transfer the outline of the

Fig. 3-11. Completed Modern Racer. Courtesy of Uncle Andy's Scrapwood Toys.

Table 3-4. Listed Are Materials for the Early Racer Project.

NUMBER OF PIECES	PART	SIZE	MATERIAL
1	body	1 5/8"x3"x8"	walnut
2	front wheels	3/4"x1 3/4" diam.	redwood
2	rear wheels	3/4"x 2 1/4" diam.	redwood
4	wheel spacers	3/4"x 1 " diam.	redwood
1	driver	3/4"x1"diam.	birch
1	driver support	1"length	1/4" birch·dowel
2	axles	4 7/8" length	1/4" birch dowel
1	top exhaust	5/8" length	1/4" birch dowel
1	top exhaust	1/2" length	1/4" birch dowel
1	top exhaust	7/16" length	1/4" birch dowel
1	rear exhaust	4"length	1/4" birch dowel
1	rear exhaust connection	1/2" length	1/4" birch dowel
1	rear exhaust coupler	9/16" length	3/4" birch dowel

body in Figs. 3-12 and 3-13 to 1 5/8-inch thick walnut. See Table 3-4 for sizes.

☐ Cut the outline of the body with a band saw.

☐ Bore 17/64-inch holes for the axles.

☐ Bore the three 1/4-inch holes on top of the body for the top exhausts.

☐ Bore the 1/4-inch hole for the driver support (neck).

☐ Sand the cockpit area with a drum sander.

☐ Roll the top edge of the body with Surform, rasp, and different grits of sandpaper.

☐ Dissolve a few drops of LePages or Franklin animal glue in a cup of hot water and apply to the body with a brush or small cloth. Apply only enough to dampen the wood. Allow to dry overnight. Sand the body with #220 sandpaper.

☐ Bore a 1/4-inch hole for the rear exhaust connection.

☐ Cut a 3/4-inch dowel stock for a coupler and bore the two holes for the connection and rear exhaust.

☐ Cut a 1/4-inch dowel stock for the rear exhaust connection and the rear exhaust.

Assembly

☐ Assemble and glue the rear exhaust, rear

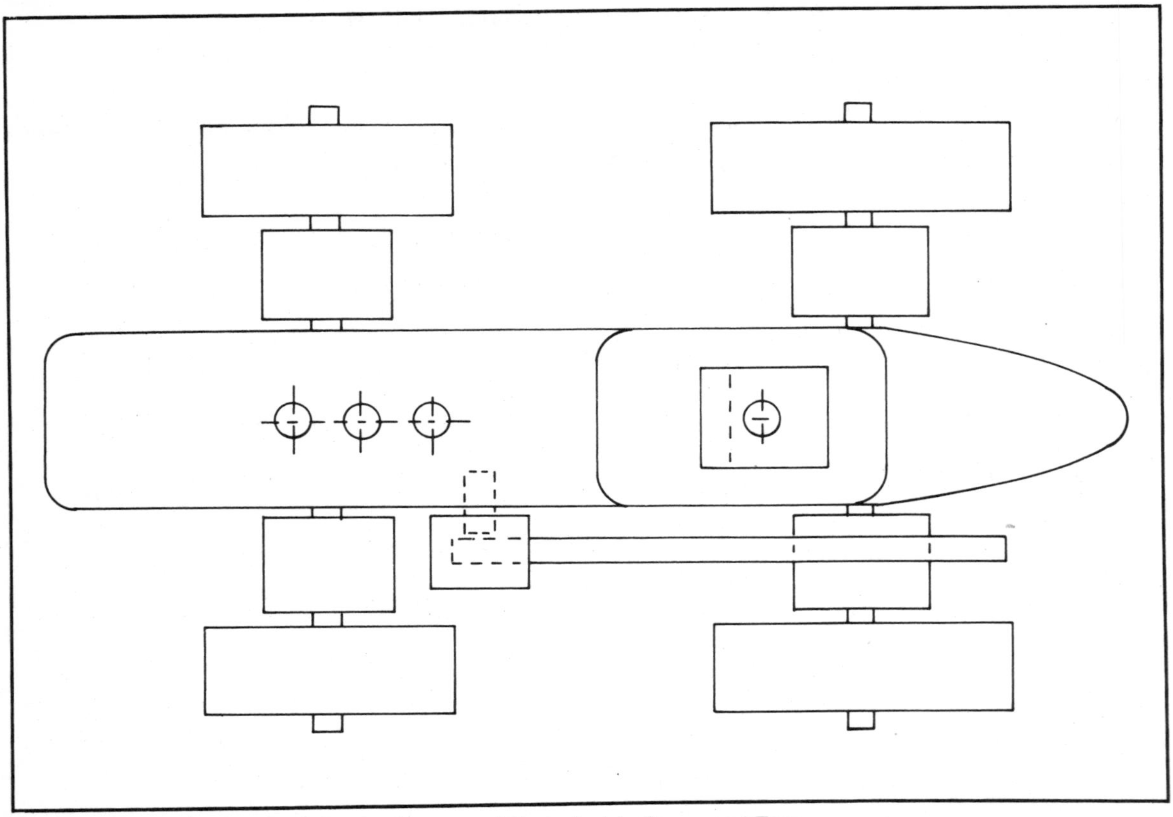

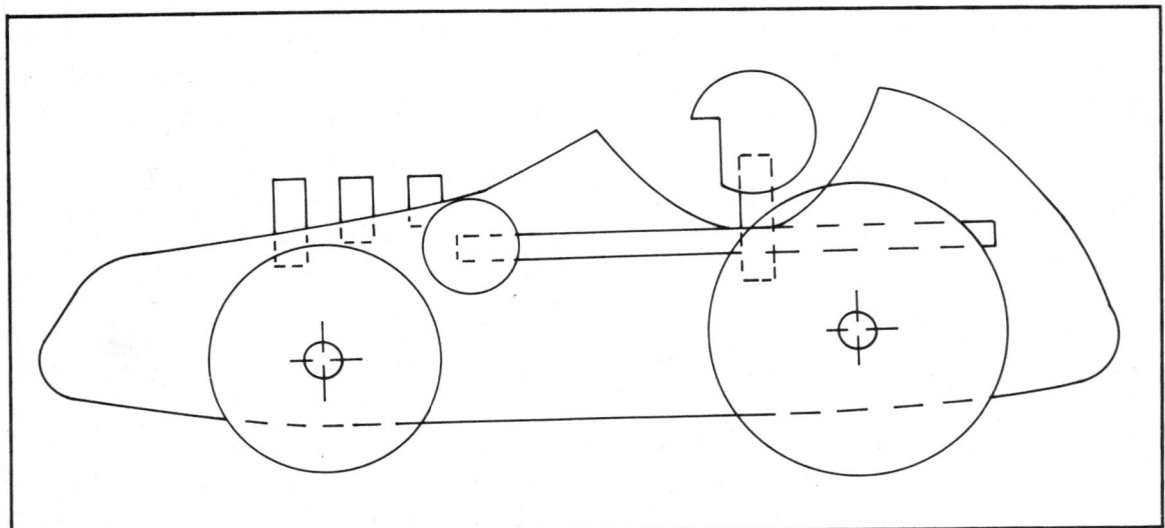

Fig. 3-12. Top view of the Early Racer. Courtesy of Uncle Andy's Scrapwood Toys.

Fig. 3-13. Side view of the Early Racer. Courtesy of Uncle Andy's Scrapwood Toys.

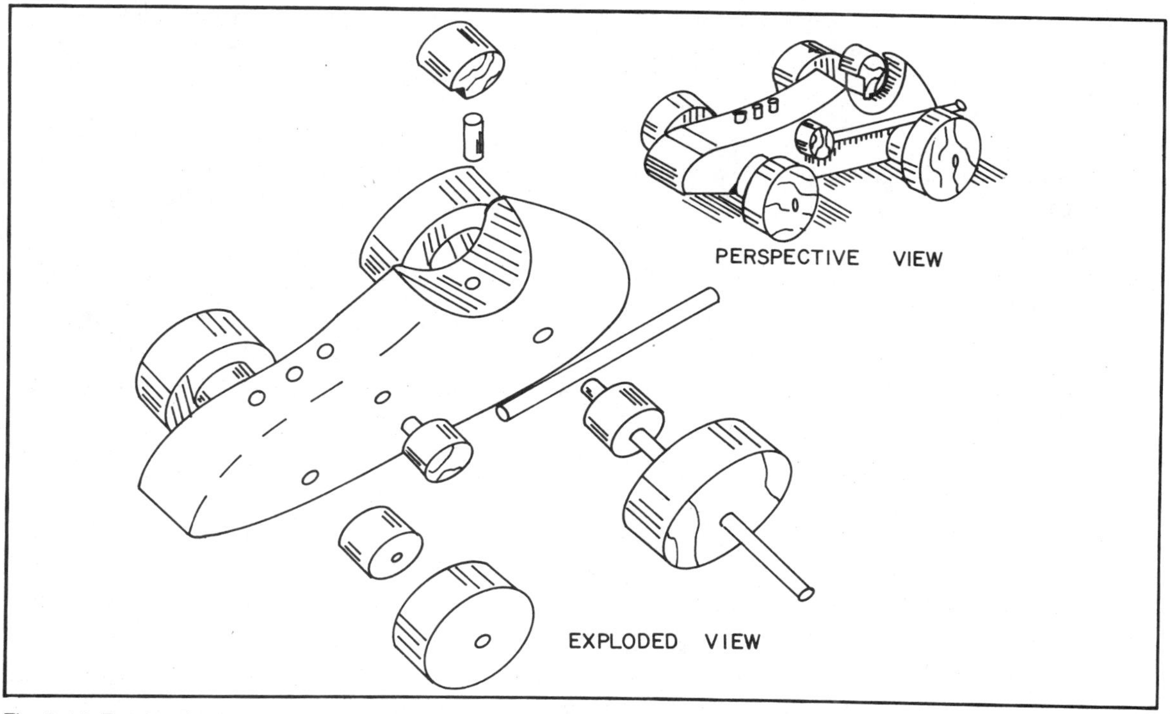

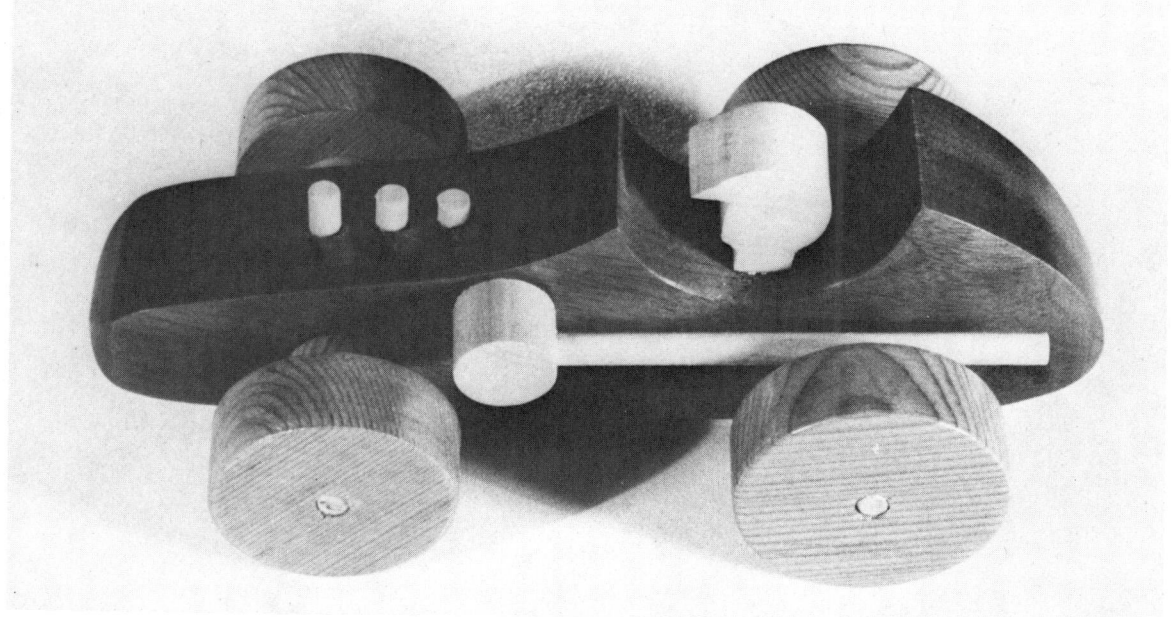

PERSPECTIVE VIEW

EXPLODED VIEW

Fig. 3-14. Perspective and exploded views of the Early Racer. Courtesy of Uncle Andy's Scrapwood Toys.

Fig. 3-15. Early Racer: Completed project. Courtesy of Uncle Andy's Scrapwood Toys.

exhaust coupler, and rear exhaust connection. When dry, insert the rear exhaust connection into the hole in the body.

☐ Cut the three top exhausts. Glue and insert them into the body holes.

☐ Bore a 1/4-inch hole into the driver's head.

☐ Cut the driver support (neck) from 1/4-inch dowel stock.

☐ Glue and insert the driver support into the driver and into the cockpit of the car.

☐ Cut the four wheels and four wheel spacers with a hole saw using the appropriate blades.

☐ Sand on the lathe with a 1/4-inch diameter mandrel fitted to a wood faceplate.

☐ Fit a wheel and spacer to an axle. Insert the axle through the body and then attach the other spacer and wheel.

Finishing

☐ When all the wheels are attached (Fig. 3-14), sand all the parts, with the exception of the body, with fine sandpaper.

☐ Apply three or four coats of clear spray Deft.

☐ When the racer is dry, sand lightly with #320 sandpaper and then rub with #0000 steel wool. Apply furniture wax and polish. Figure 3-15 shows the finished project.

4

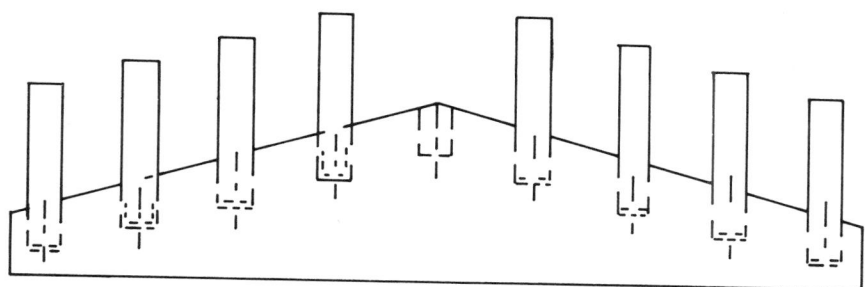

Games

This chapter contains step-by-step instructions for making three games. Illustrations and tables of materials are also included. One solution for the Up the Hill—Down the Hill Game can be found in Appendix B.

MARBLE GAME

The marble game is best played by timing the length of time that a specified number of marbles roll down the slope. The major attraction, however, is the almost hypnotic effect of the rolling marbles on the observers as they watch the marbles follow each other in their journey down the marble troughs.

Youngsters enliven the game by placing a finger on one of the troughs and so impeding their progress momentarily.

Assembly

☐ Cut the two uprights from 1 1/2-inch stock (Table 4-1).

☐ Bore a 3/4-inch hole about 2 1/2-inches deep, in one end of the tall upright.

☐ Bore another 3/4-inch hole in the side of the upright so that it will intersect the bottom of the first hole. The marbles are placed in the top of the upright and emerge out the side so that they fall on the top of the uppermost marble trough.

☐ Cut stock for the ten marble troughs. The ends should be cut at an 85-degree angle to achieve a 5-degree slope. The saw is set at 45 degrees to cut the sides of the trough.

☐ Glue the troughs to the two uprights. See Fig. 4-1.

☐ Cut five 3-inch circles from 5/8-inch stock.

☐ Place the 3-inch circles in the lathe and turn them to a 2 3/4-inch diameter. While the circles are in the lathe, turn the marble troughs as shown in Fig. 4-1.

☐ Sand the circles and remove them from the lathe. Cut the circles into 10 semicircles. Nine of them will be used as end turnarounds.

☐ Cut the nine end bumpers and the top end bumper from some flexible material, such as ve-

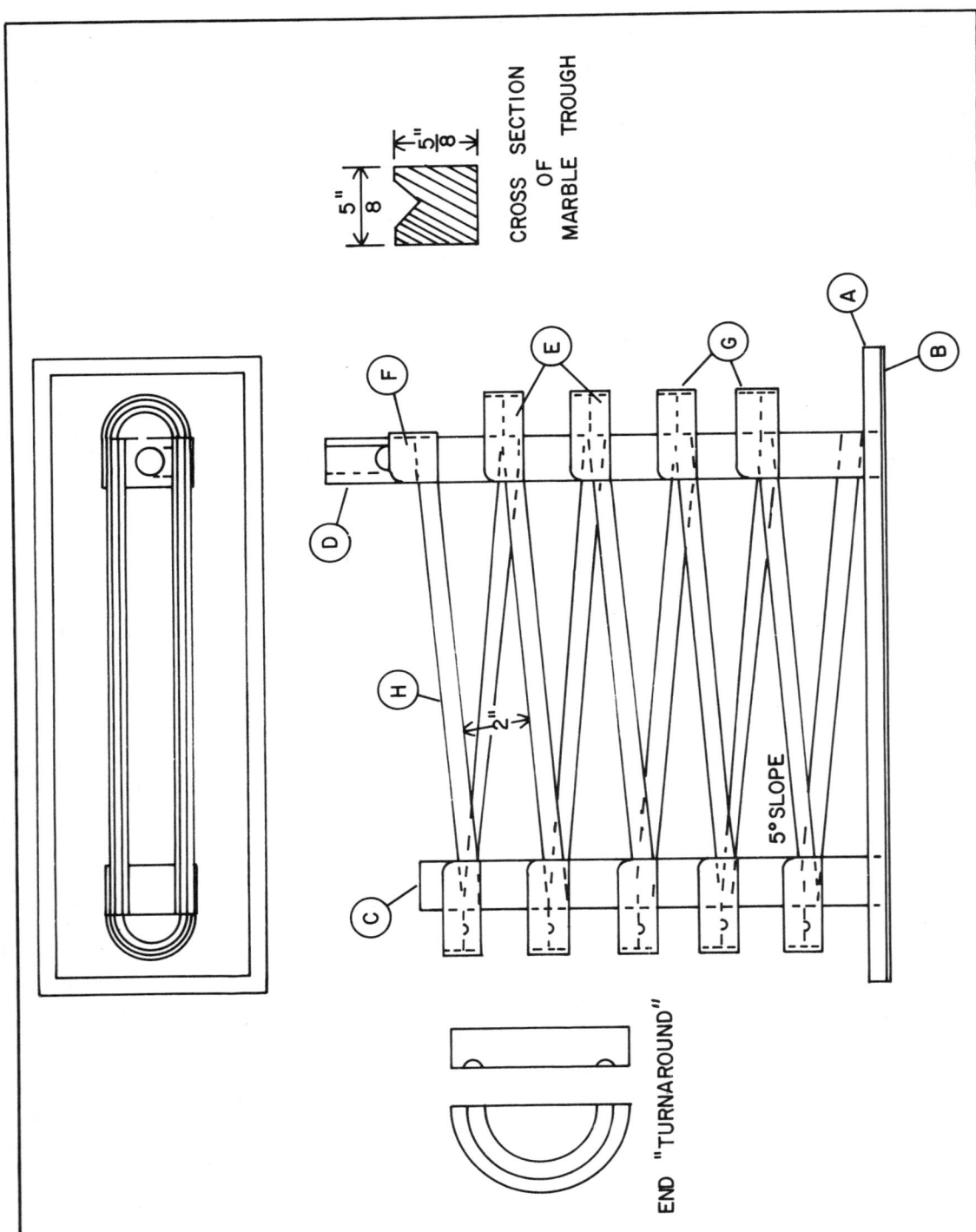

CROSS SECTION OF MARBLE TROUGH

END "TURNAROUND"

5° SLOPE

Fig. 4-1. Pattern for Marble Game parts.

NUMBER OF PIECES	CODE	PART	SIZE	MATERIAL
4	(A)	marble tray rim 2 pcs. 2 pcs.	1/2"x1/2"x20 1/2" 1/2"x1/2"x6"	pine, maple, or birch pine, maple, or birch
1	(B)	marble tray bottom	1/8"x7"x 20 1/2"	hardwood or Masonite
1	(C)	short upright	1 1/2"x1 1/2"x14 1/2"	pine, maple, or birch
1	(D)	tall upright	1 1/2"x1 1/2"x17 3/8"	pine, maple, or birch
9	(E)	end turnarounds	5/8"x1 3/8"x2 3/4"	pine, maple, or birch
1	(F)	top end bumper	1 3/4"x 3 1/2"	any flexible material
9	(G)	end bumpers	1 1/4"x 7 3/8"	any flexible material
10	(H)	marble troughs	5/8"x5/8"x 15	pine, maple, or birch

neer, plastic, or rubber. I used pieces from a rubber mopboard used for basement baseboards. Rubber step treads may also be used.

☐ Center the bumper material over each end turnaround and fasten with small, brass, roundhead nails. Extending out from the end turnarounds will be 1 1/2 inches of bumper material.

☐ Glue the end turnarounds to the uprights and to the ends of the marble troughs. By nailing the 1 1/2-inch extended portion of the bumpers to the marble troughs it will hold the end turnarounds in place until the glue is set and reinforce each end assembly.

☐ Cut the marble tray bottom of hardboard or fiberboard.

☐ Cut pieces of the marble tray rim.

☐ Glue the marble tray rim to the marble tray bottom.

Finishing

☐ Attach the upper portion of the game assembly to the marble tray with 2 1/2-inch flathead screws.

☐ Sand the complete marble game with fine sandpaper.

☐ Paint, enamel, or stain to suit. I used walnut stain and painted the bumpers a brilliant red with acrylic paint. See Fig. 4-2 for the finished project.

UP THE HILL—DOWN THE HILL GAME

Up the Hill—Down the Hill starts with four pegs on each side of the center hole. The purpose of the game is to exchange the square pegs with the birch dowels. You are permitted to jump a peg of either shape, or a peg may be moved one hole toward the other end, but it cannot be moved backward.

This game requires patience and luck and is extremely challenging. Players should try to remember the moves they have made and try to avoid wrong moves in subsequent plays.

Assembly

☐ Cut the base to size (Table 4-2). Enlarge the pattern in Fig. 4-3 to the correct proportions.

☐ Mark the nine holes for the pegs. The holes are 3/4 inch apart.

☐ Bore the holes 3/8-inch deep with a 17/64-inch bit.

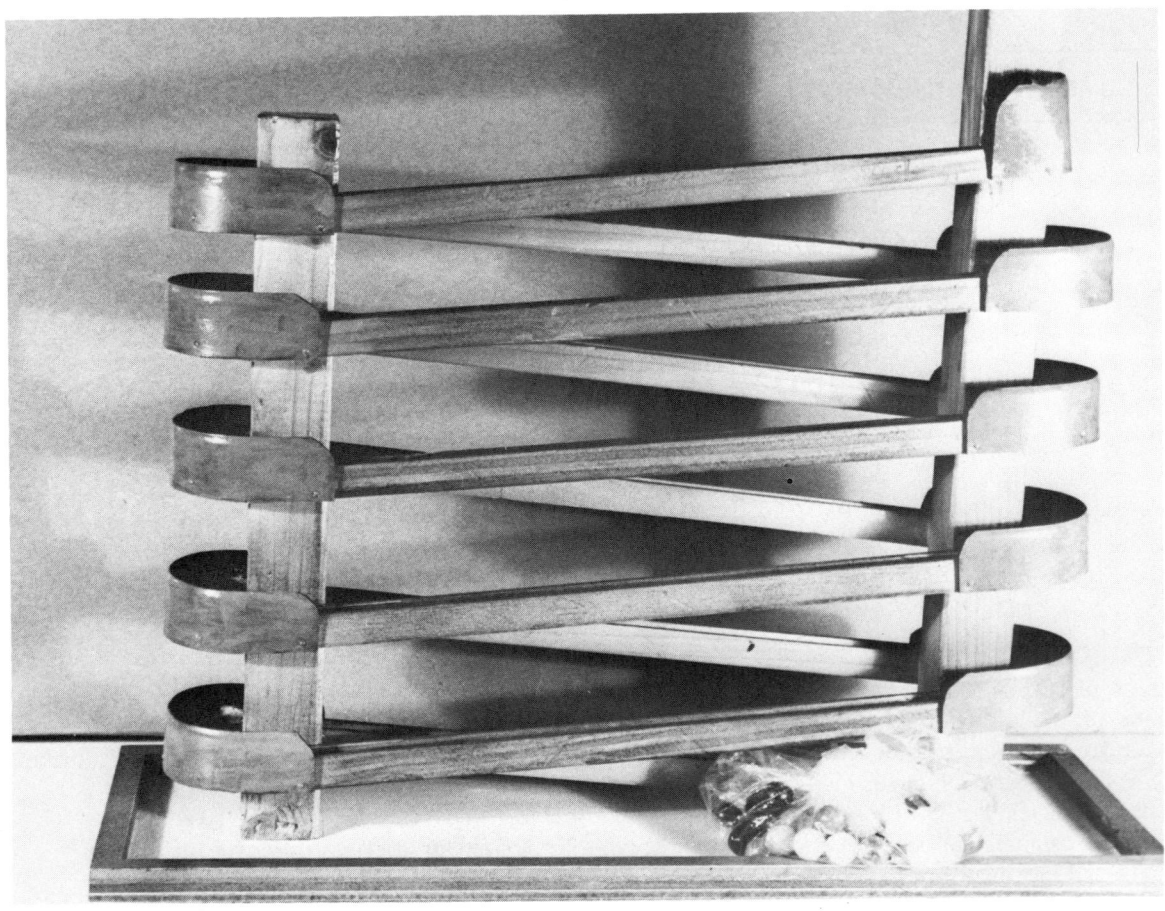

Fig. 4-2. Completed Marble Game project.

☐ Sand the base with a medium grit sandpaper.

☐ Cut the four square padauk pegs on the circular saw.

☐ Taper one end of each peg to a round point.

☐ Cut the four 1/4-inch birch dowels to length.

Finishing

☐ Sand the eight pegs and base with fine sandpaper.

☐ Apply three or four coats of clear spray Deft.

☐ When dry, rub the base and pegs with #0000 steel wool.

☐ Apply wax and polish. See Fig. 4-4 for the finished project and Appendix B for one solution.

TIC-TAC-TOE GAME

Tic-Tac-Toe, although as old as the hills, will always be new to arriving generations of children. Usually this game is played on a blackboard by drawing two sets of parallel lines at right angles to each other. One contestant marks a circle and the other contestant uses a cross or "X."

The purpose of the game is to line up three of the same symbol in a straight line, either horizontally, vertically, or diagonally, before the other contestant can do so.

This version of the game is more comfortable

Table 4-2. The Up the Hill—Down the Hill Game can be Made from the Materials Listed.

NUMBER OF PIECES	PART	SIZE	MATERIAL
I	base	13/16"x1 3/8"x 6 1/4"	walnut
4	pegs	1/4"x 1/4"x 1 1/4"	padauk
4	pegs	1 1/4" length	1/4" birch dowel

to use because the board can be used on your lap, on a table, or on the floor. This sturdy game will stand a long period of abuse and might well become a hand-me-down. I made six zero pegs and six cross pegs in case of loss.

Assembly

☐ Cut the 6-×-6-inch pieces of 1/2-inch birch plywood for base (Fig. 4-5).

☐ Set the fence of the circular saw 2 inches away from the saw.

☐ Cut the grooves for the inlays 3/16-inch deep. Use a regular saw blade, not a plywood saw, for cutting the grooves.

☐ Saw at least 2 feet of walnut inlay 1/8 × 3/16 inch.

☐ Cut the inlay pieces to the correct length and glue them in place.

☐ When glue is dry, sand the surface of the base with inlays in place until the inlays are flush with the base surface.

☐ Draw diagonals across each of the nine

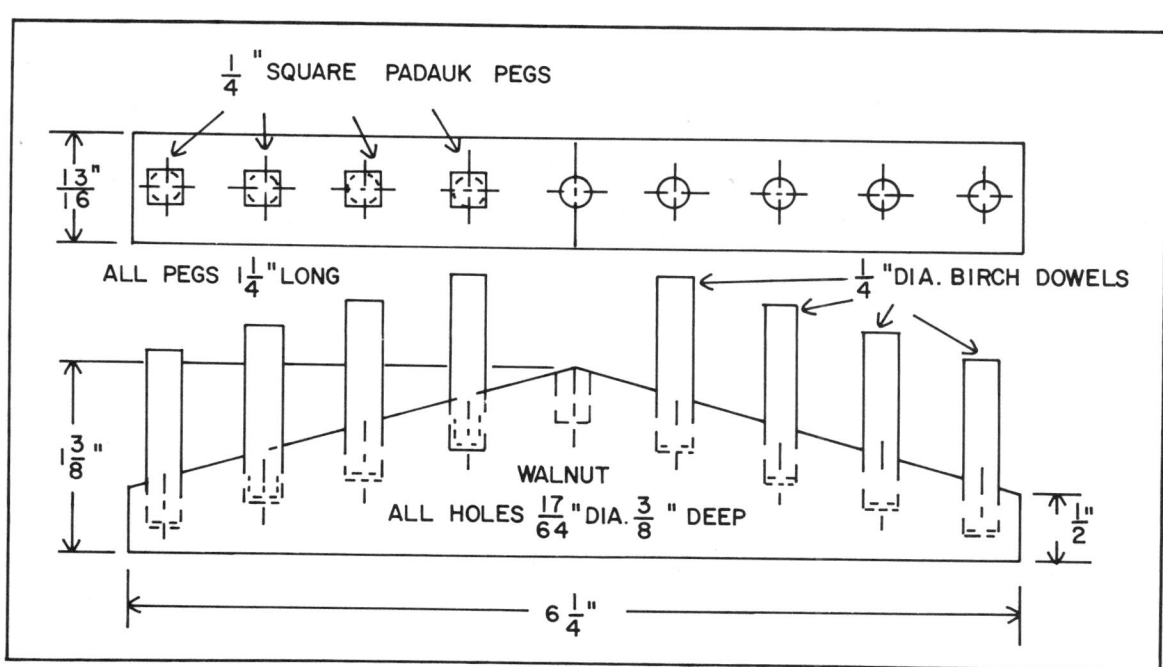

Fig. 4-3. Up the Hill—Down the Hill working plans.

Fig. 4-4. Up the Hill—Down the Hill: completed project.

squares to establish the center of each square.

☐ Mark the centers of the squares with scratch awl or center punch.

☐ Drill the nine holes 1/4-inch deep with a 17/64-inch drill.

☐ Cut the six zeros 1/2-inch long from a 1-inch diameter dowel.

☐ Make a pattern for the crosses. See Fig. 4-5.

☐ Cut padauk stock to 1/2-inch thick and trace six crosses on the stock.

☐ Cut the crosses with a band saw or jigsaw.

☐ Drill a 1/4-inch hole in the center of all the zeros and crosses to a depth of 1/4 inch.

☐ Cut 12 supports for zeros and crosses 1 1/4-inch long from 1/4-inch dowel stock.

☐ Put a small bit of glue on the ends of supports and drive into the holes you just drilled.

Finishing

☐ Sand all parts with fine sandpaper.

☐ Apply three or four coats of clear spray Deft or polyurethane.

☐ When dry, rub all parts with #0000 steel wool.

☐ Apply wax and polish. See Fig. 4-6 for the finished project.

Table 4-3. The Tic-Tac-Toe Project Uses the Listed Materials.

NUMBER OF PIECES	PART	SIZE	MATERIAL
1	base	1/2"x6"x 6"	birch plywood
6	zeros	1/2" length	1" birch dowel
6	crosses	1/2" length	1 1/4" padauk
12	supports	1 1/4" length	1/4" birch dowel
4	inlays	1/8"x 3/16"x6"	walnut

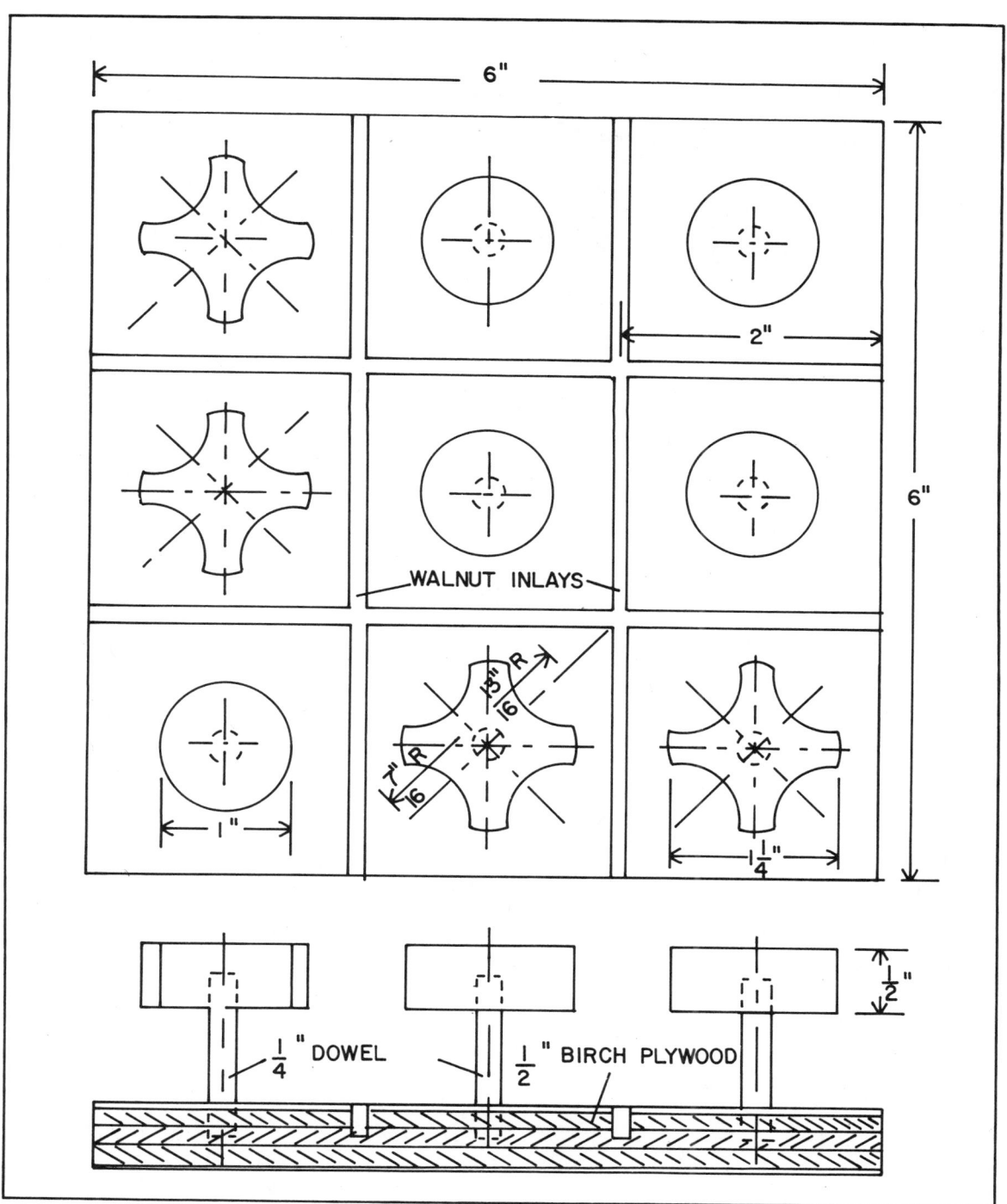

Fig. 4-5. Working plans for the Tic-Tac-Toe game.

Fig. 4-6. Finished Tic-Tac-Toe game.

5

Outdoor Toys

This chapter contains step-by-step instructions for three toys that can be used outdoors. Illustrations and tables of materials are also included to guide you in assembly of these projects.

BAMBOO SQUIRT GUN

For youngsters, this Bamboo Squirt Gun is just great for hot summer days. All that you need is the butt of an old bamboo fishing rod or pole. The diameter of the cylinder should be at least 5/8 inch. This simple toy was a favorite of farm boys during the early years of the twentieth century. It was easy to make, and the materials were readily available around the farm, although many times the plunger was made of a small branch of a tree instead of a birch dowel.

If a birch dowel is used for the plunger, it is best to apply a number of coats of wax or linseed oil before the toy is used.

When wrapping the cloth for the piston, test it during the wrapping to keep it from becoming too large. It should fit rather loosely in the cylinder because the water causes the piston to swell.

Preparation

☐ Cut the bamboo section as shown in Fig. 5-1. Be careful not to cut into the partition that separates each section and extends across the handle.

☐ Drill a small hole, 1/32 to 1/16 inch in diameter, in the center of the partition. Drill straight in, or the gun will squirt at an angle. The larger the diameter of the cylinder, the larger the hole can be.

☐ Cut the plunger about 4 inches longer than the cylinder. It should be approximately 1/2 the diameter of the inside of the cylinder.

☐ Cut a piece of dowel for the handle about 2 inches long and at least 1/4 inch larger in diameter than the plunger.

☐ Bore a hole of the same diameter as the plunger about 1/2 way through the handle.

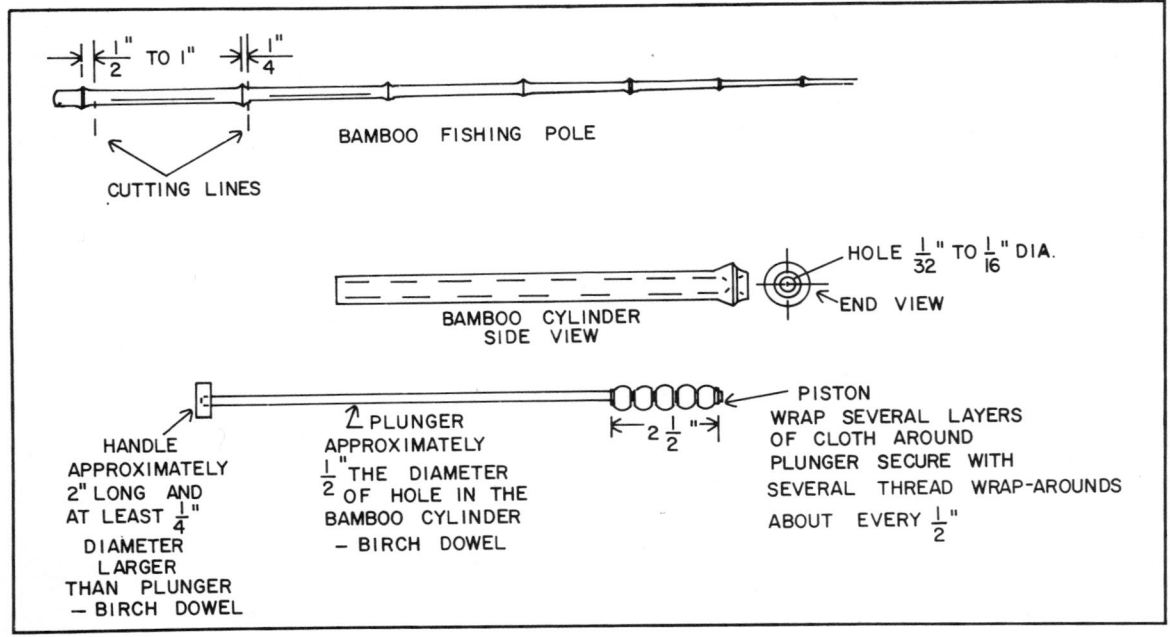

Fig. 5-1. Bamboo Squirt Gun working plans.

Assembly

☐ Glue the handle on the plunger with water-proof glue.

☐ Make the piston by wrapping cloth around the end of plunger.

☐ Tie off with thread. Wrap about 10 times around the ends and 5 or 6 times at 1/2-inch intervals. If the piston fits too tight when water is sucked into the gun, it might be necessary to untie and remove a few layers of cloth. See Fig. 5-2 for the finished project.

THE SKY PIERCER

The Sky Piercer, a simple, inexpensive toy, was a favorite of many boys before World War I. It was seldom used in villages and cities, however, because of its erratic flight pattern and the possible danger to people and property.

To operate the Sky Piercer, a shingle dart was hooked over a knot on a string which was fastened to the dart thrower. The thin, or the diamond-shaped area, was held in the left hand (for right handers). The right hand held the lower, larger end

Table 5-1. To Make the Bamboo Squirt Gun, You Need These Materials.

NUMBER OF PIECES	PART	SIZE	MATERIAL
I	dart thrower	3 1/2' x 4' length	ash or hickory branch
I	cord	3 to 3 1/2" length	chalk line or heavy fishing line
I	dart	4" wide	cedar shingle

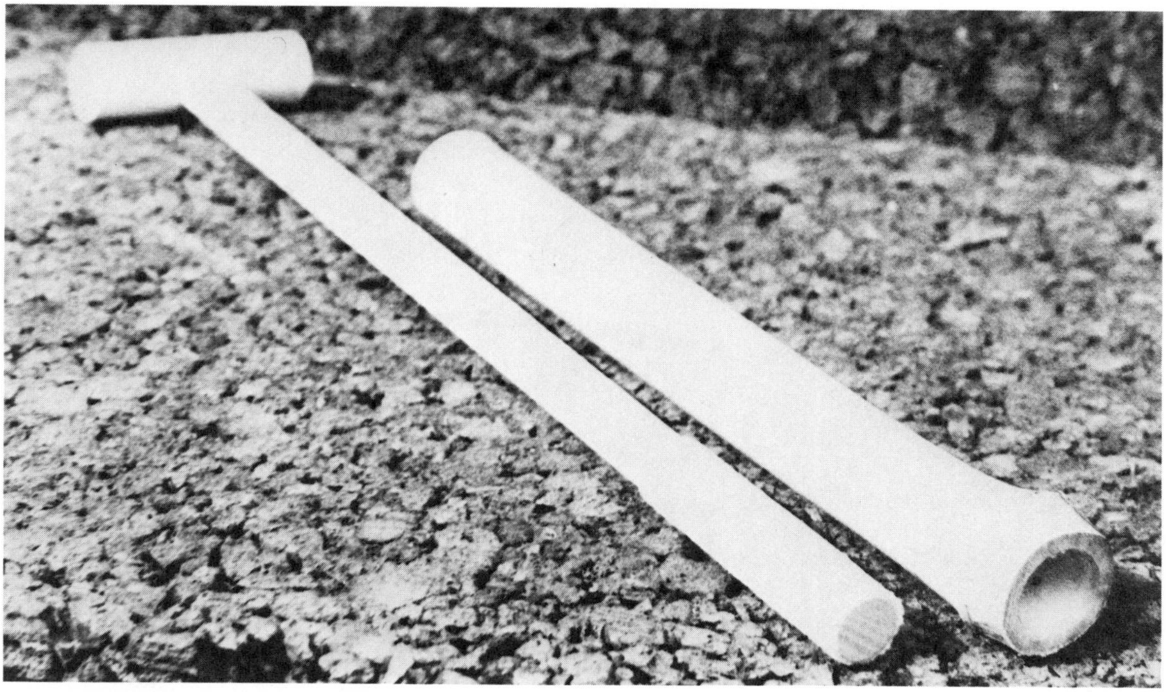

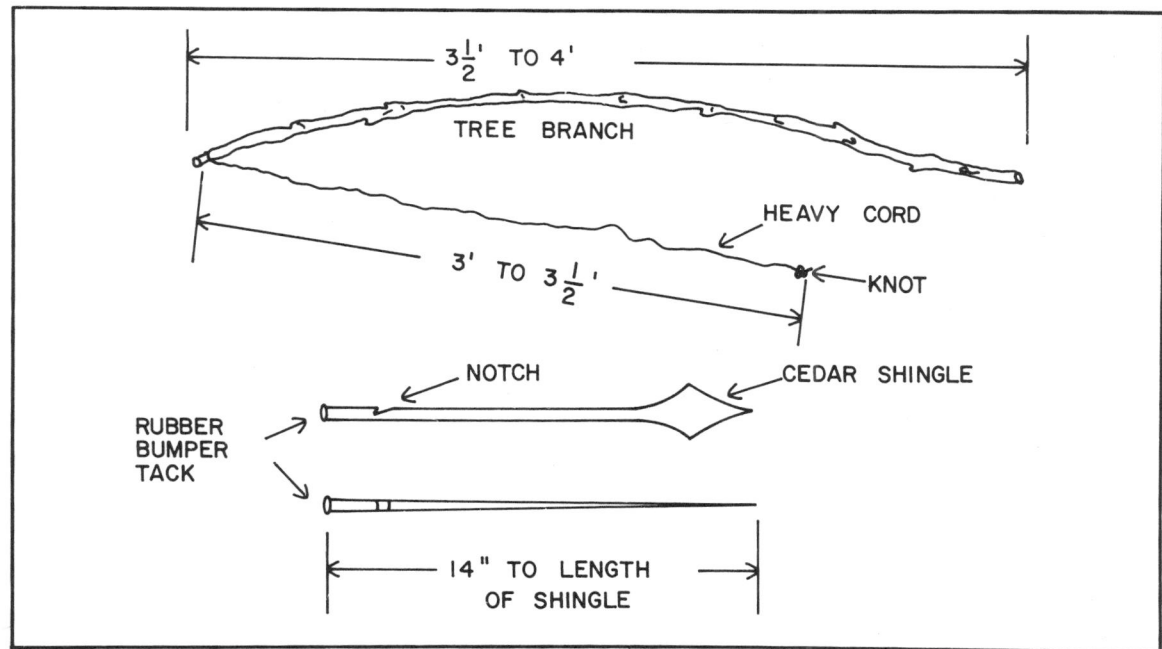

Fig. 5-2. Bamboo Squirt Gun: completed project.

3½' TO 4'

TREE BRANCH

HEAVY CORD

3' TO 3½'

KNOT

NOTCH

CEDAR SHINGLE

RUBBER
BUMPER
TACK

14" TO LENGTH
OF SHINGLE

Fig. 5-3. Working plans for the Sky Piercer.

Fig. 5-4. Completed Sky Piercer.

Table 5-2. The Super Spy Scope Can Be Made with the Listed Materials.

NUMBER OF PIECES	PART	SIZE	MATERIAL
2	top and bottom minor pieces	1/4"x3/4"x3"	birch plywood
2	top and bottom major pieces	1/4"x 3"x 12 1/8"	birch plywood
2	side pieces	1/4"x 2 1/4"x 14 7/8"	birch plywood
2	end pieces	1/4"x 2 1/2"x 3"	birch plywood
8	mirror supports	1/4"x 2 1/4"x 2 1/2"	birch plywood
2	mirrors	1/8"x 2 1/2"x 3"	

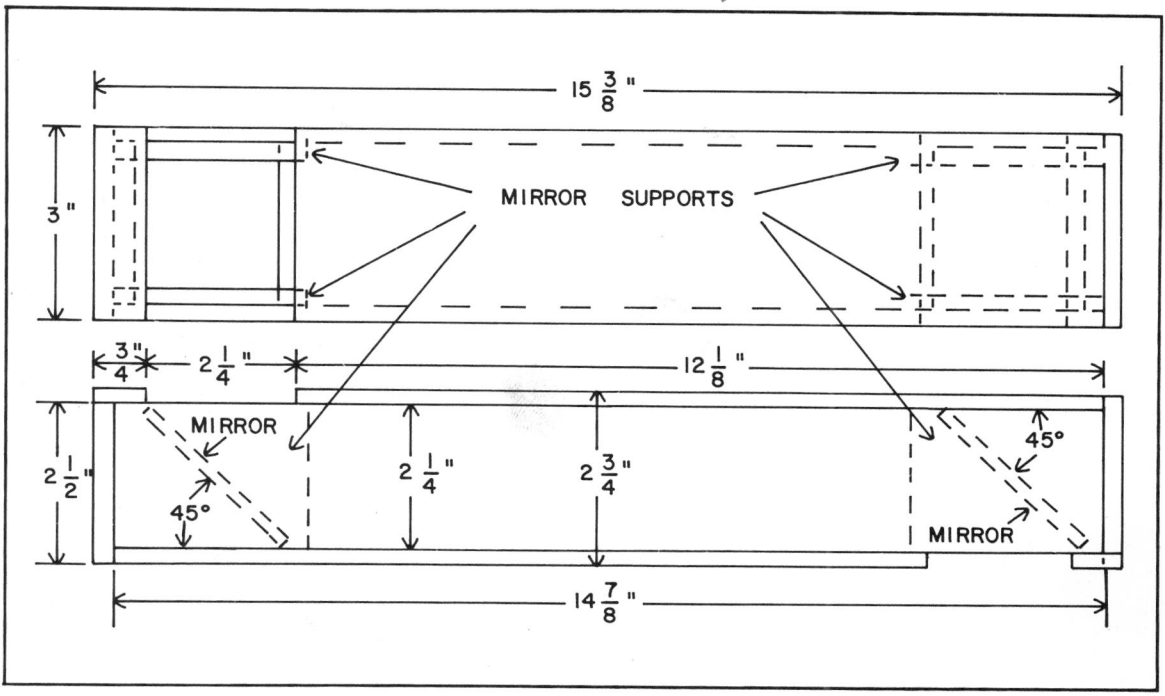

Fig. 5-5. Working plans for the Super Spy Scope.

of the tree-branch thrower. The branch was flexed with considerable tension on the dart. The right and left hands and arms were then swung back and forth before the dart was released.

This toy should be used only in a large, unpopulated area. The dart, even though fitted with a large rubber bumper on its point, can deliver a rather severe blow.

Preparation

☐ Cut a tree branch. See Table 5-1 and Fig. 5-3.

☐ Cut off the small branches, twigs, and leaves.

☐ Cut a notch around the smaller end of the branch about 3/4 inch from the end to prevent the string from slipping.

☐ Tie the cord to the end of the branch and tie a knot in the opposite end.

☐ Cut a piece of cedar shingle about 4 inches wide.

Assembly

☐ Lay out the diamond, or thin, part. The width can vary from about 2 1/2 to 4 inches.

☐ Lay out the shaft of the dart about 1/2-inch wide.

☐ Cut out the dart with any convenient tool. A heavy knife works fine.

☐ Cut the notch for the knot about 2 1/2 to 3 inches from the thick end.

☐ Attach a rubber bumper tack to the thick end. No finish is applied to either dart or thrower. See Fig. 5-4 for the finished project.

SUPER SPY SCOPE

This simple toy periscope will provide hours of enjoyment to the would-be sleuth. The design ideas and plans were furnished by Stanley Tools; however, I have made a few alterations, the most important of which is using 1/4-inch plywood instead of 1/2-inch solid stock.

Fig. 5-6. Completed Super Spy Scope.

Preparation

☐ Cut stock for the two side pieces. Enlarge the pattern in Fig. 5-5 to the correct proportions. See Table 5-2 for sizes.

☐ Cut stock for the top and bottom minor and major pieces.

☐ Cut stock for the eight mirror supports.

☐ Cut mirror stock to size with a glass cutter.

☐ Cut stock for the two ends.

Assembly

☐ Attach one mirror support to each end of the side pieces with glue and 1/2-inch brads.

☐ Attach the other four mirror supports to the side pieces using one piece of mirror as a spacer between the supports.

☐ Attach the larger, or major, bottom piece to the two sides with glue and brads.

☐ Apply flat black enamel to the sides and major bottom piece.

☐ Apply flat black enamel to the major top piece.

☐ Attach the major top piece to the sides/bottom assembly.

☐ Attach the two end pieces to the sides and bottom.

☐ Slide the mirrors between the mirror supports.

☐ Attach the minor top and bottom pieces.

☐ Apply flat black enamel around the edges of the mirror openings.

☐ Cover the mirrors with paper and masking tape.

☐ Spray the periscope with walnut stain.

☐ Apply three or four coats of clear Deft spray finish.

☐ Rub the periscope with #0000 steel wool after paper and masking tape have been removed.

☐ Apply wax and polish. See Fig. 5-6 for the finished project.

6

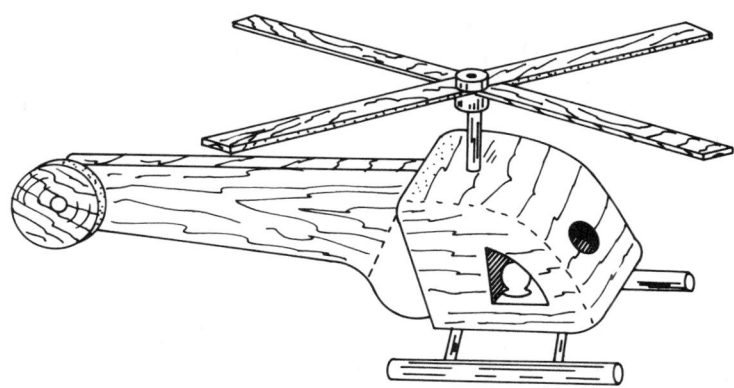

Planes

This chapter contains step-by-step instructions for making four planes. Illustrations and tables of materials are provided to assist you in the assembly of these projects.

MONOPLANE

This simple, but sturdy, Monoplane will attract the attention of small children. It is easy and quick to build (Fig. 6-1).

I took a number of liberties with the design furnished by Hayes Patterns. I made the fuselage of walnut, the wings, tail and wheel block of pine, and the propeller of brilliant red padauk. Instead of boring a 7/8-inch hole in the cockpit, a 3/4-inch hole was drilled to accommodate a "people." Instead of a nail for the propeller shaft, I used a white tack bumper to resemble a propeller hub or spinner. No brads were used, although they were recommended.

Preparation

☐ Make patterns for the body (fuselage),

front wing, rear wing (elevator), tail (rudder), and propeller. Be sure to enlarge the patterns in Figs. 6-2 and 6-3 to the correct proportions.

☐ Cut out rough stock for the body [A] (Table 6-1).

☐ Mark or transfer the profile of the body on body stock.

☐ Cut the profile on a band saw or other curve-cutting tool.

☐ Bore a hole in the cockpit.

☐ Sand the body. A disc sander and drum sander speed up the sanding.

☐ Cut out the stock for the front wing.

☐ Mark or transfer the shape of wing tips from the pattern.

☐ Cut wing tips on a band saw.

Assembly

☐ Fit the wing to the cutout on the underside of the body.

☐ Glue and clamp the wing to the body after sanding.

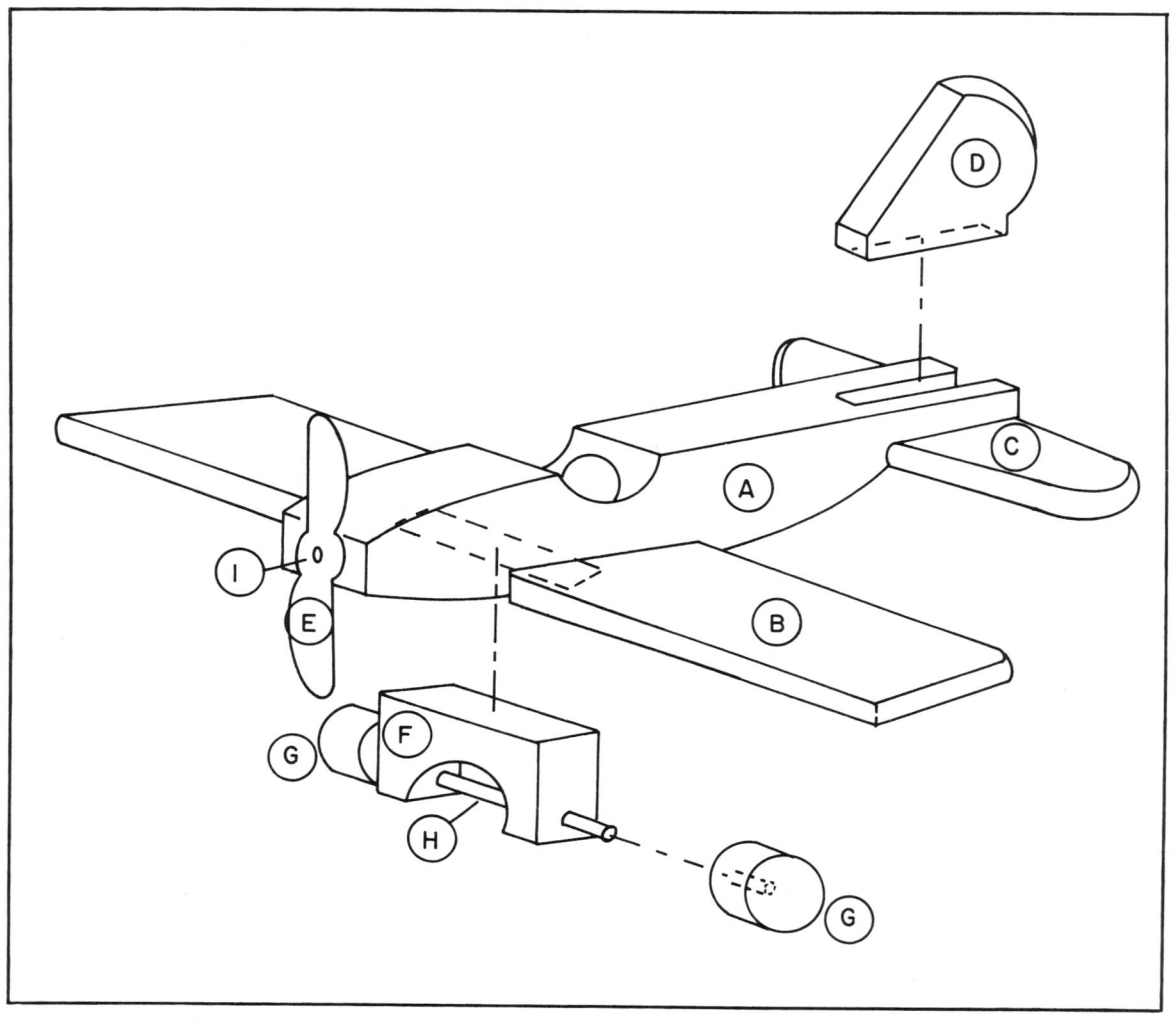

Fig. 6-1. Monoplane assembly. Courtesy of Hayes Patterns.

☐ Cut out stock for the rear wing.

☐ Mark and cut on a band saw or other curve-cutting tool.

☐ Sand and roll the edges with sandpaper.

☐ Glue to the underside of the tail section.

☐ Cut out the stock for the tail.

☐ Mark the outline and cut on a band saw or other curve-cutting tool.

☐ Sand and roll the edges.

☐ Glue it into the slot above the rear wing.

☐ Cut out the stock for the wheel block. Be sure to enlarge the pattern in Fig. 6-2.

☐ Cut the curved portion on a band saw.

☐ Drill a 17/64-inch hole for the axle and sand the wheel block.

☐ Cut the wheels with a hole saw or turn on a lathe. I used commercial wheels.

☐ Cut out the propeller after the enlarged pattern is transferred.

☐ Sand the two blades of the propeller at an angle.

☐ Fasten the propeller to the body with the nail.

☐ Glue the wheel block to the underside of

Table 6-1. Make the Monoplane with the Given Materials.

NUMBER OF PIECES	CODE	PART	SIZE	MATERIAL
1	(A)	body (fuselage)	1 1/8"x1 1/2"x8 7/8"	any appropriate material
1	(B)	front wing	3/8"x 2 3/8"x11 3/4"	any appropriate material
1	(C)	rear wing (elevator)	3/8"x2"x 5"	any appropriate material
1	(D)	trail (rudder)	3/8"x 2 1/8"x 2 5/8"	any appropriate material
1	(E)	propeller	1/8"x4 1/8"x 7/8"	any appropriate material
1	(F)	wheel block	3/4"x1 3/8"x 2 3/8"	any appropriate material
2	(G)	wheels	3/4"x 1 1/4"diam.	commercial
1	(H)	axle	3 1/4"length	1/4"birch dowel
1	(I)	nail	no. 4 common	

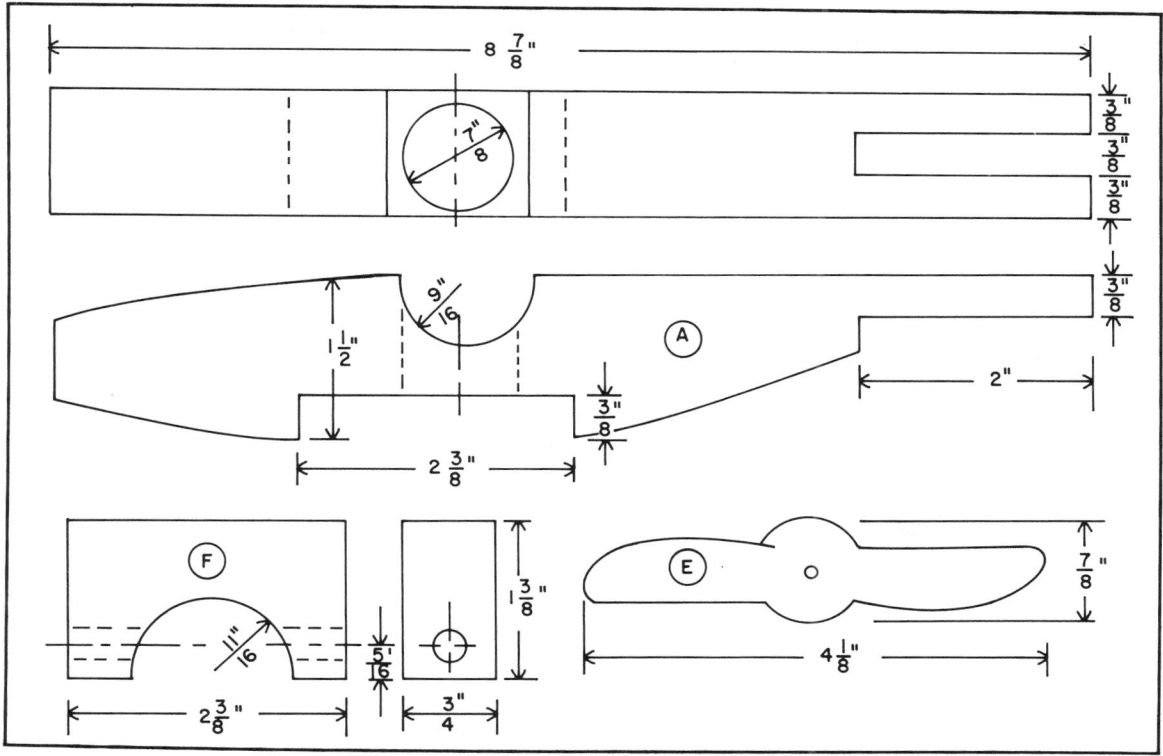

Fig. 6-2. Working plans for the Monoplane's body, wheel block, and propeller. Courtesy of Hayes Patterns.

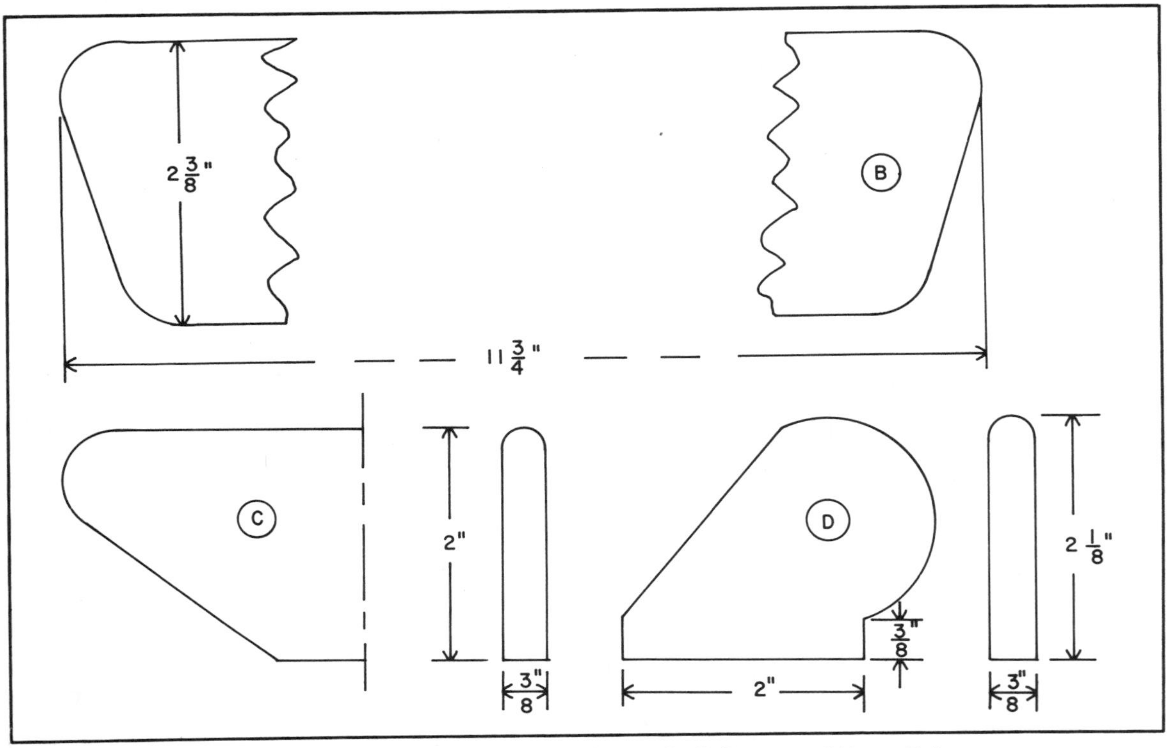

Fig. 6-3. Working plans for the Monoplane's front and rear wings and tail. Courtesy of Hayes Patterns.

Fig. 6-4. Completed Monoplane project. Courtesy of Hayes Patterns.

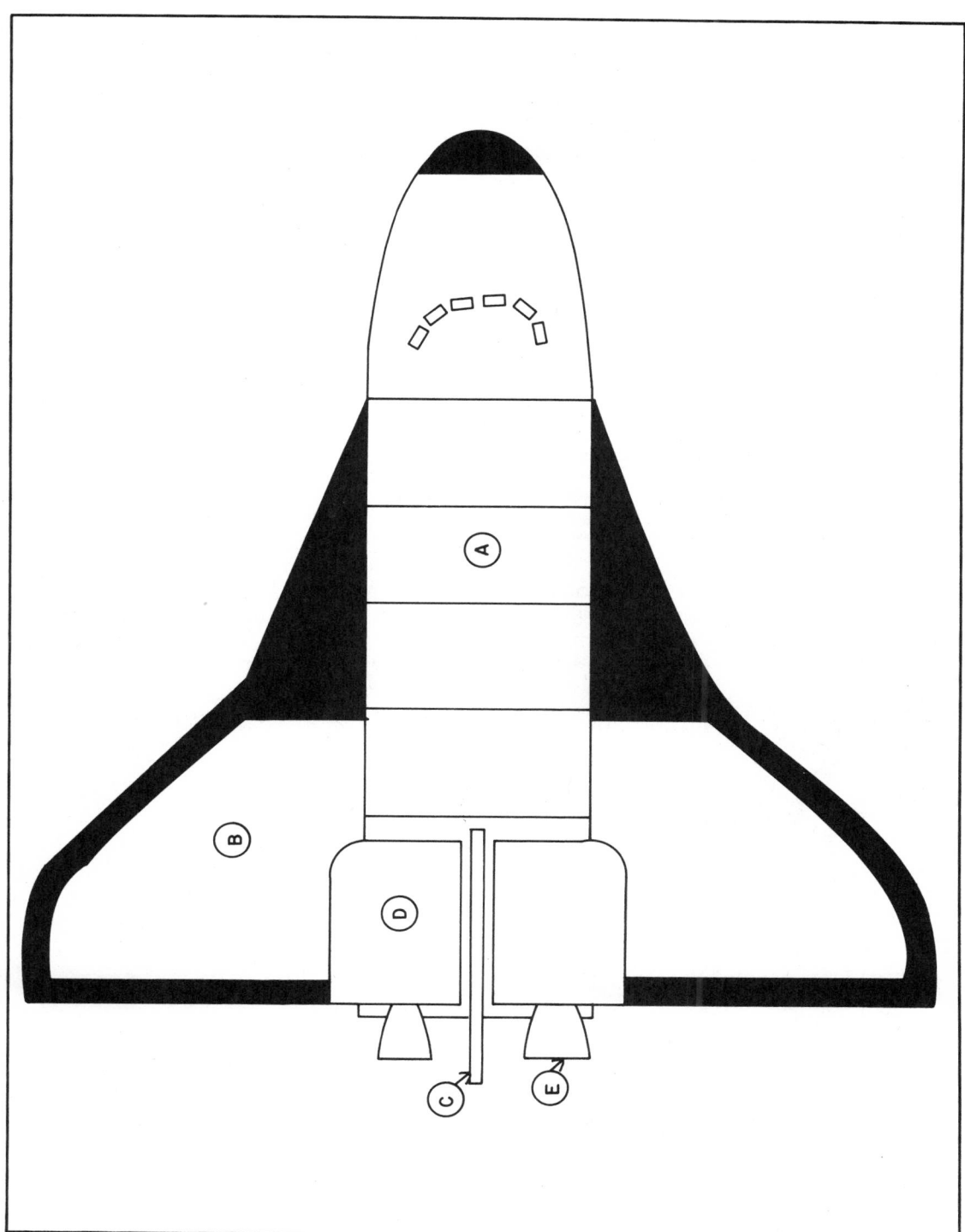

Fig. 6-5. Top view of the Space Shuttle.

Table 6-2. For the Space Shuttle, You Need the Listed Materials.

NUMBER OF PIECES	CODE	PART	SIZE	MATERIAL
1	(A)	fuselage	1 3/4"x2"x8"	maple
1	(B)	wing	1/4"x8"x 7 7/8"	redwood
1	(C)	rudder	1/8"x2 1/8"x3 7/8"	birch plywood
2	(D)	orbital maneuvering engines	1 3/8" diam. x 1 1/2"	maple or white pine
2	(E)	directional thrusters	1/2" length	1/2" padauk

the front wing and attach the wheels and axle.

Finishing

☐ Finish with clear spray Deft or polyurethane.

☐ Rub with #0000 steel wool, apply wax, and polish. See Fig. 6-4 for the finished project.

SPACE SHUTTLE

I started construction on this Space Shuttle toy even before the incredible journey of the "Columbia." This toy was prompted by a most fascinating article in the March 1981 issue of the *National Geographic* magazine.

Most American children would really like to be

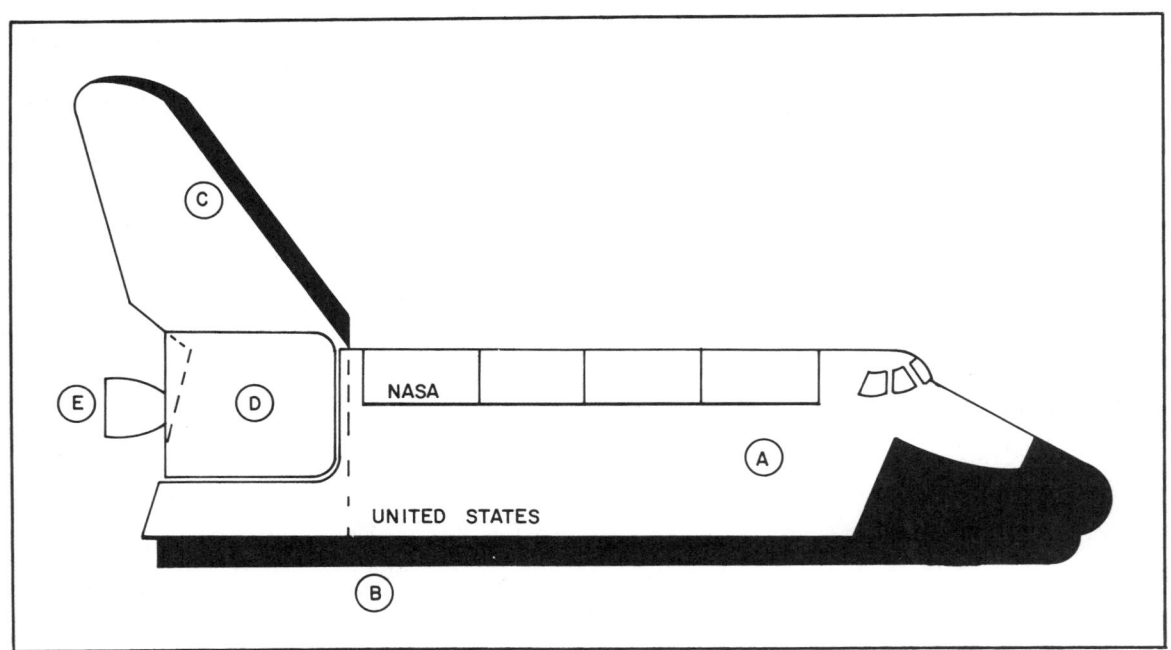

Fig. 6-6. Side view of the Space Shuttle.

involved in planning and making this toy, or at least in playing with it. The squat, chunky version of a combination rocket, airplane, and glider may include a fuel tank and rocket boosters if you desire.

Preparation

☐ Cut the fuselage stock to rough size. See Table 6-2.

☐ Place the stock in a vise and plane the cross section to a rough semicircle.

☐ Use a Surform, rasp, and different grades of sandpaper to complete the shape.

☐ Shape the nose with a band saw, chisel, rasps, and sandpaper (Figures 6-5 and 6-6).

☐ Cut the slot in the rear of the fuselage to accommodate the rudder.

☐ Cut with a band saw the recess at the rear of the fuselage for the two orbital maneuvering engines.

☐ Make a pattern for the wing, apply it to the wing stock, mark and cut it to shape on a band saw or other curve-cutting tool. Roll all the edges with a drum sander (Fig. 6-7).

☐ Turn the orbital maneuvering engines and directional thrusters on a lathe. Sand while the lathe is running.

Assembly

☐ Fasten the directional thrusters to the orbital maneuvering engines with small dowels or epoxy glue.

☐ Cut the rudder stock to size.

☐ Glue the rudder in the slot in the fuselage.

☐ Fasten the orbital maneuvering engines to the fuselage with small dowels or epoxy glue. Glue the engines to the rudder as well as to the fuselage.

Finishing

☐ Lay out the lettering and the windows on the fuselage and burn in with a burning tool. You could also paint them on the shuttle with a fine brush and black acrylic paint.

☐ Glue the fuselage to the wing.

☐ Lay out the black portions on the fuselage, rudder, and wing which represent the area covered by heat-dissipating tile.

☐ Paint with black acrylic paint.

☐ Spray on three or four coats of clear Deft or polyurethane. When dry, rub with #0000 steel wool, wax, and polish. See Fig. 6-8 for the finished project.

PROPELLER TOY

The Propeller toy by Stanley Tools is a simple, but amazing toy. No one seems to know just why it works. The fact that the propeller turns only one way also defies explanation.

The propeller turns when the dowel is rubbed

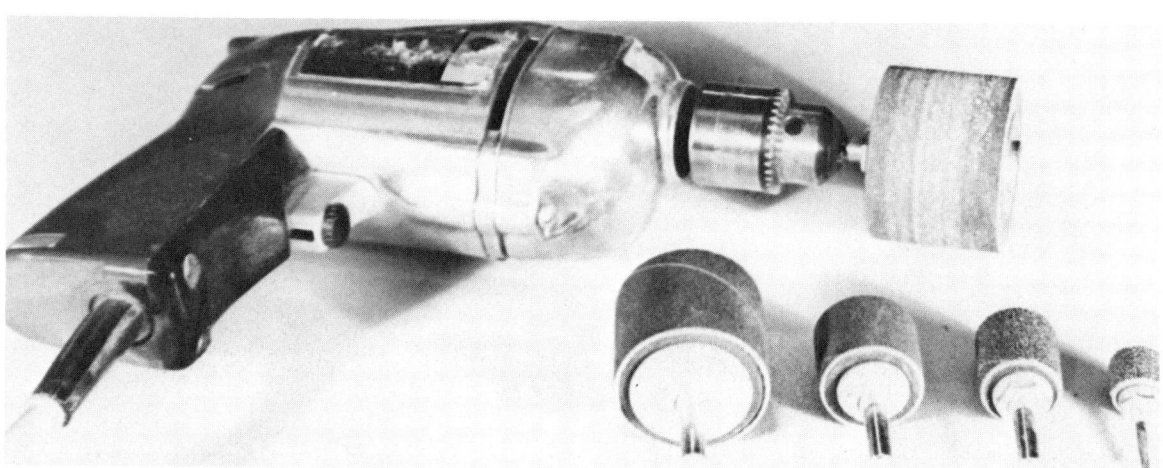

Fig. 6-7. Drum sanders are shown.

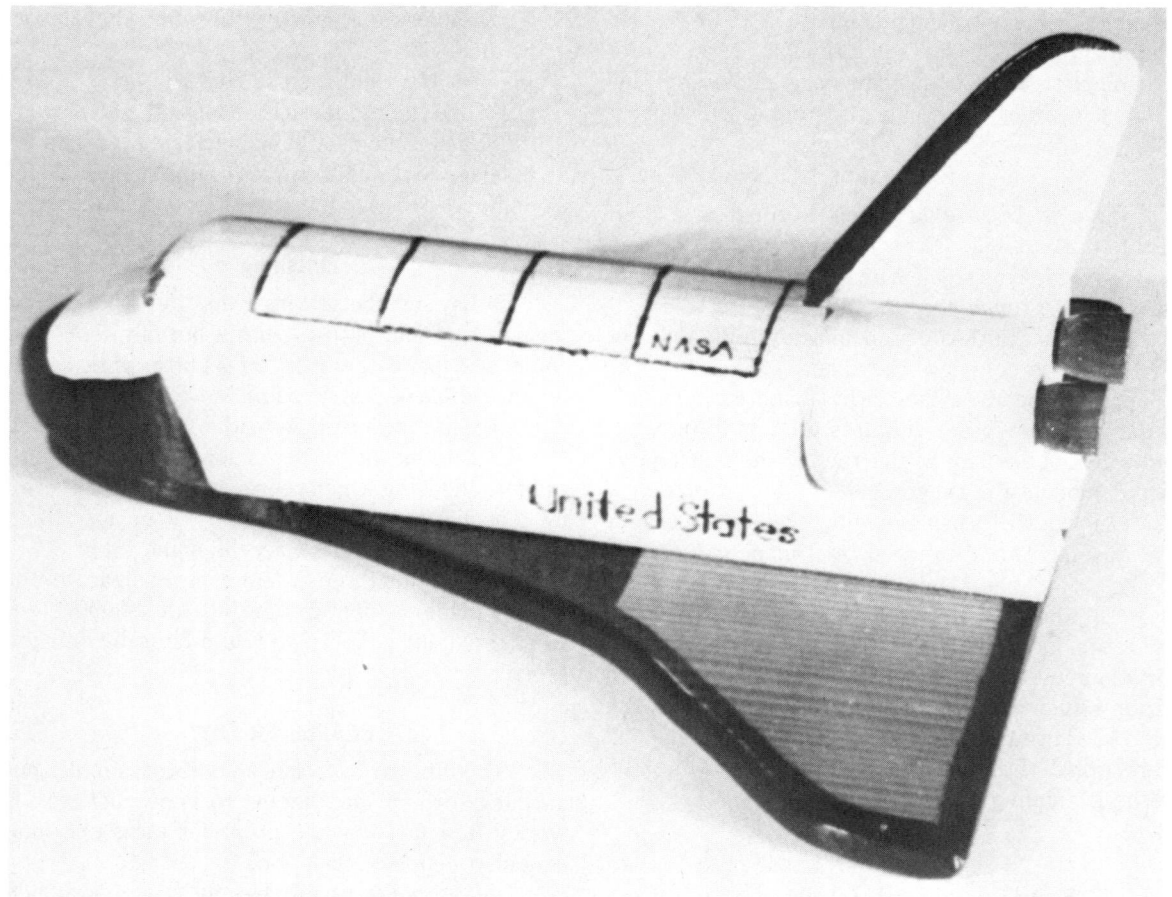

Fig. 6-8. Completed Space Shuttle project.

over the teeth on the handle. The dowel should be moved in both directions. The faster the teeth are stroked, the faster the propeller turns.

The secret of success in making this toy is in the balancing of the propeller. If one propeller blade is even slightly heavier than the other blade, it will not work.

Preparation

☐ Cut out rough stock for the handle. See Table 6-3. I used walnut.

☐ Make a pattern or drawing of handle and transfer to handle stock. Be sure to enlarge the pattern to the sizes given in Fig. 6-9.

☐ Cut the outline of the handle with a jigsaw or band saw. Care should be exercised in cutting out the teeth. They should be uniform in size and shape.

☐ Sand the handle. End up with fine grit sandpaper.

☐ Cut the propeller from 1/8-inch stock. I used cherry.

☐ Select a nail for the propeller shaft. Do not use a brad. I used a brass nail about 3/4-inch long.

☐ Drill a hole in the center of the propeller slightly larger than the diameter of the nail.

Assembly

☐ Insert the nail through the propeller's

Table 6-3. A Materials List for the Propeller Toy.

NUMBER OF PIECES	PART	SIZE	MATERIAL
1	handle	1/4"x 2"x 12"	hardwood
1	propeller	1/8"x 11/16"x 4 9/16"	hardwood
1	activator	11" length	1/4" birch dowel

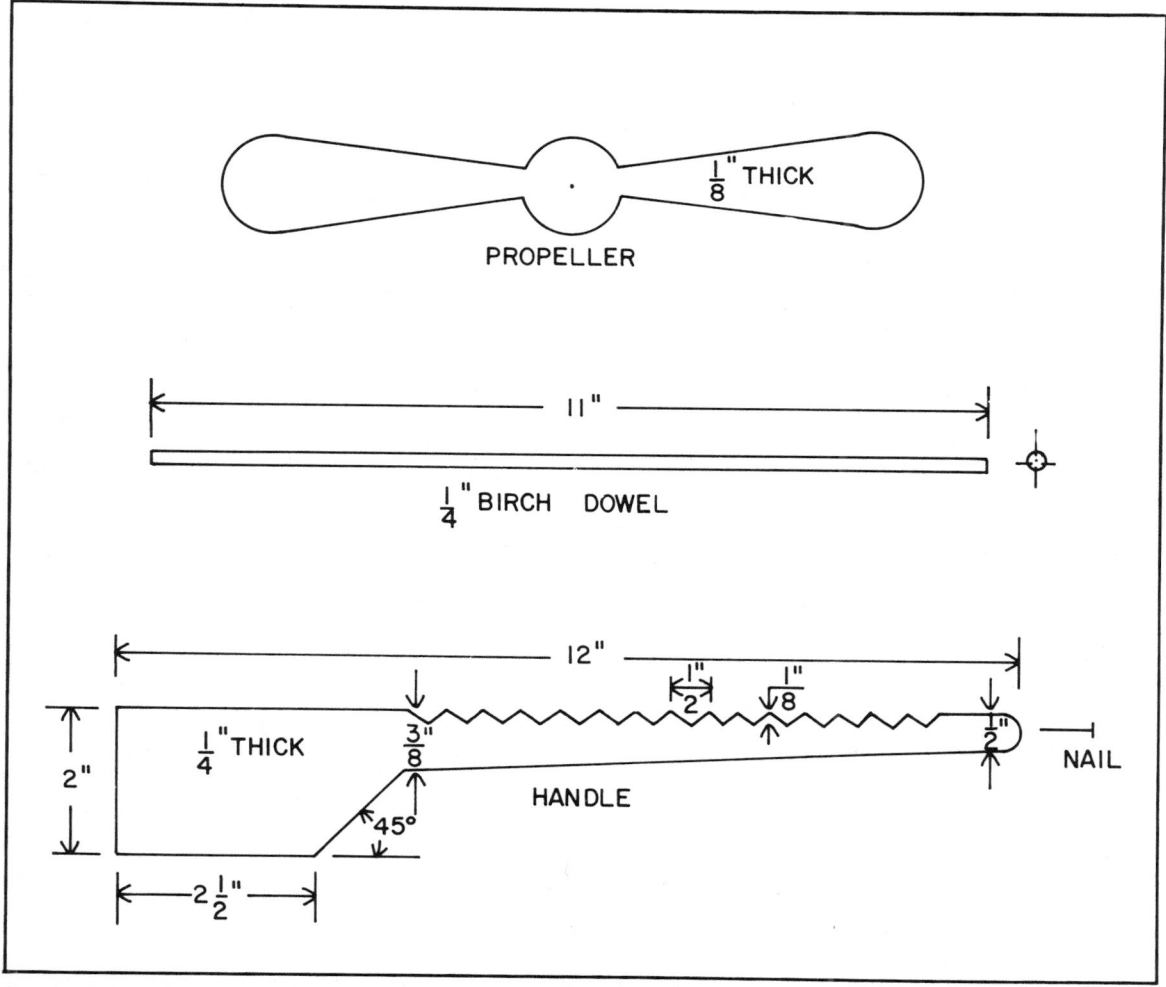

Fig. 6-9. Propeller toy working plans. Courtesy of Stanley Tools.

center hole to ascertain if the propeller is balanced.

☐ If one blade of the propeller is heavier than the other blade, sand down the heavier blade. After every few strokes of sandpaper, try the propeller on the nail. When the propeller stays in any position on the nail, complete balance has been obtained.

☐ Drill a hole in the end of the handle slightly smaller than the diameter of the nail.

☐ Place the end of the handle in the vise and drive in the nail. Hold the end of the handle tightly in the vise to help alleviate any tendency of the wood to split.

☐ Cut 11 inches of 1/4-inch dowel for the activator.

☐ Finish with three or four coats of clear spray Deft.

HELICOPTER

All youngsters are intrigued by anything that flies, but they are intensely attracted to a plane that can simulate the flight of a humming bird by hovering, or flying left, right, straight ahead, up, down, or even backward.

There are no troublesome problems presented by this project if you follow the directions. The contrast of colors between the red propeller, the dark brown cabin, and the light colored tail section, adds a great deal of eye appeal.

Assembly

☐ Make a pattern or lay out the outline of the cabin on 2 inch black walnut with the grain running from front to back of the cabin. Be sure to enlarge the pattern to the sizes given in Figs. 6-10 and 6-11.

☐ Lay out the cockpit and cut the hole with a saber saw. It is much easier to control the saber saw while the piece is in the plank than it is after the outside outline is cut out with a band saw.

☐ Cut out the outside outline of the cabin with a band saw.

☐ Sand the inside of the cockpit with emery boards.

☐ Bore the windshield hole 3/4-inch in diameter.

☐ Round over the curved corners of the cabin with Surform, rasps, and different grades of sandpaper.

☐ Cut off 1 1/4 inches of the lower part of the "people."

☐ Glue the "people" into the cockpit.

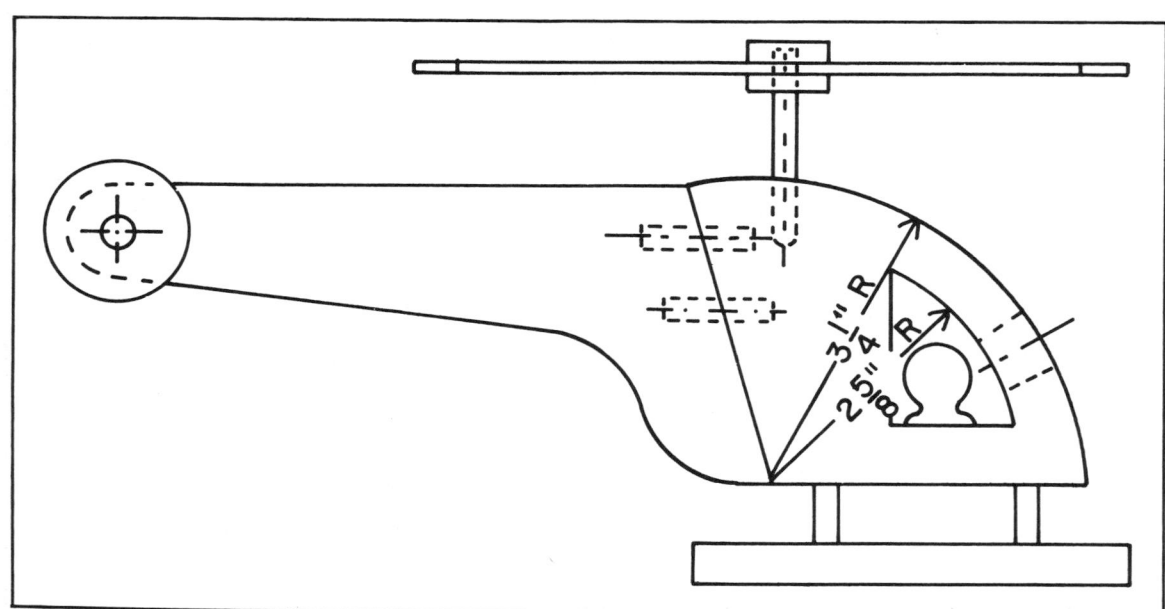

Fig. 6-10. Side view of the Helicopter is shown half size.

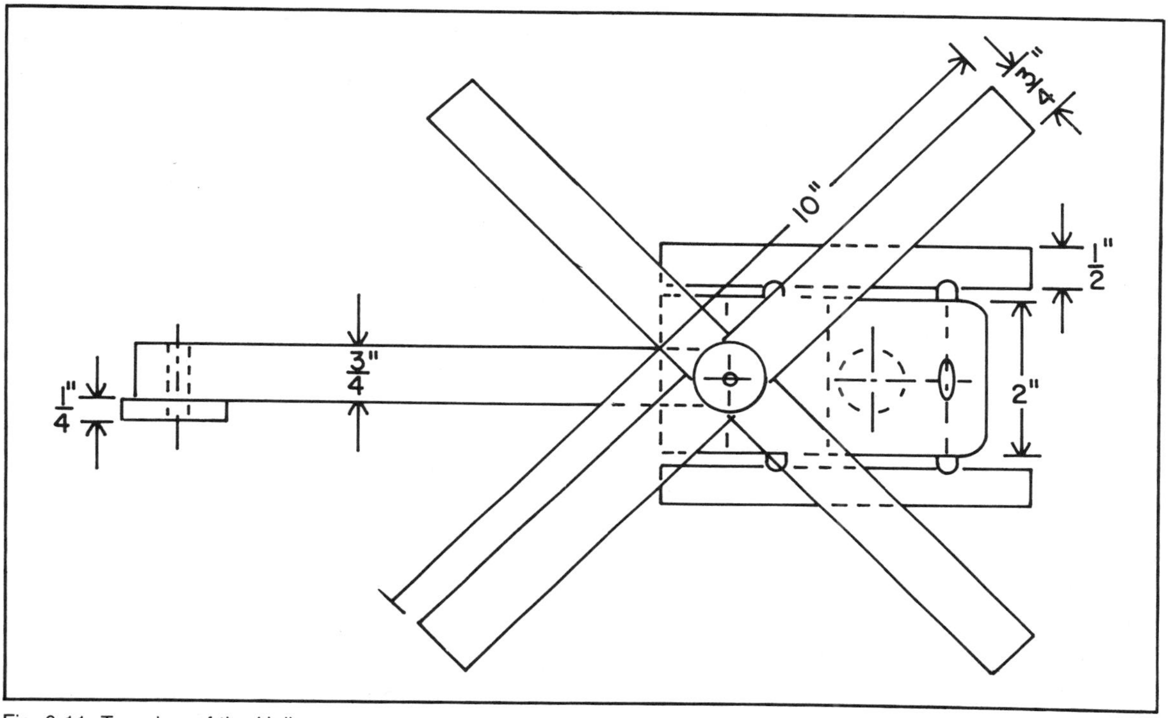

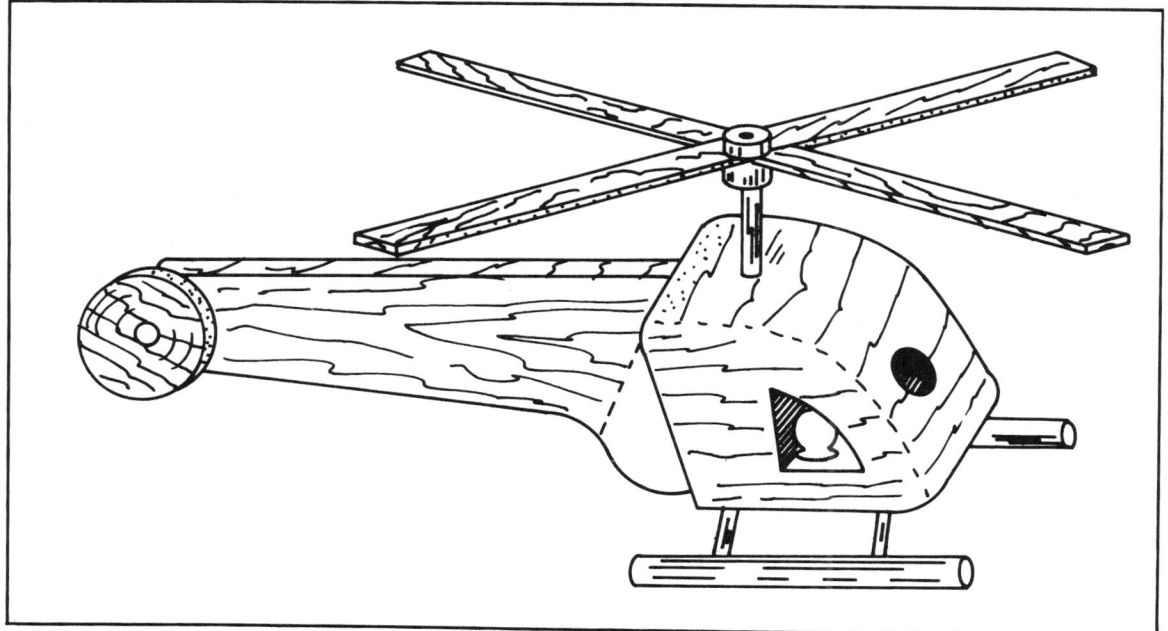

Fig. 6-11. Top view of the Helicopter.

Fig. 6-12. Perspective view of the Helicopter.

113

☐ Bore a 1/4-inch hole for the main rotor shaft about 3/4 inch deep in the top of the cabin. Make the main rotor blades and hubs (Table 6-4).

☐ Assemble the main rotor blades and hubs to the main rotor shaft (Fig. 6-12).

☐ Bore the four 1/4-inch diameter holes in the cabin for the landing gear supports at 45 degrees. Make a jig or template to make sure that the correct angle is maintained. Bore holes 3/8-inch deep.

☐ Cut the two landing gear units to 4 1/2-inch length.

☐ Cut the four landing gear supports to 5/8-inch length.

☐ Bore the four 1/4-inch holes in the landing gear units to a depth of 1/4 inch.

☐ Assemble and glue the landing gear units, landing gear supports, and cabin together.

☐ Make an enlarged pattern for the tail section and transfer to 3/4-inch white pine or maple.

Saw the outline with a band saw and sand the edges.

☐ Bore the 1/4-inch hole in the tail section for the rear rotor shaft.

☐ Locate the holes on the rear of the cabin to accommodate the two dowel joint pieces.

☐ Drive small brads into the hole locations and snip off the heads so that about 1/16 inch of the brads extend from the rear of the cabin.

☐ Place the forward part of the tail section over the brad points and tap gently with a mallet. The procedure will mark the dowel locations in the tail section.

☐ Pull out the brads with needlenose pliers and bore 1/4-inch holes 5/8 inch deep in the cabin and tail section.

☐ Place glue on the ends of the 1/4-inch dowel joint pieces and insert in the holes in the cabin and tail section. Place the tail section in a vise and force the cabin onto the dowels. Use clamps to hold the pieces until the glue is set.

Table 6-4. Materials Needed for the Helicopter.

NUMBER OF PIECES	PART	SIZE	MATERIAL
I	cabin	2" x 3" x 4"	black walnut
I	tail section	3/4" x 3 3/16" x 8"	white pine or maple
2	main rotor blades	1/8" x 3/4" x 10"	padauk
2	landing gear units	4 1/4" length	1/2" birch dowel
4	landing gear supports	1 3/8" length	1/4" birch dowel
2	main rotor hubs	1/4" length	7/8" birch dowel or turned wood
I	main rotor shaft	2 1/4" length	1/4" birch dowel
I	rear rotor	1 1/2" diam. x 1/4"	turned walnut
I	rear rotor shaft	1 1/16" length	1/4" birch dowel
I	"people"	7/8" diam. x 2 1/4"	commercial item
2	joint pieces	1 1/4" length	1/4" birch dowel

Fig. 6-13. Completed Helicopter project.

☐ Turn the rear rotor on the lathe or use a hole saw.

☐ Cut the rear rotor shaft.

☐ Glue the rear rotor shaft to the rear end of the tail section in the hole bored in the tail section, and in the hole on the rear rotor.

☐ Sand the entire project with fine sandpaper.

☐ Finish with three or four coats of clear spray Deft.

☐ Sand with #320 sandpaper.

☐ Rub with #0000 steel wool, apply wax, and polish. See Fig. 6-13 for the finished project.

7

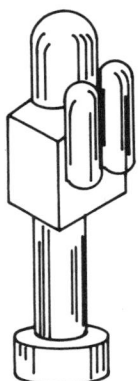

Ships and Boats

This chapter contains step-by-step instructions for making three ships and boats. Illustrations and tables of materials are also provided to give you further help in making these toys.

PADDLE WHEEL BOAT

The plans for this miniaturized version of a Mississippi river stern-wheeler were provided by Stanley Tools.

The hull can be made of any lightweight, straight-grained wood such as basswood, white pine, poplar, or redwood. I chose redwood because of its resistance to moisture. I also chose teak for the cabin, white pine for the bridge, padauk for the smokestack, and cherry for the paddle wheel. Some woods, like walnut and some tropical woods, will actually sink when placed in water.

Assembly

☐ Make a pattern of the hull and transfer to 3/4-inch stock (Table 7-1). Be sure to enlarge the pattern in Fig. 7-1 to 1-inch squares.

☐ Saw the outline on the band saw.

☐ Sand the edges of the hull with a disc sander.

☐ Cut the cabin to size and sand.

☐ Cut the bridge to size on the circular saw and round the front end with the disc sander.

☐ Cut dowel stock for the smokestack or turn on a lathe.

☐ Cut the two paddle wheels to size. Figure 7-1 gives dimensions. Cut the slot with a circular saw or band saw. Slide the two paddles together and sand.

☐ Glue the hull, cabin, bridge, and smokestack together with waterproof glue.

Finishing

☐ Sand the entire project with fine sandpaper.

☐ Finish the project with spar varnish or polyurethane.

☐ Attach the paddle wheels to the hull with two rubberbands. See Fig. 7-2 for the finished project.

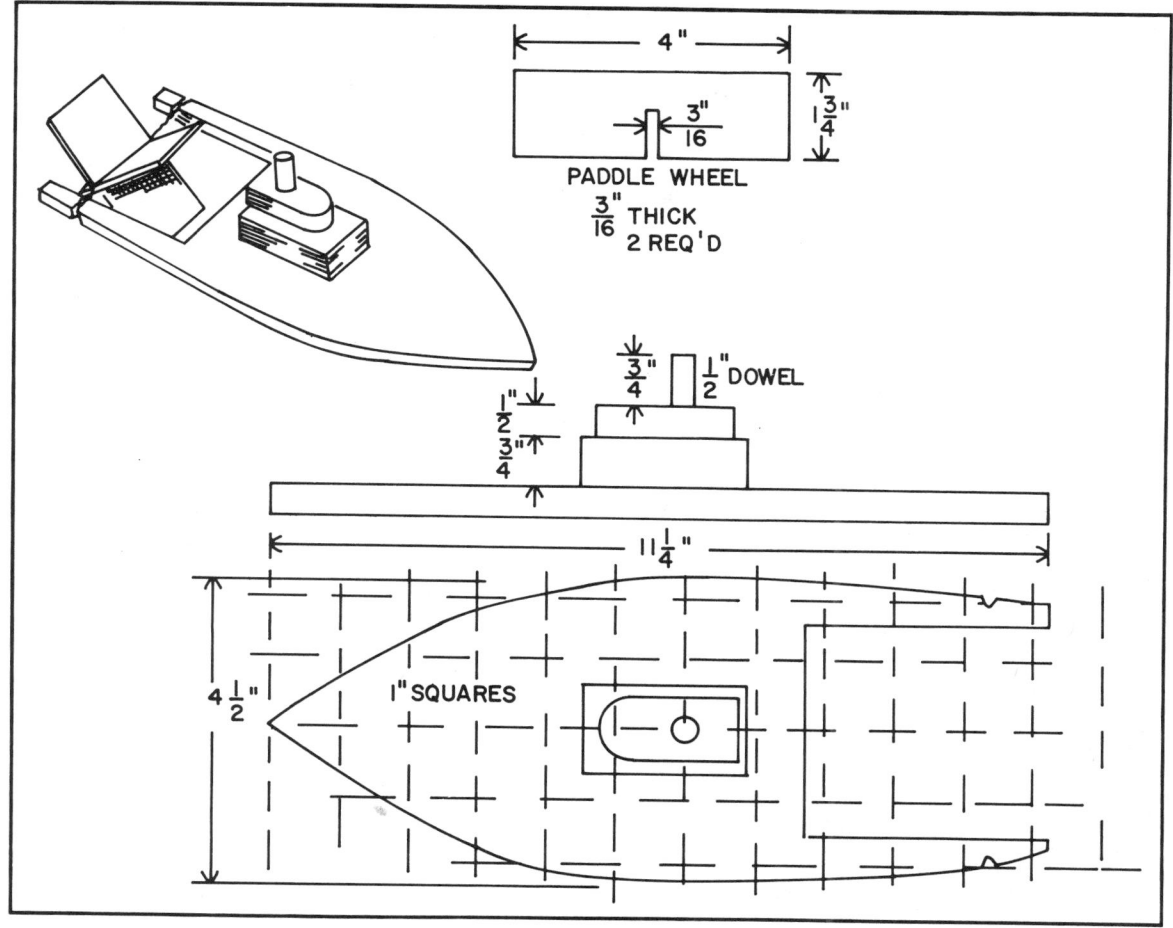

Fig. 7-1. Paddle Wheel Boat working plans. Courtesy of Stanley Tools.

☐ If the entire boat is made of light-colored wood, the hull may be enameled red, the cabin gray, and the bridge white, the smokestack gray and black, and the paddle wheels gray. These colors are recommended by Stanley; however, I prefer to use naturally colored woods for color effects rather than paint or enamel.

OCEAN LINER

The Ocean Liner, which I designed and constructed, appeals both to the child and the adult—to the child as a toy, to the adult as a collector's item or decoration piece.

If the ship will be used in water, the hull should

be made of a different wood since walnut barely floats, if at all. Ship should be finished with a water-proof varnish if it is used in water.

The imitation portholes were burned in using one of the burning tools in a kit sold by American Handicrafts Co. (Fig. 7-3). See Appendix A for suppliers' addresses.

Assembly

☐ Cut the hull to stock size. See Table 7-2 and Fig. 7-4.

☐ Make heavy paper patterns for the bow and stern.

☐ Trace the outline on the hull stock.

117

Table 7-1. The Paddle Wheel Project Is Made with the Listed Materials.

NUMBER OF PIECES	PART	SIZE	MATERIAL
1	hull	3/4"x 4 1/2"x 11 1/4"	lightweight wood
1	cabin	3/4"x 11/4"x 2 1/4"	lightweight wood
1	bridge	1/2"x 1"x 1 3/4"	lightweight wood
1	smokestack	3/4" length	1/2"birch dowel
2	paddle wheels	3/16"x 1 3/4"x 4"	lightweight wood
2	rubber bands		

☐ Set the band saw table at 20 degrees.

☐ Cut the port side of the bow with the bow pointed toward the saw.

☐ Cut the starboard side of the bow with the bow pointed toward you.

☐ Cut the stern with the same saw setting.

Fig. 7-2. Paddle Wheel Boat is shown completed. Courtesy of Stanley Tools.

Table 7-2. Make the Ocean Liner from the Listed Materials.

NUMBER OF PIECES	PART	SIZE	MATERIAL
1	hull	1 15/16" x 2 1/4" x 17 1/4"	walnut
1	lower superstructure	7/16" x 2 1/4" x 12 1/2"	white pine
1	middle superstructure	7/16" x 2 1/4" x 11 3/8"	white pine
1	upper superstructure	7/16" x 1 5/8" x 10 1/2"	white pine
1	bridge	7/16" x 1 7/16" x 2 1/4"	white pine
1	radar base	7/16" x 3/4" x 1 1/4"	white pine
1	radar screen	1/2" x 1/2" x 1"	zebrawood
1	radar screen support	2" length	1/4" birch dowel
3	funnels	3/4" x 1 3/16" x 2"	padauk (brilliant red)

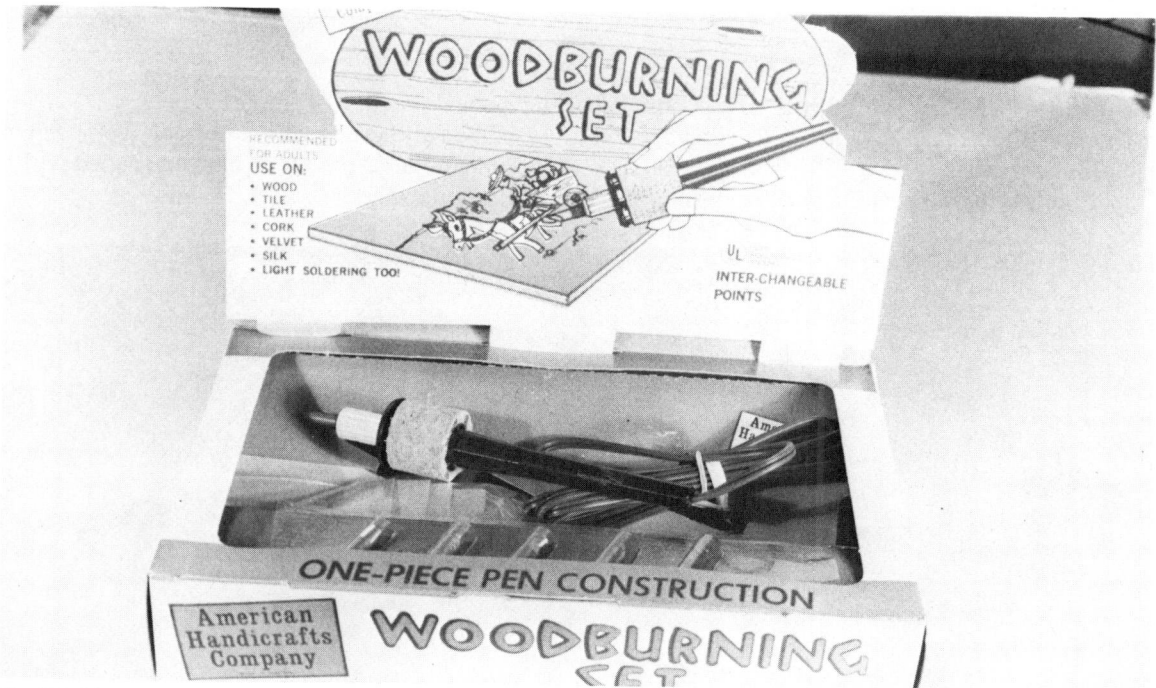

Fig. 7-3. You can buy a woodburning set from American Handicrafts Company.

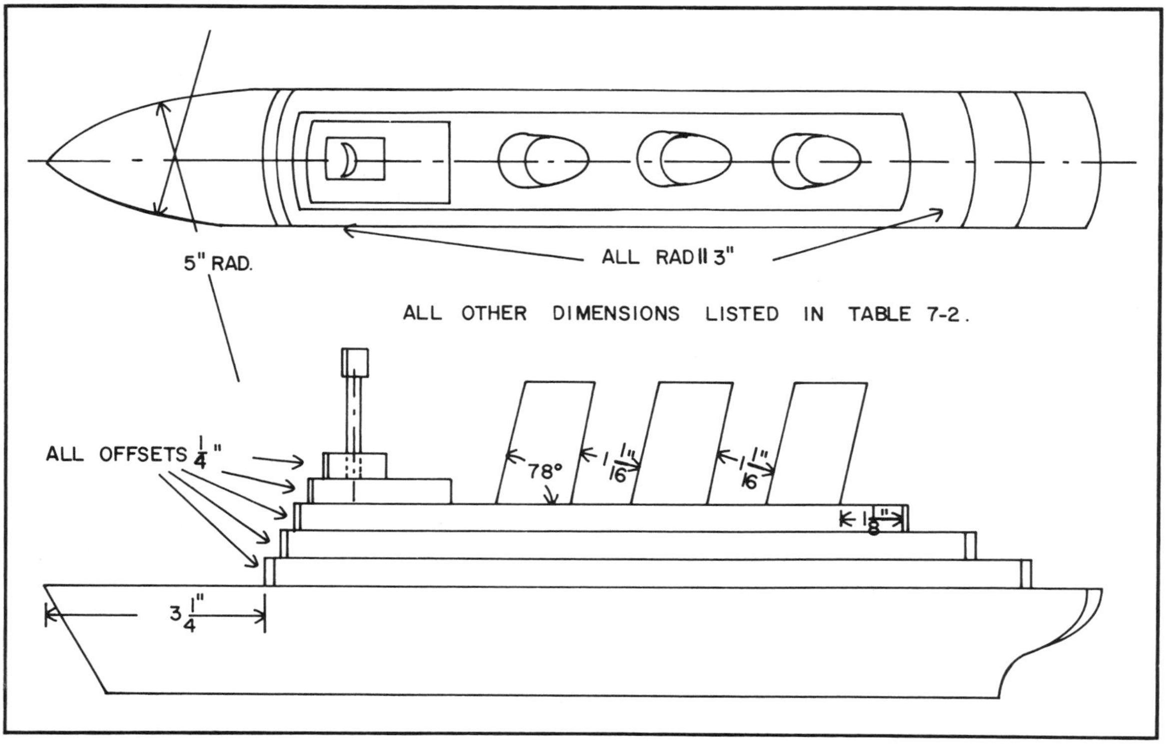

Fig. 7-4. Ocean Liner dimensions.

5" RAD.

ALL RAD ∥ 3"

ALL OTHER DIMENSIONS LISTED IN TABLE 7-2.

ALL OFFSETS $\frac{1}{4}$"

78°

$1\frac{1}{6}$"

$1\frac{1}{6}$"

$1\frac{3}{8}$"

$3\frac{1}{4}$"

□ Reset the saw blade at the normal position of 0 degrees. The blade should be 90 degrees to the table.

□ Make the undercut under the stern toward the normal position of the propeller.

□ Sand the hull with a portable belt sander. The underside of the stern may be sanded with a small drum sander.

Fig. 7-5. Completed Ocean Liner project.

120

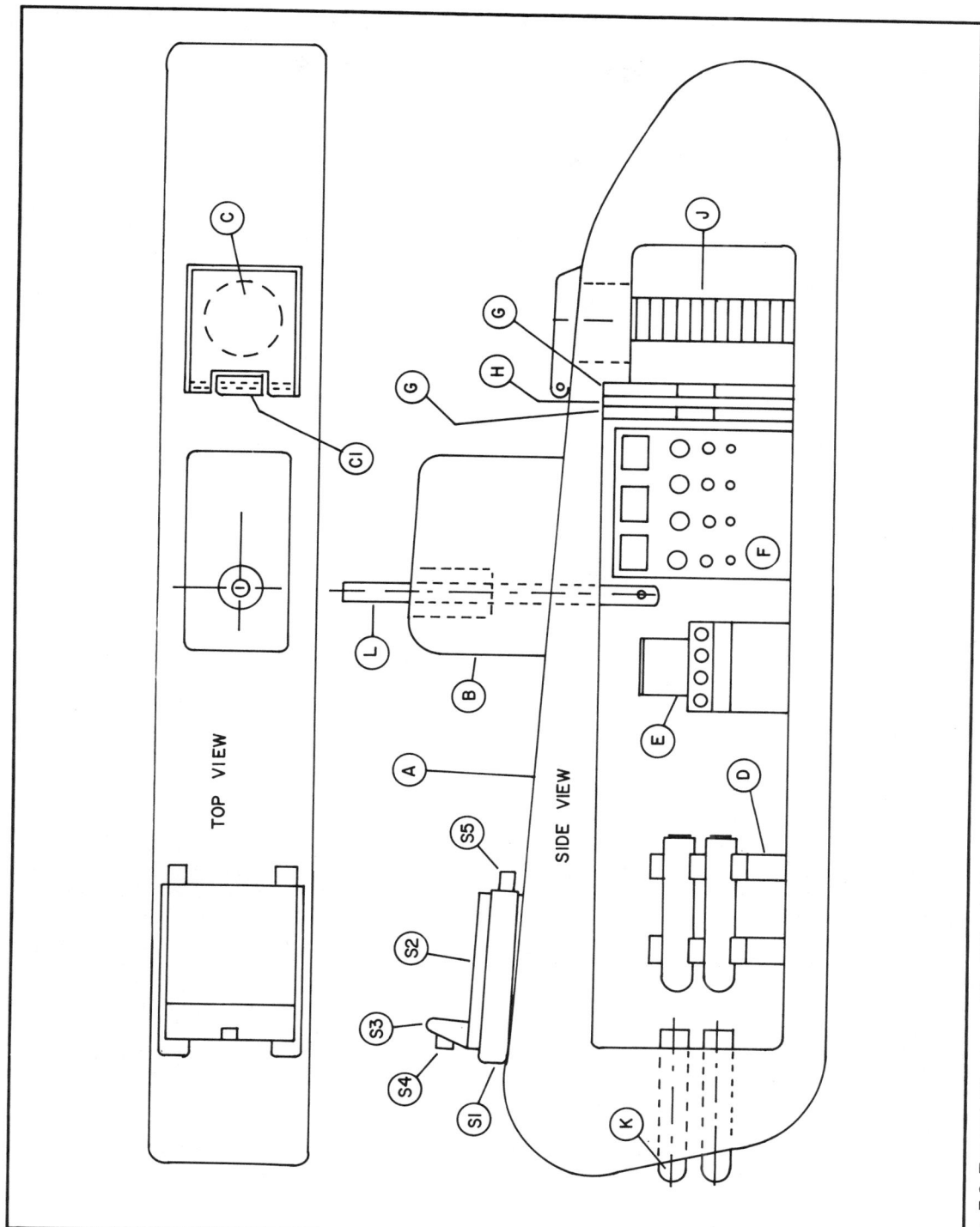

TOP VIEW

SIDE VIEW

Fig. 7-6. Top and side views of the X-Panded Play Sub. Courtesy of Criss-Cross Creations.

121

Fig. 7-7. Pattern for the hull and two parts of the X-Panded Play Sub before gluing. Courtesy of Criss-Cross Creations.

☐ Cut the parts for the three superstructures, the bridge, base for radar, and the radar screen (Table 7-2).

☐ Cut away about 1/2 of the upper 1/4 inch of radar screen support to provide a flat surface to glue on the radar screen. Glue the screen to the support with epoxy glue.

☐ Bore a hole in the radar base and glue in the support and radar screen.

☐ Sand the superstructure and bridge. Glue them to the hull.

☐ Cut the stock for the funnels 3/4-inch thick, 1 3/16-inch wide, and about 8 or 9 inches long.

☐ Shape about 6 1/2 inches of stock to an egg-shaped design shown in Fig. 7-4. Use a plane,

spokeshave, Surform, rasp, and different grades of sandpaper.

☐ Set the crosscut fence on the circular saw at 12 degrees and saw off the three 2-inch funnels. The extra rectangular length of stock provides a flat surface on the saw table to prevent rocking.

☐ Sand the funnels and attach them to the upper superstructure with epoxy glue.

Finishing

☐ Burn in the portholes. See Fig. 7-5. They are about 3/32 inch in diameter and are spaced 1/4 inch apart in the center of the edge of the superstructures.

☐ Finish with clear spray Deft or poly-

Fig. 7-8. The hull of the X-Panded Play Sub is shown assembled and glued. Courtesy of Criss-Cross Creations.

urethane. Use spar varnish if the liner will be used in water.

X-PANDED PLAY SUB

These modern submarine plans were provided by Criss-Cross Creations. Although the submarine is considered a machine of war, it is the technology and mechanical details allowing this ship to maneuver underwater that is uppermost in a child's mind.

The cutaway design lets the child play inside as well as outside the submarine. The design features an underwater entrance and exit hatch, a periscope that moves up and down, torpedo tubes, a torpedo room, control and computer panels, and a sled with divers for underwater exploration.

Hull

☐ Cut stock for the hull. See Table 7-3 and Figs. 7-6 and 7-7. Since it is difficult to obtain stock 2 1/2 inches thick and it is difficult to cut stock of that thickness with a saber saw, I used two pieces of stock 1 1/4 inches thick. After the internal design was cut out on the two pieces, both of which were oversize, the two pieces were glued together. After the glue dried, the outside design was cut on the band saw.

☐ Even up the hull with Surform, rasp, and different grits of sandpaper. A small drum sander may be used to advantage in the corners.

☐ Cut stock for the hull back.

☐ Glue the hull back to the hull. See Fig. 7-8.

☐ Bore torpedo holes, 1/2 inch in diameter, as shown in Fig. 7-9.

☐ Bore a 1/2-inch hole in the top of the hull to anchor the jet-powered underwater sled.

☐ Bore a 1 1/2-inch hole for the escape hatch. Do not bore the periscope hole at this time.

Conning Tower

☐ Cut stock for the conning tower. See Table 7-3 and Fig. 7-10. I used mahogany.

☐ Round the corners on a disc sander.

☐ Glue in place on the hull.

☐ Bore the holes as shown in Figs. 7-5 and

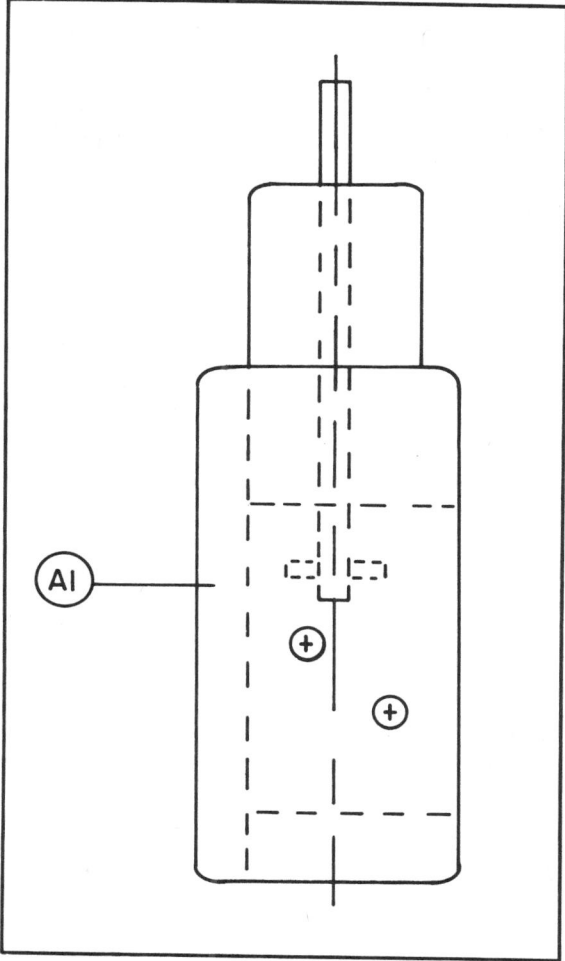

Fig. 7-9. Front view of the X-Panded Play Sub, approximately half size. Courtesy of Criss-Cross Creations.

7-9. The periscope holes should extend through the top of the hull (Fig. 7-11).

Hatch

☐ Cut stock for the hatch door. I used black walnut.

☐ Bevel the edges as shown in Fig. 7-12.

☐ Cut the hinge from dowel stock.

☐ Bore a 5/32-inch hole through the hinge. Sand a flat portion for gluing.

☐ Bore a 1/8-inch hole through the hatch door.

Table 7-3. Materials Needed for the X-Panded Play Sub Project.

NUMBER OF PIECES	CODE	PART	SIZE	MATERIAL
Hull				
1	A	hull	2 1/2"x6"x 22"	maple or pine
1	AI	hull back	1/2"x6"x22"	maple or pine
1	B	conning tower	2"x 2 5/8"x 4"	any material
Hatch				
1	C	hatch door	1/2"x2 1/4"x 2 5/8"	any material
1	CI	hinge	7/8" length	5/8" birch dowel
1		hinge pin	2 1/4" length	1/8" birch dowel
Torpedo Cradle				
2	D	torpedo cradle	1/2"x 2 1/4"x 2 3/4"	maple or birch
Computer				
1	E	computer base	7/8"x 1 7/8"x 2"	any hardwood
1	E	computer top	1/2"x 7/8"x 1 1/8"	any wood that contrasts with base
4	E	computer dials	5/8" length	5/16" birch dowel
Control Panel				
1	F	control panel base	3/8"x3"x 3 3/8"	any dark hardwood
3	F	rectangular dials	1/8"x 5/8"x3/4"	maple or birch
4	F	round controls	1/2" length	1/2" birch dowel
4	F	round controls	1/2" length	3/8" birch dowel
4	F	round controls	1/2" length	1/4" birch dowel
Watertight Bulkhead				
2	G	opening	1/4"x2 1/2"x 3 5/8"	any hardwood
1	H	sliding door	1/8"x 2 1/2"x 3 9/16"	plywood, tempered masonite, or hardwood
1	J	ladder	1/4"x3/4"x 3 "	any hardwood

NUMBER OF PIECES	CODE	PART	SIZE	MATERIAL
Torpedoes				
2	(K)	torpedoes	3" length	1/2" birch dowel
Periscope				
1	(L)	periscope	6" length	3/8" birch dowel
1	(L)	periscope handle	1" length	3/16" birch dowel
Jet Powered Underwater Sled				
2	(S1)	jet motor	3 1/2" length	5/8" birch dowel
1	(S2)	platform	1/4" x 2 1/2" x 3"	any suitable wood
1	(S3)	control panel	3/4" x 3/4" x 2 1/2"	any suitable wood
1	(S4)	light	1/2" length	3/8" birch dowel
2	(S 5-6)	nozzles	1" length	3/8" birch dowel
1		anchor	1 1/2" length	1/2" birch dowel
Crewman				
1		head	1/2" diam. bead	birch
1		neck	1 1/8" length	3/16" birch dowel
1		torso	3/4" length	5/8" birch dowel
1		legs	1 1/4" length	3/8" birch dowel
1		feet	1/4" length	5/8" birch dowel
Scuba Driver				
1		helmet	5/8" length	1/2" birch dowel
1		neck	1 1/8" length	3/8" birch dowel
1		torso	5/8" x 5/8" x 3/4"	maple or birch
1		legs	1 1/4" length	3/8" birch dowel
1		feet	1/4" length	5/8" birch dowel
2		tanks	3/4" length	1/4" birch dowel

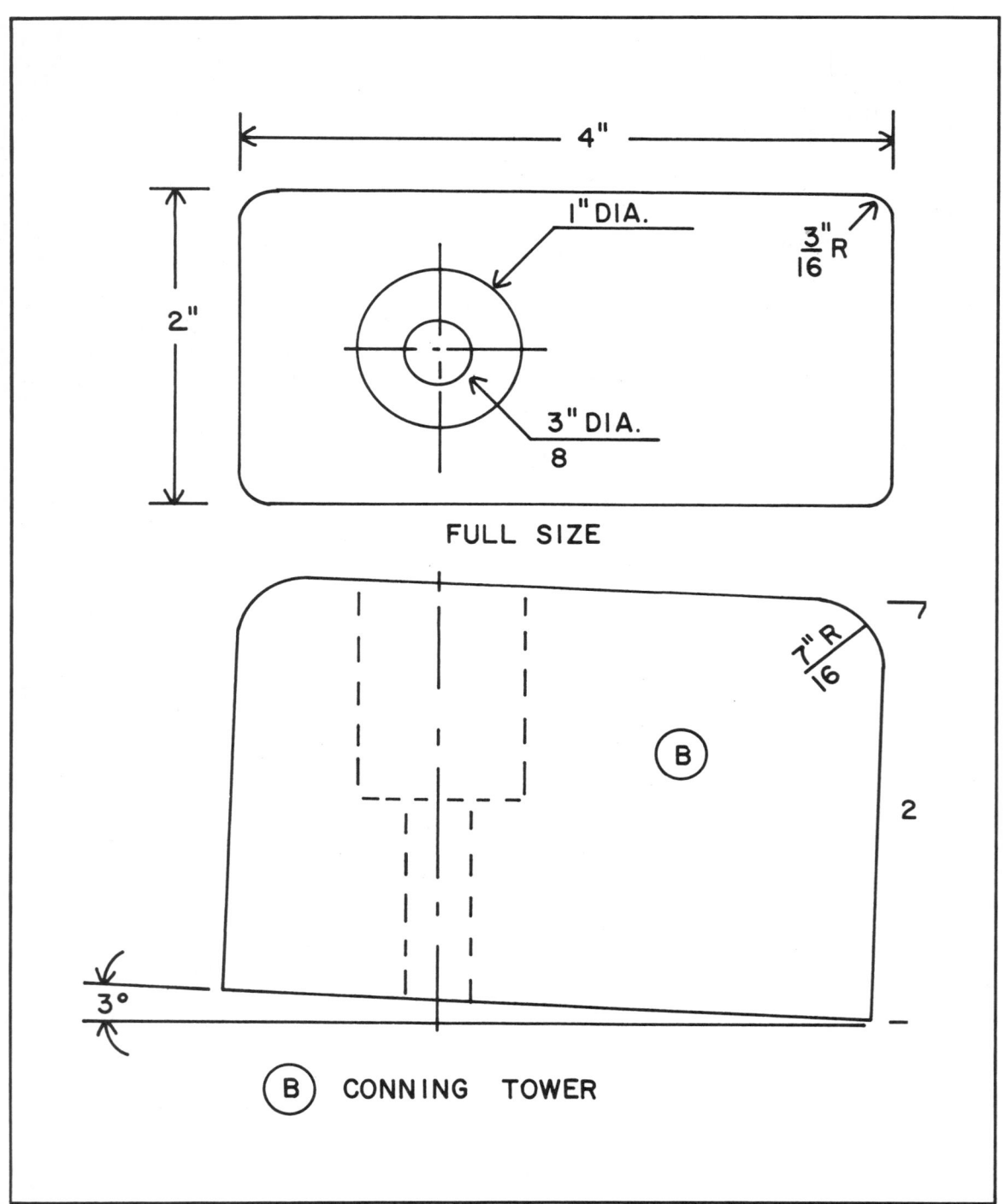

Fig. 7-10. X-Panded Play Sub conning tower, shown full size. Courtesy of Criss-Cross Creations.

Fig. 7-11. Conning tower for the X-Panded Play Sub is shown completed. Courtesy of Criss-Cross Creations.

BEVEL SIDE

$2\frac{5}{8}$ "

$\frac{5}{8}$ "

$\frac{7}{8}$ "

CI

$\frac{5}{8}$ "

1 "

© C

TOP

$2\frac{1}{4}$ "

$\frac{5}{32}$ " DIA.

SAND OFF THIS
AREA FOR GLUING
SURFACE

$\frac{1}{8}$ " DIA.

SIDE

$\frac{1}{2}$ "

USE $\frac{1}{8}$ " DOWEL AS HINGE PIN

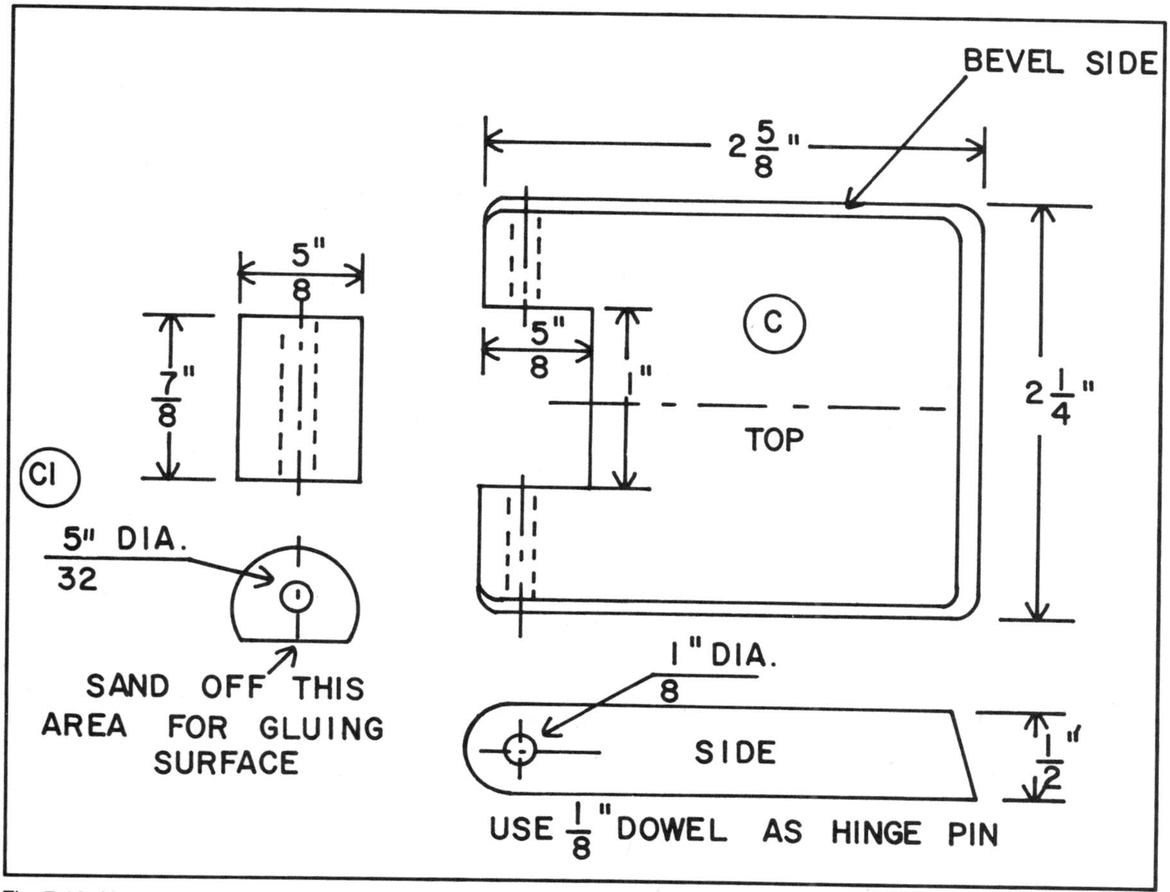

Fig. 7-12. Hatch details of the X-Panded Play Sub are shown. Courtesy of Criss-Cross Creations.

127

☐ Insert a 1/8-inch dowel through the hatch door and hinge. Apply a small amount of glue on the ends of a 1/8-inch dowel before completing the insertion.

☐ Glue the hinge dowel stock in place on the hull so that the door covers the 1 1/2-inch hole in the hull (Fig. 7-13).

Torpedo Cradle

☐ Cut stock for torpedo cradle. See Fig. 7-14. I used cherry.

☐ Cut the curved portions with a jigsaw or butt the two pieces together and cut a 1/2-inch hole through both pieces.

Computer

☐ Cut stock for the computer base. I used teak. See Fig. 7-15.

☐ Cut the computer dials to length using a 5/16-inch dowel.

☐ Bore the four holes in the computer base.

☐ Apply a small amount of glue to the short dowels and drive in place.

☐ Cut stock for the computer top. I used maple.

☐ Glue the computer top to the computer base.

Control Panel

☐ Cut stock for the control panel base. I used padauk. See Fig. 7-16.

☐ Bore holes for 12 round controls in the panel base.

☐ Cut the birch dowel for the round controls to length.

☐ Apply a small amount of glue to the ends of the short dowels and drive in place. Sand dowels to an even height after the glue is set. The contrast between the nearly white dowels and the dark red padauk provides an interesting design (Fig. 7-17).

☐ Cut the rectangular dials to size and glue in place.

Watertight Bulkhead

☐ Cut the two openings. I used walnut. See Fig. 7-18.

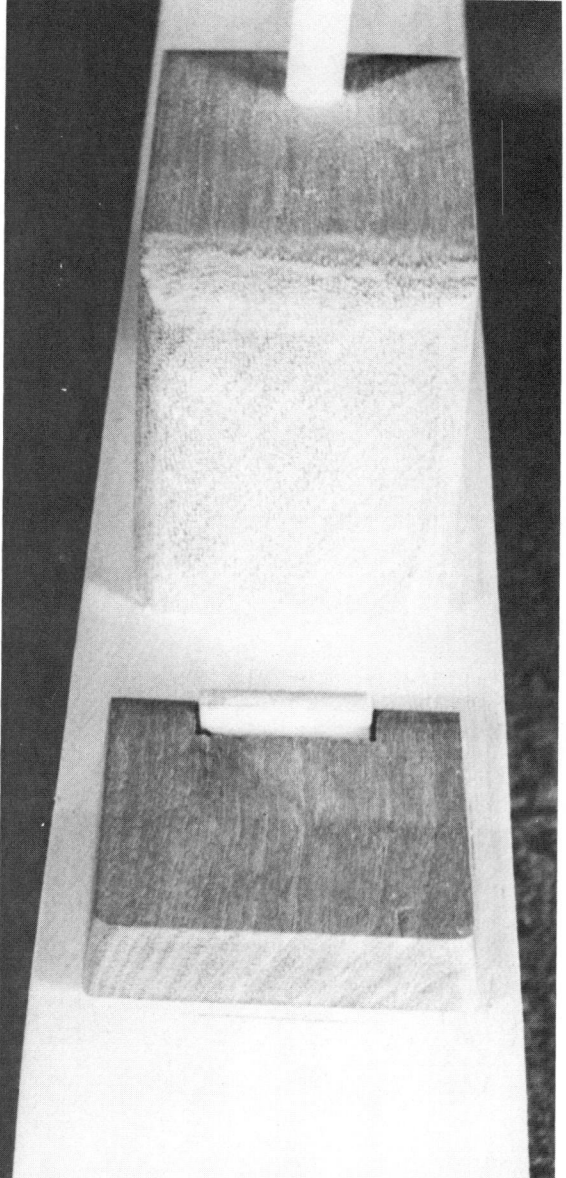

Fig. 7-13. The hull of the X-Panded Play Sub is seen from the stern. Courtesy of Criss-Cross Creations.

☐ Cut the opening holes with a jigsaw. Be sure the length is consistent with the hull opening.

☐ Cut the semicircle in the edge of both pieces with a jigsaw, band saw, or other curve-cutting tool.

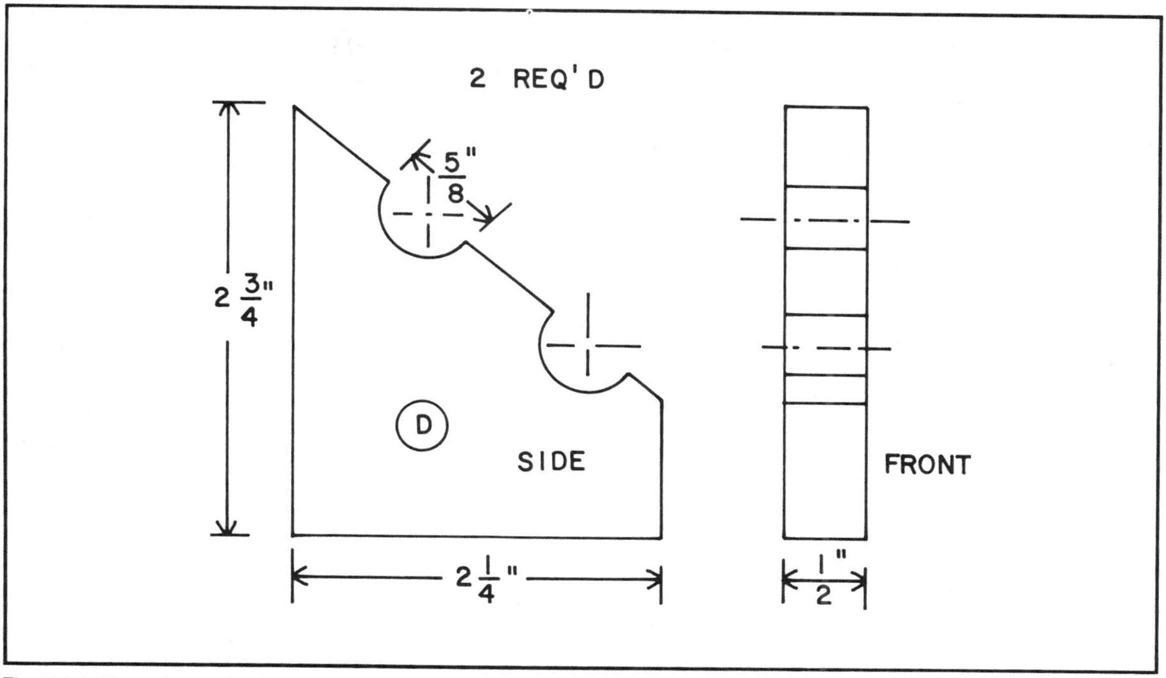

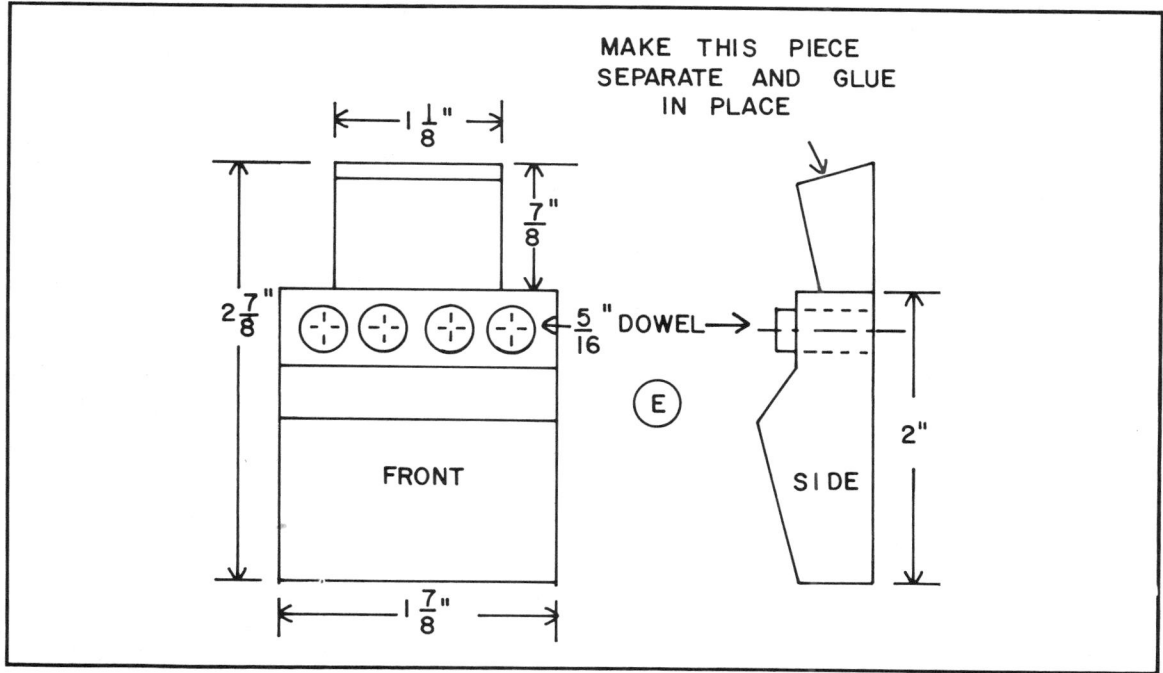

2 REQ'D

$\frac{5}{8}$"

$2\frac{3}{4}$"

D

SIDE

FRONT

$2\frac{1}{4}$"

$\frac{1}{2}$"

Fig. 7-14. Torpedo cradle detail of the X-Panded Play Sub. Courtesy of Criss-Cross Creations.

MAKE THIS PIECE SEPARATE AND GLUE IN PLACE

$1\frac{1}{8}$"

$\frac{7}{8}$"

$2\frac{7}{8}$"

$\frac{5}{16}$" DOWEL →

E

FRONT

SIDE

2"

$1\frac{7}{8}$"

Fig. 7-15. Computer detail for the X-Panded Play Sub. Courtesy of Criss-Cross Creations.

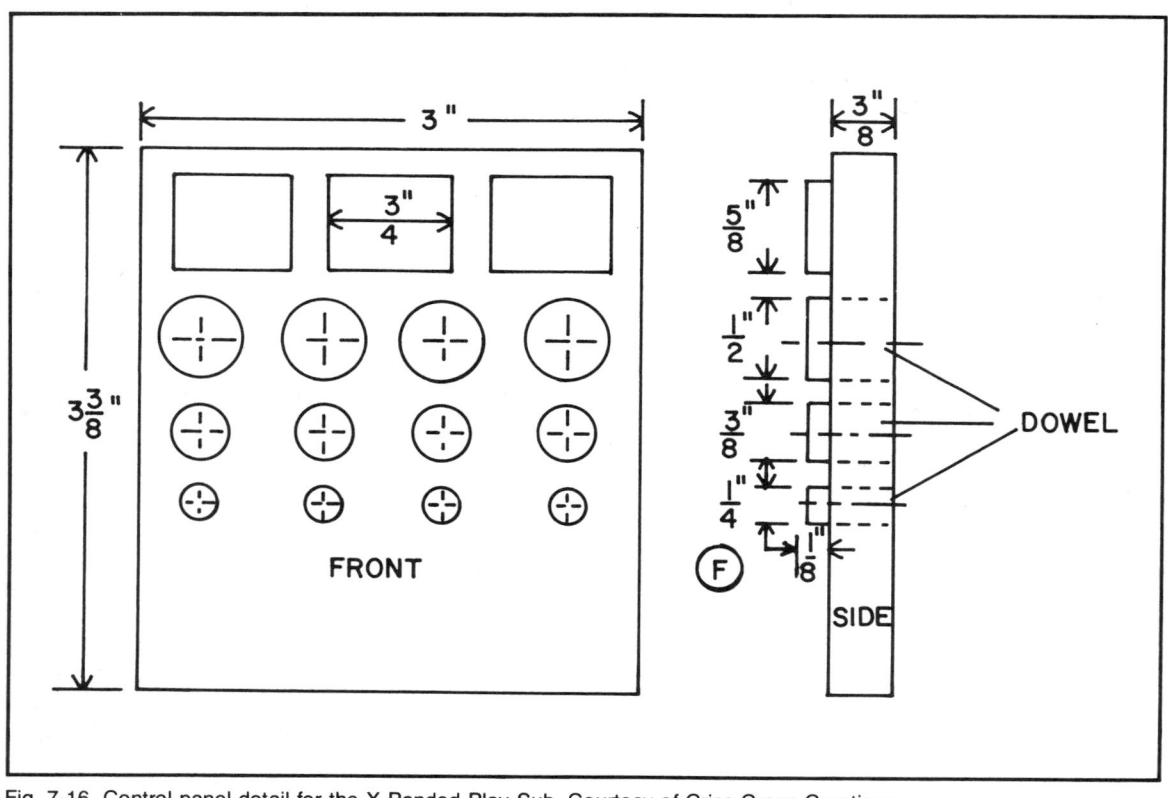

Fig. 7-16. Control panel detail for the X-Panded Play Sub. Courtesy of Criss-Cross Creations.

☐ Cut the sliding door to size. I used Masonite fiberboard.

Ladder

☐ Cut the stock for the ladder. See Fig. 7-19.

☐ Make simulated rungs with a file or small saw. I opted to make a more realistic ladder. The two side members are 1/8 × 3/16 × 3 inches, and the rungs are 1/16-inch birch dowels.

Torpedoes

☐ Cut the stock for the two torpedoes from 1/2-inch birch dowel. See Fig. 7-19.

☐ Round over one end on the disc sander and different grits of sandpaper.

Periscope

☐ Cut stock for the periscope from 1 3/8-inch birch dowel. See Fig. 7-19.

☐ Cut stock for the periscope handle.

☐ Bore a 3/16-inch partial hole at the top of the periscope and a 3/16-inch through hole for the handle.

☐ Apply a little glue to the handle and insert in the hole in the lower end of the periscope.

Jet-Powered Underwater Sled

☐ Cut the two jet motors from a 5/8-inch dowel. See Fig. 7-20.

☐ Cut stock for the platform.

☐ Bore a 1/2-inch anchor hole.

☐ Cut an anchor 1 1/2 inches long from a 1/2-inch dowel.

☐ Glue the anchor into the anchor hole.

☐ Bore a 3/8-inch hole, 7/16-inch deep, in one end of the two jet motors for the nozzles.

☐ Cut the two nozzles 1-inch long from a 3/8-inch dowel.

130

□ Apply glue to the ends of the nozzles and insert into the holes in the jet motors.

□ In the other ends of the jet motors bore a 1/4-inch hole 1/2-inch deep.

□ Countersink the holes bored in the last step.

□ Flatten one side of each of the jet motors to provide a gluing surface.

□ Cut stock for the control panel.

□ Bore a 3/8-inch hole in the control panel for the light.

□ Cut the light from a 3/8-inch dowel 1/2-inch long.

□ Apply glue to the light and insert it in the hole in the front of control panel.

□ Assemble and glue all the parts together (Fig. 7-21).

Crewman

□ Cut all the dowel parts as shown in Fig. 7-22. Use a 1/2-inch wooden bead for the head.

□ Drill holes for the insertion of dowels. As-

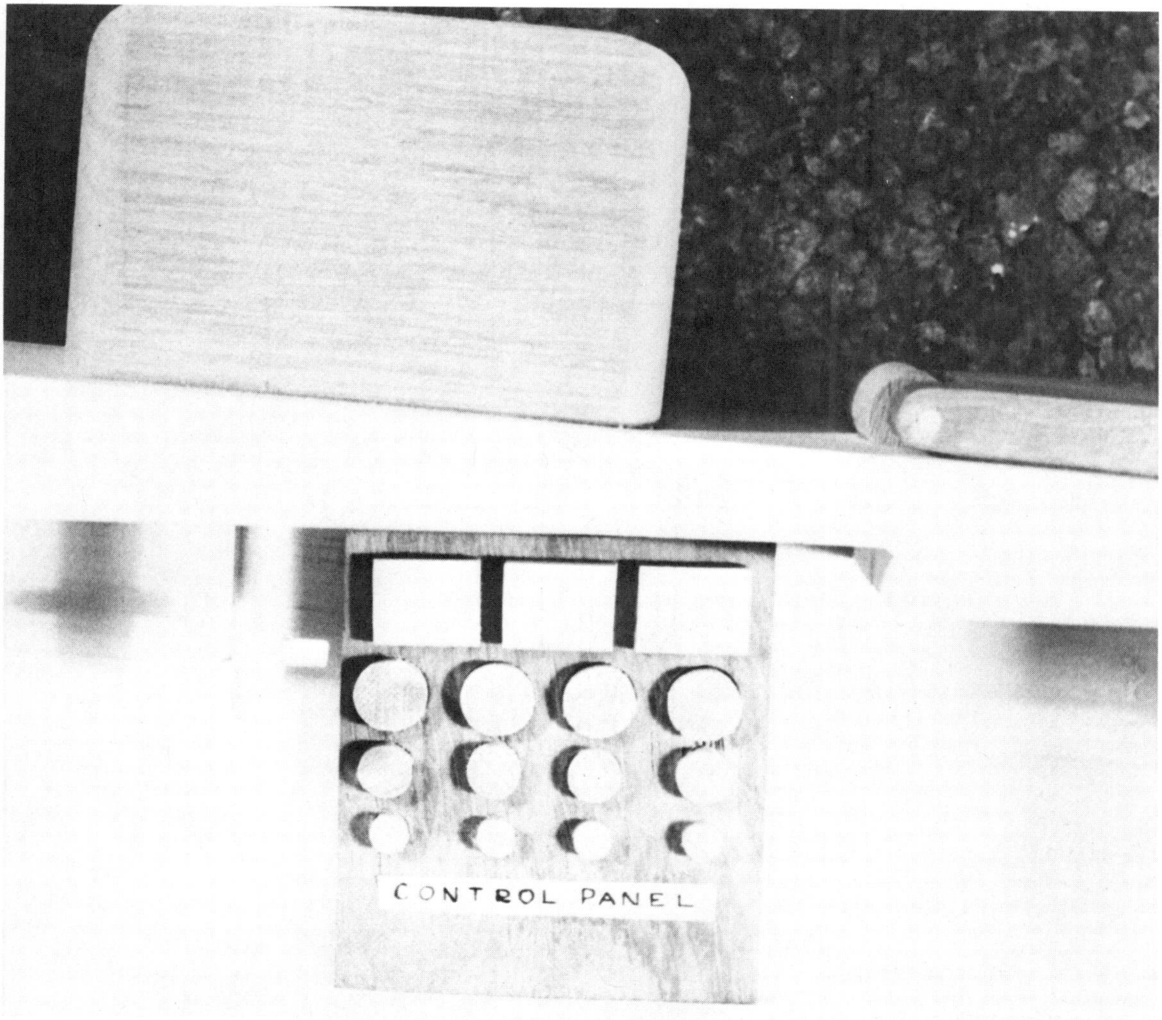

Fig. 7-17. Completed control panel is shown assembled in the sub. Courtesy of Criss-Cross Creations.

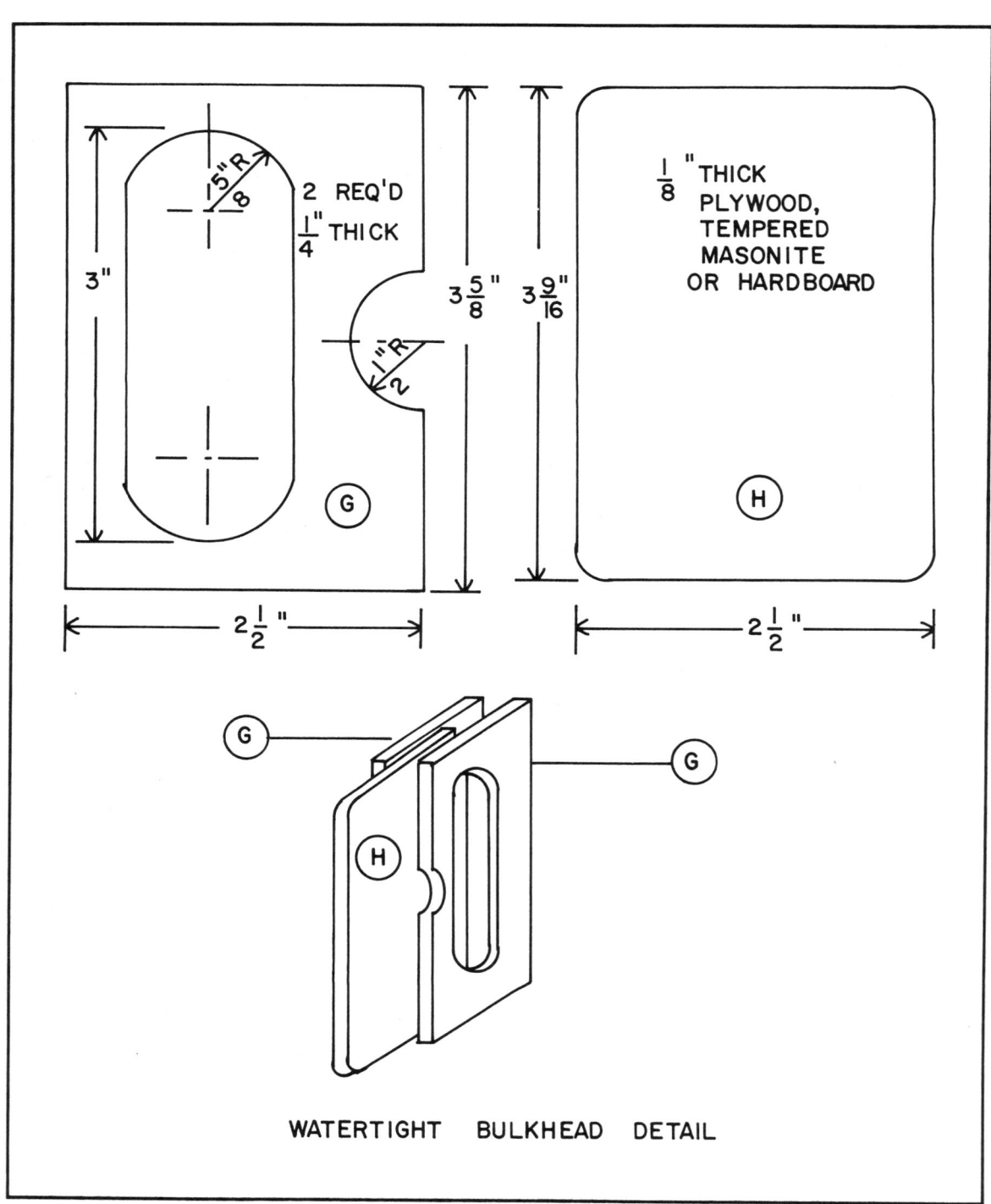

3"

5/8"R

2 REQ'D
1/4" THICK

3 5/8"

3 9/16"

1/2"R

G

1/8" THICK
PLYWOOD,
TEMPERED
MASONITE
OR HARDBOARD

H

2 1/2"

2 1/2"

G

H

G

WATERTIGHT   BULKHEAD   DETAIL

Fig. 7-18. Watertight bulkhead detail is shown for the X-Panded Play Sub. Courtesy of Criss-Cross Creations.

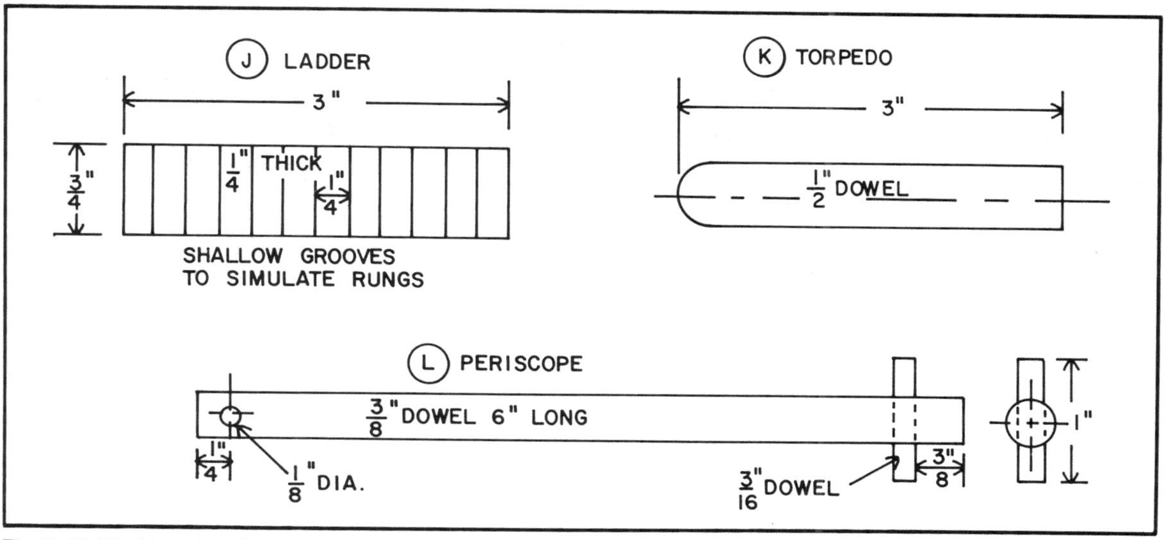
J LADDER
3"
1/4" THICK
1/4"
3/4"
SHALLOW GROOVES
TO SIMULATE RUNGS
K TORPEDO
3"
1/2" DOWEL
L PERISCOPE
3/8" DOWEL 6" LONG
1/4"
1/8" DIA.
3/16" DOWEL
3/8"
1"

Fig. 7-19. Working plans for the sub's ladder, torpedo, and periscope are shown. Courtesy of Criss-Cross Creations.

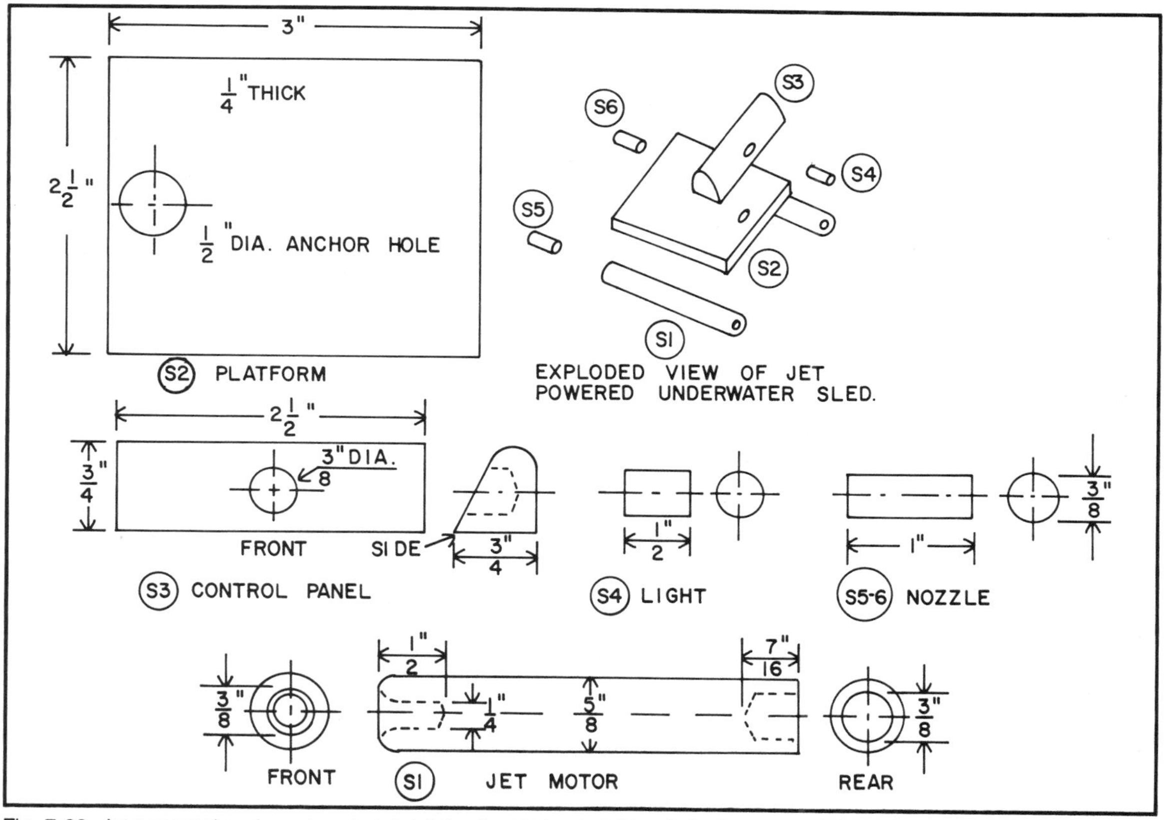
3"
1/4" THICK
2 1/2"
1/2" DIA. ANCHOR HOLE
S2 PLATFORM
S3
S6
S4
S5
S2
S1
EXPLODED VIEW OF JET
POWERED UNDERWATER SLED.
2 1/2"
3/4"
3/8" DIA.
FRONT
SIDE
3/4"
S3 CONTROL PANEL
1/2"
S4 LIGHT
1"
3/8"
S5-6 NOZZLE
1/2"
7/16"
3/8"
1/4"
5/8"
3/8"
FRONT
S1 JET MOTOR
REAR

Fig. 7-20. Jet-powered underwater sled detail for the X-Panded Play Sub. Courtesy of Criss-Cross Creations.

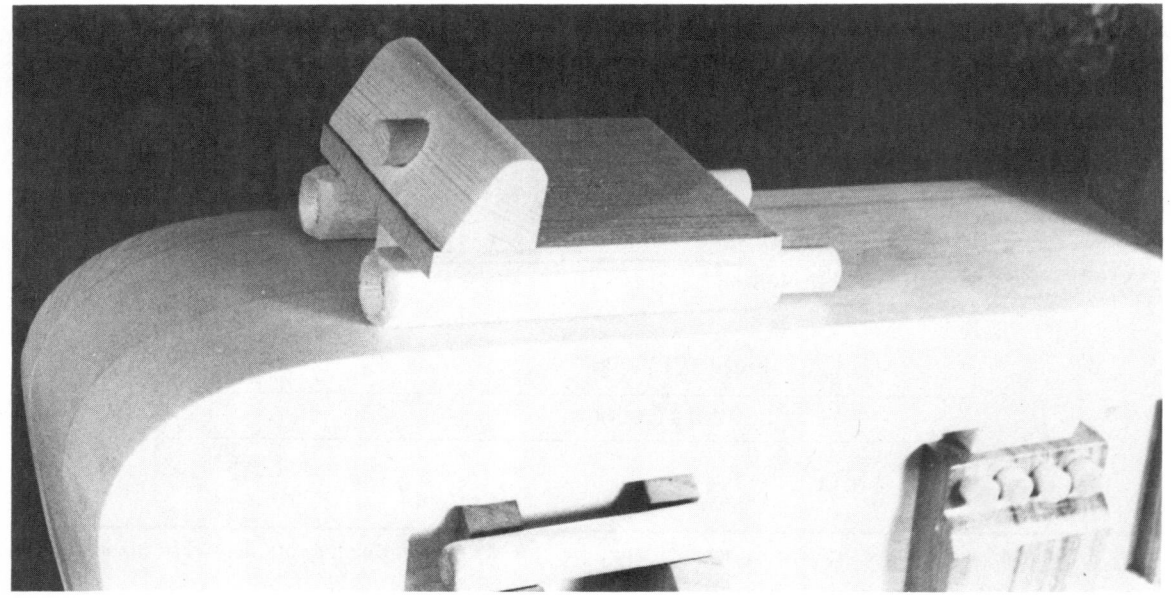

Fig. 7-21. The jet-powered underwater sled for the sub is shown here completed. Courtesy of Criss-Cross Creations.

semble and glue. I chose to turn the entire piece on a lathe, which took much less time. If you possess a lathe you are advised to use this method (Fig. 7-23).

Scuba Diver

☐ Cut all dowel parts as shown in Fig. 7-22.

☐ Cut the square torso of maple or birch.

☐ Bore holes to insert dowels.

☐ Assemble and glue.

☐ Flatten the two tanks to provide a gluing surface.

☐ Glue the tanks to the torso.

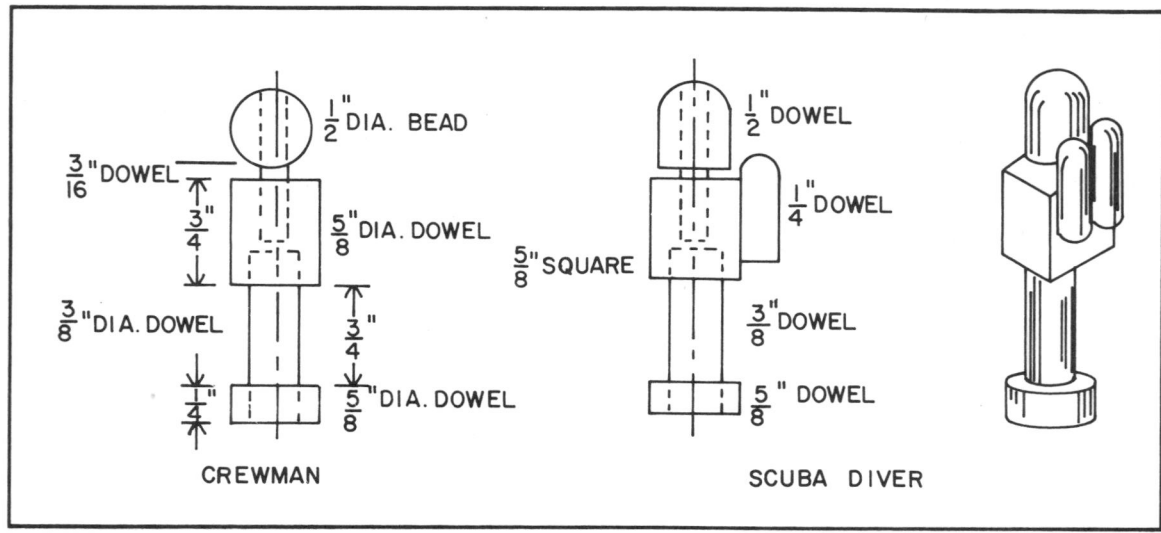

Fig. 7-22. Details for the crewman and scuba diver are shown. Courtesy of Criss-Cross Creations.

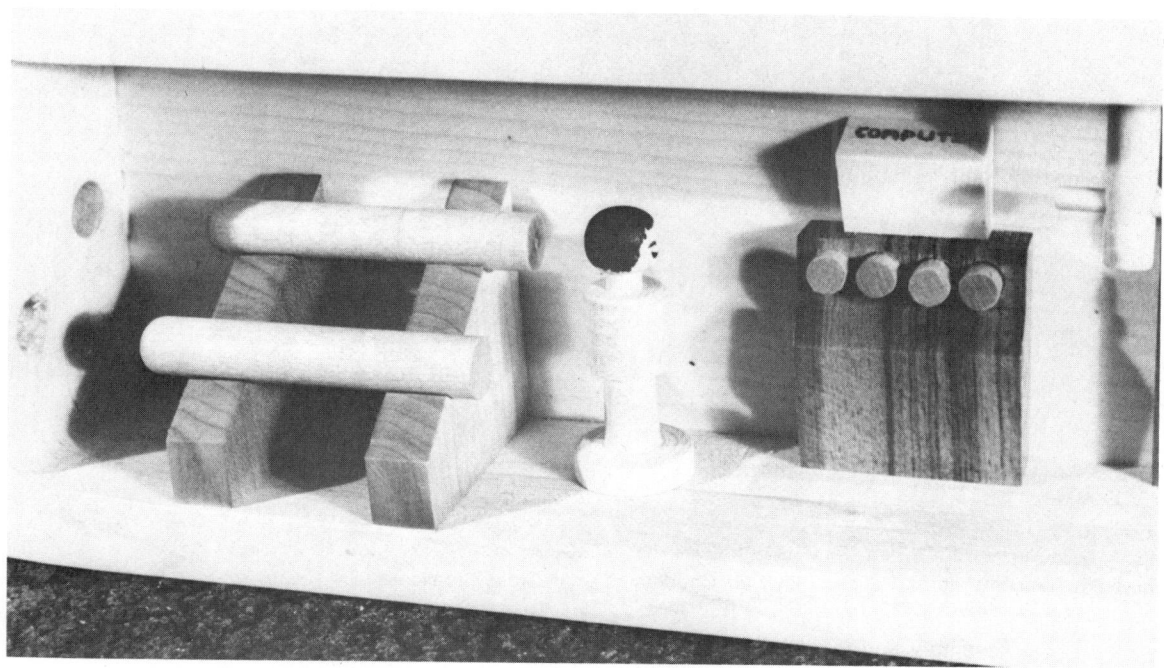

Fig. 7-23. Shown completed are the torpedoes, cradle, crewman, and the computer for the sub. Courtesy of Criss-Cross Creations.

Fig. 7-24. The control panel, watertight bulkhead, scuba diver, ladder, and hatch for the X-Panded Play Sub. Courtesy of Criss-Cross Creations.

Fig. 7-25. The completed X-Panded Play Sub. Courtesy of Criss-Cross Creations.

Assembly and Finishing

☐ Sand all the assembled parts with #220 sandpaper.

☐ Finish all separate parts with one or two spray coats of clear Deft or polyurethane. Be sure to avoid getting finish on the surfaces that are to be glued to the hull.

☐ Glue the torpedo cradle, computer, control panel, the opening of the watertight bulkhead, and the ladder to their respective positions in the hull (Fig. 7-24). The anchor on the underwater sled, the torpedoes, the crewman, the scuba diver, the slid-ing door of the watertight bulkhead, and the periscope are not glued in place.

☐ So the periscope can move up, down, and around, carefully sand the periscope column. The movement should require some effort. Avoid a sloppy fit.

☐ Apply two or three more coats of clear Deft or polyurethane.

☐ Sand lightly with #320 sandpaper after the finish is dry. Rub with #0000 steel wool.

☐ Apply wax and polish. The finished project is shown in Fig. 7-25.

8

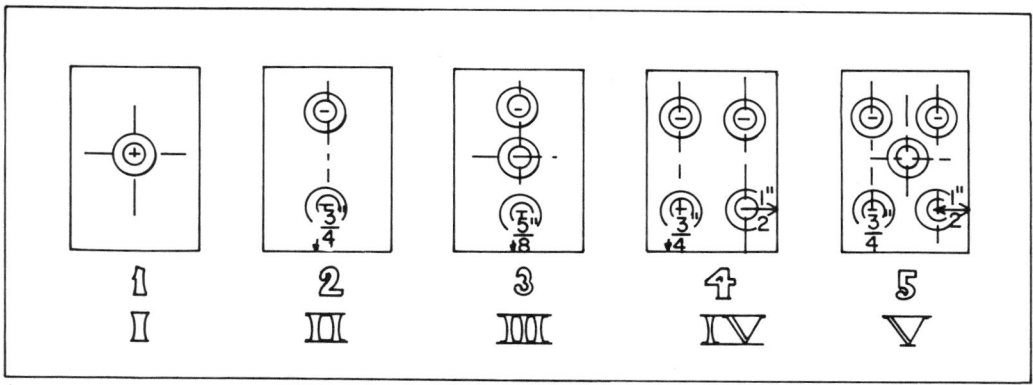

Teaching/Learning Toys

In this chapter you will find step-by-step instructions for making three teaching/learning toys. Tables of materials and illustrations are also provided to aid you in assembly.

NUMBERS ASSOCIATION TOY

The Numbers Association Toy is a teaching/learning device used to introduce children to counting and number concepts. The teacher should remove all the number blocks from the board and slowly replace them on the board, verbally counting "one," "one, two," "one, two, three," etc. At the same time the teacher should point to the arabic and roman numerals. The number of holes, the number of pegs, the number of blocks, and the numerical symbols will help reinforce the learning process.

A spin-off of this game is the association of the different kinds of woods and their distinct coloration with numbers. Print the names of the different woods and their numbers on self-adhesive paper and place them on the underside of the board.

Preparation

☐ Cut the base to size. See Table 8-1 and Fig. 8-1.

☐ Cut the 15 blocks to size.

☐ Sand the base and the blocks.

☐ Bore the 5/8-inch holes in the blocks after carefully locating the center of each hole. Place a piece of scrap wood under each block, or bore in from both sides, to prevent splintering.

☐ Place the bottom block from each set on the base and mark location. The blocks should be 1 inch in from the edge of base and spaced 1 inch apart.

☐ In the center of the marked circles bore the 15 3/8-inch holes 1/2-inch deep in the base.

☐ Cut the 15 pegs to length and chamfer one end at 45 degrees.

Assembly

☐ Mark on the arabic and roman numerals. Be sure to use guidelines. Paint the numerals with yellow acrylic paint.

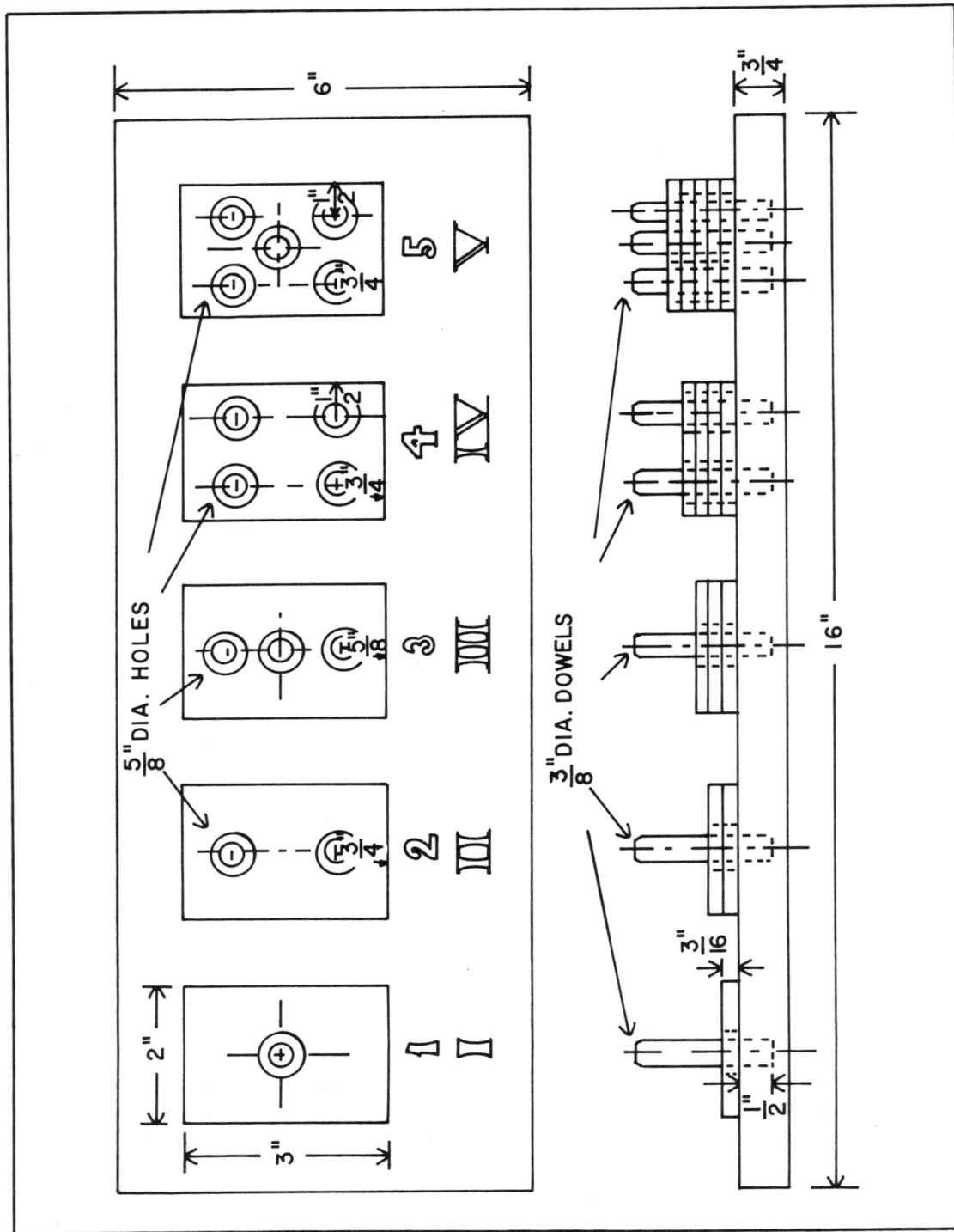

Fig. 8-1. Working plans for the Numbers Association Toy.

Table 8-1. The Numbers Association Toy Uses These Materials.

NUMBER OF PIECES	PART	SIZE	MATERIAL
1	base	3/4"x6"x16"	redwood
1	No.1 block	3/16"x2"x3"	zebrawood
2	No.2 blocks	3/16"x2"x3"	teakwood
3	No.3 blocks	3/16"x2"x3"	bubinga
4	No.4 blocks	3/16"x2"x3"	black walnut
5	No.5 blocks	3/16"x2"x3"	white pine
15	pegs	2"length	3/8" birch dowel

☐ Place a small amount of white glue on the end of each peg opposite the chamfered end and drive it into a hole.

☐ Finish the blocks and base with clear spray Deft or polyurethane. Allow sufficient drying time.

☐ Rub the blocks and base with #0000 steel wool. Apply paste wax and polish. See Fig. 8-2 for the finished project.

CLOCK

Youngsters are not only entertained by this simulated clock, but they learn how to tell time while they play with it. With some help from an adult they will soon learn that as the shorter arm moves from one number to another the longer arm makes a complete turn around the clock.

This teaching/learning toy can also be used as a game for two or more players. Individuals can compete with each other by telling the time set on the clock by a third person. A score is kept of the number of correct answers.

Preparation

☐ Cut the clock face from any 1/4-inch hardwood plywood. I used Philippine mahogany plywood.

☐ Draw diagonals across the face to establish the center.

☐ Set the compass for 1 7/8 inches radius and draw a light circle using the center established in the last step.

☐ Divide the circle into 12 equal parts with a

Fig. 8-2. The completed Numbers Association Toy.

compass or dividers. Be sure that a line connecting numbers 12 and 6 is parallel to the sides of the clock.

☐ Draw the numerals 3/4 inches high on 1/8-inch hardboard, Masonite fiberboard, or plywood.

☐ Cut out the numerals on the jigsaw.

☐ Sand the edges with emery boards.

☐ Drill a 13/64-inch hole through the center of the clock face.

Assembly

☐ Lay the clock face on a flat surface. Position the numerals using the points established for numbers 12 and 6. The inside edges, closest to center of the clock, of the numerals should be temporarily placed about 1/8 inch from the circle you have already drawn. Mark the positions with a pencil. Be sure that balance is attained and the entire clock face looks right.

☐ Place the numerals on sheets of self-adhesive paper. Paint the top and edges with a light-colored enamel, lacquer, or acrylic. A spray enamel or lacquer is the quickest way; however, I brushed on white acrylic paint.

☐ After the finish is dry, glue the numerals in the positions you established two steps ago.

☐ Draw the two arms on the same material as used for the numerals. Cut the arms on the jigsaw.

☐ Drill a 13/64-inch hole in each arm to accommodate the machine bolt and sand the edges.

☐ Finish the arms with the same finish as used for the numerals.

☐ After the finish is dry, thread the parts on the machine bolt as shown in Fig. 8-3. First thread the longer arm, then one of the flat washers. Follow with the shorter pointer arm, the second washer, the clock face, and the lock or split washer. Finally, thread the nut.

☐ Paint a 1/4-inch wide edge around the clock face to simulate a frame. I used flat black enamel.

☐ Cut the two clock supports. I used black walnut.

☐ Glue the supports to the clock face 1 inch in from each side.

☐ Spray the back of clock with walnut stain.

Table 8-2. Make the Clock Toy from the Given Materials.

NUMBER OF PIECES	PART	SIZE	MATERIAL
1	clock face	1/4"x 6 1/4"x 6 1/4"	plywood
2	clock supports	1/2"x 1 1/4"x 5"	hardwood
1	short pointer arm	1/8"x 5/8"x 1 3/4"	hardboard, masonite, fiberboard, or plywood
1	long pointer arm	1/8"x 5/8"x 2 1/4"	hardboard, masonite, fiberboard, or plywood
1	machine bolt	10-32 x 1"	
2	flat washers	#10	
1	split or lock washer	#10	
1	nut	#10-32	

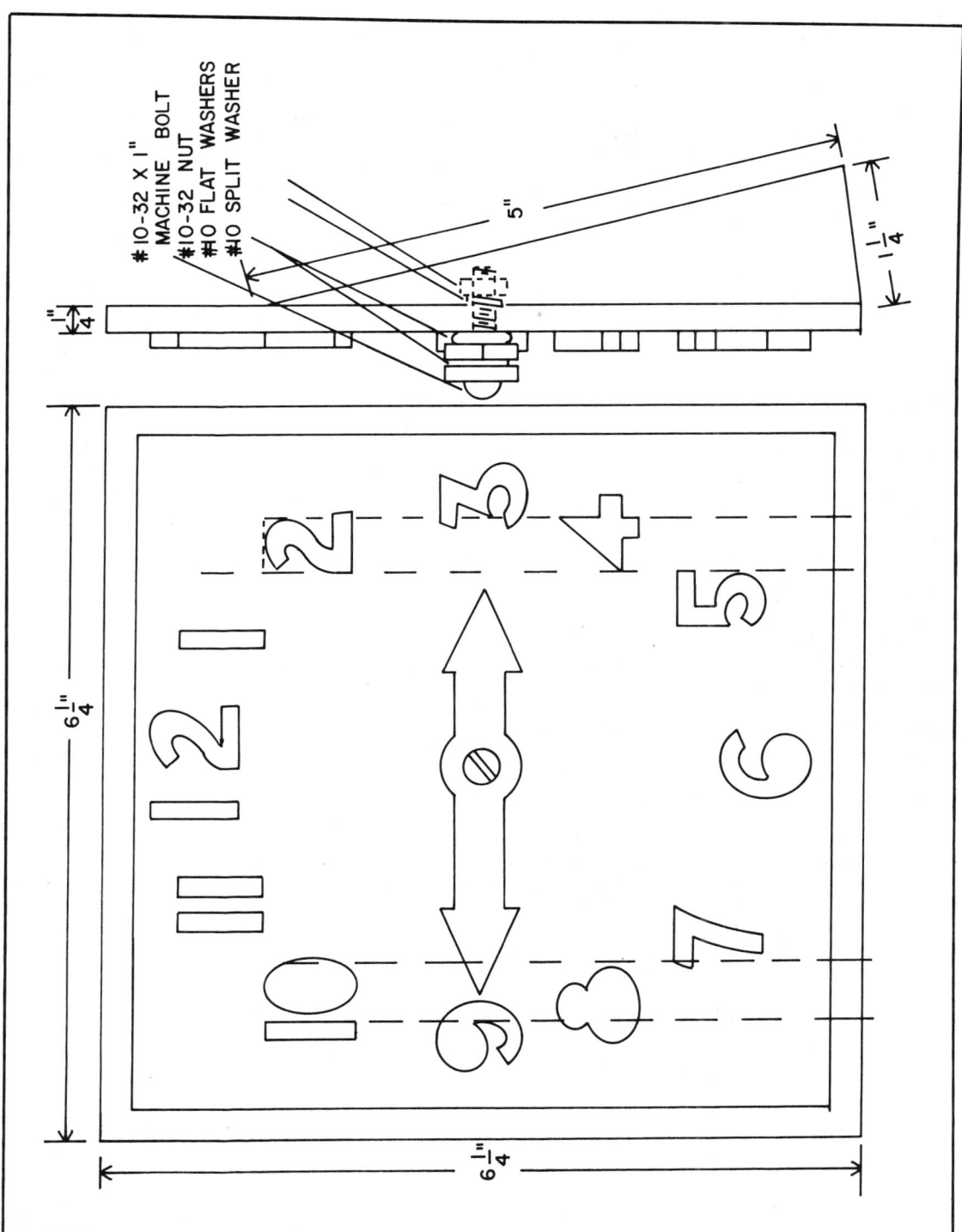

Fig. 8-3. Details for the Clock.

141

Fig. 8-4. Completed Clock project.

□ Spray the entire clock with two or three coats of clear Deft finish. Figure 8-4 shows the finished project.

SIZE/SHAPE DISCRIMINATION TOY

This teaching/learning toy is a miniaturized version of the Minnesota Spatial Relations Test. The original performance test used an elaborate set of 4 form boards, each of which had about 60 pieces varying in size and shape. It was used to measure mechanical aptitude.

The score is the number of seconds needed to complete the assembly. Used in this fashion it can double as a competitive game. The winner of the game is the person who completes the assembly in the fewest number of seconds. The blocks are placed in a jumbled pile before starting.

Preparation

□ Cut the form board to size. See Table 8-3 and Fig. 8-5.
□ Lay out the eight forms with a compass and

142

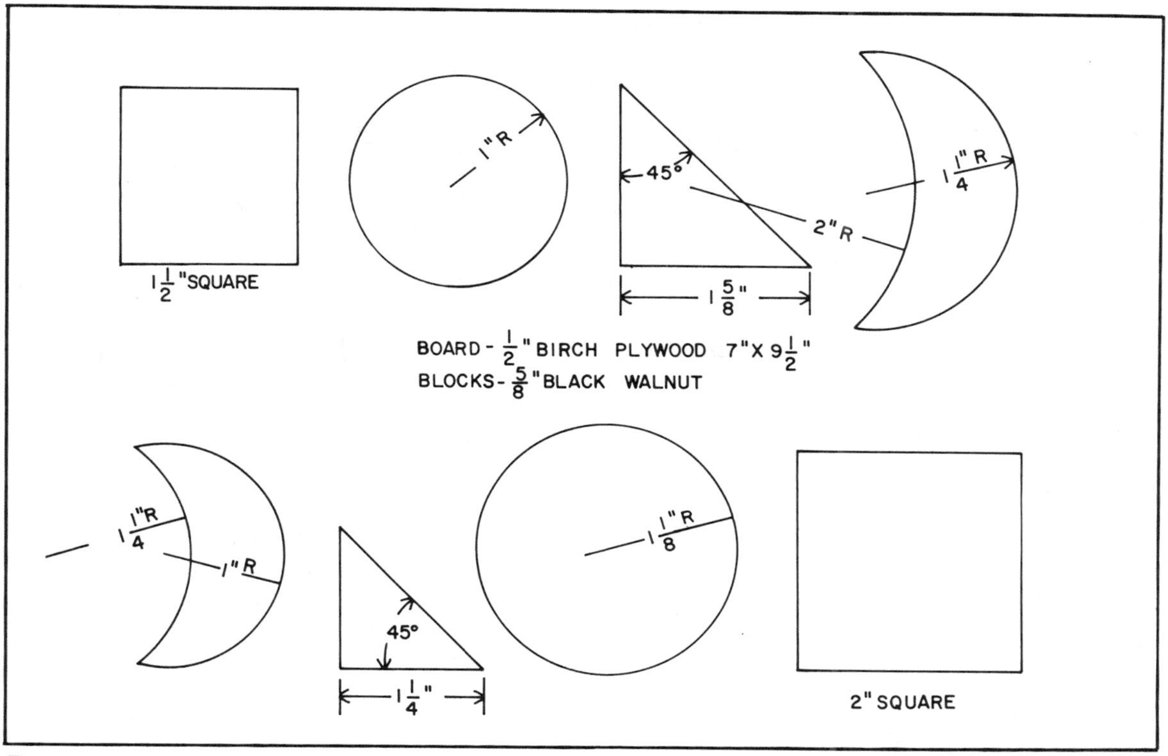

Fig. 8-5. Details for the Size/Shape Discrimination Toy.

BOARD - $\frac{1}{2}$" BIRCH PLYWOOD 7" X 9$\frac{1}{2}$"
BLOCKS - $\frac{5}{8}$" BLACK WALNUT

1$\frac{1}{2}$" SQUARE

1" R

45°

2" R

1$\frac{1}{4}$" R

1$\frac{5}{8}$"

1$\frac{1}{4}$" R

1" R

45°

1$\frac{1}{4}$"

1$\frac{1}{8}$" R

2" SQUARE

Fig. 8-6. The complete Size/Shape Discrimination Toy.

NUMBER OF PIECES	PART	SIZE	MATERIAL
1	form board	1/2"x7"x9 1/2"	birch plywood
1	retainer	7"x9 1/2"	heavy cardboard
1	small square block	5/8"x1 1/2"x1 1/2"	black walnut
1	large square block	5/8"x2"x2"	black walnut
1	large circular block	5/8"x 1 1/8" radius	black walnut
1	small circular block	5/8"x1" radius	black walnut
1	large crescent block	5/8"x1 1/2"x2 1/2"	black walnut
1	small crescent block	5/8"x1 1/4"x2"	black walnut
1	large triangular block	5/8"x1 5/8"x1 5/8"	black walnut
1	small triangular block	5/8"x1 1/4"x1 1/4"	black walnut

square on one face of the form board.

☐ Cut out the openings with a jigsaw, coping saw, or saber saw.

☐ Smooth up the edges of the holes with rasps, files, emery boards, and drum sanders.

☐ Place the form board on a piece of 5/8-inch thick black walnut.

☐ Trace around the inside edges of each form with a sharp pencil.

☐ Cut out the walnut form blocks with a band saw. See Fig. 8-5.

☐ Sand the blocks with a disc sander, drum sander, and by hand. End up with #220 sandpaper.

Assembly

☐ Mix a few drops of liquid animal glue in a cup of hot water. Apply this sizing mixture to the walnut blocks and allow to dry overnight.

☐ Sand the blocks with #320 sandpaper.

☐ Glue the retainer to the underside of the form board to prevent the walnut blocks from falling out when the form board is lifted.

☐ Apply three or four coats of clear spray Deft to the form board and blocks.

☐ When dry rub with #0000 steel wool, apply wax and polish. Figure 8-6 shows the finished project.

9

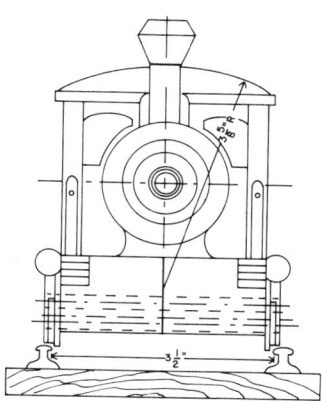

Trolleys and Trains

This chapter contains step-by-step instructions for four trolley and train toys. Illustrations and tables of materials are also included to show you assembly procedures.

1887 TROLLEY

Criss-Cross Creation's replica is based on the famous Richmond trolley, designed by Frank J. Sprague and used by the Union Passenger Railway Co., in Richmond, Va. in 1887.

Preparation

☐ Transfer the outline of parts to wood. Be sure to enlarge pattern to dimensions given in Figs. 9-1 through 9-4. If the model is to be constructed with hand tools, be sure to leave enough stock for planing and sanding the parts to the finished size (Table 9-1).

☐ Cut the floor and floor tread first. Note the dotted outline on Fig. 9-1. This locates the axle-bearing struts that are glued to the bottom of the floor.

☐ Cut out the two side walls. (See Fig. 9-2.) The grain runs lengthwise.

☐ Make the score line shown in the side walls with an X-Acto knife or utility razor knife and a straight edge.

☐ Cut the wood about 1/2 way through and bend to the angle shown.

☐ Cut out the four end walls and score as shown in Fig. 9-2.

☐ Assemble and glue the side walls and end walls onto the floor using Fig. 9-2 as a guide.

☐ Cut out the six seat frames, arranging three frames on each side of the trolley (Fig. 9-2). The end seat frames are placed against the end walls with the third frame placed in the middle. Glue the frames in place.

☐ Plank the seat frames over with 1/16-inch zebrawood planking using Fig. 9-5 as a guide. The zebrawood is a good imitation of upholstery. This planking material is not listed in Table 9-1 since it must be cut to fit.

☐ Cut out the roof sections (Fig. 9-3). The

145

dotted outline on the third section is where the second section is glued and also where the roof slopes out to the edge on all sides.

Car Assembly

☐ Assemble the roof parts by first centering the first section over the top part of the second section. The first section must be clamped in place because of the radius on top of the second section.

☐ Cut out the panel guards (Fig. 9-4). Be sure the grain runs across the width, not the length, of the panel guards. Score the panels in the same manner as for the side walls. Bend to shape and glue in place.

☐ Assemble and glue the steps and step ends in place.

☐ Assemble and glue the axle-bearing struts, axles, wheels, truck assembly guards, and assembly axle guards together (Fig. 9-6).

☐ Glue truck assembly guard (P) of the truck assembly to the bottom of the side wall.

☐ Cut out the controllers, one for each end of the trolley. Cut the handle from an ice cream stick, cracking the end portion, bending upward and gluing to hold shape. Glue the handle in place on the controller.

Trolley Pole Assembly

☐ Cut out the pole base, rounding off edges and drill four 1/8 inch holes at a 45-degree angle (Fig. 9-7). The angle of the drill bit should be toward the center of the base. When the dowels are set in the holes they should form a pyramid as shown in Fig. 9-7.

☐ Set the 1/8-inch dowels for the pole struts in each hole, apply glue, and bring together at the center. Use a piece of masking tape wrapped around the dowels to hold them in place.

☐ Apply a dab of glue at the joint where the dowels meet and drop the trolley pole holder into place.

☐ After the glue has set, place the trolley pole in the slot on the holder and apply glue. Allow the glue to set.

☐ Glue the base of the trolley pole assembly to the first roof section. Attach the trolley wheel to the pole.

Gluing Tips

☐ The closer the fit of the joint, the stronger it will be.

☐ Do not use excessive amounts of glue. It is difficult to control as it will be squeezed out of the

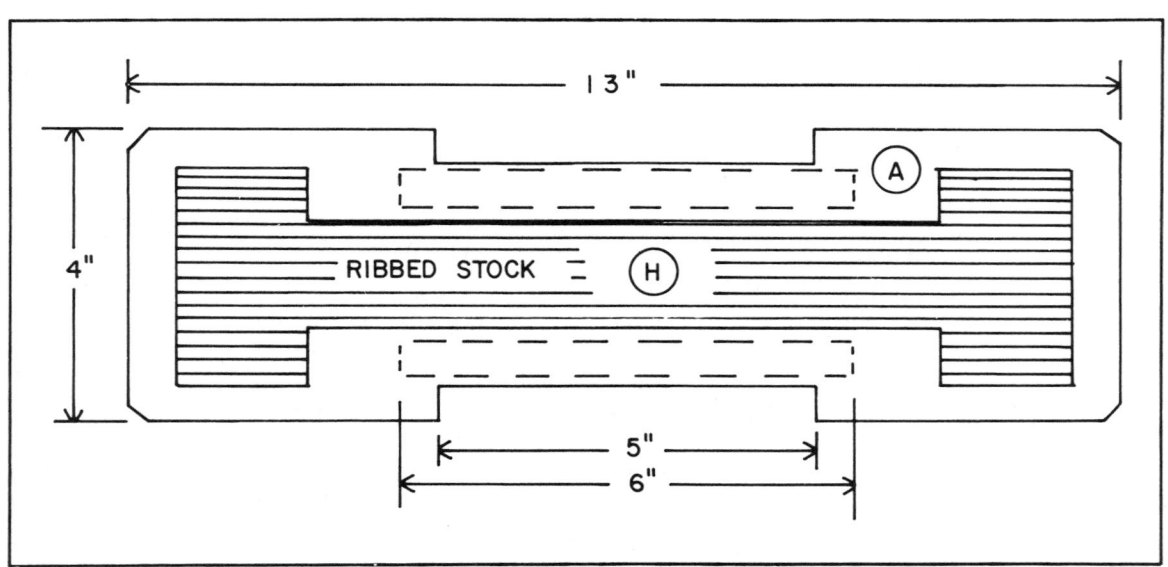

Fig. 9-1. Floor and floor tread details for the 1887 Trolley. Courtesy of Criss-Cross Creations.

Table 9-1. Materials Needed for the 1887 Trolley.

NUMBER OF PIECES	CODE	PART	SIZE	MATERIAL
1	A	floor	1/4"x4"x 13 "	white pine
2	B	axle bearing struts	1/2"x 1/2"x 6"	maple or birch
2	C	axles	3 1/2" length	1/4"birch dowel
4	D	wheels	3/8"x1 3/4"x 1 3/4"	cherry
2	E	sidewalls	1/4"x4"x8"	maple
4	F	end walls	1/4"x 1 1/2"x3 3/4"	maple
6	G	seat frames	1/8"x1"x1 1/2"	maple
1	H	floor tread	1/16"x3"x 11 3/4"	ribbed stock ✻
1	I	third roof section	3/8"x 5 1/2"x 13"	white pine
1	J	second roof section	1/2"x3"x 8"	white pine
1	K	first roof section	1/8"x3 1/2"x9"	black walnut
4	L	steps	1/16"x1 "x 2"	ribbed stock ✻
8	M	step ends	1/8"x3/8"x 1 1/8"	maple
2	N	panel guard	1/4"x 1 1/2"x3 3/4"	maple
2	O	truck assembly guard	1/8"x3/8"x 4 1/4"	black walnut
8	P	truck assembly guards	1/2" length	1/4" birch dowel
4	Q	truck assembly axle guard	3/8"x 3/8"x 3/8"	padauk
1	R	trolley pole base	1/8"x2 "x 2"	maple
1	S	trolley pole holder	5/8" length	5/8" birch dowel
1	T	trolley pole	6 1/2" length	3/16" birch dowel
4	U	trolley pole struts	1 1/2" length	1/8 "birch dowel
1	V	trolley wheel	1/4" length	5/8" birch dowel
2	W	contollers	1/2"x 3/4"x 1 1/4"	padauk

Ribbed stock is available at many craft shops.

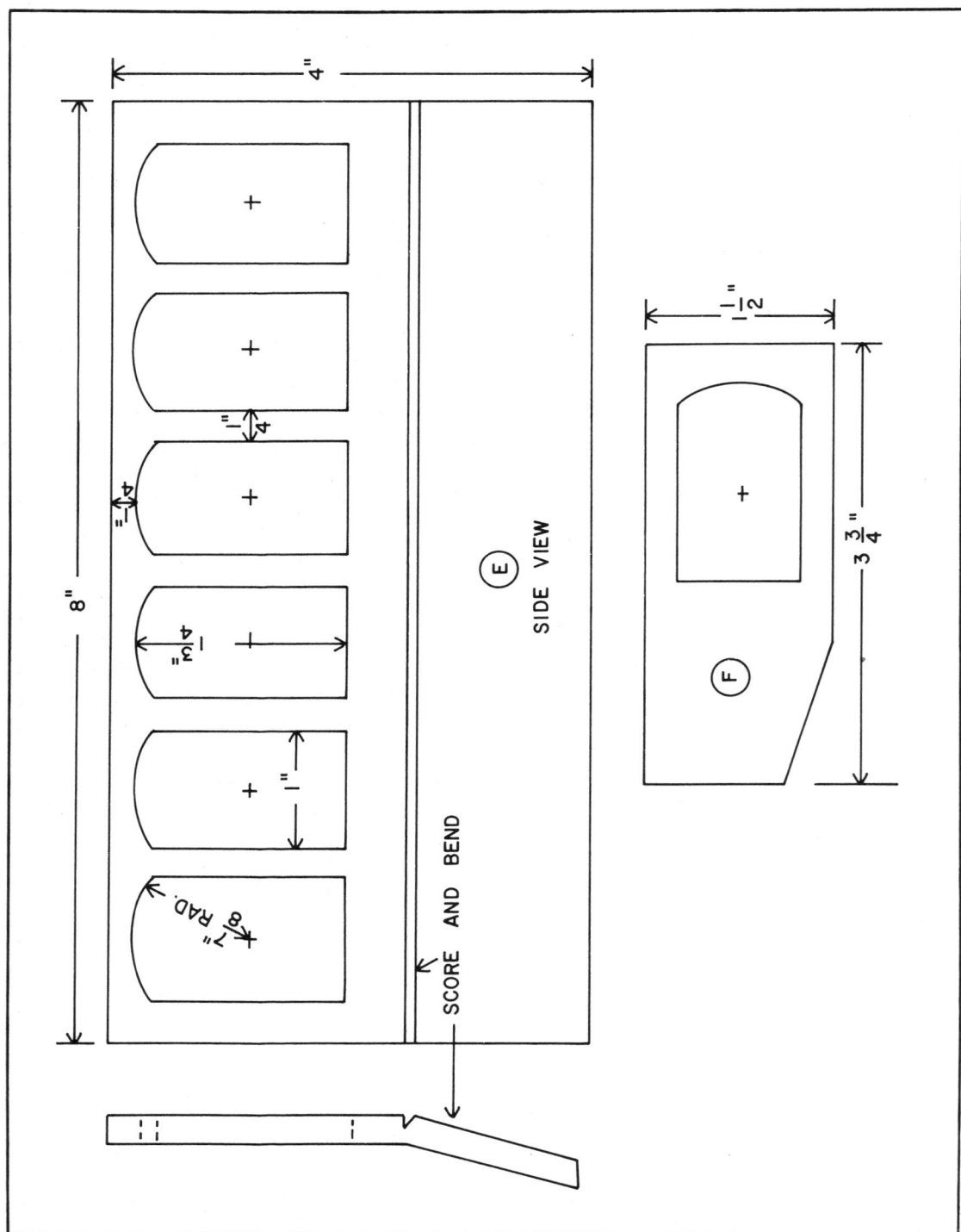

Fig. 9-2. Trolley sidewalls and endwalls are shown. Courtesy of Criss-Cross Creations.

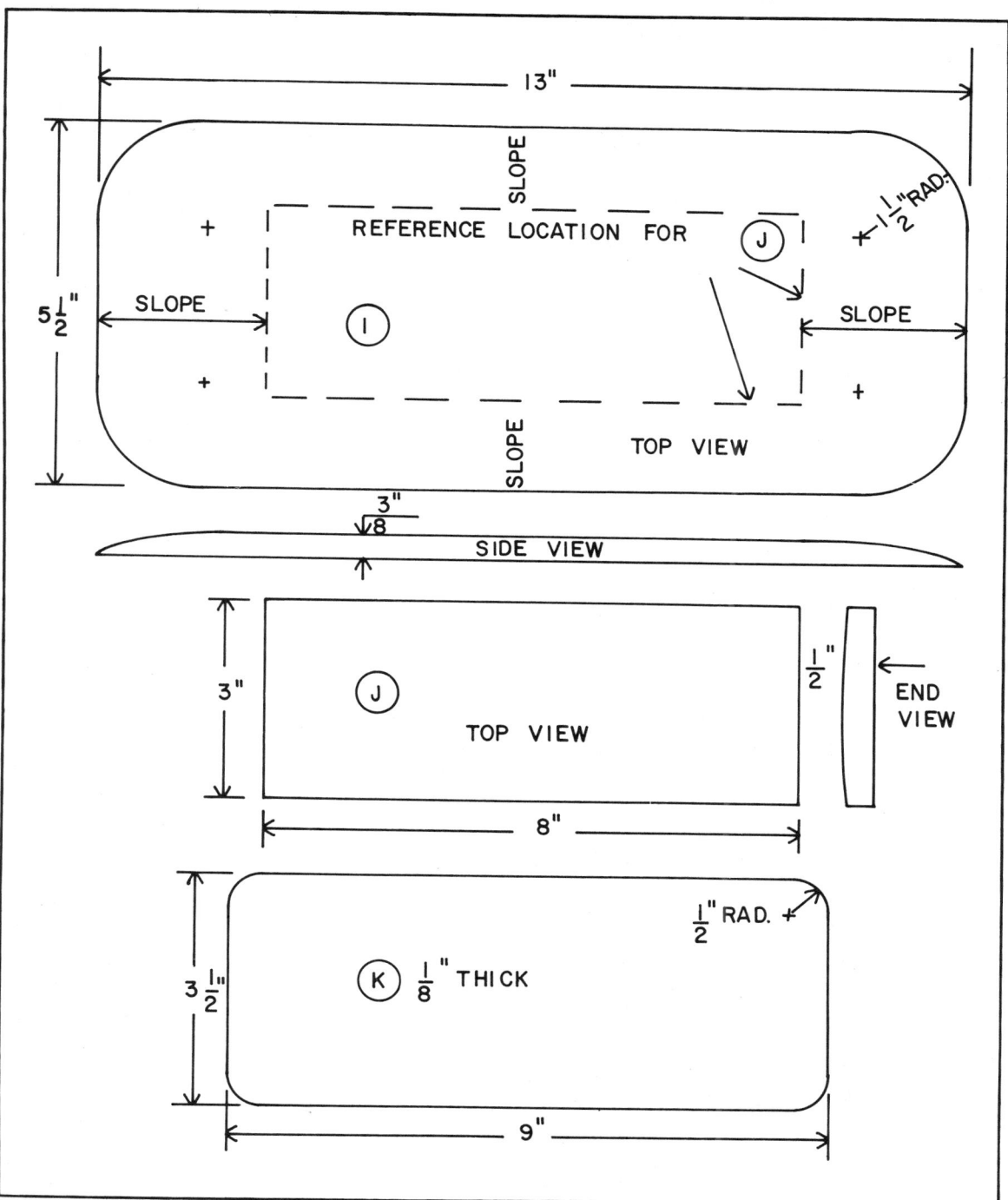

Fig. 9-3. The first, second, and third roof sections for the 1887 Trolley are shown, as viewed from the top. Courtesy of Criss-Cross Creations.

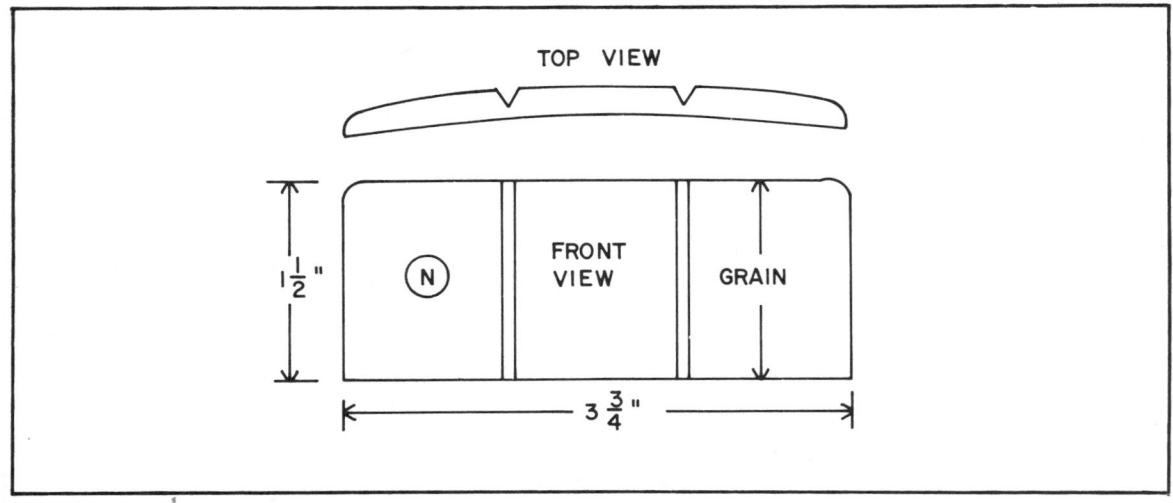

TOP VIEW

FRONT VIEW

(N)

GRAIN

$1\frac{1}{2}$ "

$3\frac{3}{4}$ "

Fig. 9-4. 1887 Trolley panel guard. Courtesy of Criss-Cross Creations.

PLANK #1

PLANK #2

PLANK #3

PLANK #4

(G)

(G)

(G)

(G)

HANDLE MADE FROM ICE CREAM STICK

CRACK, BEND AND GLUE

(W)

TOP VIEW

FRONT VIEW

GLUE

GLUE THIS SIDE TO PANEL

(N)

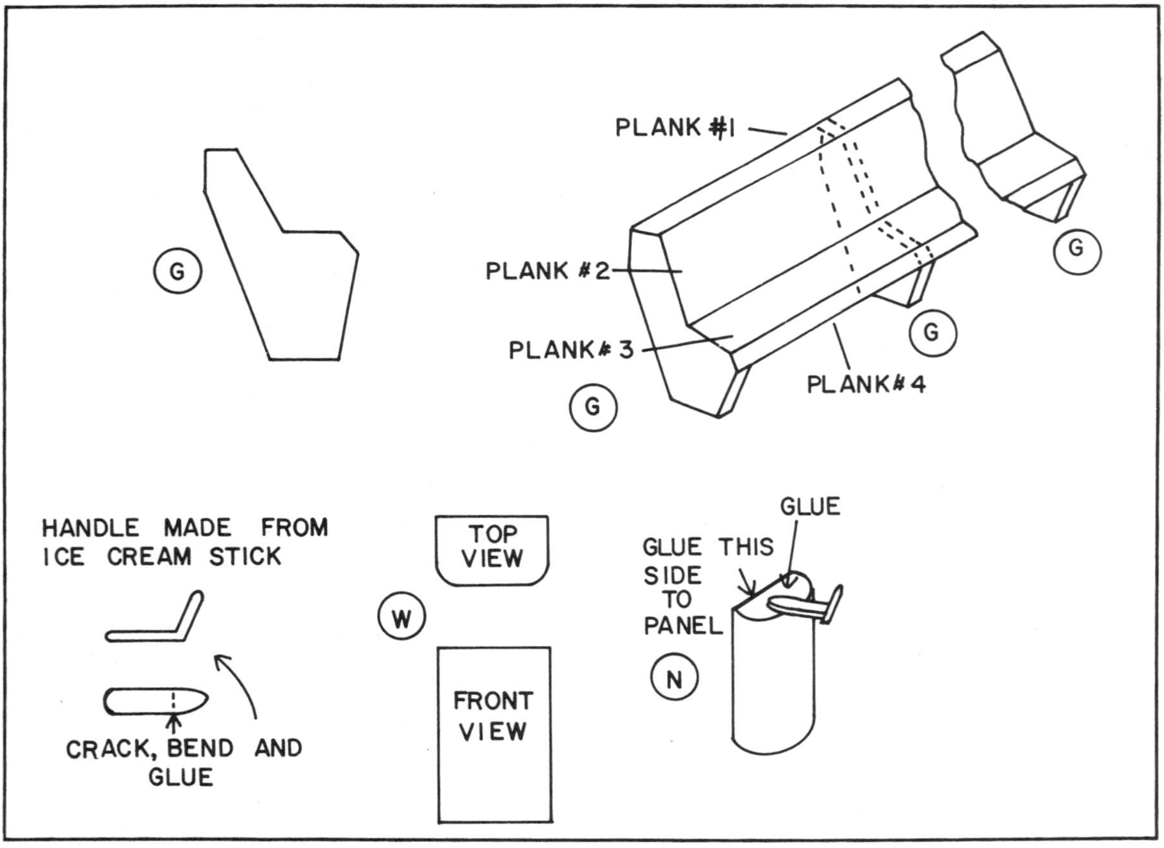

Fig. 9-5. Seat and controller detail for the 1887 Trolley. Courtesy of Criss-Cross Creations.

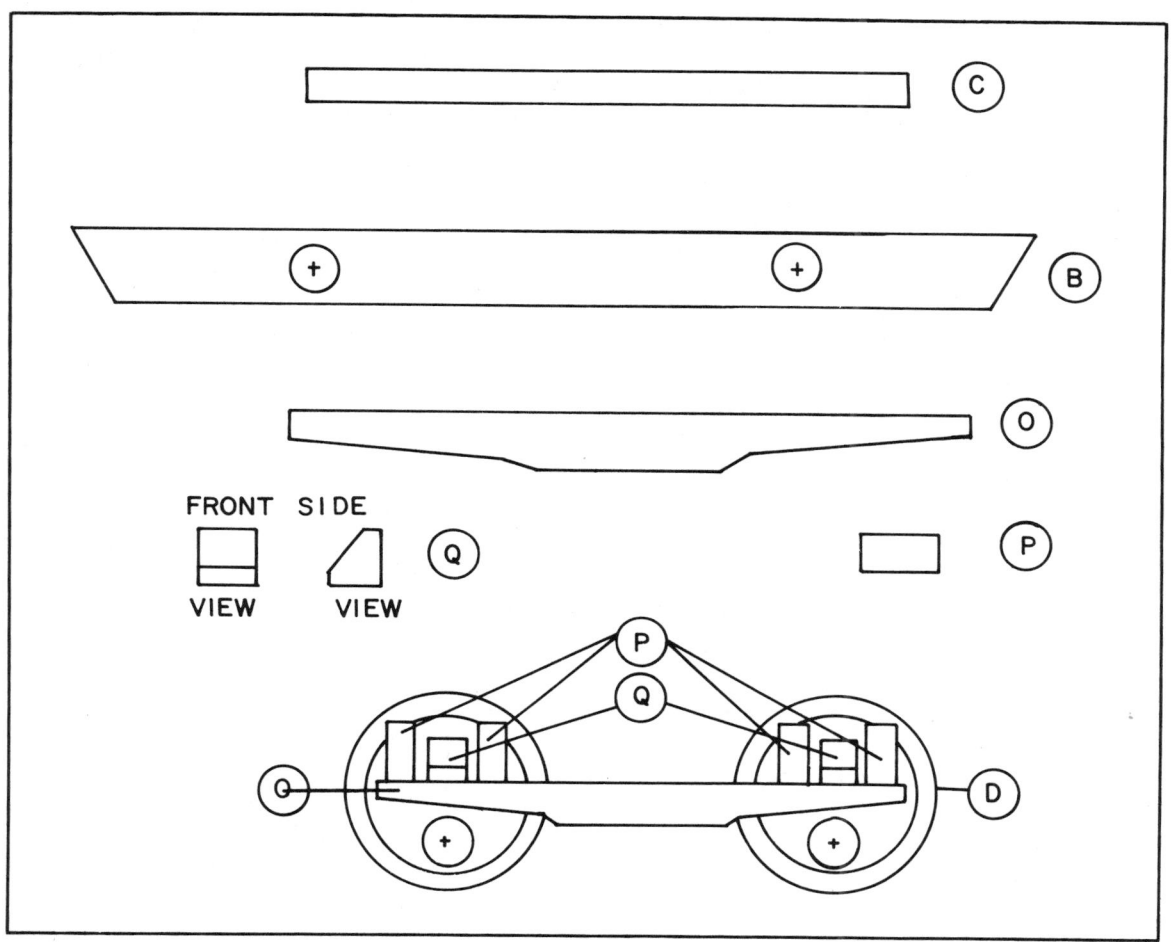

Fig. 9-6. 1887 Trolley truck parts and assembly are shown. Courtesy of Criss-Cross Creations.

joint and over the work when clamped. If this happens, wipe off the excess glue immediately with a damp cloth. A thin film of glue is stronger than a thick one.

☐ Preassemble the parts that you are going to glue and decide just how you are going to clamp these parts and what materials you will need for the operation when the glue is applied.

☐ Before actually applying glue, check all fits to be sure everything is in alignment. Be sure to have all your tools and materials on hand and ready.

☐ In general, hardwoods need a longer clamping time than softwoods.

☐ If you are gluing scrap wood together in order to obtain larger pieces, try to keep the grain matched.

Finishing

☐ Thoroughly sand wood removing all tool marks and irregularities. When sanding is finished, be sure all wood dust is cleaned from the surface.

☐ If you intend to do any staining, plan accordingly. For instance, if you are going to stain the interior of the trolley, be sure you do so before you glue the roof on. Before applying stain, apply a very thin coat of lacquer sealer or white shellac.

☐ The undercarriages (truck assembly) of trolleys were usually painted in a black or dark

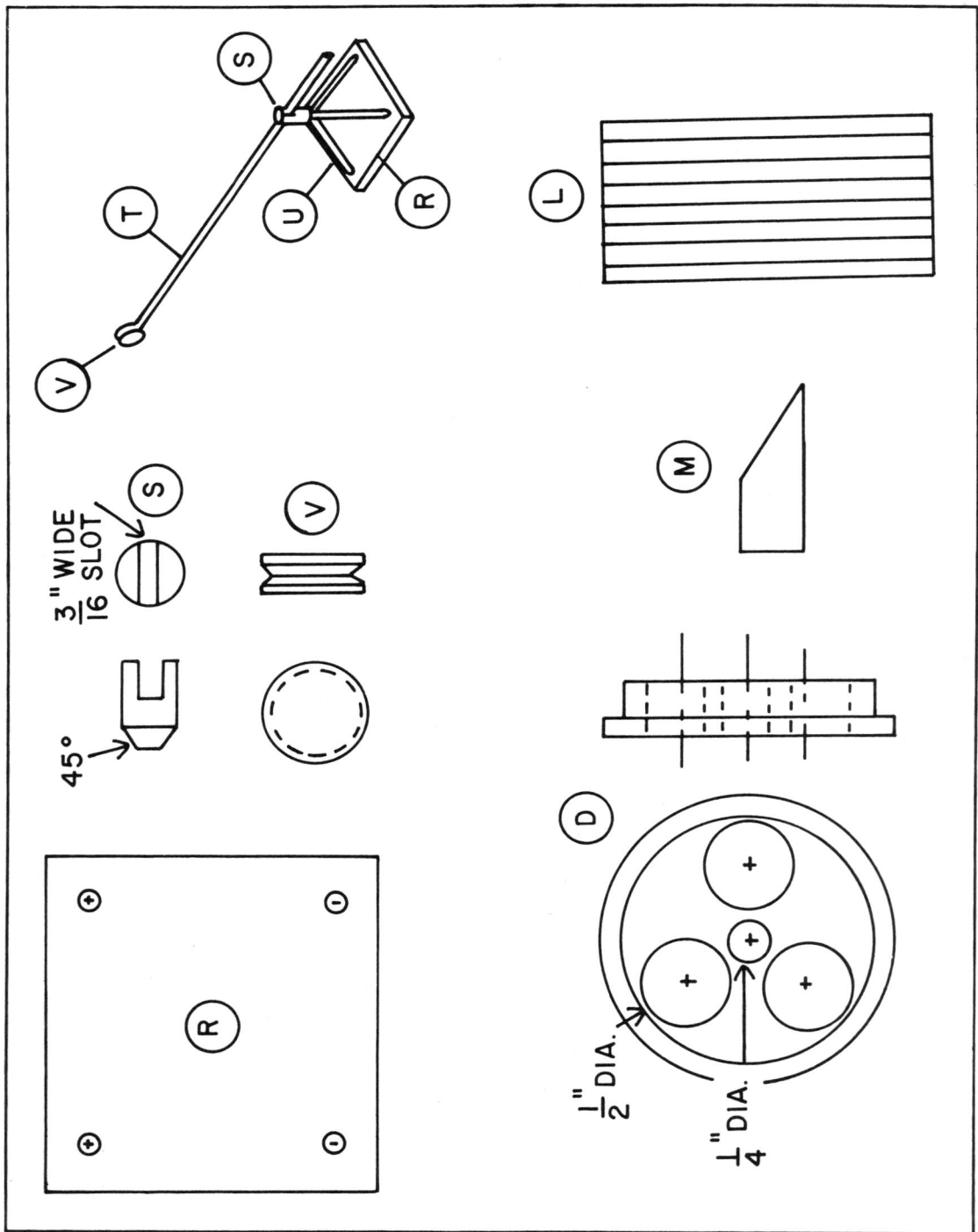

Fig. 9-7. 1887 Trolley pole parts and assembly, including wheel detail (bottom left) and step details (bottom right). Courtesy of Criss-Cross Creations.

Fig. 9-8. The 1887 Trolley, shown complete. Courtesy of Criss-Cross Creations.

finish and for this reason you may want to stain this section of your trolley in a darker tone, if the rest of the trolley is stained, to give it a nice accent.

☐ Finish with clear spray Deft or polyurethane. Figure 9-8 shows the finished project.

EARLY SWITCHING LOCOMOTIVE

This early switching engine was used at roundhouses and switching yards at the turn of the century for moving one or two cars at a time.

This strong, sturdy toy will stand a lot of child abuse. Softwoods or hardwoods may be used throughout, with the exception of the axle blocks which should be made of hardwood. I selected pine for the chassis, maple for the axle blocks, mahogany for the cab, boiler, and cowcatcher, and walnut for the cab roof. The design is by Toy Designs (Fig. 9-9).

Preparation

☐ Cut stock for chassis. See Table 9-3 and Fig. 9-10.

☐ Drill the hole for the hitch pin.

☐ Glue the axle blocks to chassis.

☐ Cut stock for cowcatcher. To cut the cowcatcher on a table saw, set both the miter gauge and the blade at 30 degrees. To cut the cowcatcher by hand, mark 30-degree angles on both the top and side and follow both marks with a handsaw.

☐ Glue the cowcatcher to the chassis.

☐ Drill holes for the axles.

☐ Cut stock for the boiler (Fig. 9-11). Three pieces of 3/4-inch thick stock may be glued together instead of using solid stock.

☐ Cut the corners of the boiler with the saw set at 45 degrees, or stock can be marked and planed off by hand.

☐ Drill the holes for the axle peg, buttons, and smokestack. These holes may be bored before the corners are cut off.

Table 9-2. The Early Switching Locomotive Uses These Materials.

NUMBER OF PIECES	PART	SIZE	MATERIAL
1	cab	2 1/4"x2 1/4"x4"	any suitable material
1	boiler	2 1/4"x2 1/4"x3"	any suitable material
1	roof	3/4"x2 3/4"x3 1/2"	any suitable material
1	cow catcher	3/4"x1"x2 1/2"	any suitable material
1	chassis	3/4"x 2 1/2"x8"	any suitable material
2	axle blocks	3/4"x1"x2 1/2"	hardwood
1	axle block	3/4"x1 1/2"x2 1/2"	hardwood
4	large wheels	2 1/2" diam.	commercial component
2	small wheels	1 1/2" diam.	commercial component
1	smokestack		commercial component
2	buttons (screw covers)		commercial component
1	axle peg	3/8" diam.	commercial component
1	hitch pin	3/8" diam. x 1 1/2"	commercial component
2	axles	4 1/8" length	3/8" birch dowel
1	axle	3 5/8" length	1/4" birch dowel

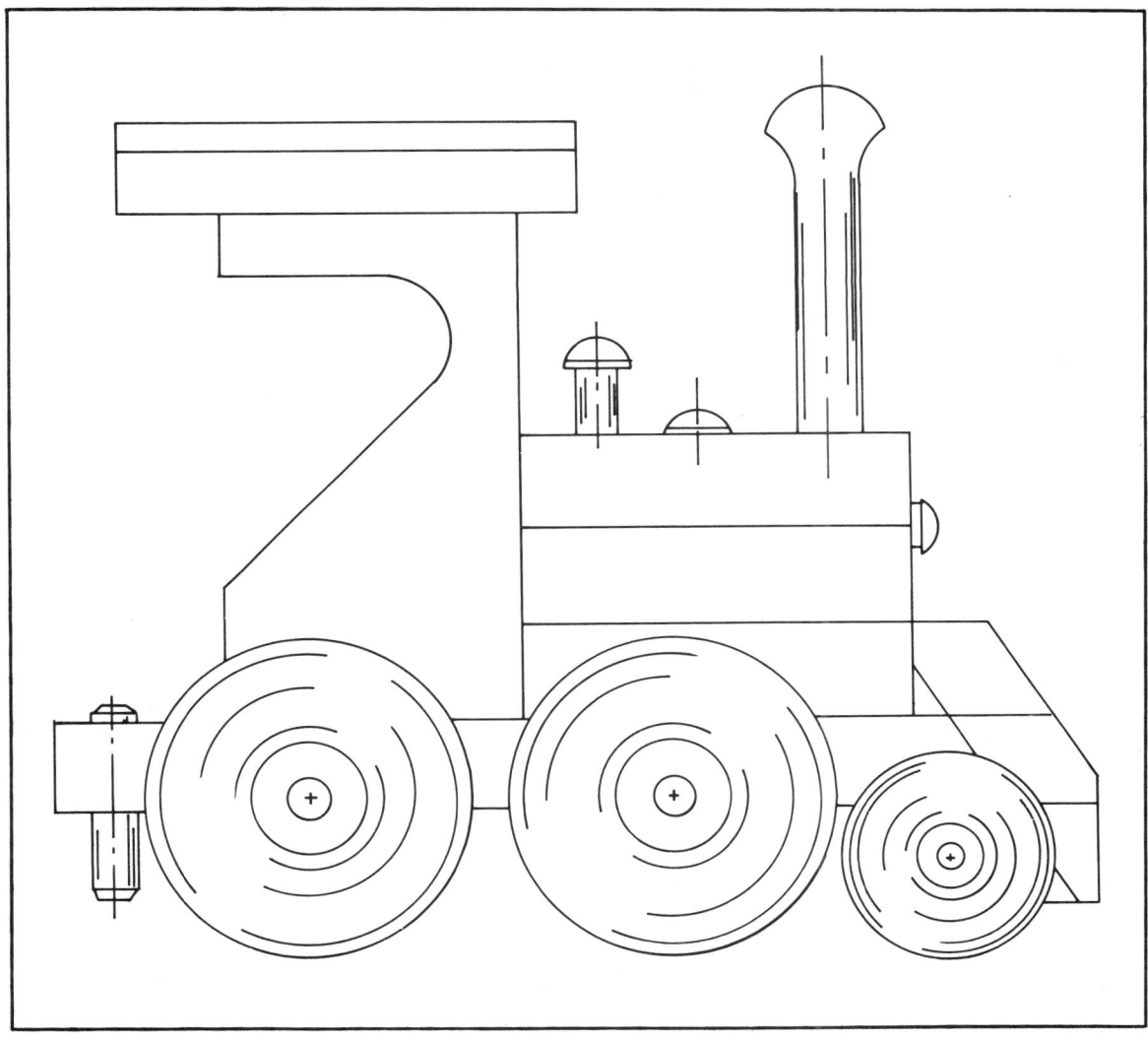

Fig. 9-9. Early Switching Locomotive: perspective view. Courtesy of Toy Designs.

☐ Cut the axle blocks.

☐ Make the pattern for cab and transfer to 2 1/4-inch stock (Fig. 9-11).

☐ Cut the outline of the rear of the cab with a band saw or saber saw. An alternate method is to bore a 1-inch hole and saw into it.

☐ Cut the stock for cab roof (Fig. 9-10). Set the saw at 15 degrees for the roof angle.

Assembly

☐ Glue the axle pin, buttons, and smokestack to the boiler and glue the whole assembly to the chassis.

☐ Glue the roof to the cab and glue both parts to the chassis in back of the boiler. Use clamps wherever possible.

☐ Glue the hitch pin in place.

☐ Assemble the wheels, axles, and axle blocks.

☐ Sand all surfaces, particularly the edges and corners.

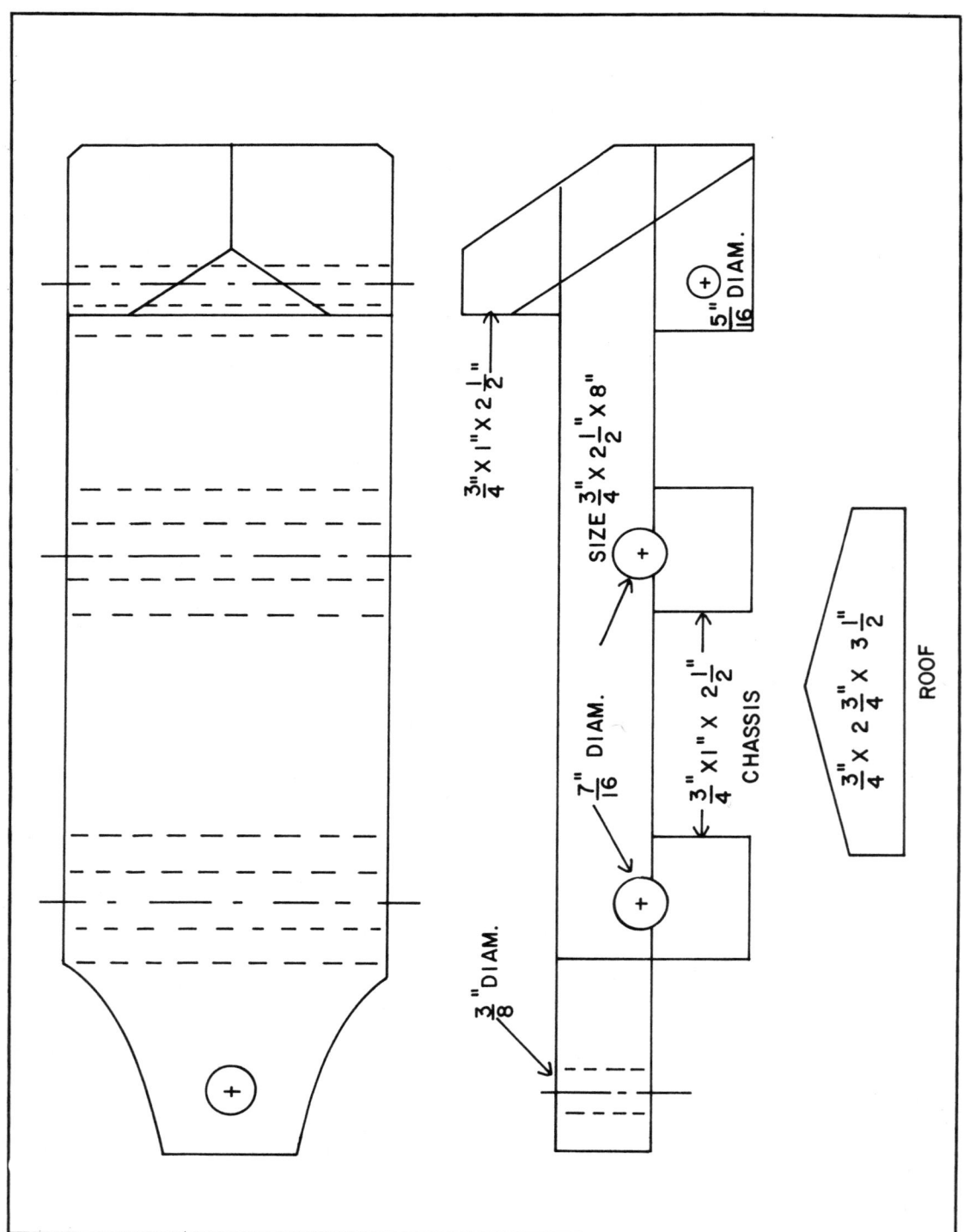

Fig. 9-10. Chassis and roof details for the Early Switching Locomotive. Courtesy of Toy Designs.

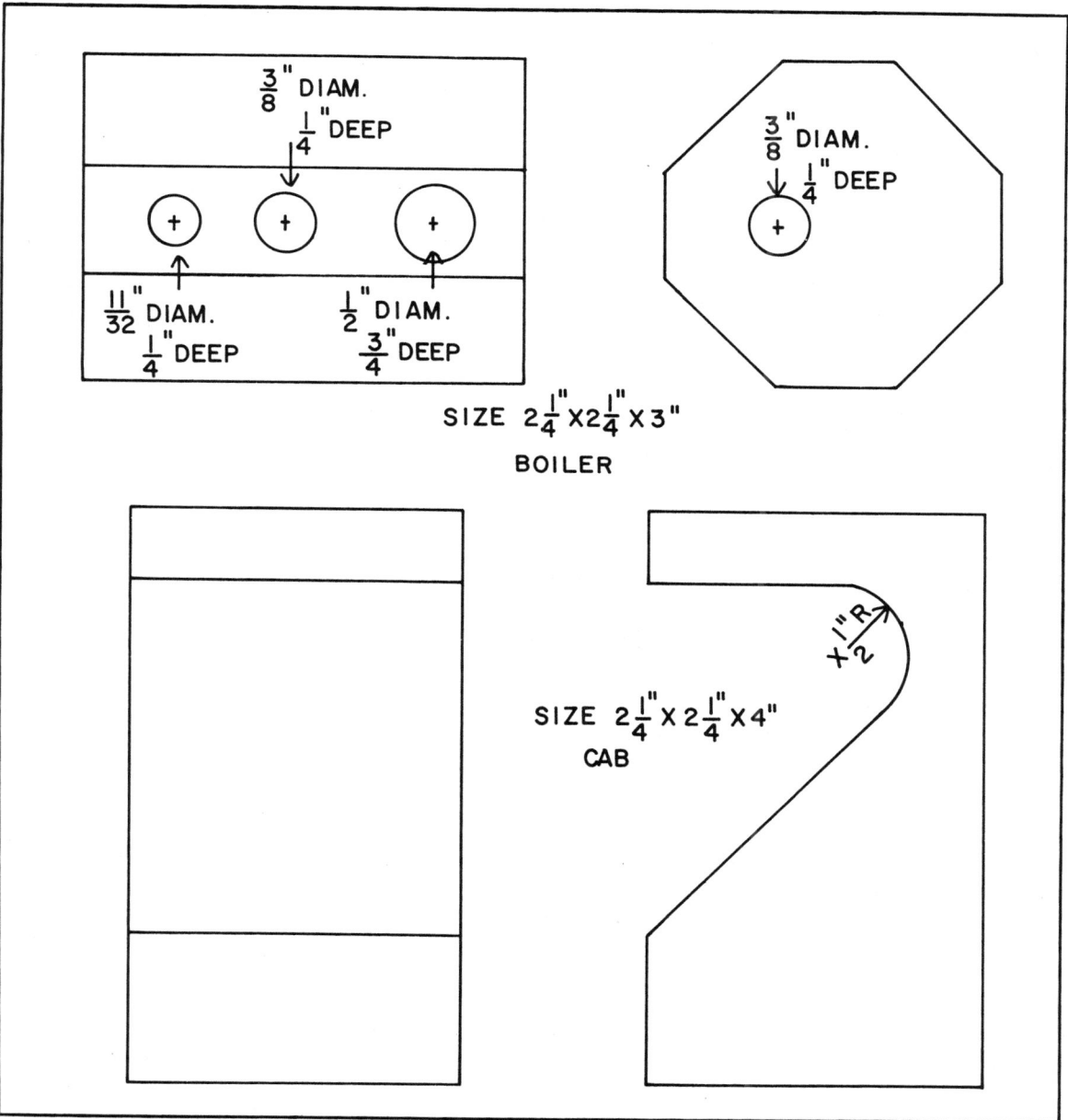

$\frac{3}{8}$" DIAM.
$\frac{1}{4}$" DEEP

$\frac{11}{32}$" DIAM.
$\frac{1}{4}$" DEEP

$\frac{1}{2}$" DIAM.
$\frac{3}{4}$" DEEP

$\frac{3}{8}$" DIAM.
$\frac{1}{4}$" DEEP

SIZE $2\frac{1}{4}$" X $2\frac{1}{4}$" X 3"
BOILER

SIZE $2\frac{1}{4}$" X $2\frac{1}{4}$" X 4"
CAB

$\frac{1}{2}$" R

Fig. 9-11. Boiler and cab details for the Early Switching Locomotive. Courtesy of Toy Designs.

☐ Apply three or four coats of clear spray Deft or polyurethane.

☐ After 48 hours, rub the engine with #0000 steel wool, then apply wax and polish. Figure 9-12 shows the finished project.

STEAM LOCOMOTIVE

Anyone older than 50 will fondly remember the mournful whistle of the steam locomotive. Youngsters are still thrilled by the noisy roar of any locomotive as it pulls into a station.

This locomotive, which I designed, is an electric model derived from the study of many steam locomotive plans, drawings, and photos. No paint or enamel is used, and, as in many of the other toys, color is achieved by the use of a number of naturally colored woods.

Preparation

☐ Cut the stock for the boiler. Table 9-3 gives dimensions. Bore holes for the smokestacks, domes, and whistle while the boiler is still in the square (Fig. 9-13). It is difficult to bore holes in round stock.

☐ Turn the boiler in the lathe (Fig. 9-14).

☐ Mark the lines for the rivets while the lathe is turning.

☐ Mark the location of the rivets using marked masking tape.

☐ Bore the 3/16-inch holes for the rivets 1/4-inch deep. Place the 3/16-inch drill bit in a portable electric drill and drill toward the center of the boiler while resting the drill on the lathe tool rest.

☐ Cut the 3/16-inch rivets from dowel stock about 3/8-inch long.

Assembly

☐ Drive the rivets into the holes in the boiler after a small amount of glue is placed on each rivet.

☐ After the glue is dry, cut off each rivet with a fine tooth saw leaving approximately 1/32 inch protruding from the boiler.

Fig. 9-12. The completed project of the Early Switching Locomotive. Courtesy of Toy Designs.

Table 9-3. A Materials List for the Steam Locomotive.

NUMBER OF PIECES	CODE	PART	SIZE	MATERIAL
1	A	boiler	6" 1 1/16" length	2" mahogany
1	B	base	1 1/4" x 3 1/4" x 10"	pine or maple
1	C	cap top	9/16" x 3 1/2" x 2 1/2"	walnut
2	D	cab sides	5/16" x 2 1/8" x 2 5/8"	pine or maple
1	E	cab front	5/16" x 2 5/8" x 2 1/2"	pine or maple
1	F	top headlight	1/2" x 1/2" x 1/2" 1/16" length	walnut 3/8" padauk
1	G	boiler headlight	1/16" length	3/8" padauk
1	H	smokestack	1 7/8" length	7/8" bubinga
1	I	auxiliary smokestack	1 3/8" length	1/2" commercial
1	J	front dome	1" length	3/4" teakwood
1	K	rear dome	1 1/4" length	3/4" cherry
1	L	whistle	1" length	1/4" birch dowel
4	M	rail supports	1 5/8" length	3/16" birch dowel
2	N	rails	5 1/4" length	1/16" birch dowel
2	O	boiler cradles	3/8" x 1" x 1 1/2"	walnut
2	P	piston cylinders	7/8" length	1/2" padauk
1	Q	coupling	1 1/8" length	1/4" birch dowel
4	R	drive wheels	5/16" length	1 5/8" walnut
8	S	idler wheels	1/4" length	15/16" walnut
6	T	axles	3 3/4" length	1/4" birch dowel
2	U	simulated steel rails	7/16" x 1/2" x 19 3/4"	redwood for engine and tender
12	V	ties	1/2" x 1/2" x 5"	pine or maple for engine tender

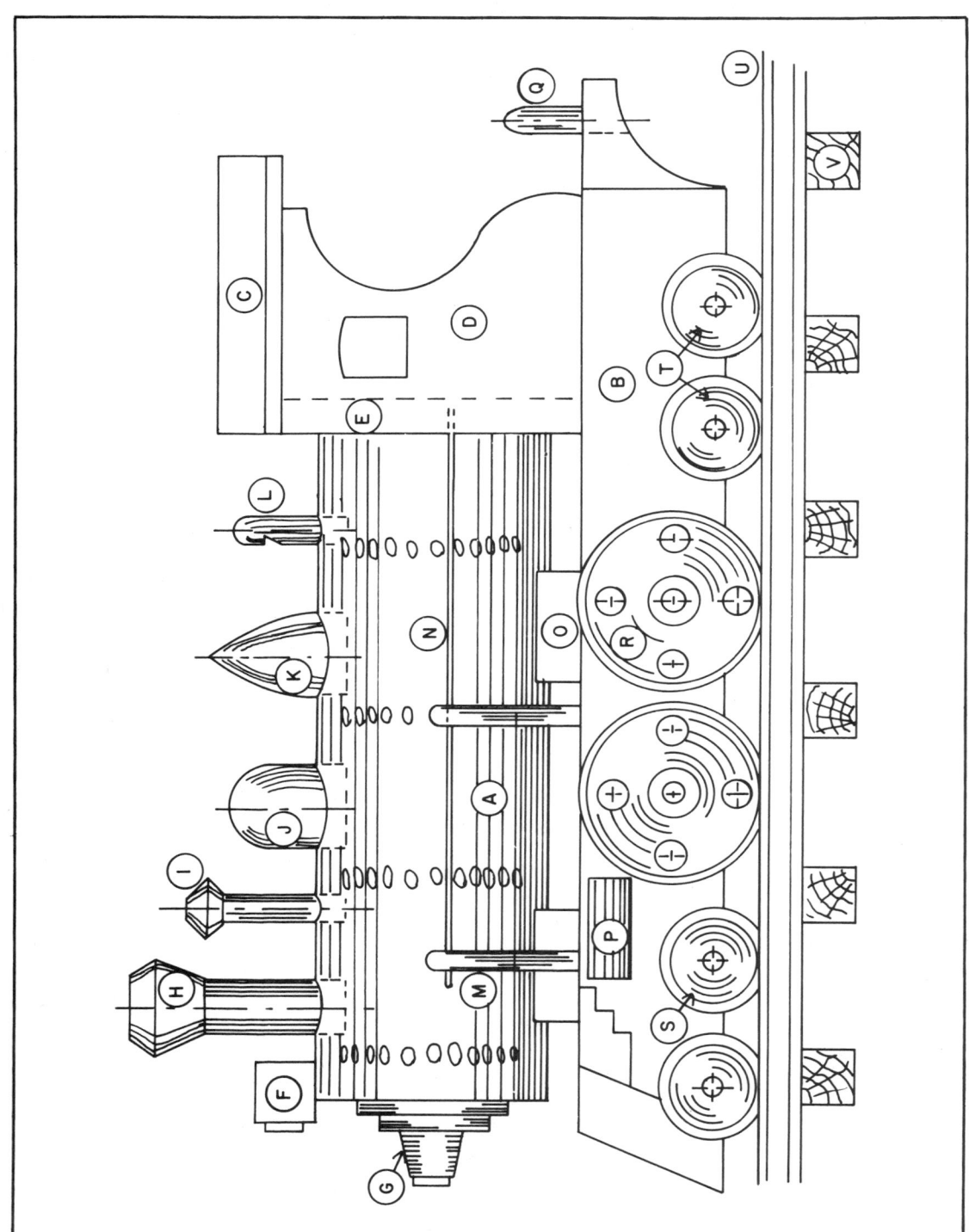

Fig. 9-13. Side view of the Steam Locomotive.

☐ Sand down the rivets to a uniform height.

☐ Turn the large smokestack and the two domes to shape and cut the notch in the whistle stock.

☐ Cut the top headlight which is a cube. Cut the small 3/8-inch diameter padauk part and glue it to the walnut cube. At the same time, the padauk boiler headlight can be cut and glued to the front of the boiler. It is best to turn a short piece of padauk 3/8-inch diameter and then slice off the 1/16-inch thick portions.

☐ Glue in the smokestacks, domes, and whistle.

☐ Glue on the top headlight with epoxy glue.

☐ Cut and shape the two boiler cradles and glue to the underside of the boiler (Fig. 9-15).

☐ Cut the base to size (Table 9-3) and carve the steps on the front end. Bore the six axle holes with a 17/64-inch bit.

☐ Cut the cab sides to size. Cut out the windows and curved edges with the jigsaw after making a paper pattern.

☐ Cut the cab front to size and cut out the windows with the jigsaw. A coping saw may be used as well.

☐ Cut out the stock for the cab top. The curve has a 3 5/8-inch radius. Cut the radius with the band saw. Sand the top with two or three grades of sandpaper starting with the coarsest grade.

☐ Assemble and glue the parts of the cab together.

☐ Glue the cab to the base.

☐ When the glue is dry, glue the boiler subassembly and boiler cradles to the cab and to the base. Attach the rail supports and rails.

☐ Cut all the wheels to rough size with the hole saw.

☐ Turn the wheels to shape on the lathe by using the 1/4-inch diameter dowel mandrel in the center of a wood faceplate.

☐ Turn the piston cylinders to size and flatten one side for gluing to the base.

☐ Extend the axles through the base and attach the wheels. Place push nuts over the ends of the axles of the four drive wheels.

☐ Glue the piston cylinders to the base. Attach the coupling.

☐ Sand the entire locomotive with fine sandpaper.

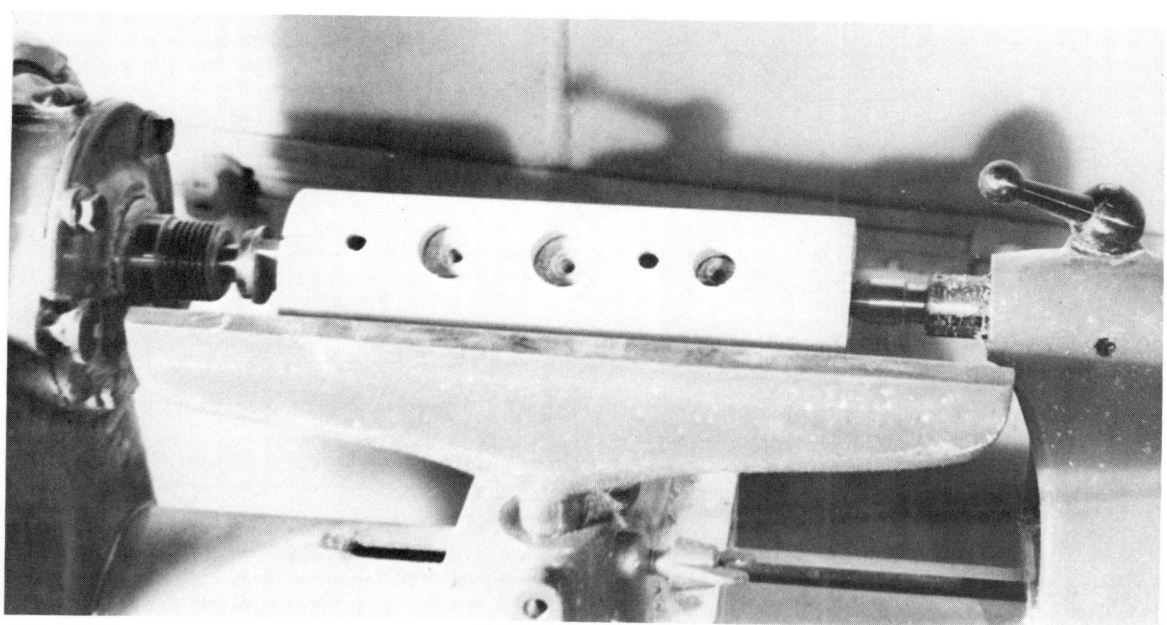

Fig. 9-14. You can turn the boiler on a lathe.

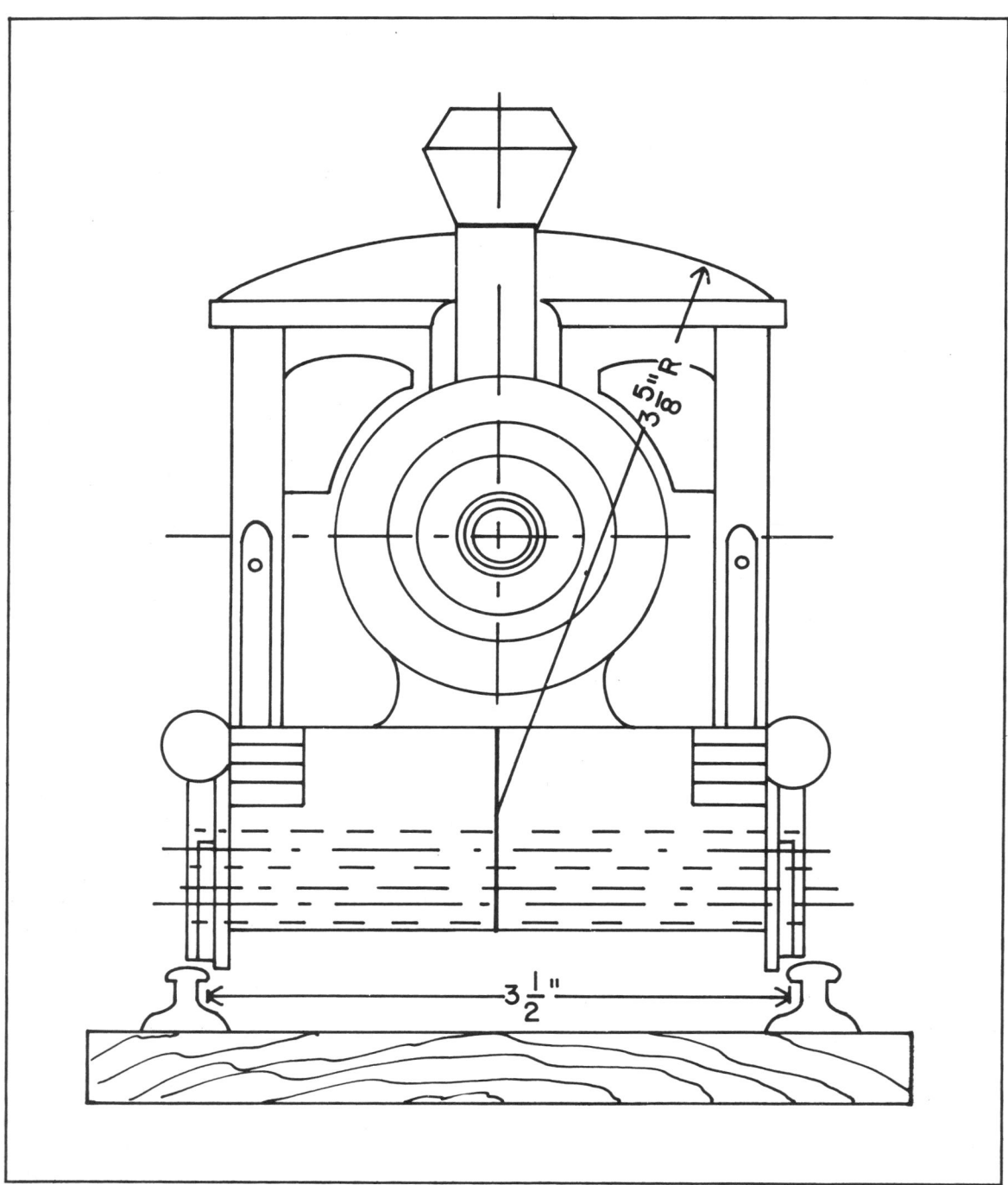

Fig. 9-15. Front view of the Steam Locomotive.

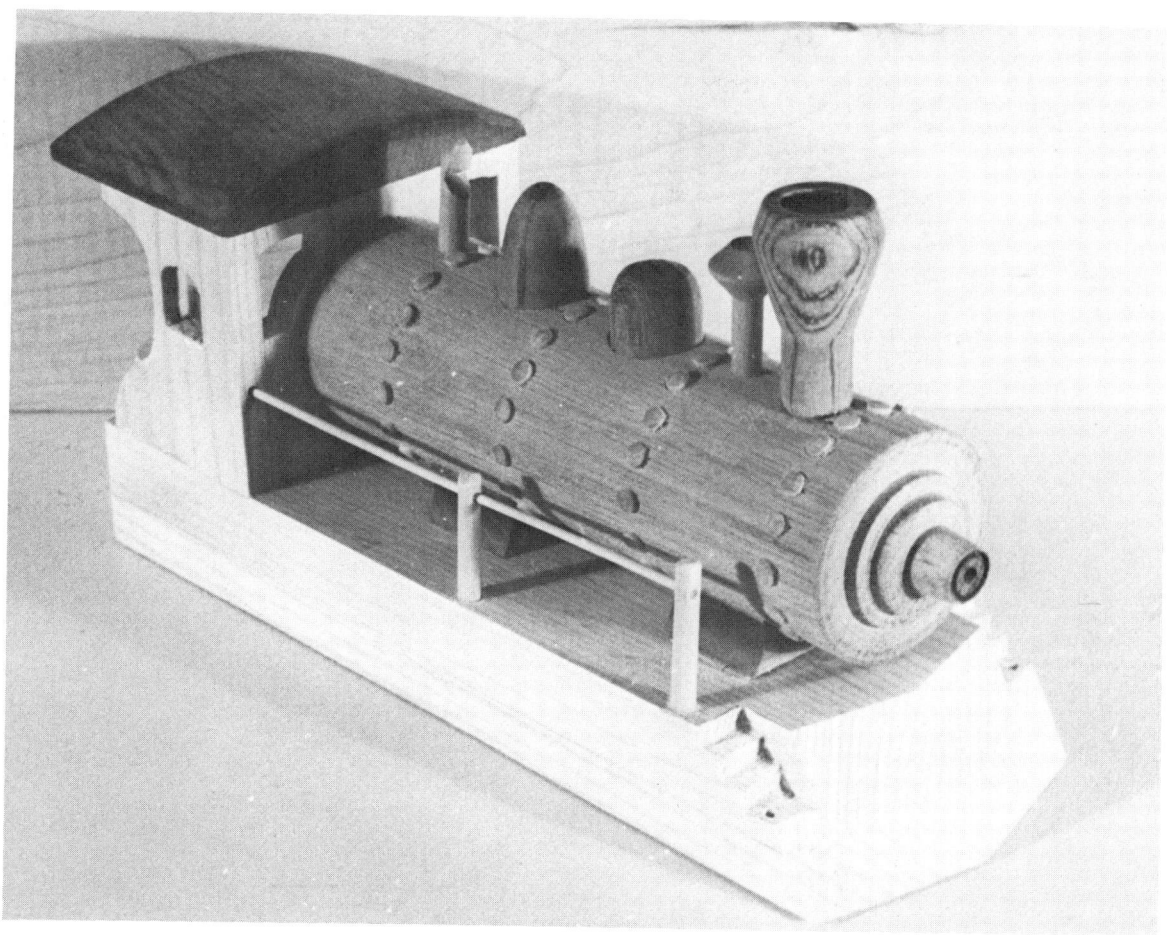

Fig. 9-16. The Steam Locomotive, shown complete without wheels.

☐ Apply three or four coats of clear spray Deft or polyurethane.

☐ When dry, rub with #0000 steel wool.

☐ Apply wax and polish.

Simulated Steel Rails and Ties (for locomotive and tender)

☐ Cut the simulated rails to rough size.

☐ Shape the rails with a router. Fasten the router in a vise, upside down, and make a fence which can be clamped to the router base to adjust the depth of cut.

☐ Cut the 12 ties to size and sand.

☐ Attach rails to the ties. The ties should be spaced 1 1/2 inches apart between centers. Be sure that the ties are square with the rails. The inside top edges of the rails should be 3 1/2 inches apart.

☐ Spray the rail and tie assembly with clear spray Deft or polyurethane. Figure 9-16 shows the project, without wheels.

STEAM LOCOMOTIVE TENDER

The tender, hooked directly behind the engine, was the vehicle that stored the wood or coal for the engine, and is many times considered an integral part of the locomotive.

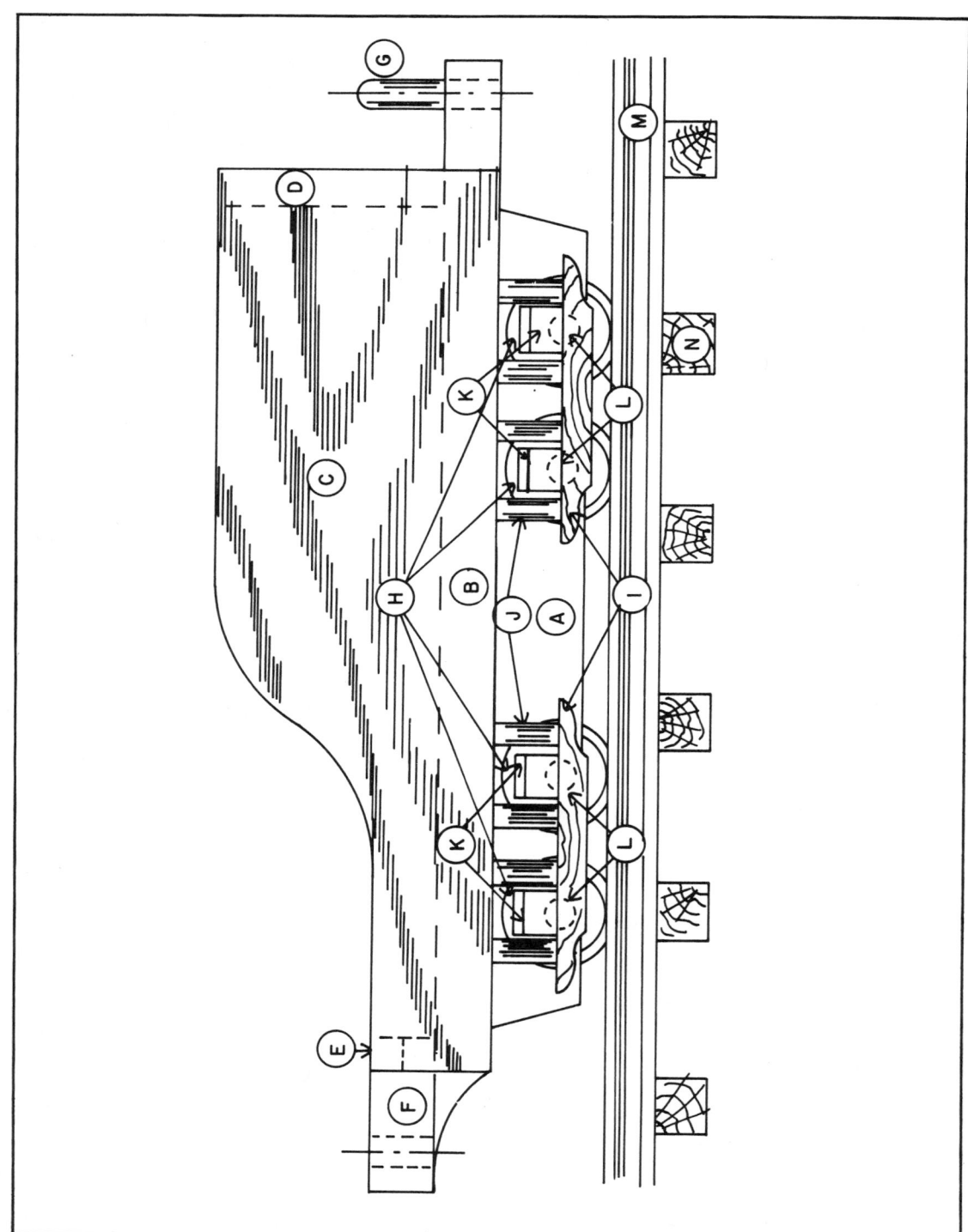

Fig. 9-17. Side view of the Steam Locomotive Tender.

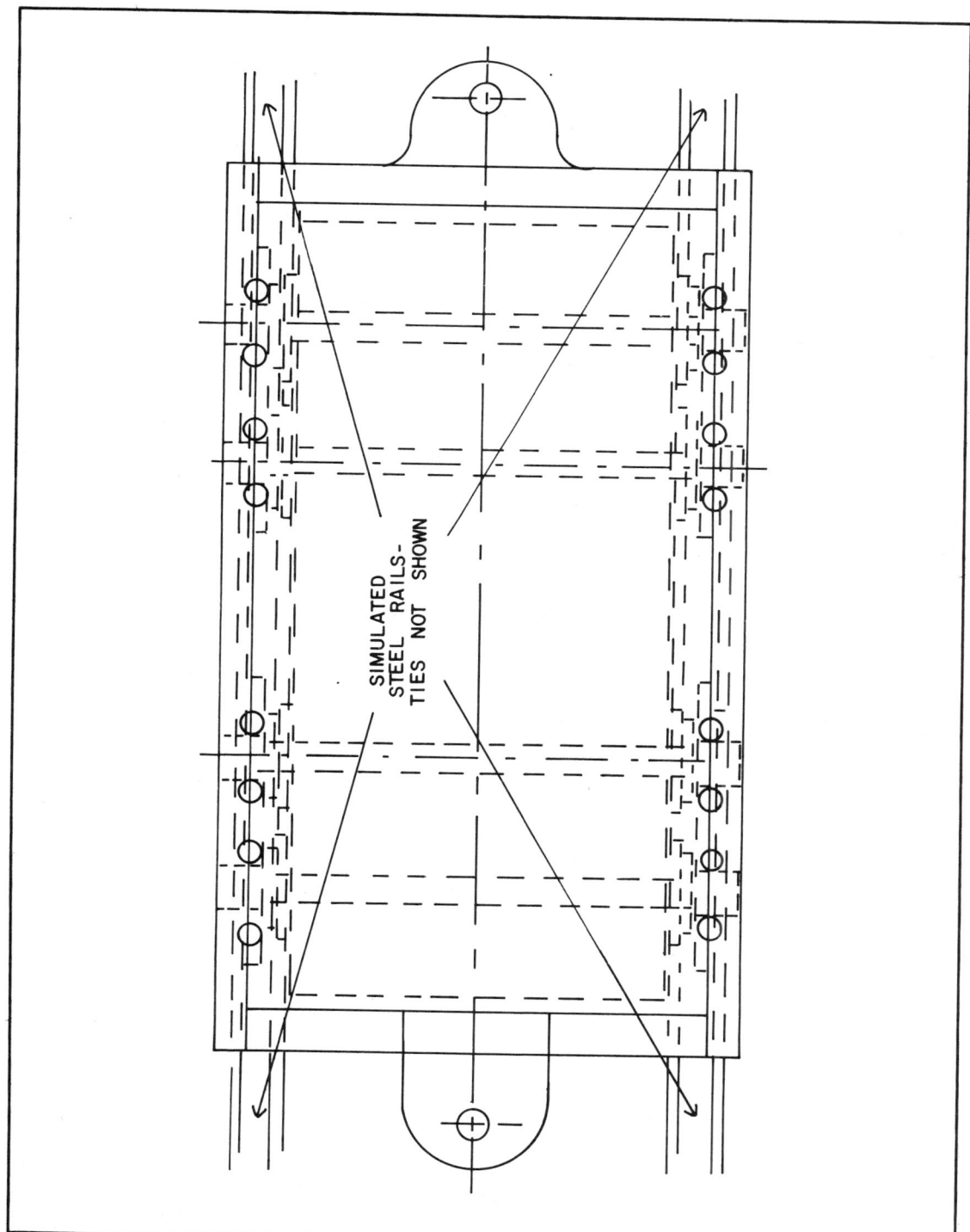

SIMULATED STEEL RAILS-
TIES NOT SHOWN

Fig. 9-18. Top view of the Steam Locomotive Tender.

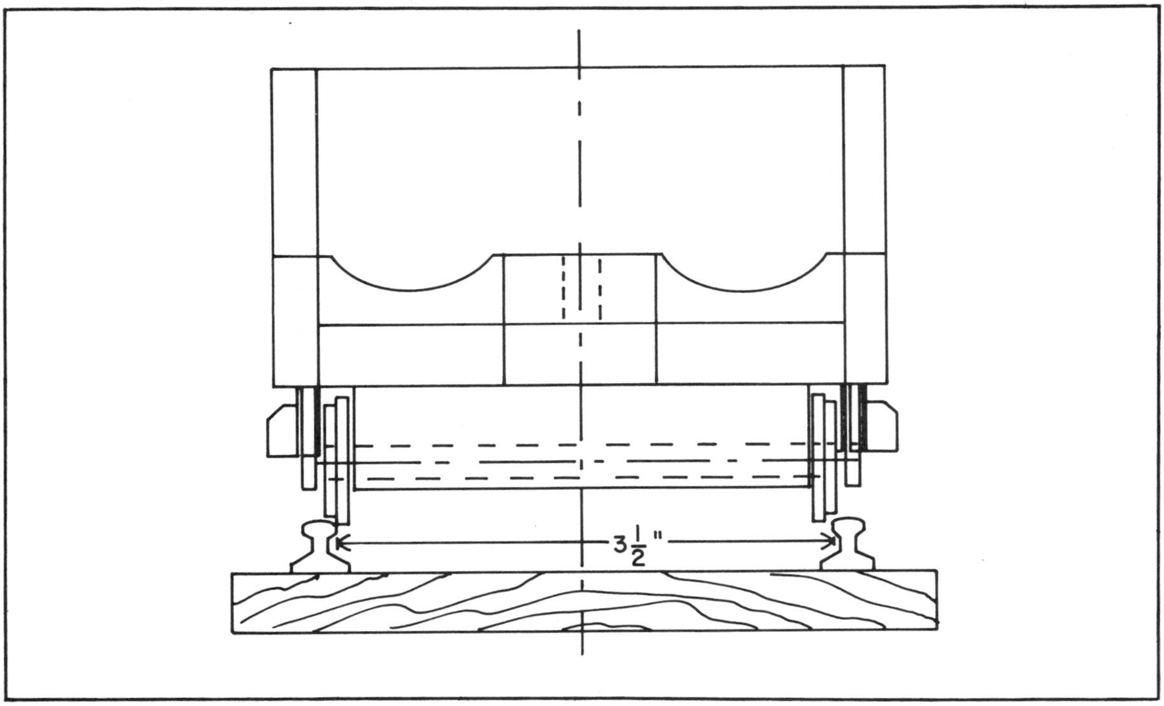

Fig. 9-19. Front view of the Steam Locomotive Tender.

Fig. 9-20. Completed Steam Locomotive Tender.

This railroad car (Figs. 9-17 through 9-19) is much easier to build than the engine and should pose few, if any, difficult problems.

Preparation

☐ Cut the base to size (Table 9-4).

☐ Bore the axle holes in the base 17/64 inch in diameter.

☐ Cut the bottom of the tender to size.

☐ Cut the tender sides stock. Make a pattern and transfer to sides. Table 9-4 gives dimensions. Cut the curves on a curve-cutting tool, band saw, jigsaw, or coping saw.

☐ Cut the tender back to size.

☐ Cut the tender front to size. Make a pattern and transfer to stock (Table 9-4). Cut the curves with a curve-cutting tool.

☐ Bore a hole in the bottom of the tender, 1/4

inch in diameter, to accept the rear coupling. Glue in the rear coupling.

Assembly

☐ Assemble and glue the tender sides, back, front, and bottom.

☐ Cut the front coupling to the size indicated in Table 9-4. Bore the hole before the curved parts are cut. Cut the curved parts with a curve-cutting tool. This part is easily sanded on a disc and drum sander.

☐ Glue the front coupling to the partial tender assembly.

☐ Glue the partial assembly to the base.

☐ Insert the axles through the axle holes.

☐ Attach the wheels to the axles.

☐ Cut the wheel guards.

☐ Cut the wheel guard supports.

Table 9-4. List of Materials for the Steam Locomotive Tender.

NUMBER OF PIECES	CODE	PART	SIZE	MATERIAL
1	A	base	3/4"x 3 1/4"x 7 "	pine or maple
1	B	bottom of tender	1/2"x3 7/8"x8 3/4"	pine or maple
2	C	tender sides	5/16"x2 3/8"x7 3/4"	pine or maple
1	D	tender back	5/16"x1 7/8"x 3 7/8"	pine or maple
1	E	tender front	5/16"x1/2"x3 7/8"	pine or maple
1	F	front coupling	1"x1 1/4"x 1 3/16"	pine or maple
1	G	rear coupling	1 3/16"length	1/4" birch dowel
8	H	wheels	1/4"length	15/16"walnut
4	I	wheel guards	1/8"x1/4"x 2 1/2"	walnut
16	J	wheel guard supports	1/2"length	3/16"birch dowel
8	K	axle housing	3/8"x3/8"x3/8"	padauk
4	L	axles	3 5/8"length	1/4"birch dowel

Fig. 9-21. Steam Locomotive with Tender is shown.

□ Glue the wheel guard supports to the wheel guards.

□ Glue the assembled wheel guards and wheel guard supports to the underside of the tender bottom. Use epoxy glue because the area is small.

□ Cut the axle housings and glue them in place on the wheel guards and between the wheel guard supports.

□ Sand the entire project with fine sandpaper.

□ Spray on three or four coats of clear Deft or polyurethane.

□ When the finish is dry, rub with #0000 steel wool. Wax and polish. See Fig. 9-20 for the finished project.

□ Attach the tender to the engine and place on the railroad track (Fig. 9-21).

10

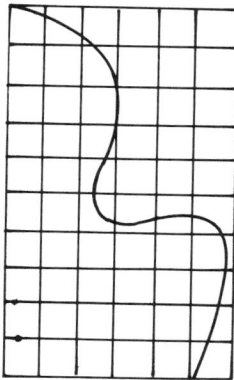

Tractors and Heavy Equipment

This chapter contains step-by-step instructions for seven heavy vehicles. Tables of materials and illustrations are also provided to help you assemble these toys.

FARM TRACTOR AND WAGON

This Farm Tractor and Wagon, designed by Uncle Andy's Scrapwood Toys, is naturally appealing to children, particularly boys (Fig. 10-1). The tractor is easily controlled by the youngster because the smaller hand can readily encompass the 1 1/2-inch thick toy.

I have taken a few liberties with the original design. The tractor seat was made of zebrawood which simulates upholstery material. Plastic/ rubber wheels on the tractor were substituted for the wooden ones on the original plan. These wheels are available from Woodcraft Supply and are made by Hobbies and Handicrafts, Ltd., England (see Appendix A).

The wheels on the wagon were made of redwood, and the sides and ends were glued on perma-

nently to make it more sturdy. The original plans called for detachable sides and ends. Basswood or poplar may be substituted for pine, maple, or birch.

Farm Tractor

☐ Make a pattern for the tractor body and transfer the profile to 1 1/2-inch stock. Table 10-1 and Fig. 10-2 give dimensions.

☐ Cut the outline with a band saw or other curve-cutting tool.

☐ Bore the two 1-inch holes in the body.

☐ Complete the elongated hole to expose the engine cylinders by cutting the sides with a saber saw, or chisel out the remainder of stock between the two holes.

☐ Drill 1/4-inch holes for the engine cylinders, the power take-off pulley axle, the steering wheel post, and the coupling.

☐ Drill a 17/64-inch hole for the rear tractor wheel axle.

☐ Sand the body with drum sanders and by hand.

169

Table 10-1. The Farm Tractor and Wagon Are Made from These Materials.

NUMBER OF PIECES	CODE	PART	SIZE	MATERIAL
Farm Tractor				
1	A	tractor body	1 1/2"x3 5/16"x 8 3/16"	pine, maple, or birch
1	B	steering wheel	3/8" length	1" birch dowel
1	C	steering wheel post	1 1/2" length	1/4" birch dowel
1	D	exhaust pipe	2" length	1/4" birch dowel
4	E	engine cylinders	1 1/4" length	1/4" birch dowel
2	F	front tractor wheels	1 7/8"diam.x 3/4"	pine, maple, or birch
1	G	front tractor wheel axles	2 5/8" length	1/4" birch dowel
1	H	front tractor wheel axle housing	3/4"x 1 1/8"x 1 3/4"	pine, maple, or birch
4	I	rear tractor wheels	3 1/4"diam.x 3/4"	pine, maple, or birch
2	J	rear tractor wheel extenders	1 5/8" diam.x 3/4"	pine, maple, or birch
1	K	tractor seat	3/4"x 7/8"x 1 3/8"	pine, maple, or birch
1	L	coupling	1 1/2" length	1/4" birch dowel
1	M	power take-off pulley	3/8" length	1" birch dowel
1	N	power take-off pulley axle	3/4" long	1/4" birch dowel
Farm Tractor Wagon				
1	O	wagon tongue	1 1/2"x1 5/8"x 3 3/4"	pine, maple, or birch
8	P	wagon wheels	1 7/8"diam. x 3/4"	pine, maple, or birch
2	Q	wagon wheel axles	5 1/4" length	1/4" birch dowel

Note: Cut a third length of 1/4" dowel about 5 3/4" long for the rear tractor wheels and extenders.

1	R	wagon wheel axle housing	1 1/2"x 1 3/4"x 2 1/4"	pine, maple, or birch
1	S	wagon bed	1/2"x5"x7"	pine, maple, or birch
2	T	wagon sides	1/2"x3"x6"	pine, maple, or birch
2	U	wagon ends	1/2"x3"x5"	pine, maple, or birch

Note: This information conforms with the original plans and instructions.

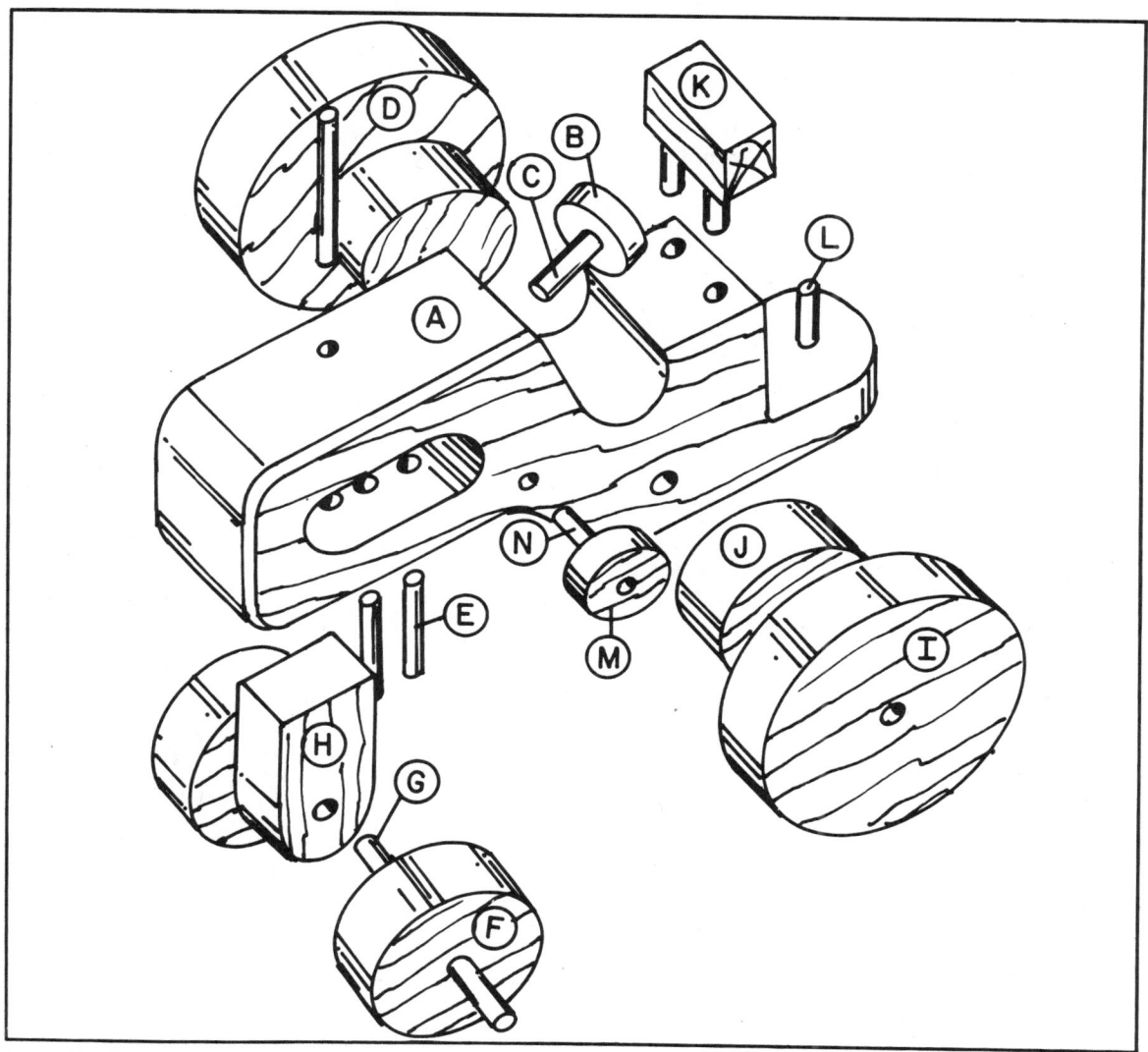

Fig. 10-1. Assembly of the Farm Tractor. Courtesy of Uncle Andy's Scrapwood Toys.

☐ Cut a 3/8-inch length of 1-inch dowel for the steering wheel. Mark the center with a centering jig and drill a 1/4-inch hole through the 3/8-inch length.

☐ Cut the steering wheel post from a 1/4-inch birch dowel and glue the post into the steering wheel. Glue the steering wheel post into the tractor body.

☐ Cut the four engine cylinders and glue them into the tractor body.

☐ Cut the exhaust pipe and glue it into the tractor body.

☐ Cut the power take-off pulley and the power take-off pulley axle. Place a center mark on the pulley and drill for the axle. Glue the axle to the pulley and glue the assembly into the tractor body.

☐ Cut the front and rear tractor wheels with the appropriate hole saw. The wagon wheels may be cut at the same time.

☐ Cut the seat and glue to the body.

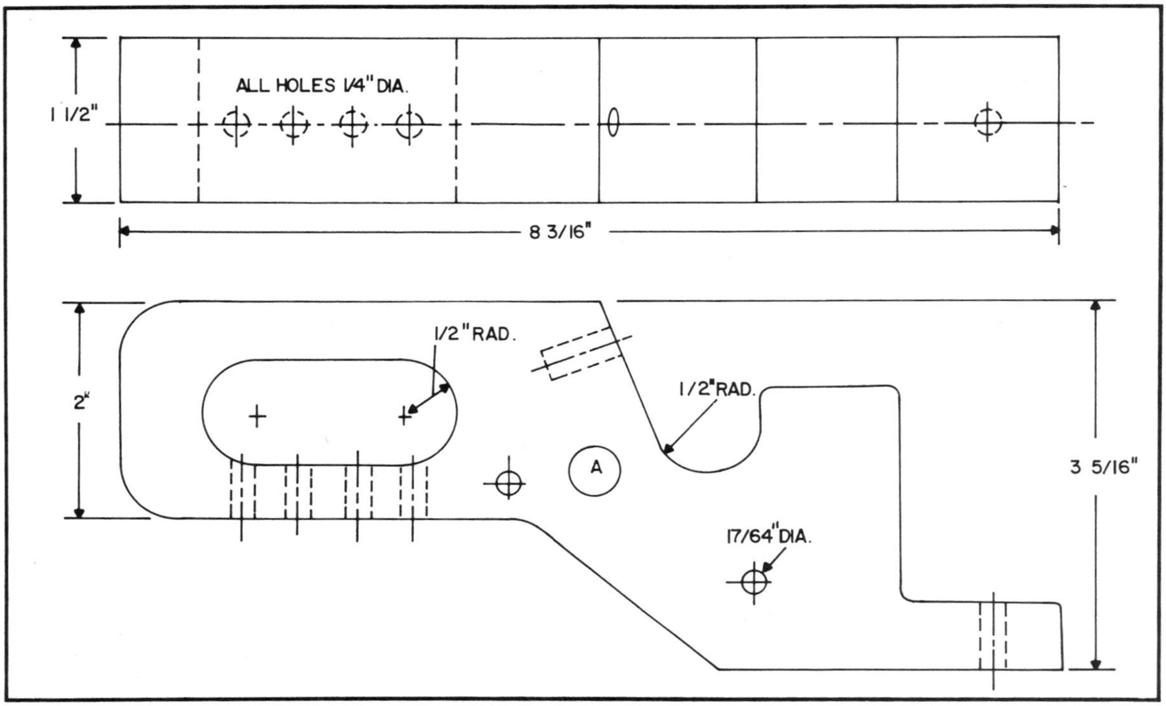

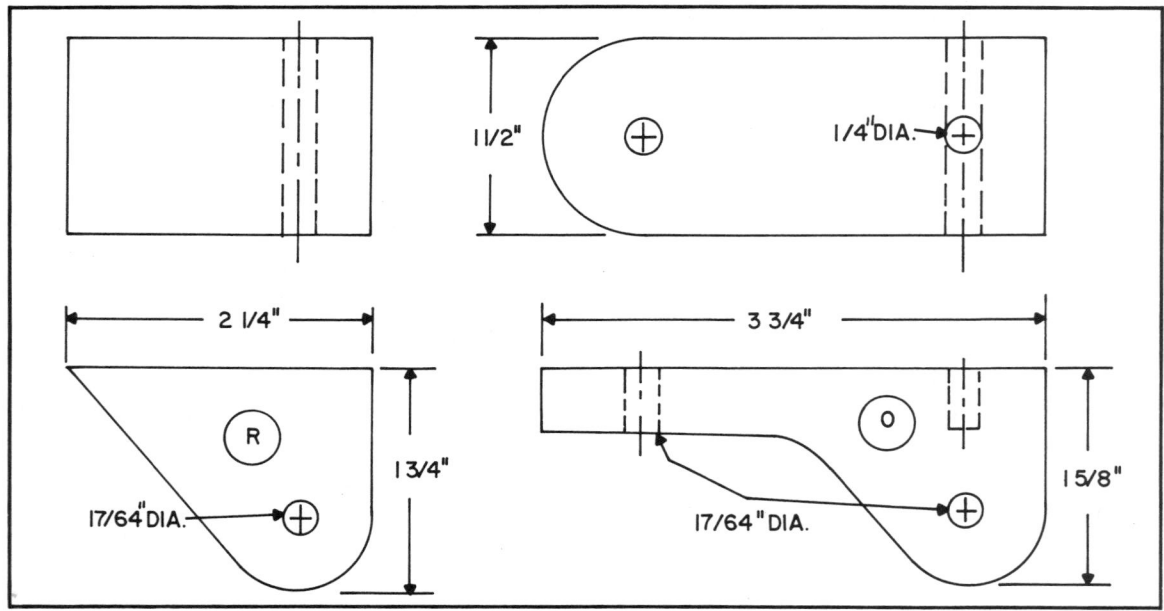

Fig. 10-2. Details of the Farm Tractor body. Courtesy of Uncle Andy's Scrapwood Toys.

Fig. 10-3. Wagon wheel axle housing and wagon tongue details for the Farm Wagon. Courtesy of Uncle Andy's Scrapwood Toys.

172

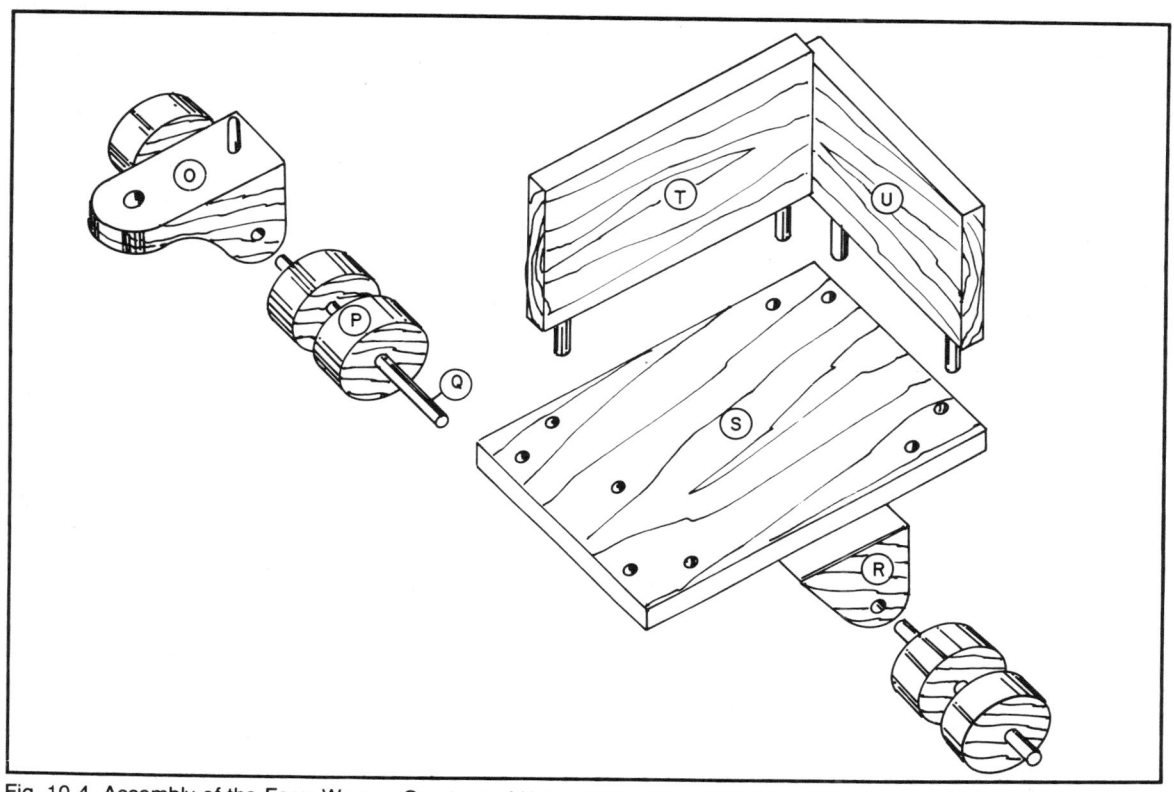

Fig. 10-4. Assembly of the Farm Wagon. Courtesy of Uncle Andy's Scrapwood Toys.

☐ Cut the front tractor wheel axle and the rear tractor wheel axle.

☐ Cut and glue the front tractor wheel axle housing to the body.

☐ Insert the front tractor wheel axle through the hole in the housing and attach the front tractor wheels.

☐ Insert the rear tractor wheel axle through the hole in the body and attach the rear wheels and extenders.

☐ Cut the coupling and glue it into the rear of the tractor body. The end of the coupling dowel should be rounded over.

☐ Sand and finish the tractor with clear spray Deft or polyurethane (Fig. 10-5).

Farm Wagon

☐ Make patterns for the wagon wheel axle housing and the wagon tongue or transfer profile to

1 1/2-inch stock (Fig. 10-3). Cut out the stock with a band saw or other curve-cutting tool.

☐ Mark and drill the 17/64-inch holes in both pieces.

☐ Mark and drill the 1/4-inch hole in the tongue.

☐ Cut the wagon bed, the wagon sides, and the wagon ends.

☐ Glue or dowel the sides and ends to the wagon bed (Fig. 10-4).

☐ Glue the wagon wheel axle housing to the underside of the wagon bed.

☐ Insert the wagon wheel axle into the axle housing and attach the wheels.

☐ Sand the wagon and wagon tongue and finish both parts with clear spray Deft or polyurethane.

☐ Attach the wagon and wagon tongue to the tractor.

Fig. 10-5. Completed Farm Tractor and Wagon. Courtesy of Uncle Andy's Scrapwood Toys.

ROAD GRADER

The rugged road grader by Design Group will appeal to all youngsters. I took a few liberties with the original design; for example, I cut an opening in the windshield to make it more realistic, and I omitted the lights since they added nothing to the overall design. For contrast, I made the wheels and cab roof of black walnut and the engine simulator of brilliant red padauk. For added accent, Palnuts were placed over the ends of the rear axles.

I recommend that the rear wheels be made first and fitted to the axles after extending them through the body. Then while holding the four wheels in contact with a flat surface, measure the distance from the flat surface to the center of the front axle hole. This measurement will determine the correct radius of the front wheels and eliminate any measurement discrepancies which might have occurred.

Preparation

☐ Make a pattern for the body. Be sure to enlarge the pattern in Fig. 10-6 to 1-inch squares. Table 10-2 gives dimensions.

☐ Trace the pattern on 1 1/2-inch stock and cut on a band saw or other curve-cutting tool.

☐ Drill the three axles' holes with a 17/64-inch drill so that 1/4-inch axles will rotate freely.

☐ Saw the scraper at an angle so that the top

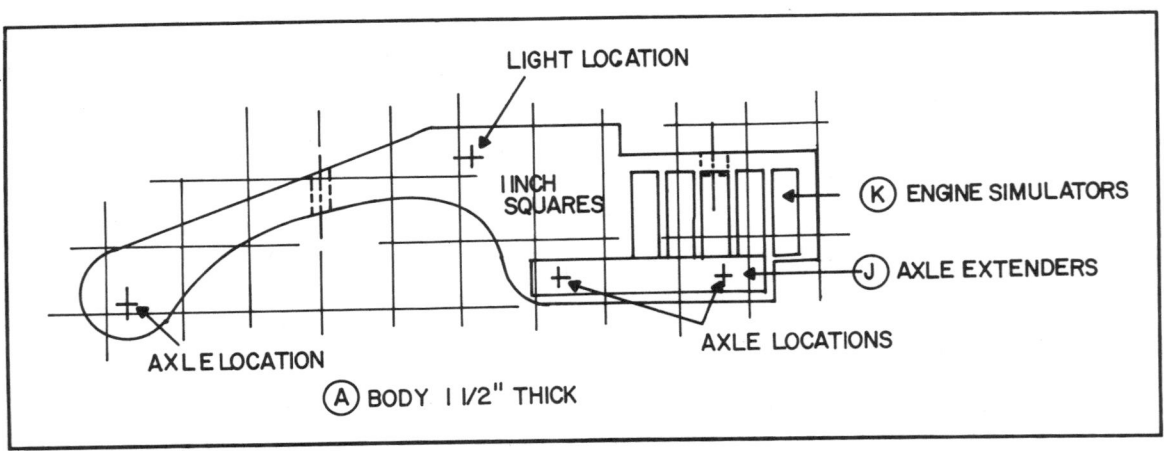

Fig. 10-6. Road Grader body details. Courtesy of Design Group.

Table 10-2. To Make the Road Grader, You Need the Materials Listed.

NUMBER OF PIECES	CODE	PART	SIZE	MATERIAL
1	(A)	body	1 1/2"x 2 5/8"x 10 3/8"	pine, maple, or birch
1	(B)	cab roof	5/8"x 1 5/8"x 3 1/2"	pine, maple, or birch
1	(C)	windshield	1/4"x 1 1/4"x 1 1/2"	pine, maple, birch, or 1/4" birch plywood
1	(D)	cab back	5/8"x 1 1/4"x 1 1/2"	pine, maple, or birch
4	(E)	large wheels (rear)	11/16"x 2 1/4" diam.	pine, maple, or birch
2	(F)	lights	1/2" length	1/2" birch dowel
1	(G)	rear control	1/4" length	1" birch dowel
1	(H)	rear control support	1" length	1/2" birch dowel
2	(J)	axle extenders	3/16"x 9/16"x 3 1/4"	pine, maple, or birch
10	(K)	engine simulators	3/16"x 5/16"x 1 1/4"	pine, maple, or birch
2	(L)	small wheels (front)	1 5/8" diam.x 11/16"	pine, maple, or birch
1	(M)	scraper	7/8"x 1 1/4"x 5"	pine, maple, or birch
1	(N)	scraper control	3/8" length	7/8" birch dowel
1	(O)	scraper control axle	2 1/2" length	1/4" birch dowel
2	(P)	rear axles	3 1/4" length	1/4" birch dowel
1	(Q)	front axle	2 3/4" length	1/4" birch dowel

edge is 1/4-inch thick, and the bottom edge is 7/8-inch thick.

☐ Drill the hole for the scraper control axle in the center of the top scraper edge with a 1/4-inch drill.

☐ Mark the positions for lights, axle extenders, and engine simulators.

☐ Mark and drill a 1/2-inch hole for the rear control support.

Assembly

☐ See Fig. 10-7 for the correct placement of parts.

☐ Glue the rear control to the rear control support. When the glue is dry, glue the rear control support into the 1/2-inch hole in the body.

☐ Drill a 1/4-inch hole in the center of the scraper control and glue the scraper control axle in place.

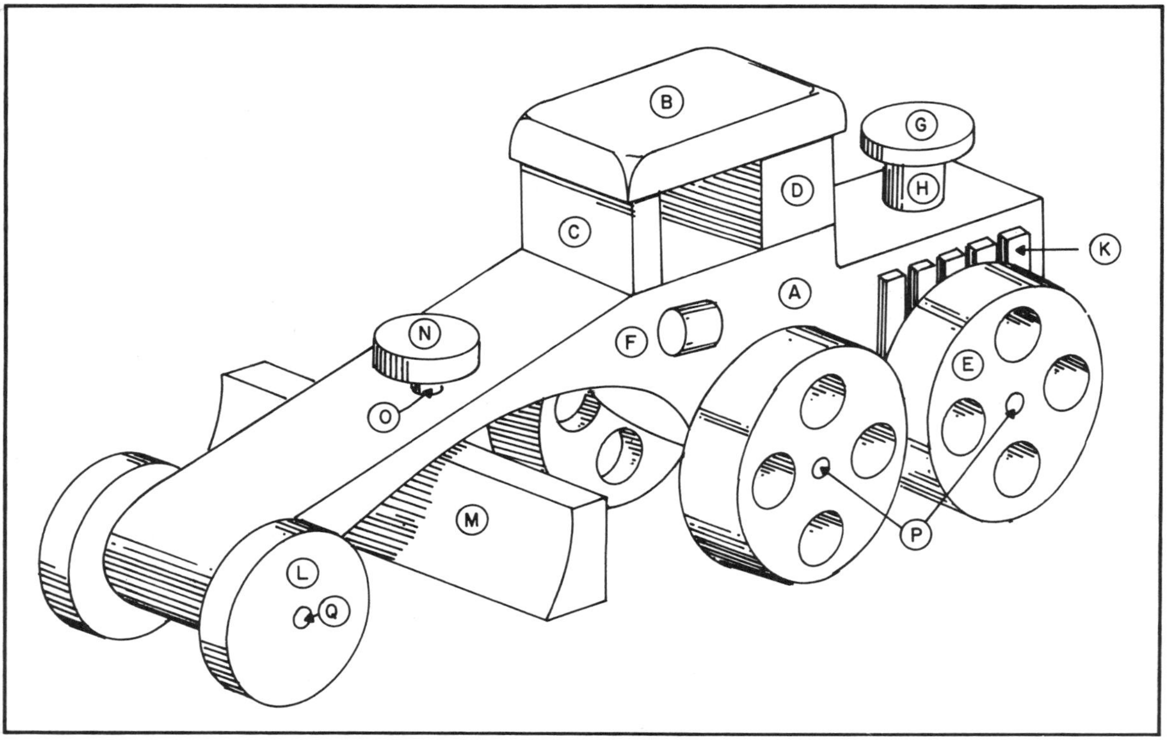

Fig. 10-7. Assembly of the Road Grader. Courtesy of Design Group.

Fig. 10-8. Completed Road Grader. Courtesy of Design Group.

□ Sand the scraper control axle lightly so that it will barely turn in the hole in the front of the body.

□ Place glue on the end of the scraper control axle and insert it into the scraper, pushing the axle through the hole in the body.

□ Cut the simulators and axle extenders and glue them in place.

□ Cut the four rear wheels with a hole saw or turn in a lathe.

□ Bore four 1/2-inch holes in the four rear wheels at right angles to each other.

□ Cut the two front wheels with a hole saw or turn on a lathe.

□ Cut, assemble, and glue the cab and attach it to the body with glue.

□ Sand all parts with fine sandpaper.

□ Glue one end of the wheel axles into the wheels.

□ Insert the wheel axles through holes in the body and axle extenders and glue on the second wheel.

□ Finish with clear spray Deft or polyurethane. See Fig. 10-8 for the finished project.

LARGE FARM TRACTOR

This farm tractor is considerably larger than other wooden toys depicted in this book. It is a sturdy, heavily constructed tractor that is intended for the 8- to 12-year-old child. It will take longer than many other toys to construct, primarily because of the large number of parts involved.

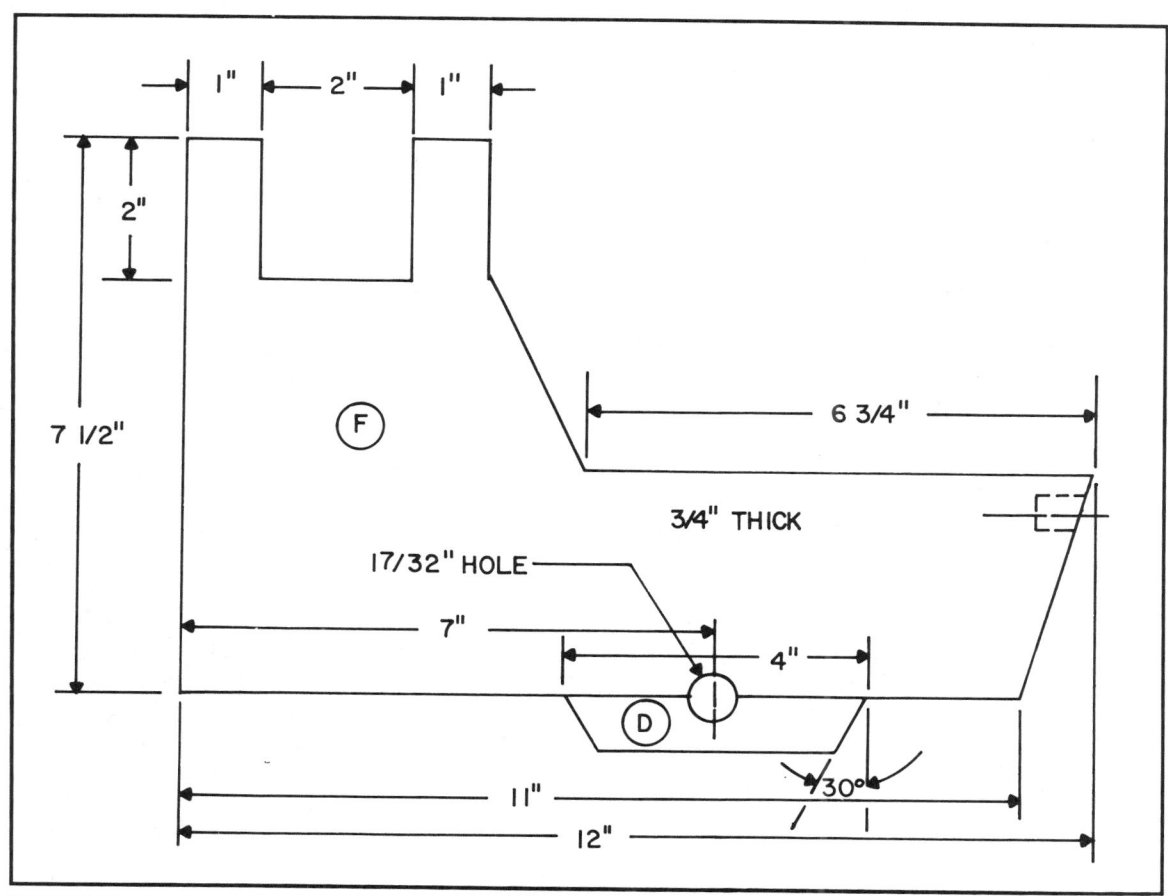

Fig. 10-9. Cab sides and axle support details for the Large Farm Tractor. Courtesy of Sleepy's Toys.

The larger parts should be made of lightweight wood such as pine, poplar, or basswood. If made entirely of hardwood it would be much too heavy and cumbersome. All parts should be carefully sanded and all corners rounded over.

A Grain Wagon and a Corn and Wheat Combine complement the large farm tractor. They are built to the same scale as the tractor. It is a good idea to study carefully the instructions and drawings before starting to build the tractor since it is rather complicated. It will save time in the long run.

Tractor Body Assembly

☐ Make a pattern for the cab sides. Be sure to enlarge the pattern in Fig. 10-9 to the correct dimensions.

☐ Trace around the pattern on 3/4-inch stock (Table 10-3).

☐ Place this piece of stock on another piece of stock of the same size.

☐ Drive brads through the first piece into the second, but only in the waste parts.

☐ Cut out the two cab sides with a band saw or saber saw.

☐ Sand all the edges, first with medium sandpaper, and then with fine sandpaper.

☐ Make a pattern for the four axle supports. Trace it on 3/4-inch stock. Be sure to enlarge the pattern to the dimensions given in Fig. 10-9.

☐ Cut the axle supports on the circular saw. Two axle supports will be used in the next step and the other two later.

☐ Glue the axle supports on each of the bottom edges of the cab sides centered 7 inches from the back of the sides.

☐ Drill a 17/32- or 9/16-inch hole 7 inches from the back edge of each of the cab sides centered between the sides and the axle supports. These holes are bearings for the axle.

☐ Bore a 1/2-inch diameter hole, 1/2-inch deep, 1/2 inch down from the top and centered on the front part of each of the cab sides.

☐ Cut and glue the 1/2-inch diameter by 1/2-inch long dowels for headlights in these holes.

☐ Taper a space 1 1/2 inches high, on the back side of both cab sides up 1 1/2 inches from the

bottom on the inside edges. This space will give the swiveling back portion and rear wheels of the tractor more room to articulate at the pivot point.

☐ Cut the part for the grill on the circular saw. Cut the ends at the same angle as the front part of the cab sides.

☐ Cut the cab bottom back and the cab top back on the circular saw (Fig. 10-10).

☐ Bore a 3/8-inch diameter hole vertically through the center of the bottom back.

☐ Bore a 3/8-inch diameter hole up 1 inch into the center of the bottom of the top back.

☐ Assemble and glue the cab sides, grill, bottom back and top back together. The bottom back must be even with the bottom of the sides. When the top back is glued in place, it must be 1 1/2 inches from the top of the bottom back. When the top and bottom backs are glued in place, there must be a 3/8-inch diameter dowel through the bottom back and into the top back to align the holes with each other.

☐ Cut the cab floor (Fig. 10-10). When it is assembled and glued it must not extend below the cab top back.

☐ Cut the cab front, which is also the dash, on the circular saw. See Table 10-3 for the correct dimensions.

☐ Bore a 1/4-inch diameter hole in the center of the dash to accept the steering wheel (Table 10-3). Glue the steering wheel and the steering wheel post together and glue the combined parts into the hole on the dash.

☐ Cut out the hood on the circular saw. See Fig. 10-11 for the correct dimensions.

☐ Bore two 1/2-inch diameter holes back 2 1/2 inches from the front and 3/4 inch from the sides of the hood. They are to accommodate the muffler and the air breather.

☐ Shape the muffler from stock. Use a plane, rasp, or Surform to shape the muffler before sanding. See Fig. 10-12 for correct dimensions.

☐ Bore a 1/2-inch diameter hole 1/2 inch deep in the center of both ends of the muffler. Cut one piece of 1/2-inch dowel 1 1/2 inches long and another 1-inch long. Glue the two dowels into the holes just bored.

Table 10-3. Materials List for the Large Farm Tractor.

NUMBER OF PIECES	CODE	PART	SIZE	MATERIAL
2	(A)	axles	10 1/2" length	1/2" birch dowel
4	(B)	wheels	4 1/2" diam. x 1 1/2"	redwood
4	(C)	washers	1/2"	steel
4	(D)	axle supports	3/4" x 3/4" x 4"	pine
2	(E)	head lights	1/2" length	1/2" birch dowel
2	(F)	cab sides	3/4" x 7 1/2" x 12"	pine
1	(F F)	grill	3/4" x 2" x 3 3/4"	pine
1	(G)	hood	3/4" x 3 1/2" x 7 1/4"	pine
1	(H)	muffler	3/4" x 1 1/2" x 2 1/2" with 1/2" dowels on both ends.	pine 1" dowel
1	(I)	air breather	2 1/2" length 1 1/4" length	1/2" dowel
1	(J)	cab front	3/4" x 2" x 3"	pine
1	(K)	cab bottom back	3/4" x 1 1/2" x 2"	pine
1	(L)	cab floor	1/4" x 2" x 3 3/4"	pine
1	(M)	cab top back	3/4" x 2" x 2 1/2"	pine
1	(N)	cab roof	3/4" x 5" x 5"	pine
1	(O)	air conditioner	3/4" x 1 1/2" x 2"	pine
1	(P)	front filler piece	3/4" x 1 1/2" x 2"	pine
1	(R)	swivel pin	5" length	3/8" birch dowel
1	(S)	hitch	3/4" x 2" x 2 1/2"	pine
1	(T)	back filler piece	3/4" x 1" x 2"	pine
1	(U)	swivel tongue	1 1/2" x 2" x 8"	pine
2	(V)	swivel tongue sides	3/4" x 3" x 5 1/4"	pine
1	(W)	seat	1 1/2" x 2" x 2 1/2"	zebrawood
1	(X)	steering wheel	1" length 1/4" length	1/4" birch dowel 3/4" birch dowel

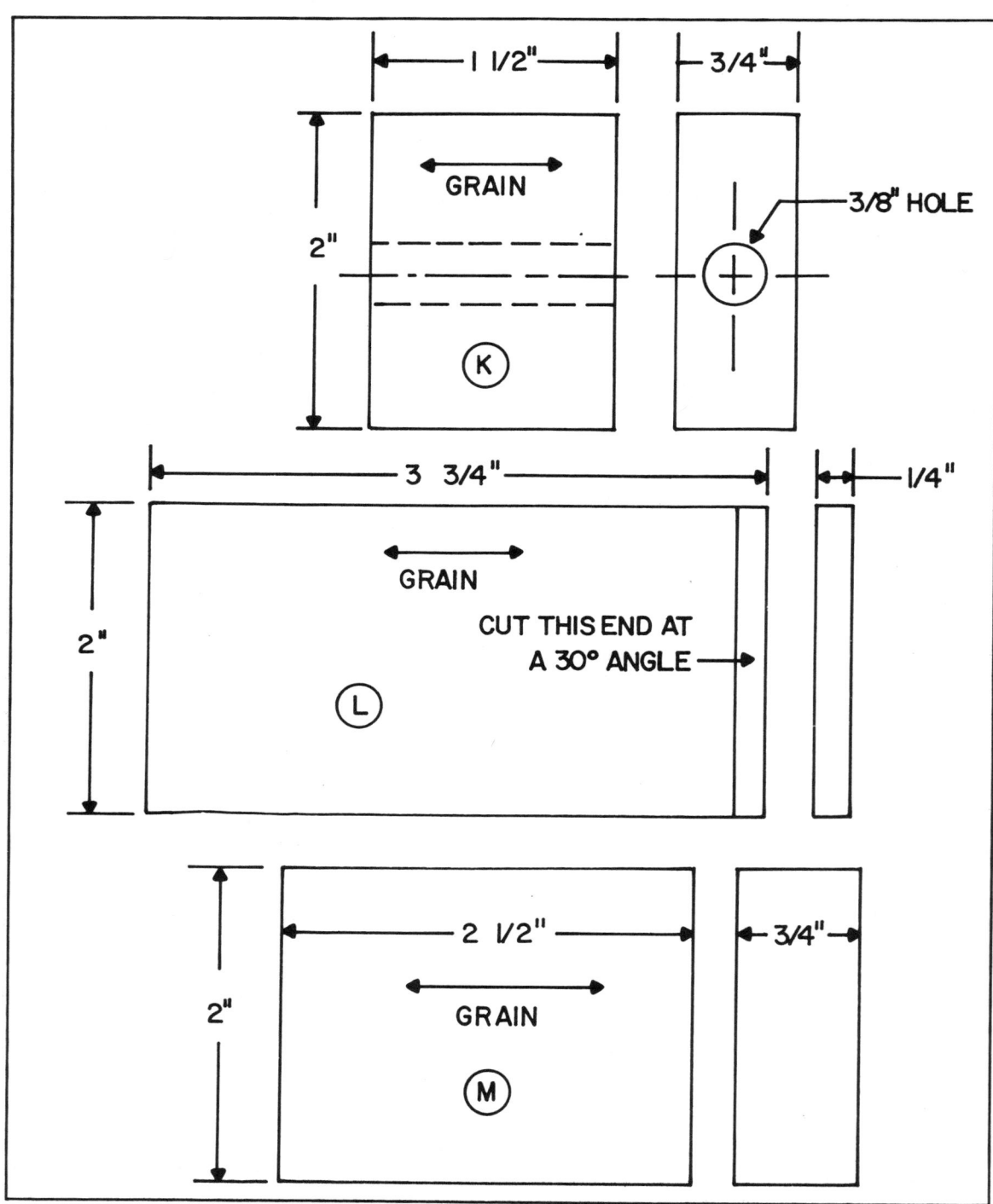

Fig. 10-10. Cab bottom, floor, and top back for the Large Farm Tractor. Courtesy of Sleepy's Toys.

180

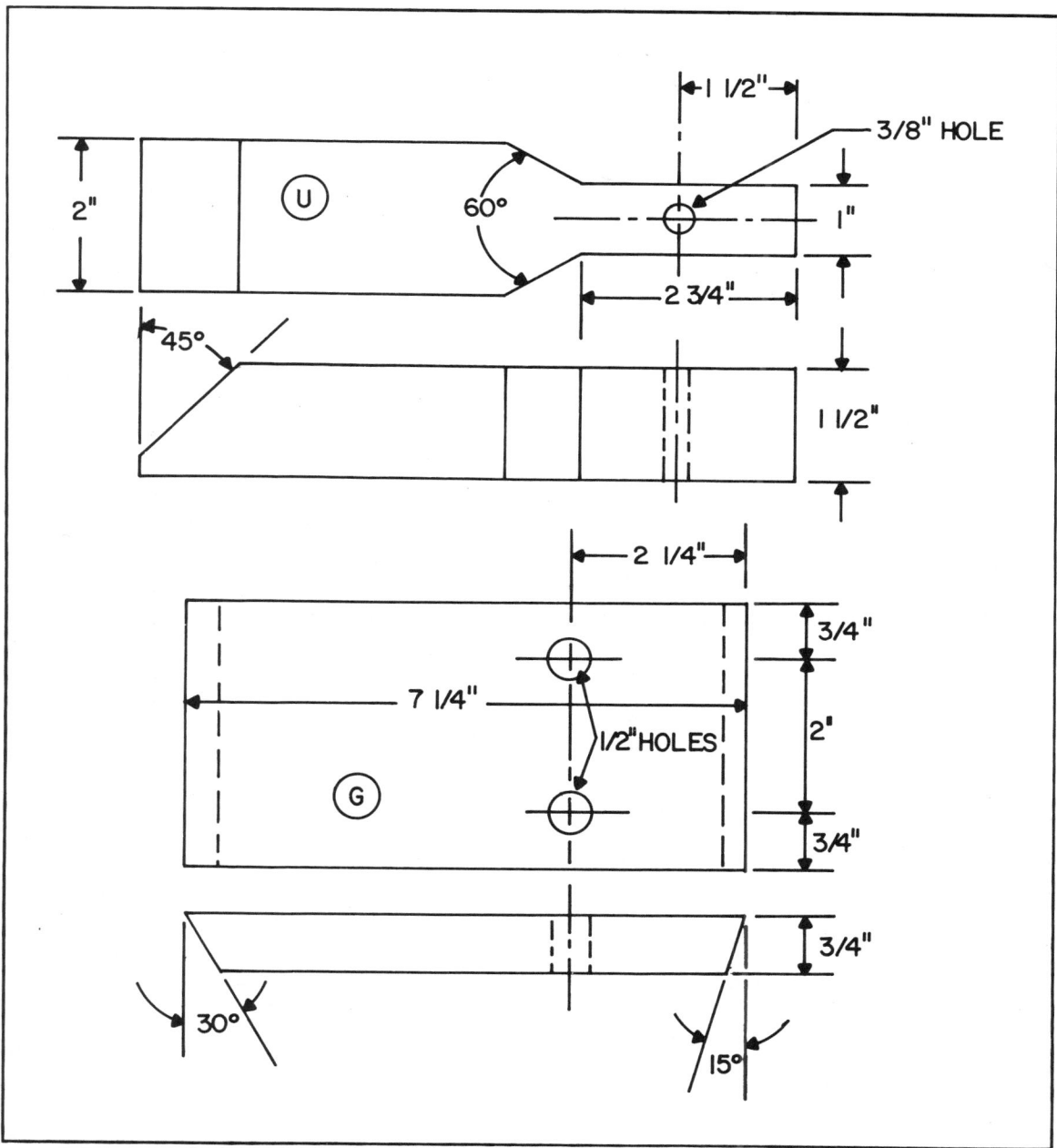

Fig. 10-11. Swivel tongue and hood details for the Large Farm Tractor. Courtesy of Sleepy's Toys.

□ Cut a piece of 1-inch diameter dowel 1 1/4 inches long for the air breather. Taper one end about 1/4 inch down from the top at about a 30-degree angle. On the opposite end from the taper mark the centering lines with a centering jig. Bore a 1/2-inch diameter hole at the center 1/2-inch deep. Cut a 1/2-inch diameter dowel 1 1/2 inches long and glue it into the hole.

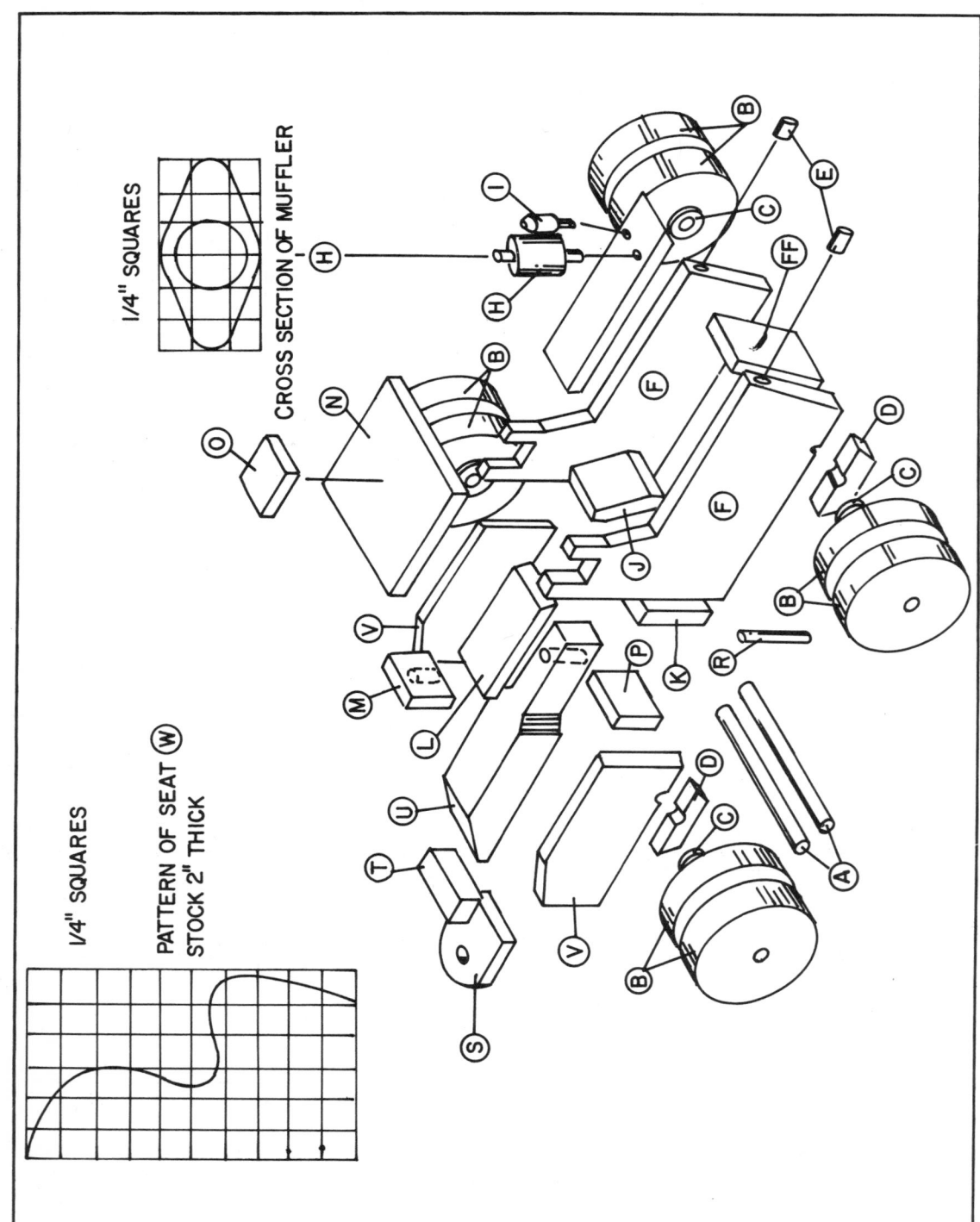

1/4" SQUARES

CROSS SECTION OF MUFFLER

1/4" SQUARES

PATTERN OF SEAT W
STOCK 2" THICK

Fig. 10-12. Assembly of the Large Farm Tractor. Courtesy of Sleepy's Toys.

☐ Cut the cab roof with the circular saw. See Table 10-3 for the correct dimensions. Sand the edges. The top edge is rounded over.

☐ Cut the air conditioner on the circular saw. Sand the edges. See Table 10-3 for correct sizes.

☐ Glue the air conditioner to the center of the cab roof.

☐ Glue the combined parts to the top of the cab with 1/2 inch exposed behind it.

☐ Cut the seat from 2-inch thick zebrawood. Be sure to enlarge the pattern in Fig. 10-12 to the correct dimensions.

☐ Glue the seat to the cab top back on the inside of the cab after the seat has been sanded on a drum sander.

☐ Glue the muffler and air breather into the holes on the hood.

☐ Cut the swivel tongue from 1 1/2-inch stock or from two pieces of 3/4-inch stock glued together with a circular saw and a band saw. See Fig. 10-11 for the correct dimensions.

☐ Bore a vertical 3/8-inch diameter hole centered 1 1/2 inches back from the front end.

☐ Cut 1/2 inch off each side 2 3/4 inches back from the front end of the swivel tongue. Taper outward from this point at 30 degrees.

☐ Cut the back top corner of the swivel tongue at an angle of 45 degrees.

☐ Cut the swivel tongue sides one for each side with the circular saw. See Fig. 10-13 for the correct dimensions and for how the two sides differ.

☐ Glue the two remaining cut axle supports to the bottom side of the swivel tongue sides 1/2 inch from the back side of each.

☐ Bore a 17/32- or 9/16-inch diameter hole, 2 1/2 inches forward from the back edge of the swivel tongue sides centered between the sides and the axle supports.

☐ Cut the filler pieces, and hitch on the circular saw. See Table 10-3 and Fig. 10-13 for the correct dimensions.

☐ Bore a 17/32- or 9/16-inch hole in the hitch. Mark the curve with a compass and cut the curve on a band saw (Fig. 10-13).

☐ Assemble and glue the swivel tongue, tongue sides, filler pieces, and hitch together, making sure that all parts are properly aligned.

☐ After the glue is dry, round over all sharp corners.

Wheel Assembly

☐ Mark the eight wheels with a compass on 1 1/2-inch stock. The diameter of the wheels is 4 1/2 inches.

☐ Cut out the eight wheels on the band saw. Saw about the width of the compass circle line outside the compass circle. Saw slowly and carefully. It will save time in the long run.

☐ Bore 1/2-inch diameter holes through the wheels at the center point.

☐ Cut a circle at least 4 1/2 inches in diameter from 3/4-inch or heavier stock, preferably plywood. This circle will form the base for a mandrel jig to finish turning and sanding the wheels.

☐ Center and attach this wood faceplate to the regular lathe aluminum or steel faceplate with flathead screws.

☐ Place a 1/2-inch bit in a Jacobs chuck and mount it in the tailstock.

☐ Advance the 1/2-inch bit into the wood faceplate while the lathe is turning. Bore the hole at least 1/2-inch deep.

☐ Cut a piece of 1/2-inch diameter dowel long enough so that about 1 3/4 inches extend out from the wood faceplate. Glue the dowel into the wood faceplate.

☐ Drive a number of small brads into the wood faceplate. Cut off the heads with side cutters leaving about 1/32 to 1/16 inch extending out from the wood faceplate. Sharpen the brad points to a sharp point with a small file.

☐ Place the mandrel jig and regular faceplate on the lathe.

☐ Place one of the wheels on the mandrel jig. It may be necessary to tap the wheel with a mallet to seat the wheel on the brads. The brads keep the wheels from slipping during the turning and sanding.

☐ Set the outside calipers at 4 1/2 inches and turn the wheel to this diameter. Sand with medium sandpaper while the lathe is turning. Continue until all eight wheels are turned and sanded.

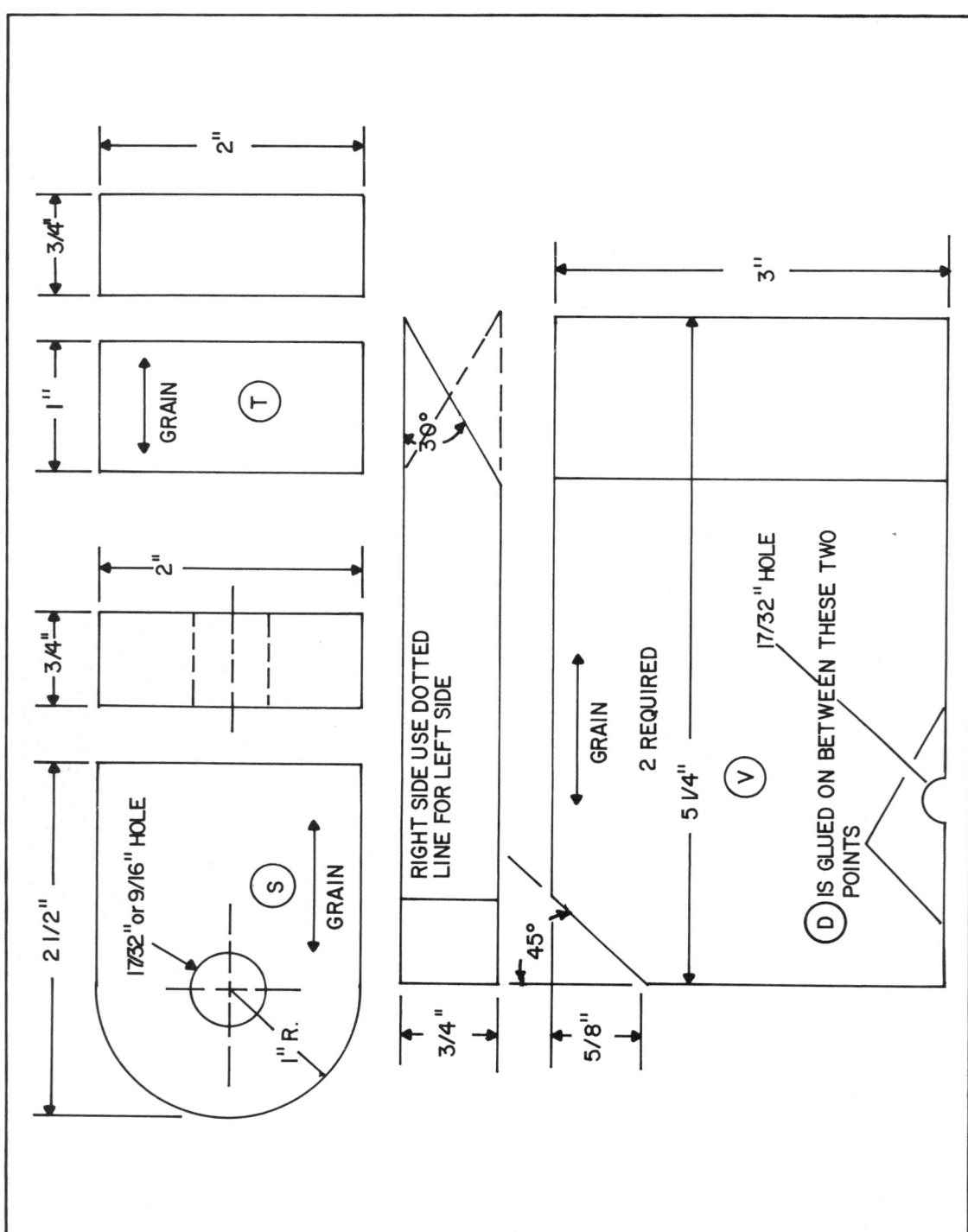

3/4"

2"

GRAIN

T

3/4"

2"

2 1/2"

17/32" or 9/16" HOLE

S

GRAIN

1" R.

RIGHT SIDE USE DOTTED
LINE FOR LEFT SIDE

30°

45°

3/4"

5/8"

3"

GRAIN

2 REQUIRED

5 1/4"

17/32" HOLE

V

D IS GLUED ON BETWEEN THESE TWO
POINTS

Fig. 10-13. Hitch, filler piece, and rear sides for the Large Farm Tractor. Courtesy of Sleepy's Toys.

☐ Cut the two axles 10 1/2 inches long from 1/2-inch birch dowel.

☐ Assemble the wheels and the axles using a 1/2-inch washer between the axle supports and inside wheel.

☐ Place the 3/8-inch swivel pin in from the bottom of the cab bottom back through the hole in the swivel tongue and into the cab top back. Cut the dowel flush with the bottom of the bottom back.

Finishing

☐ Apply three or four coats of spray clear Deft or polyurethane.

☐ When dry, rub with #0000 steel wool. Apply wax and polish. See Figs. 10-14 through 10-16 for the finished project.

GRAIN WAGON

The Grain Wagon is another large toy by Sleepy's Toys designed to be a companion piece to the Large Farm Tractor.

This strong, sturdy toy is more suitable to the older child. Because of its size it is best to use lightweight wood. Hardwoods would make the toy much too heavy. Both the Grain Wagon and the Large Farm Tractor are planned to turn on a very short radius.

Beans, peas, or small marbles may be placed in the Grain Wagon to simulate grain. The "grain" may be ejected through the gate by lifting the grain slide gate.

Wagon Body Assembly

☐ Lay out the two sides of the grain box on 3/4-inch stock (Table 10-4). Be sure to enlarge the pattern to the correct dimensions in Fig. 10-17.

☐ Cut out the two sides of the grain box on a circular saw or band saw.

☐ Sand the surfaces and edges with medium sandpaper.

☐ On one of the two sides lay out the opening for the grain slide. See Figs. 10-17 and 10-18.

Fig. 10-14. Side view of the completed Large Farm Tractor. Courtesy of Sleepy's Toys.

□ Cut the grain opening 1 × 1 1/2 inches, with a jigsaw, saber saw, keyhole saw or compass saw.

□ Cut the two tapered ends of the grain box on the circular saw.

□ Taper the two ends of each of the ends of the grain box at 40 degrees.

□ Cut away a 3/4-inch notch at the bottom end of both sides of both parts of the tapered ends to connect the wagon side frames. See Fig. 10-17.

□ Cut the grain side gate and the slide gate handle.

□ Glue the handle to the gate about 3/4 inch from one end and centered.

□ Cut the two slide rails by cutting a 1/4-inch groove in the corner of 1/2-inch square pieces.

□ Position and glue the bottom end of these slide rails 5 inches from the top of each of the grain

Fig. 10-15. Front view of the completed Large Farm Tractor. Courtesy of Sleepy's Toys.

Fig. 10-16. Rear view of the Large Farm Tractor. Courtesy of Sleepy's Toys.

box sides and 1 1/4 inches apart and centered over the grain dump hole.

☐ Cut the grain box top ends and the grain box top sides to size.

☐ Glue the top ends, top sides, tapered ends, and box sides together, making sure all parts are square before clamping.

☐ Cut the wagon side frames, wagon frame end, rear frame floor, frame front, and front frame floor.

☐ Glue all six parts together after checking for squareness. Since the side frames will later be

Table 10-4. Grain Wagon Materials are Listed.

NUMBER OF PIECES	CODE	PART	SIZE	MATERIAL
1	(A)	grain box bottom	1/2"x1 1/2"x4 1/2"	pine
2	(B)	grain box top ends	3/4"x2"x 6"	pine
2	(C)	grain box top sides	3/4"x2"x 15 1/8"	pine
2	(D)	tapered ends of grain box	3/4"x6"x9 3/4"	pine
2	(E)	sides of grain box	3/4"x6 1/4"x15 1/8"	pine
2	(F)	wagon side frame	3/4"x1 1/2"x 15 1/8"	pine
4	(G)	grain box braces	3/4"x3/4"x2 1/2"	pine
1	(H)	wagon frame end	3/4"x1 1/2"x4 1/2"	pine
1	(I)	rear frame floor	3/4"x1 1/2"x4 1/2"	pine
1	(J)	steering gear pin	2 1/2" length	3/4" birch dowel
1	(K)	frame front	3/4"x3/4"x 4 1/2"	pine
2	(L)	front steering gear axle supports	3/4"x 3"x4"	pine
1	(M)	steering gear top	3/4"x4"x 4 1/2"	pine
1	(N)	front frame floor	3/4"x4"x4 1/2"	pine
2	(P)	steering gear tongue supports	3/4"x1 1/8"x1 3/4"	pine
1	(R)	tongue swivel dowel	2 1/2" length	3/8" birch dowel
1	(S)	wagon tongue	3/4"x1"x 6"	pine
1	(T)	hitch pin	2" length	3/8" birch dowel
4	(U)	wheels	3 1/2" diam.x 1 1/2" wide	pine
4	(V)	washers	1/2"	
2	(X)	rear axle supports	3/4"x3"x 4 "	pine
2	(Y)	axles	9 1/2" length	1/2" birch dowels
1	(A A)	grain slide gate	3/16"x1 1/4"x 3 1/2"	walnut

NUMBER OF PIECES	CODE	PART	SIZE	MATERIAL
1	B-B	slide rails	1/2" x 1/2" x 3 1/2"	pine
1	C-C	slide gate handle	3/8" x 3/8" x 3/8"	walnut
1	D-D	slide gate base	3/4" x 2 1/4" x 2 1/2"	pine
1	E-E	slide gate chute	3/4" x 2" x 2 1/2"	pine

slid between the bottom parts of the box sides and the tapered ends you may want to check the fit before the glue is set.

□ Cut the four axle supports. See Fig. 10-17 for the correct dimensions.

□ Bore a 9/16-inch hole in the four axle supports centered 3/4 inch from the bottom.

□ Cut the steering gear top to size (Table 10-4).

□ Bore a 3/4-inch hole in the center of the top.

□ Cut the steering gear tongue supports. The front edge of the top and both sides of the supports are cut at the same angle as the angles on the front axle supports. I opted to cut one piece 4 1/2 inches long to extend across the underside of the gear top and glued 3/4 inch back from the front part of it. After the glue was set, I marked and used a center punch for the location of the tongue swivel axle on the glue line between the axle supports and the gear top on both sides of the top.

Instead of using a drill press to bore the hole, I placed a Jacobs chuck and a 3/8-inch bit in the headstock of the lathe. I then placed the two marked and punched locations between the bit and the tail center in the tailstock and advanced the tailstock and tailstock center until a perfect hole was bored.

□ Cut the slot in the front edge of the steering gear top to receive the wagon tongue. Cut the slot 1 1/8 inches wide and 1-inch deep, which will also cut away the center section of the tongue supports.

□ Cut the wagon tongue to size and bore a 3/8-inch hole in both ends. Bore the front hole vertically through the 3/4-inch thick stock and 5/8 inch back from the front end. Bore the hole in the back of the tongue horizontally through the 1-inch width centered 1/2 inch from the back end of the tongue.

□ Round over the back end of the tongue so that the tongue swings freely up and down. Also partially round over the front end of tongue, but at right angles to the rounded back end.

□ Slide the tongue swivel dowel through the steering gear top and tongue supports and through the back end of the tongue.

□ Glue the front steering gear axle supports to the sides of the gear top. Make sure they are square and straight.

□ Cut the hitch pin dowel and glue it into the hole in the front end of the tongue.

□ Glue the rear axle supports, which were cut earlier, to the bottom side of the wagon side frames 1/2 inch forward from the rear of the frames.

□ Cut the grain box braces to length and cut the taper on one end. See Fig. 10-19.

□ Place the grain wagon box on the wagon frame. Be sure it is centered and the top edges of the grain wagon box are parallel to the wagon frame. Glue in place and glue the grain box braces in place.

Wheel Assembly

□ Mark the four wheels with a compass on 1 1/2-inch stock. Set the compass to mark a 3 1/2-inch circle.

□ Cut the four wheels on a band saw. Saw about the width of the compass line outside the circle. Saw slowly and carefully to save time later.

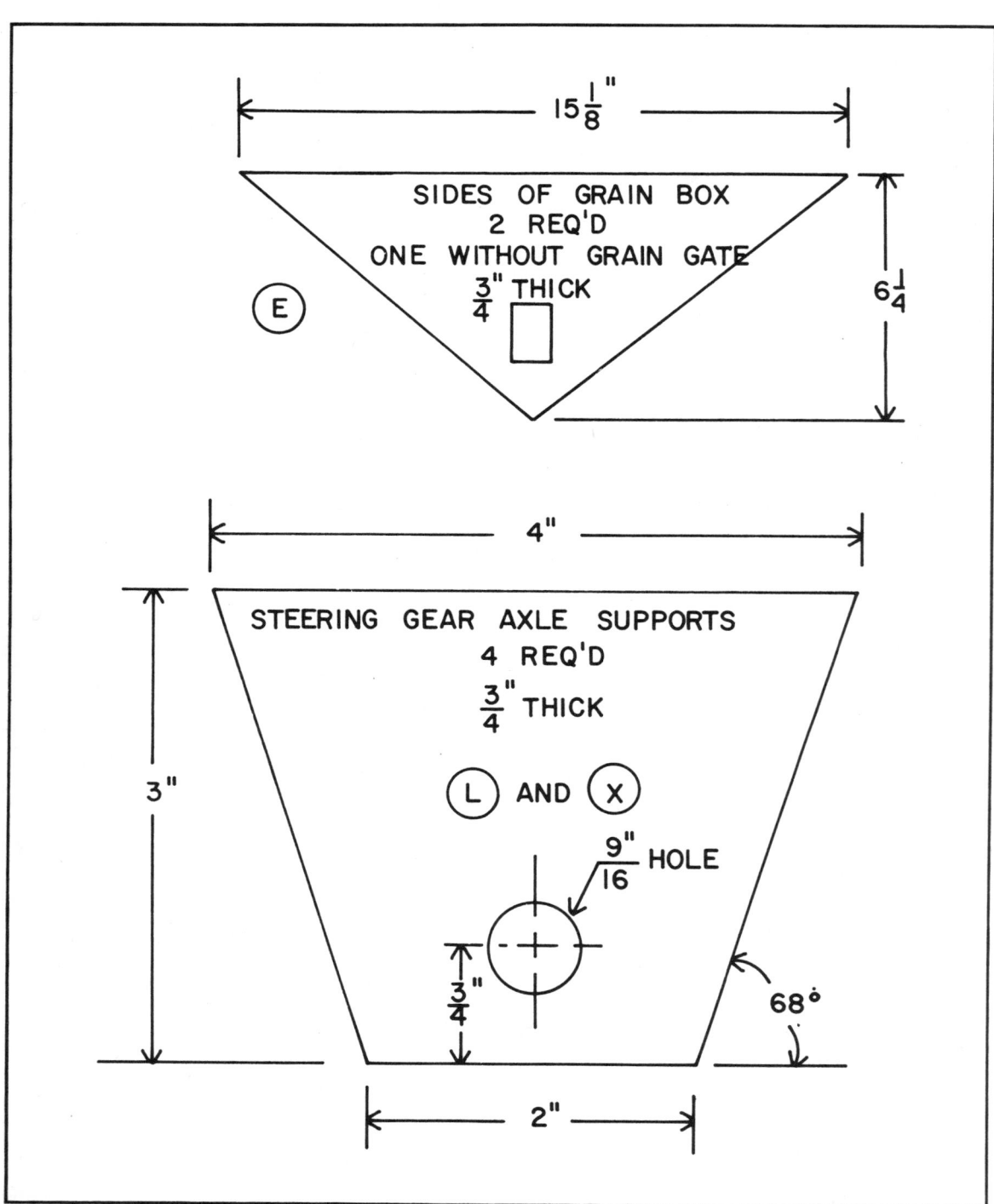

SIDES OF GRAIN BOX
2 REQ'D
ONE WITHOUT GRAIN GATE
$\frac{3}{4}$" THICK

E

$15\frac{1}{8}$"

$6\frac{1}{4}$

STEERING GEAR AXLE SUPPORTS
4 REQ'D
$\frac{3}{4}$" THICK

L AND X

4"

3"

$\frac{9}{16}$" HOLE

$\frac{3}{4}$"

68°

2"

Fig. 10-17. Details of the Grain Wagon. Courtesy of Sleepy's Toys.

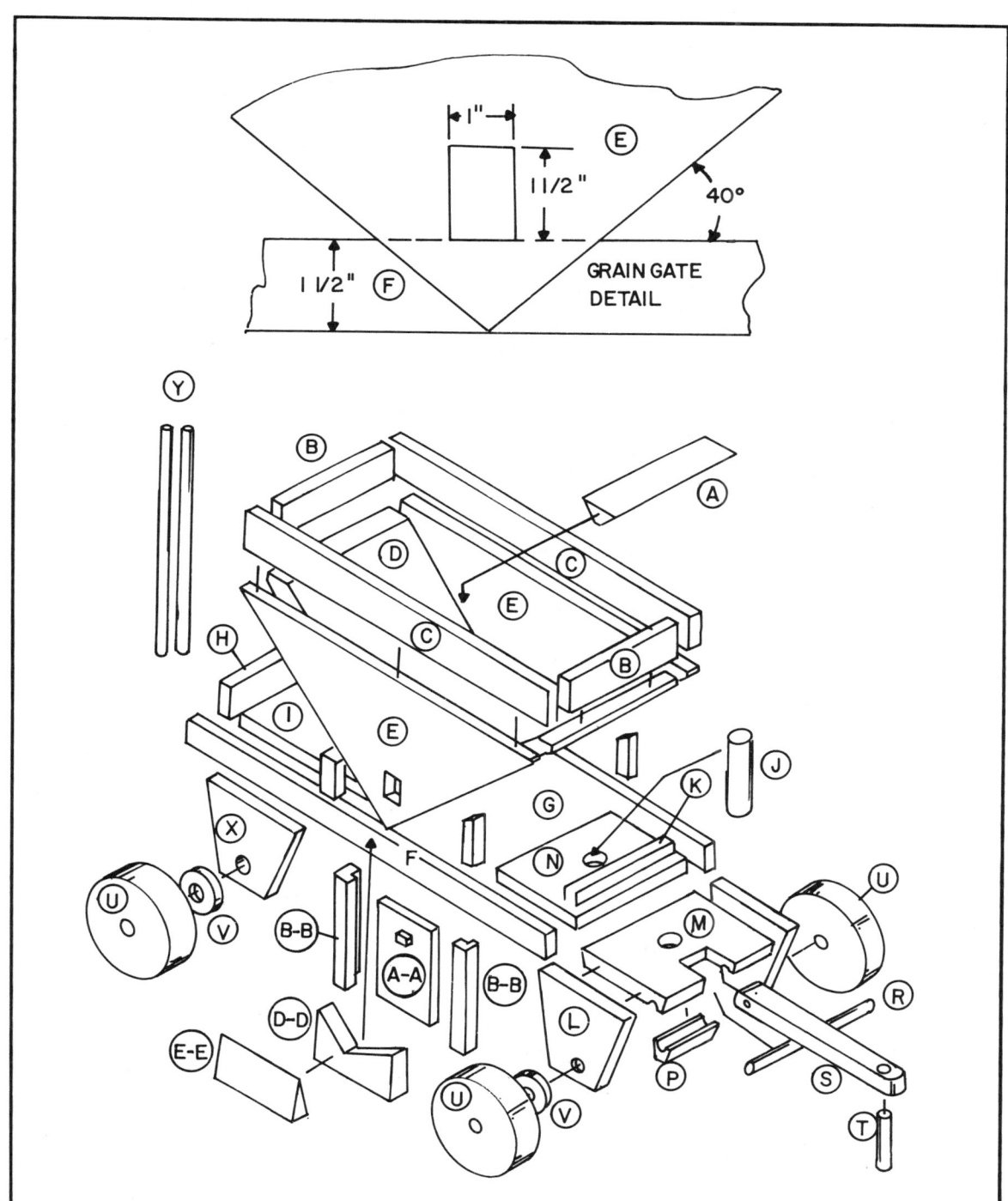

Fig. 10-18. Grain Wagon detail and assembly. Courtesy of Sleepy's Toys.

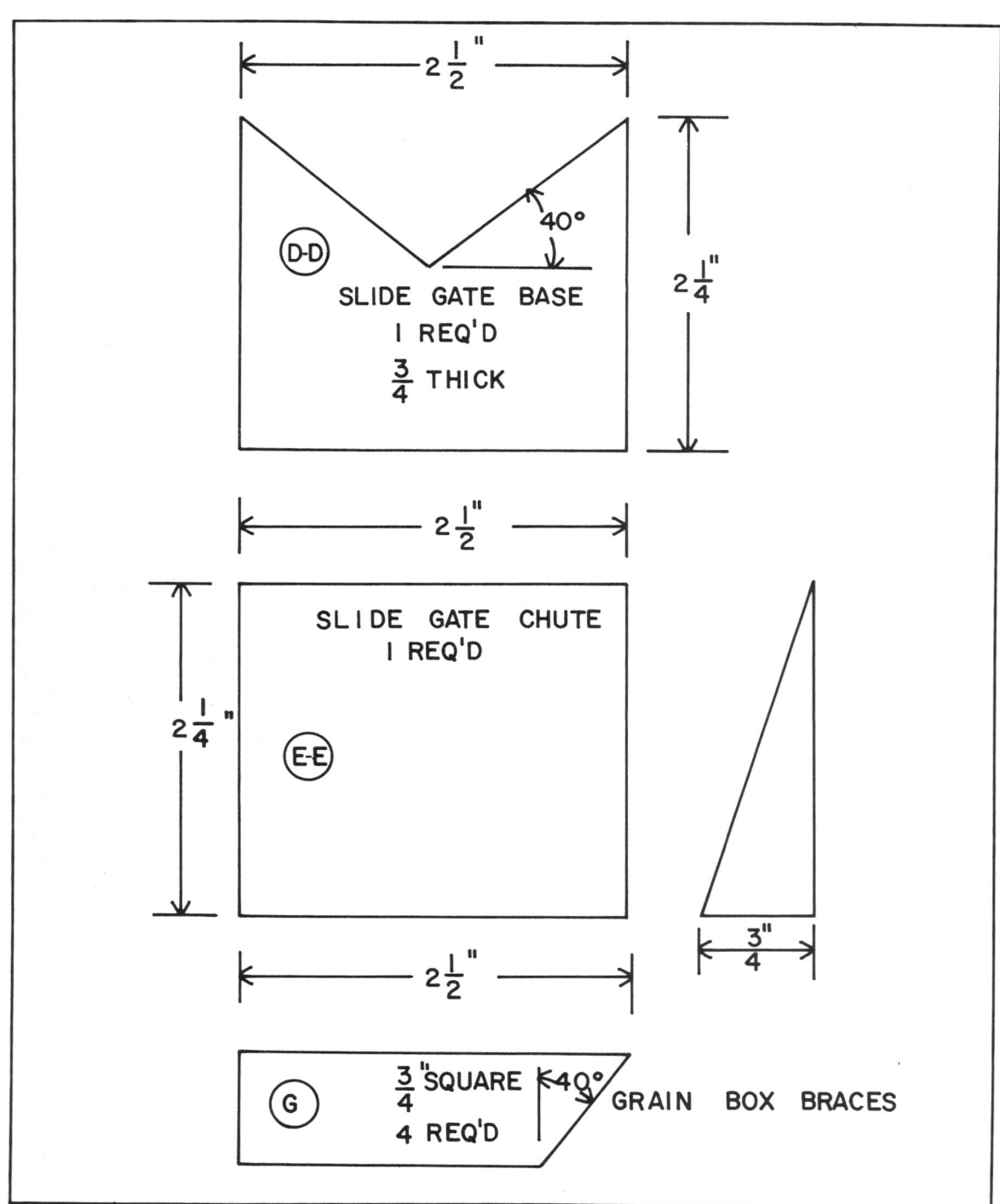

2 1/2"

D-D

40°

SLIDE GATE BASE
I REQ'D
3/4 THICK

2 1/4"

2 1/2"

SLIDE GATE CHUTE
I REQ'D

2 1/4 "

E-E

2 1/2"

3"
4

G

3/4" SQUARE

4 REQ'D

40°

GRAIN BOX BRACES

Fig. 10-19. Detail of three parts of the Grain Wagon. Courtesy of Sleepy's Toys.

Fig. 10-20. Use a lathe mandrel jig for turning the wheels.

☐ Bore 1/2-inch diameter holes through the wheels at the center point after the center points have been deepened with a center punch.

☐ Cut a circle of wood at least 3 1/2 inches in diameter from 3/4-inch or heavier stock, preferably plywood with the band saw. This circle will form the base for a lathe mandrel jig to finish turning and sanding the wheels. See Fig. 10-20.

☐ Center and attach this wood faceplate to the regular aluminum or steel faceplate with flat head screws.

☐ Place a 1/2-inch bit in the Jacobs chunk and mount in the tailstock.

☐ Advance the bit into the wood faceplate while the lathe is running. Bore the hole at least 1/2 inch deep.

☐ Cut a piece of 1/2-inch diameter dowel long enough to extend about 1 3/4 inches out from the wood faceplate. Glue the dowel into the wood faceplate.

☐ Drive a number of small brads into the wood faceplate around the dowel. Cut off the heads with side cutters leaving about 1/32 to 1/16 inch protruding out from the wood faceplate. Sharpen the brads to a sharp point with a small file.

☐ Place the lathe mandrel jig and regular faceplate on the lathe headstock.

☐ Place the wheels on the mandrel jig. It may be necessary to tap the wheel with a mallet to seat the wheel on the brads. The brads keep the wheels from slipping around the dowel during the turning and sanding.

☐ Set the outside calipers for 3 1/2 inches and turn the wheels to this diameter. If any of the four wheels do not "clean up" at this diameter, set the calipers from 1/64 to 1/32 inch smaller than the 3 1/2 inches and turn all four wheels again.

☐ Sand the four wheels with medium sandpaper while the lathe is turning.

☐ Cut the two axles 9 1/2 inches long from a 1/2-inch diameter dowel.

☐ Glue two of the wheels to the ends of the axles.

☐ When the glue is dry, slip a washer over the ends of the axles and insert the axles through the holes in the axle supports. Slip on the other two washers and glue on the remaining wheels, but first be sure that the axles turn freely in the axle holes.

Finishing

☐ Cut the slide gate base to fit under the bottom corner of the sides of the grain box. See Fig. 10-19.

☐ Cut the slide base chute. See Fig. 10-19.

☐ Glue the chute to the gate base together to the bottom of the sides of the grain box and the side of the frame.

☐ Cut the grain box bottom and glue to the bottom inside of the grain box.

☐ Sand the entire project with fine sandpaper.

☐ Spray on three or four coats of clear Deft or polyurethane.

☐ When finish is dry, rub with #0000 steel wool. Apply paste wax and polish. Figure 10-21 shows the finished project.

FARM COMBINE

The Farm Combine is a companion piece to the Large Farm Tractor and the Grain Wagon and is another design of Sleepy's Toys. This large toy will appeal to the older, 9- to 12-year-old, child and will

Fig. 10-21. The Grain Wagon is shown attached to the Large Farm Tractor. Courtesy of Sleepy's Toys.

194

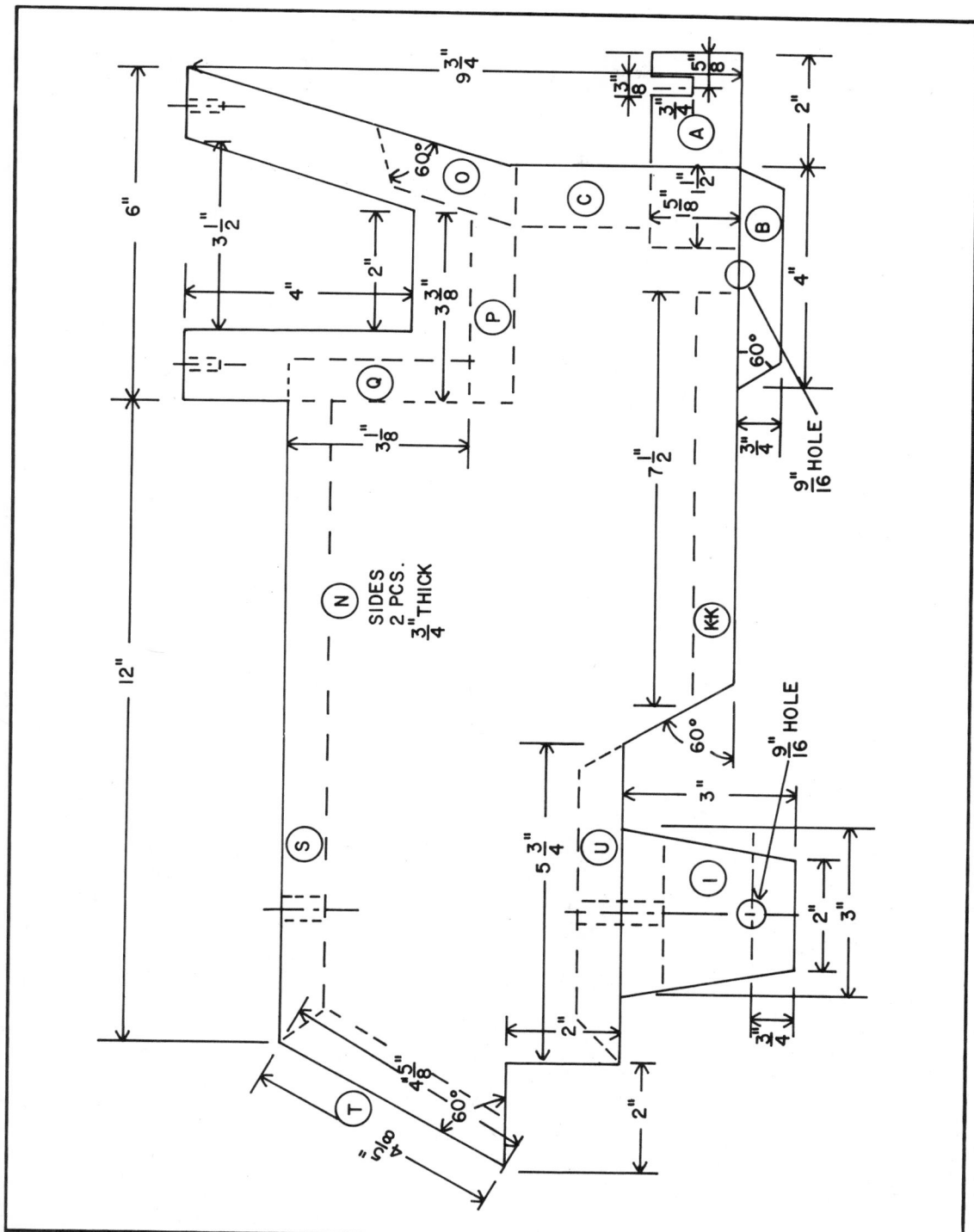

Fig. 10-22. Details for the Farm Combine's sides. Courtesy of Sleepy's Toys.

Table 10-5. To Make the Farm Combine, Use the Materials Given.

NUMBER OF PIECES	CODE	PART	SIZE	MATERIAL
2	(A)	header platform	3/4"x1 1/2"x3 1/2"	white pine
2	(B)	axle supports	3/4"x 3/4"x4"	white pine
1	(C)	combine front	3/4"x2 3/8"x3"	white pine
2	(D)	front wheels	1 1/2"x4 1/2"diam.	white pine
1	(E)	front axle	8" length	1/2" birch dowel
1	(F)	top rear axle support (part of steering gear)	3/4"x2 3/4"x3"	white pine
1	(G)	hopper auger and handle	7 1/2"length	3/8"birch dowel
2	(H)	rear wheels	3/4"x 3 1/2"diam.	white pine
2	(I)	rear axle supports (part of steering gear)	3/4"x 3/4"x3"	white pine
2	(J)	grain elevator	3/4"x3/4"x12"	white pine
2	(K)	grain box sides	3/4"x6"x12"	white pine
2	(L)	grain box front and back	3/4"x3 1/4"x4 1/2"	white pine
2	(M)	cab side	3/4"x3/4"x5"	white pine
2	(N)	combine side	3/4"x9 3/4"x20"	white pine
1	(O)	cab front and dash	3/4"x2 1/2"x3"	white pine
1	(P)	cab floor	3/4"x3"x3 3/8"	white pine
1	(Q)	cab back	3/4"x3"x3 1/8"	white pine
1	(R)	cab roof	1"x5 1/2"x 8 1/4"	mahogany
1	(S)	combine top	3/4"x3"x 12"	white pine
1	(T)	combine rear	3/4"x3"x4 5/8"	white pine
1	(U)	combine bottom and straw rack	3/4"x3"x5 3/4"	white pine
1	(V)	steering wheel	3/4"x2 1/2"diam.	padauk

NUMBER OF PIECES	CODE	PART	SIZE	MATERIAL
1	(W)	washer	1/2" hole	steel
1	(X)	seat	1 1/2" x 2" x 2 7/8"	zebrawood
1	(Z)	steering wheel	1/4" dowel through a 3/4" dowel	
1	(AA)	grain auger	1 1/2" length	3/4" birch dowel
1	(BB)	grain auger	7" length	3/4" birch dowel
1	(CC)	grain auger swivel	4 3/4" length	1" birch dowel
2	(DD)	grain auger mount	3/4" x 1 3/4" x 1 3/4"	white pine
1	(EE)	rear axle	5 3/4" length	1/2" birch dowel
1	(FF)	header platform cover	3/4" x 1" x 3"	white pine
1	(GG)	steering shaft	9 1/2" length	1/2" birch dowel
2	(JJ)	belt guard	3/4" x 1 1/2" x 3 1/2"	white pine
1	(KK)	combine bottom	3/4" x 3" x 7 1/2"	white pine
2	(RR)	headlights	1/2" length	1/2" birch dowel
1	(2)	corn header bottom	3/4" x 2 1/2" x 11 1/4"	white pine
1	(3)	corn header back	3/4" x 3" x 11 1/4"	white pine
2	(4)	corn header side	3/8" x 1" x 1"	white pine
2	(5)	bean header sides	3/4" x 2 1/2" x 3"	white pine
1	(6)	bean header back	3/4" x 2 1/4" x 12"	white pine
1	(7)	bean header bottom	3/4" / 2 1/2" x 12"	white pine
1	(8)	reel 4 pieces	13 1/2" length	3/8" birch dowel
			3/16" x 5/8" x 12"	white pine
2	(9)	header attachment cover	3/4" x 1 1/8" x 4 1/2"	white pine
4	(10)	header attachment sides	3/4" x 1 1/8" x 3"	white pine

especially please the farm boy because of his close association with farm machinery. With the two companion pieces, youths can pretend they are operating their father's expensive farm equipment.

Although this toy is not particularly difficult to construct, it is rather time-consuming because of the large number of parts involved.

Combine Assembly

☐ Make a pattern of cardboard or heavy paper for the two combine sides. See Fig. 10-22 for the correct dimensions.

☐ Cut two pieces of stock (Table 10-5).

☐ Trace the outline of the pattern on the two pieces. As an option, the two pieces may be joined together with brads through the waste material; one of the tracings can then be eliminated.

☐ Cut out the outline of the two pieces with a band saw or other curve-cutting tool.

☐ Round over the outside edges of the two combine sides with a router or with a rasp or Surform followed by different grades of sandpaper. Do not round over the edges of the cab parts.

☐ Cut the two axle supports.

☐ Glue the axle supports to the bottom of the combine sides, even with the front end of the sides.

☐ Bore a 17/32- or 9/16-inch hole, 2 inches from the front part of the combine sides.

☐ Sand the edges of the sides and axle supports.

☐ Mark the diameters of the two front wheels, 1/16 to 1/8 inch oversize on 1 1/2-inch thick stock with a compass.

☐ Bore 1/2-inch diameter holes through the two wheels at the center point made by the compass.

☐ Slide the wheels on a 1/2-inch faceplate mandrel.

☐ Turn the two wheels down to size and sand while turning in a lathe.

☐ Cut out parts for the header platform and glue to the inside of the combine sides. Make sure that the parts are straight and level. See Fig. 10-22 for the correct dimensions.

☐ Cut the combine front to size and sand one face which will be the front of the combine.

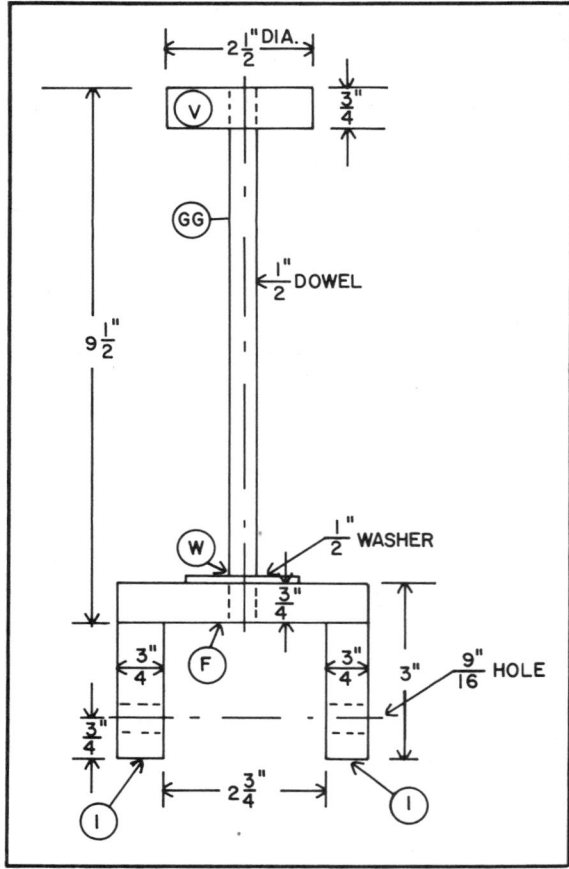

Fig. 10-23. Steering gear details for the Farm Combine. Courtesy of Sleepy's Toys.

☐ Cut the cab front and dash to size. One edge is cut to the same angle as the front edge of the cab, and the other edge is cut at 60 degrees. See Fig. 10-22.

☐ Cut the seat to size. Be sure to enlarge the pattern in Fig. 10-24 to 1/4-inch squares.

☐ Cut the cab floor to size. One edge is cut to the same angle as the front edge of the cab. See Table 10-5.

☐ Cut the cab back to size.

☐ Cut the combine top to size. One end is cut to a 60-degree angle.

☐ Cut the combine rear to size. One end is cut to a 60-degree angle.

☐ Cut the combine bottom and straw rack to

198

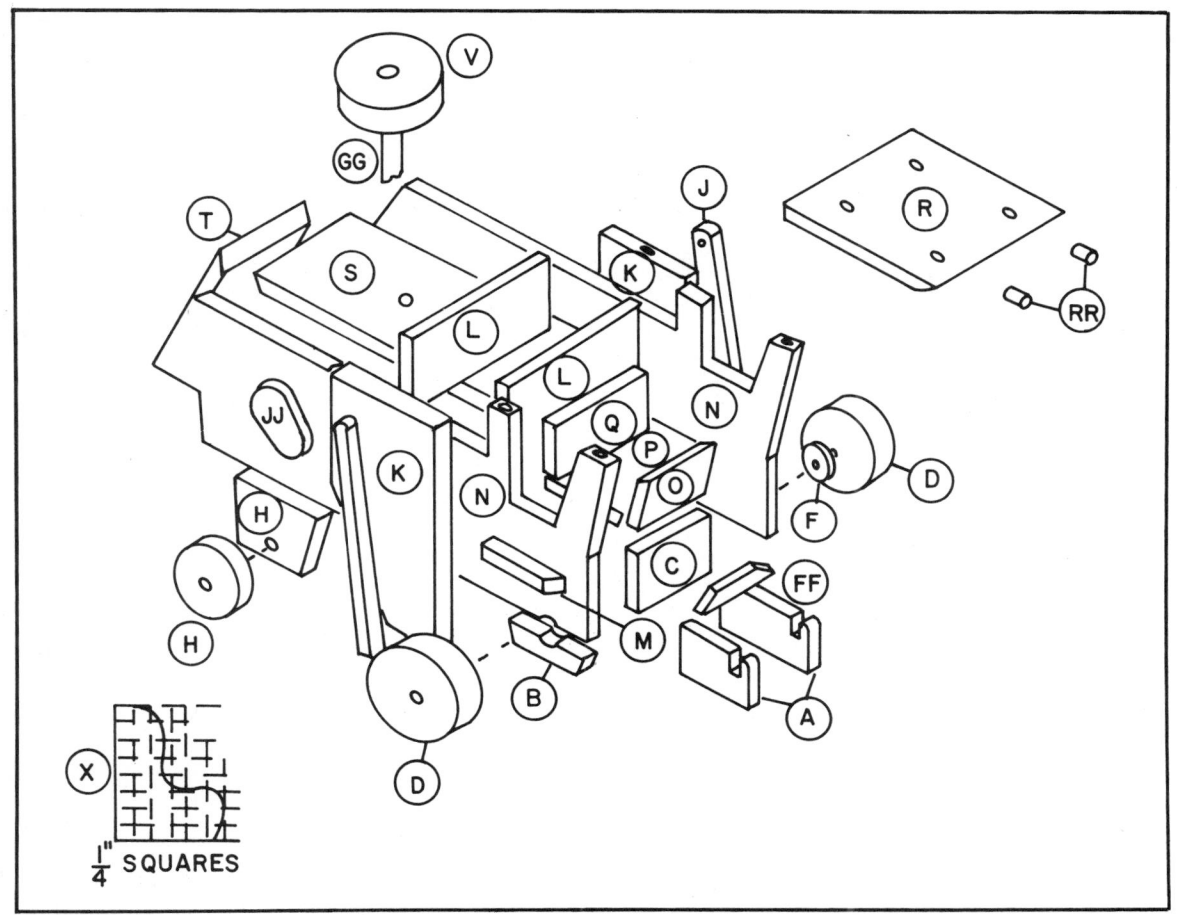

Fig. 10-24. Assembly of the Farm Combine. Courtesy of Sleepy's Toys.

size. One end is cut to a 45-degree angle, the other to a 60-degree angle. See Fig. 10-22.

☐ Cut the combine bottom to size. One end is cut to a 60-degree angle.

☐ Bore a 17/32- or 9/16-inch hole in the combine top and the bottom and straw rack for the steering post. See Fig. 10-22 and Fig. 10-23.

☐ Bore a 1/4-inch hole in the dash and make a small steering wheel of 3/4-inch dowel 1/4-inch long. Bore a 1/4-inch hole in the center and glue a 1/4-inch dowel 1-inch long into the steering wheel. The other end is glued into the dash.

☐ Lay one side of the cab side flat on its side.

☐ Glue and place the combine front, front and dash, cab floor, cab back, combine top, combine rear, combine bottom and straw rack and combine bottom to the cab side (Fig. 10-24).

☐ Glue the seat to the inside of the cab assembly.

☐ Glue and place the other combine side, inside down on the parts listed in the last step. Make sure all parts are in place, straight, and square. Clamp and let the glue set.

☐ Cut the grain box sides to size (Fig. 10-25). Round over the outside edges.

☐ Cut the grain box front and back to size. Round over the top outside edges.

☐ Glue the grain box sides 1 1/4 inch behind

the cab back and even with the bottom of the combine side straight up and down.

☐ Glue the grain box front and back into place, aligned with the edge of the grain box sides.

☐ Cut the grain elevator parts to size (Fig. 10-25). Bore a 3/8-inch hole 1/2 inch down from the top end and round over both ends.

☐ Glue the grain elevator to the sides of the grain box. The elevator should be centered with the bottom of the sides and even with the bottom of the sides. The top should be 2 inches from the front edge of the sides.

☐ Glue a 3/8-inch diameter dowel 7 1/2 inches long through both grain elevator parts.

☐ Cut the cab sides to size (Fig. 10-26). One end is cut to a 45-degree angle.

☐ Glue the cab sides 3 1/2 inches from the bottom of the combine side and butted against the grain box sides.

☐ Make a pattern for the belt guard (Fig. 10-25). Trace an outline on 3/4-inch stock. Cut out with a band saw or other curve-cutting tool. Sand

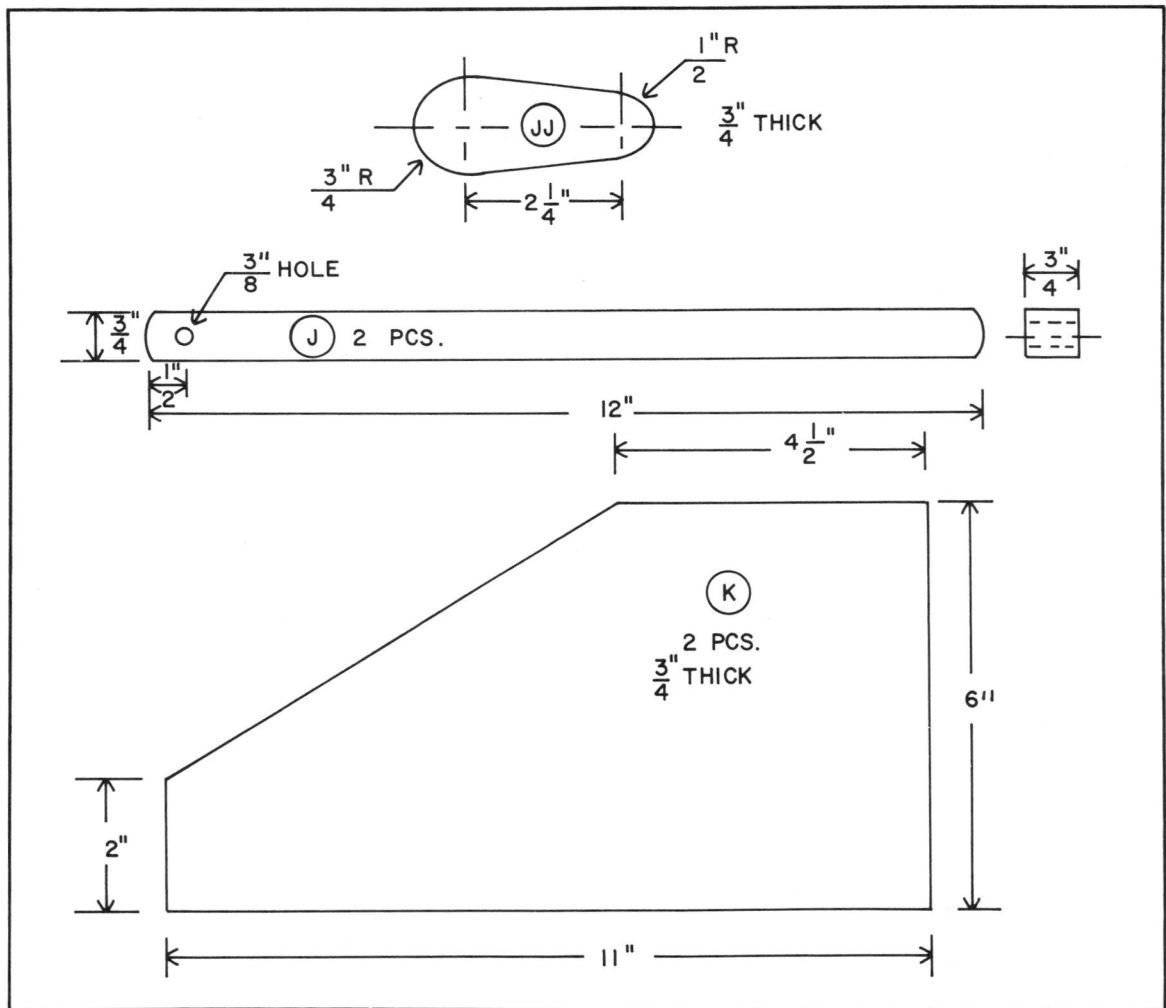

Fig. 10-25. Belt guard, grain elevator, and grain box sides of the Farm Combine are detailed. Courtesy of Sleepy's Toys.

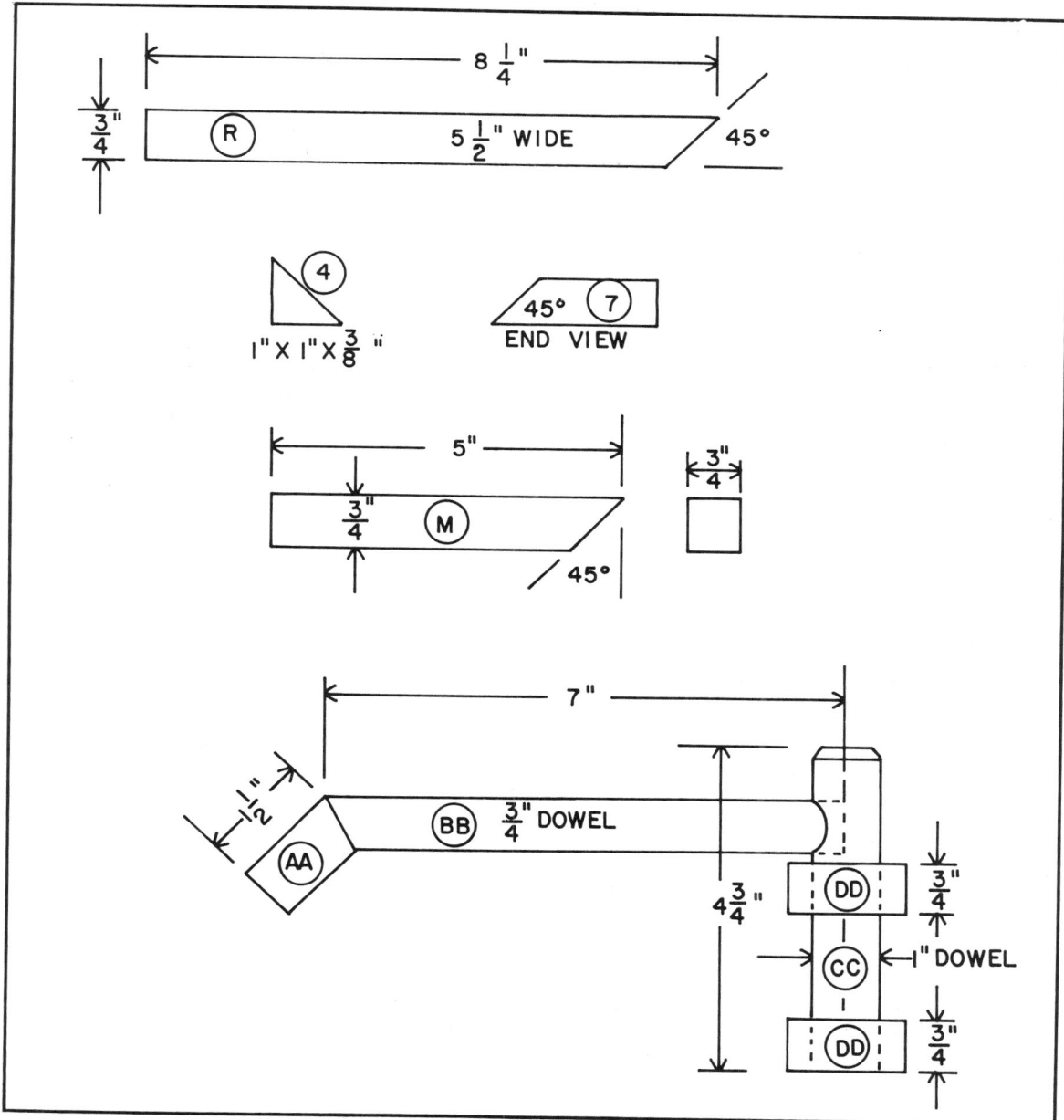

Fig. 10-26. Details of the cab roof, Corn Header side, Bean Header bottom, cab side, and grain auger are shown. Courtesy of Sleepy's Toys.

the edges with a disc sander. Glue to the combine sides to the rear of the grain box sides.

☐ Cut the header platform covers to size (Table 10-5). The ends are cut at a 45-degree angle. Glue the covers to the top of the header platform.

☐ Cut out the cab roof to size (Fig. 10-26).

Round over the roof with a plane so that edges are 1/2-thick and the center is 1-inch thick. Taper the front edge to 45 degrees.

☐ Center and glue the cab roof with the back edge against the grain box front.

☐ Bore 1/4-inch holes through the cab roof and into each of the four cab posts. Glue a 1/4-inch dowel into each.

☐ Bore two 1/2-inch diameter holes 1/4-inch deep into the 45-degree angle portion of the cab roof. Glue 1/2-inch diameter birch dowels 1/2-inch long in these holes for the headlights.

☐ Cut the rear axle supports to size. See Fig. 10-22.

☐ Bore a 17/32- or 9/16-inch hole in each rear axle support centered 3/4 inch from the bottom.

☐ Cut the top rear axle support to size, and drill a 1/2-inch diameter hole in the center. See Fig. 10-23. Taper the two edges of the top rear axle support to match the front and back edges of the rear axle support.

☐ Cut the steering shafts from a 1/2-inch diameter dowel 9 1/2 inches long. See Fig. 10-23.

☐ Cut out the steering wheel from 2 1/2-inch round padauk 3/4-inch thick. Bore a 1/2-inch diameter hole in the center of the steering wheel. Glue the wheel to the steering shaft. See Fig. 10-23.

☐ Place the rear axle assembly below the 17/32- or 9/16-inch hole in the combine bottom and straw rack and the combine top.

☐ Place the steering shaft down through the hole in the combine bottom and straw rack and the combine top.

☐ Place a 1/2-inch washer on the shaft and glue into the hole in the top part rear axle support.

☐ Glue the wheels to the front and rear axles using a 1/2-inch washer between the wheel and the axle supports. The rear wheels are made in the same fashion as the front wheels.

☐ Cut the grain auger (AA) from 3/4-inch diameter dowel 1 1/2 inches long. Cut one end to 30 degrees.

☐ Cut the grain auger (BB) from 3/4-inch diameter dowel 7 inches long. Cut one end at 30 degrees.

☐ Cut the grain auger swivel from 1-inch diameter dowel 4 3/4 inches long.

☐ Glue the two grain auger parts (AA and BB) together.

☐ Bore a 3/4-inch hole halfway through the auger swivel centered 3 5/8 inches from one end.

☐ Glue the end of grain auger (BB) into the hole bored in the auger swivel.

☐ Round off the top edge of the grain auger swivel.

☐ Cut two grain auger mounts to size (Fig. 10-26).

☐ Bore a 1 1/16-inch hole in the center of each of the grain auger mounts.

☐ Glue the grain auger mounts in the left rear corner of the grain box; one in the bottom of the grain box, and the other 3/4 inch from the top of the box.

Corn Header Assembly

☐ Cut the corn header bottom to size. See Fig. 10-27. It has greater strength if it is cut across the grain of a 1-foot wide board.

☐ Layout the snoots and cut the snoots with a band saw. See Fig. 10-27.

☐ Round the top edges of the snoots.

☐ Cut the corn header back.

☐ Round the top outer edges to a 1-inch radius and round the forward edge slightly.

☐ Cut the header attachment sides to size. See Fig. 10-28.

☐ Bore the 3/8-inch holes and place a 3/8-inch diameter dowel 4 1/2 inches long through these holes.

☐ Glue these parts 3 1/8 inches apart, centered on the back of the corn header back even with the bottom.

☐ Cut and glue the header attachment cover to the top of the header attachment sides.

☐ Cut and glue the corn header side in place.

Bean Header Assembly

☐ Cut the bean header bottom with the grain of the wood, and taper the front edge at 45 degrees. See Fig. 10-26 and 10-28.

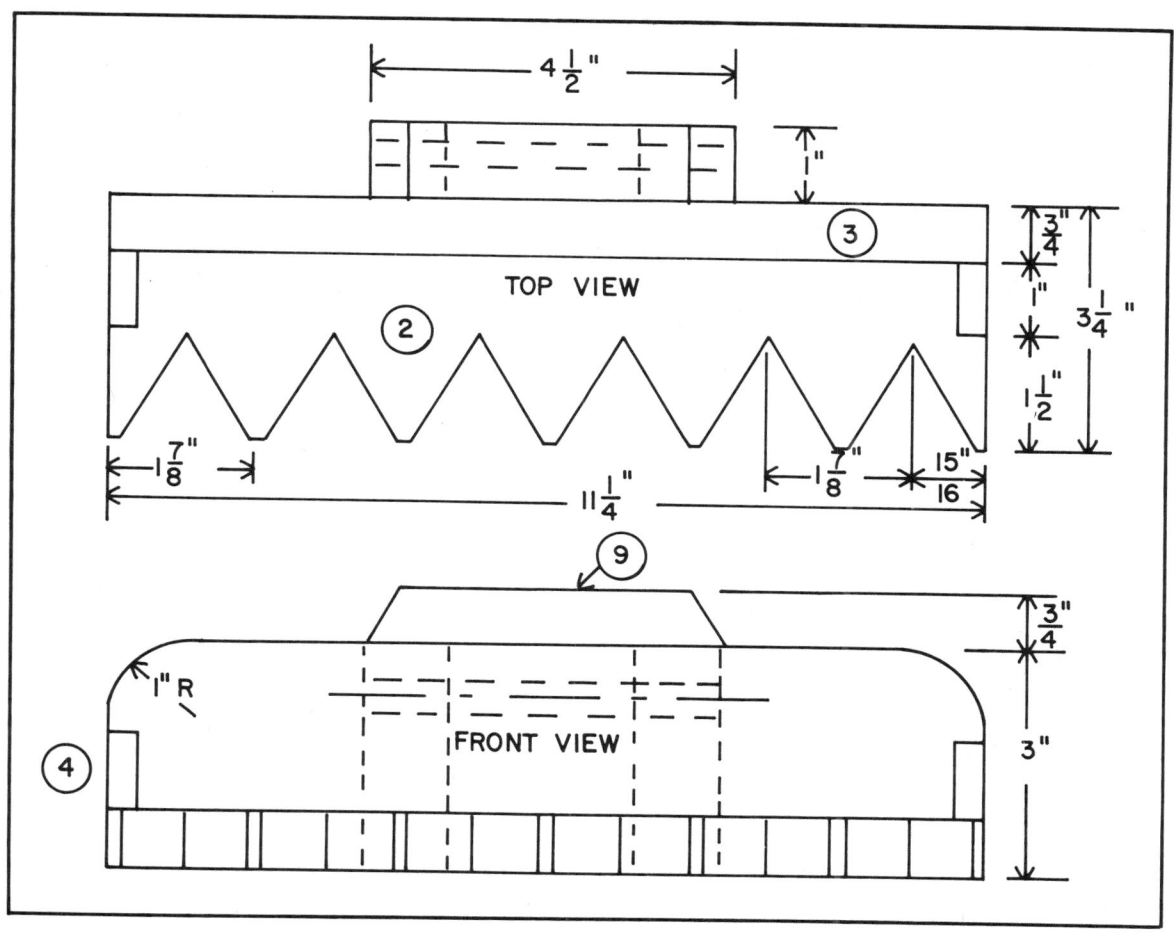

Fig. 10-27. Corn Header details for the Farm Combine. Courtesy of Sleepy's Toys.

☐ Cut the bean header back to size. See Fig. 10-28.

☐ Cut the bean header sides to size (Fig. 10-28). Bore a 3/8-inch diameter hole and taper the front edge to 45 degrees.

☐ Cut four pieces for the reel (Fig. 10-28).

☐ Glue the four blades to a 3/8-inch diameter dowel 13 1/2 inches long.

☐ Place the end of the reel through the bean header sides.

☐ Glue the sides, back, bottom, and reel together.

☐ Cut and glue the header attachment cover and the header to back of the bean header back in the same manner as in the corn header.

Finishing

☐ Finish the combine and headers with three or four coats of clear spray Deft. After the Deft is dry, rub with #0000 steel wool, apply furniture wax, and polish. See Figs. 10-29 through 10-32 for the finished project.

BIG HAULER TRUCK

Although the Big Hauler Truck and Trailer are companion projects, they are treated here as separate projects (Figs. 10-33 and 10-34). The design is another of Uncle Andy's Scrapwood Toys, which are noted for their sturdiness and simplicity.

Although there are a large number of parts,

Table 10-6. The Big Hauler Truck Uses the Materials Given.

NUMBER OF PIECES	CODE	PART	SIZE	MATERIAL
1	(A)	body	1 3/8"x 3 3/8"x 1/2"	white pine
1	(B)	cab	1 1/2"x3 1/4"x4"	white pine
1	(C)	cab roof	1/2"x2 1/4"x5 1/2"	black walnut
1	(D)	platform	1/2"x5 1/2"x8 1/2"	white pine
2	(E)	side racks	1/2"x1 1/2"x7 3/4"	white pine
1	(F)	rear rack	1/2"x1 1/2"x4"	white pine
1	(G)	platform safety wall	1/2"x4"x 5 1/2"	white pine
2	(H)	fenders	1 1/2"x1 1/2"x3 1/2"	white pine
6	(I)	wheels	3/4"x2 3/8"diam.	white pine
2	(J)	washer wheels	3/4"x 1 1/4"diam.	white pine
2	(K)	headlights	5/8" length	3/4" birch dowel
2	(L)	take-off pulleys	1/2" length	3/4" birch dowel
1		front axle	4" length	1/4" birch dowel
1		rear axle	4 1/2" length	1/4" birch dowel
6		platform dowels	1 1/4"length	1/4" birch dowel
2		headlight dowels	3/4"length	1/4"birch dowel
2		take-off pulley dowels	1" length	1/4" birch dowel

these projects are easy to construct and assemble. Believe it or not, the most tiring part of these projects is the boring of 84 holes in the 14 wheels. Almost any straight-grained wood is suitable for the truck and trailer.

Preparation

☐ Make a pattern for the body. Be sure to enlarge the patterns in Figs. 10-35 and 10-36 to 1-inch squares.

☐ Trace or transfer outline to 1 3/8-inch stock (Table 10-6).

☐ Saw the outline with a band saw or saber saw.

☐ Sand the edges with a drum sander.

☐ Mark and bore the axle holes 17/64 inch in diameter.

☐ Mark and bore the holes for the headlight dowels and power take-off pulleys 1/4 inch in diameter.

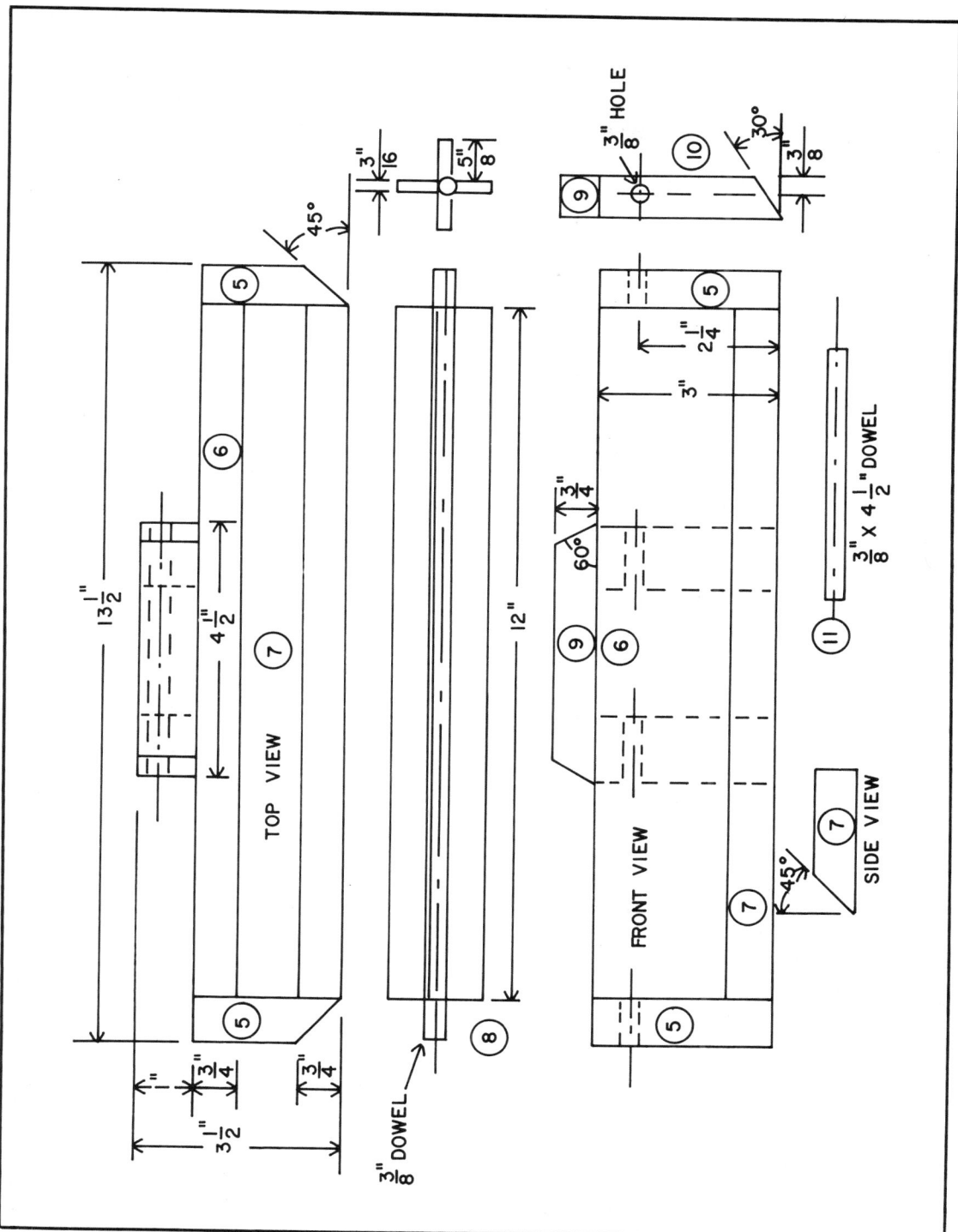

Fig. 10-28. Bean Header details for the Farm Combine. Courtesy of Sleepy's Toys.

Fig. 10-29. The completed Farm Combine, without header, is shown. Courtesy of Sleepy's Toys.

Assembly

☐ Cut the cab stock to rough size. Enlarge the pattern in Fig. 10-36 to 1-inch squares.

☐ Mark the semicircular cut 1 5/8 inches in diameter on the side of the cab stock.

☐ Cut the semicircular cut with the band saw or saber saw. Note: This cut must be made before the sides of the cab are tapered.

☐ Cut the tapered sides of the cab on the circular saw.

☐ Cut the top of the cab at the proper angle.

☐ Sand the cab with medium grit sandpaper.

☐ Cut the cab roof to size (Fig. 10-35). Be sure to enlarge the pattern.

☐ Glue the cab roof to the top of the cab.

☐ Cut the platform to size and sand. Be sure to enlarge the pattern in Fig. 10-35.

☐ Lay out and bore the six 1/4-inch diameter platform dowel holes.

☐ Cut the two side racks and the rear rack at the same time, since they are the same width and thickness (Figs. 10-35 and 10-36).

☐ Cut the platform safety wall to size and sand (Fig. 10-36).

☐ Make a pattern for the fenders (Fig. 10-36).

☐ Trace or transfer the outline to 1 1/2-inch stock.

☐ Cut the fenders with a band or saber saw.

☐ Sand with a drum sander.

☐ Glue the fenders to the sides of the body and clamp (Fig. 10-37).

☐ Glue the platform safety wall to the platform (Fig. 10-37).

☐ Bore dowel holes in the side racks and rear rack.

☐ Cut the six platform dowels to length.

☐ Insert the platform dowels into the side racks and end rack and then insert dowels into the platform.

☐ Glue the cab, cab roof, platform, platform safety wall, and racks to the body (Fig. 10-37).

☐ Cut the stock for the headlights and power take-off pulleys.

☐ Bore holes to receive the headlight and take-off pulley dowels.

☐ Cut dowels for the headlights and take-off pulleys.

☐ Glue the dowels into the headlights and take-off pulleys. Place glue on the ends of the dowels and insert them into the body.

Fig. 10-30. Rear view of the Farm Combine, with Bean Header. Courtesy of Sleepy's Toys.

Fig. 10-31. The Farm Combine, Grain Wagon, and Bean Header are all attachable. Courtesy of Sleepy's Toys.

☐ Cut the 14 wheels for both truck and trailer at the same time with a hole saw.

☐ Cut the 2 washer wheels with a hole saw.

☐ Sand the wheels and washer wheels by placing them on a lathe faceplate mandrel. Sand the edge while the wheels are turning.

☐ Make a wheel pattern from heavy paper or cardboard. In addition to the outside diameter of the wheel, mark a circle with a compass 1 1/4 inches in diameter. Divide the circle into six equal 60-degree parts. Where these lines cross the 1 1/4-inch circle,

prick a small hole with a scratch awl. Apply the wheel pattern to all the wheels and prick the center of the holes to be bored.

☐ Bore 3/8-inch holes in the 14 wheels.

☐ Cut the axle rods and attach the wheels to the completed assembly.

Finishing

☐ Sand the entire project with fine sandpaper.

☐ Apply three or four coats of clear spray Deft.

Fig. 10-32. The Farm Tractor can also be attached to the Grain Wagon and Combine. Courtesy of Sleepy's Toys.

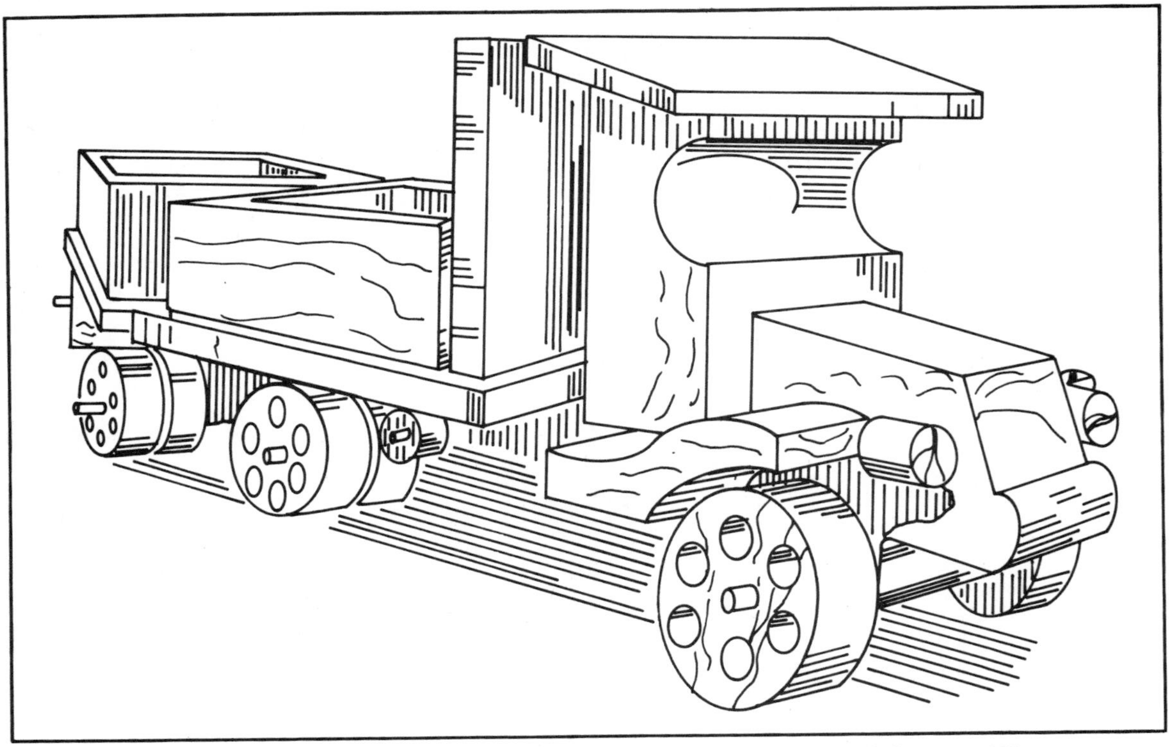

Fig. 10-33. Perspective view of the Big Hauler Truck and Trailer. Courtesy of Uncle Andy's Scrapwood Toys.

Fig. 10-34. The Big Hauler Truck and Trailer are attachable. Courtesy of Uncle Andy's Scrapwood Toys.

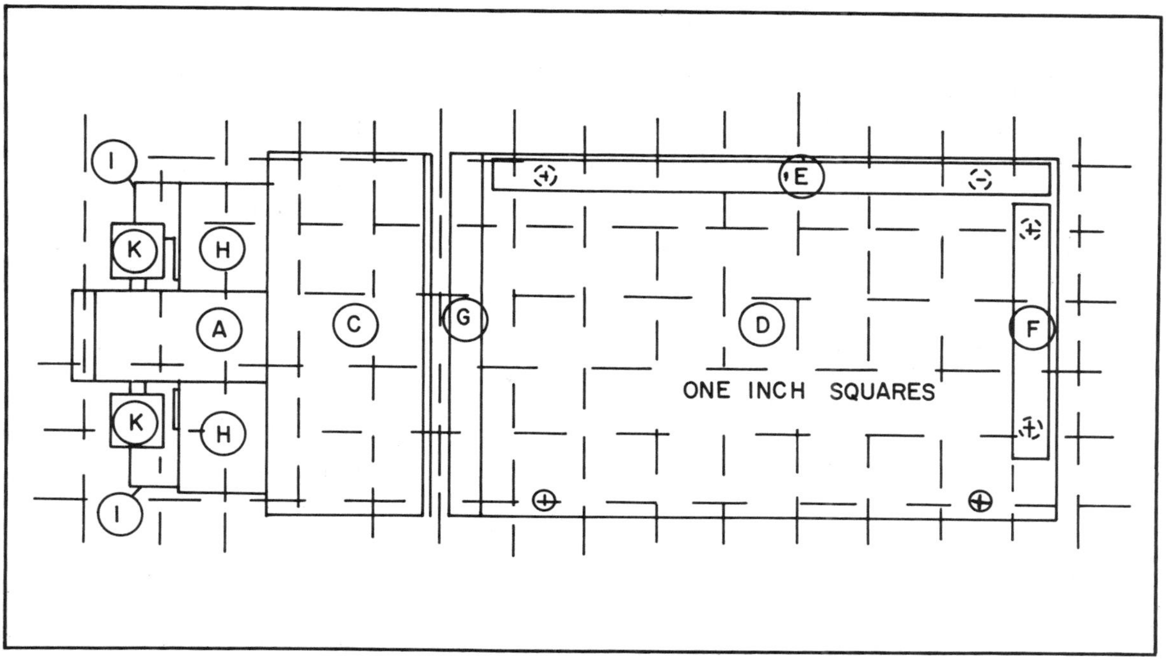

Fig. 10-35. Top view of the Big Hauler Truck. Courtesy of Uncle Andy's Scrapwood Toys.

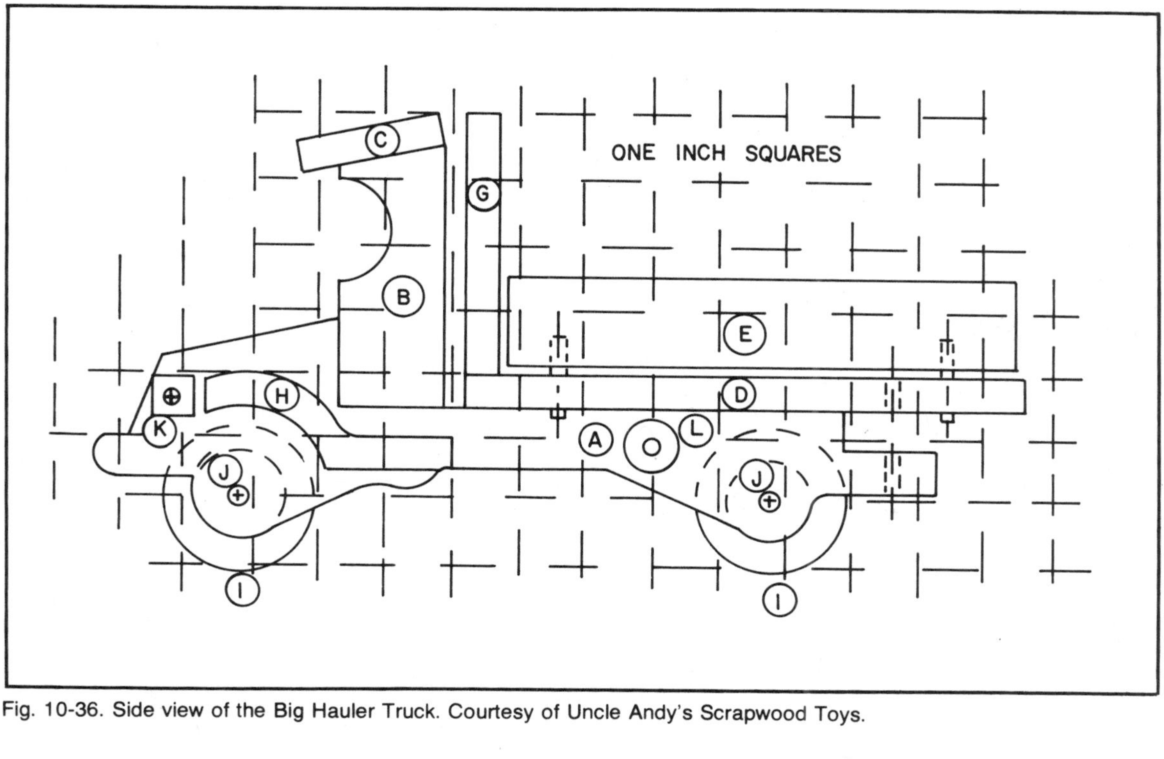

Fig. 10-36. Side view of the Big Hauler Truck. Courtesy of Uncle Andy's Scrapwood Toys.

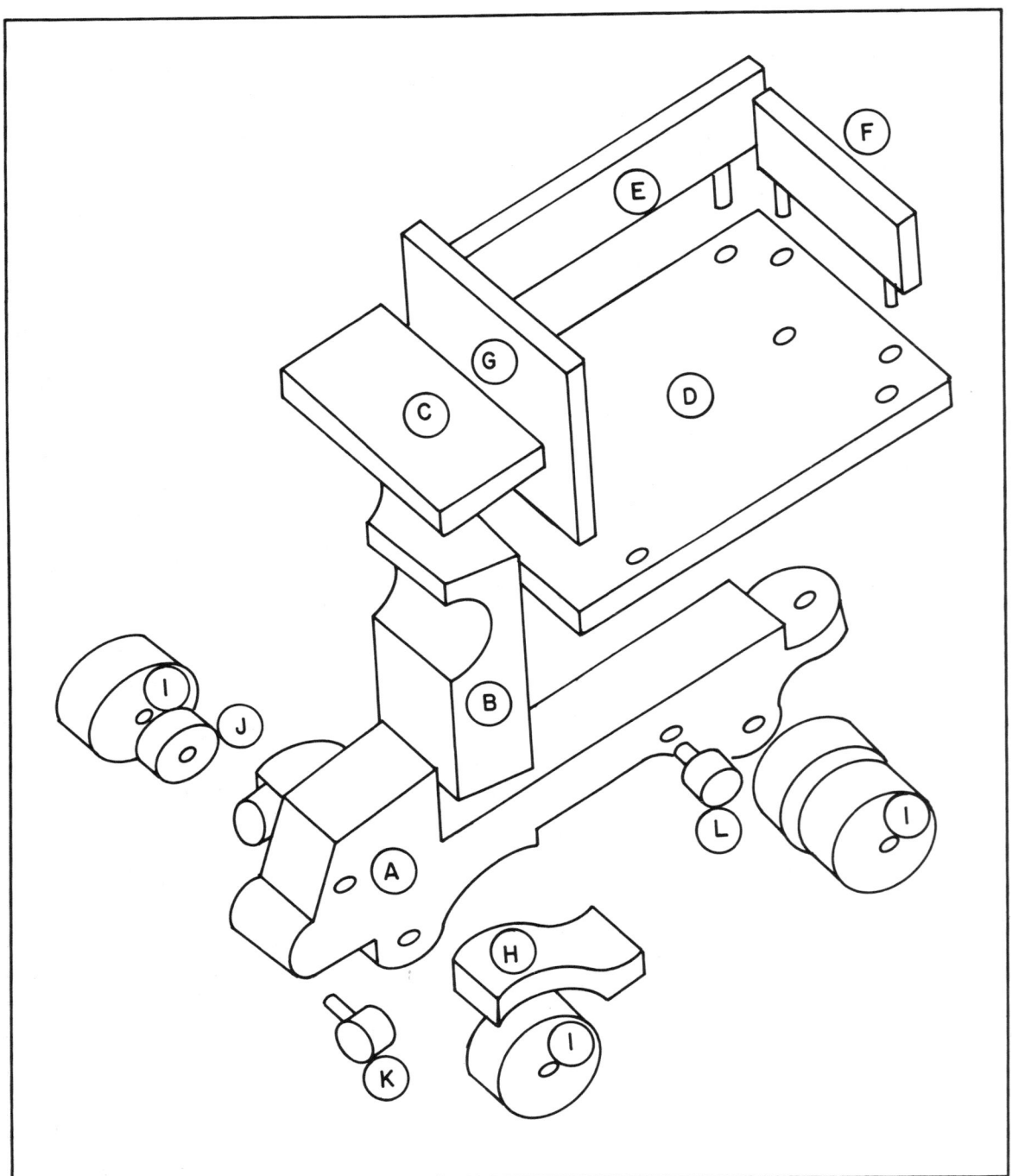

Fig. 10-37. Assembly of the Big Hauler Truck. Courtesy of Uncle Andy's Scrapwood Toys.

Fig. 10-38. Completed Big Hauler Truck. Courtesy of Uncle Andy's Scrapwood Toys.

Table 10-7. The Big Hauler Trailer Materials Are Listed.

NUMBER OF PIECES	CODE	PART	SIZE	MATERIAL
1	(M)	platform	1/2"x5 1/2"x8 3/4"	white pine
1	(N)	rear axle housing	1 3/4"x2"x3"	white pine
1	(O)	front axle housing	1 3/8"x 2"x 4 3/8"	white pine
2	(P)	axles	5" length	1/4" birch dowel
1	(Q)	front axle coupling	1 1/4" length	1/4" birch dowel
1	(R)	pivot pin	1 1/2" length	1/4" birch dowel
			1/2" length	3/4" birch dowel
2	(E E)	side racks	1/2"x 1 1/2"x 7"	white pine
2	(F)	end racks	1/2 x 1 1/2"x4"	white pine
8		platform dowels	1 1/4" length	1/4" birch dowel

213

☐ Rub the finish with #0000 steel wool when the Deft is dry.

☐ Apply furniture wax and polish. See Fig. 10-38 for the finished project.

BIG HAULER TRAILER

The Big Hauler Trailer attaches to the Big Hauler Truck and will give children more fun. Remember that the wheels for the trailer were made when the truck wheels were made.

Preparation

☐ Make a pattern for front end of the platform. Be sure to enlarge the pattern in Fig. 10-39 to 1-inch squares.

☐ Transfer the pattern to 1/2-inch stock (Table 10-7).

☐ Cut the front end of the platform with the band saw or saber saw and the other three sides with the circular saw. Sand the edges.

☐ Bore the eight 1/4-inch holes for the platform dowels.

☐ Bore the front axle coupling hole 17/64 inch in diameter.

☐ Cut the platform dowels.

☐ Cut the side racks and the end racks. Be sure to enlarge the patterns in Figs. 10-39 and 10-40 to 1-inch squares.

☐ Bore 1/4-inch holes in the side and end racks to receive the platform dowels.

☐ Make a pattern for the rear axle housing and transfer the outline to 1 3/8-inch stock. Be sure to enlarge the pattern in Fig. 10-40 to 1-inch squares.

☐ Cut the rear axle housing with a band saw or saber saw.

☐ Sand the edges on a disc sander.

☐ Bore a 17/64-inch axle hole in the rear axle housing.

☐ Make an enlarged pattern for the front axle housing and transfer the outline to 1 3/8-inch stock (Fig. 10-40).

☐ Cut the front axle housing with a band saw or saber saw.

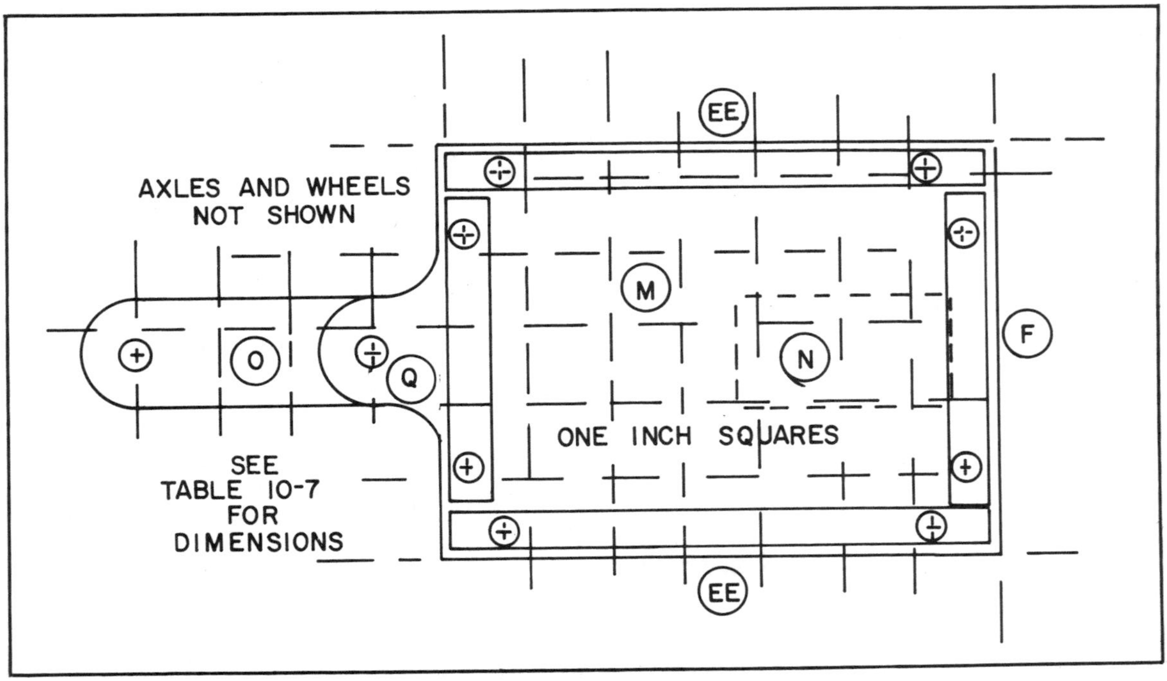

Fig. 10-39. Top view of the Big Hauler Trailer. Courtesy of Uncle Andy's Scrapwood Toys.

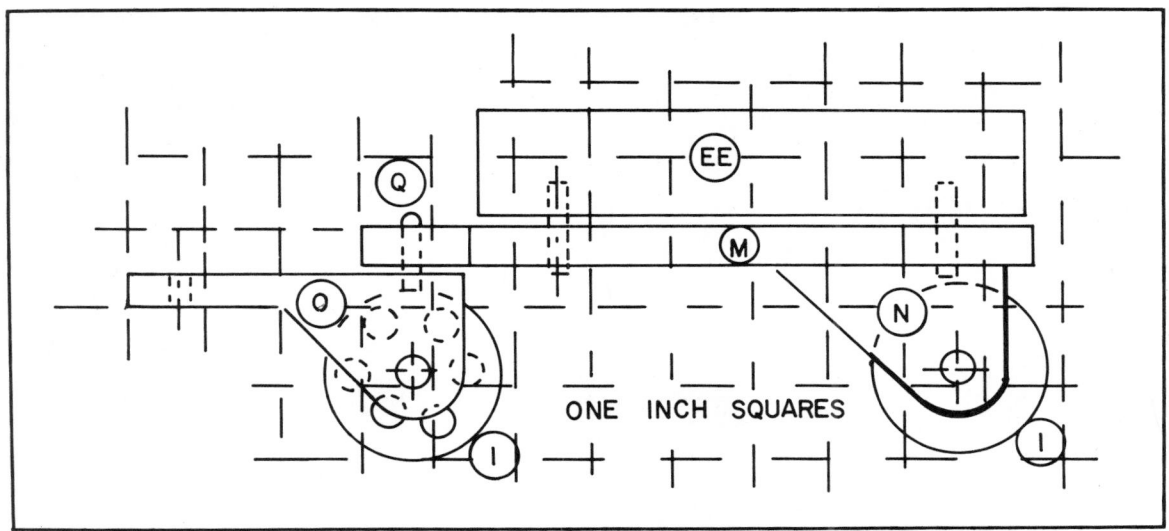

EE
Q
M
O
N
ONE INCH SQUARES
I
I
Fig. 10-40. Side view of the Big Hauler Trailer. Courtesy of Uncle Andy's Scrapwood Toys.

R
M
I
Q
N
I
P
I
Fig. 10-41. Assembly of the Big Hauler Trailer. Courtesy of Uncle Andy's Scrapwood Toys.

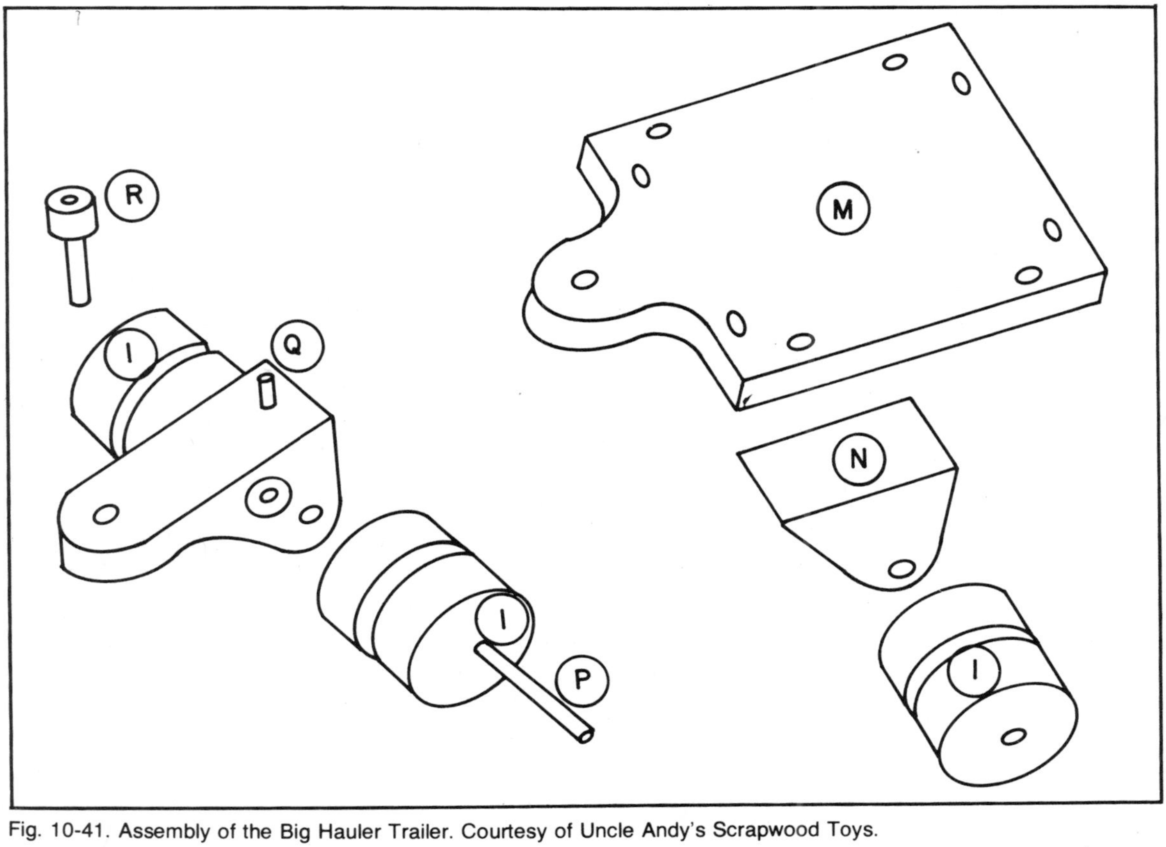

Fig. 10-42. The completed Big Hauler Trailer is shown. Courtesy of Uncle Andy's Scrapwood Toys.

☐ Sand the edges with disc and drum sanders.

☐ Bore a 17/64-inch hole in the front axle housing to receive the pivot pin.

☐ Bore a 1/4-inch hole in the front axle housing to receive the front axle coupling.

Assembly

☐ Cut the front axle coupling from a 1/4-inch diameter dowel and glue in place in the front axle housing.

☐ Cut a 1/4-inch diameter dowel, 1 1/2 inches long and a 3/4-inch diameter dowel 1/2-inch long for the pivot pin. Bore a 1/4-inch hole in the center of the 3/4-inch dowel and glue the 1/4-inch dowel into the hole.

☐ Insert the platform dowels into the side racks, end racks, and platform. Glue the rear axle housing to the underside of the platform (Fig. 10-41).

☐ Cut the axles to length and insert them through the wheels and the front and rear axle housing after a small drop of glue has been placed on the ends of the axles.

Finishing

☐ Sand the entire project with fine sandpaper.

☐ Apply three or four coats of clear spray Deft.

☐ When dry, rub with #0000 steel wool.

☐ Apply furniture wax and polish.

☐ Attach the platform to the front axle housing by placing the hole in the front end of the platform over the front axle coupling to complete the trailer assembly.

☐ Attach the trailer assembly to the big hauler truck by sliding the front end of the front axle housing under the rear end of truck. Line up the pivot pin hole of the front axle housing with the two holes in the truck body and platform and insert the pivot pin. See Fig. 10-42 for the finished project.

11

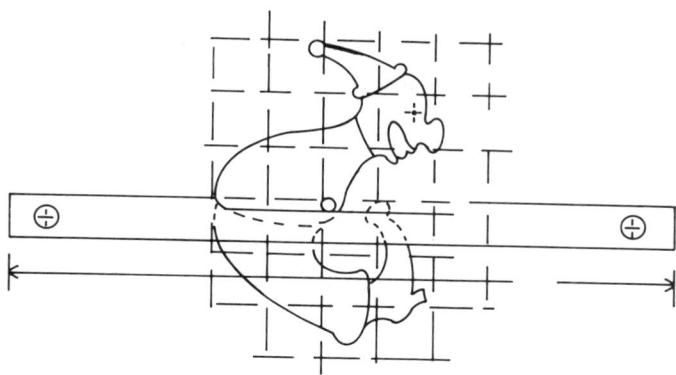

Miscellaneous Toys

A Rattlin' Roller and a Spinning Clown can be made from the step-by-step instructions given in this chapter. Tables of materials and illustrations will also help you in assembly.

RATTLIN' ROLLER

The Rattlin' Roller has a definite appeal to small children. The varied sounds emitted when the roller is rolled at different speeds is an attention getter for both young and old.

I used walnut for the top and bottom (the ends when the roller is rolling) and birch dowels for the rattler rods and support rods.

☐ Turn the bottom and top on a lathe or cut with hole saw.

☐ Cut the small and large rattler rods.

☐ Make indentations with a prick punch 3/8 inch from one end of the three rattler rods.

☐ Drill a 7/16-inch diameter hole through the rods at the indentations.

☐ Chamfer both ends of the three rattler rods.

☐ Cut the support rods to length (Table 11-1).

☐ Mark the holes, equally spaced, in the top and bottom for the support rods, 5/8 inch in from the edges of top and bottom. Drill 3/8-inch holes 3/8-inch deep.

☐ Sand, assemble, and glue the support rods in place, after inserting the support rods through the rattler rods (Fig. 11-1).

☐ Finish with clear spray Deft or polyurethane. See Fig. 11-2 for the finished project.

SPINNING CLOWN

This jolly Spinning Clown, which instantly captures the heart of every youngster, is another Stanley Tool toy, depicted in *Six Toy Patterns No. P-2*.

The clown spins his way down two horizontal bars. The secret of successful performance is to slowly and carefully raise one of the handles. The clown moves down the center portion of the horizontal bars. It is restricted in its movements by recessed portions in the central part of the bars. By raising and lowering each handle alternately the clown will continue spinning indefinitely.

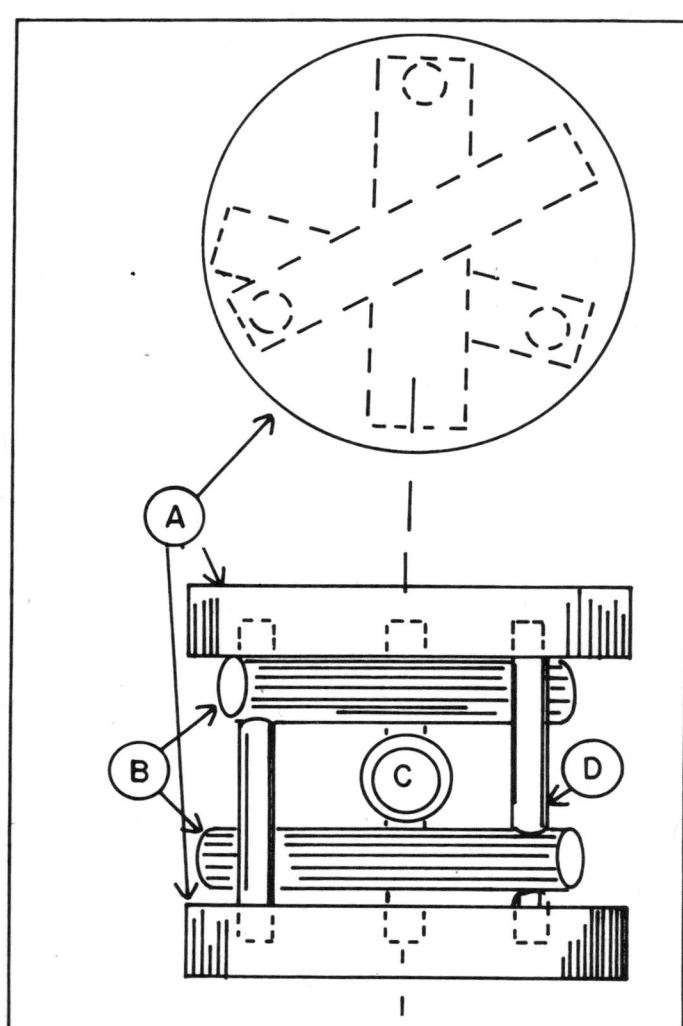

Fig. 11-1. Assembly of the Rattlin' Roller.

Table 11-1. Make the Rattlin' Roller from the Materials Listed.

NUMBER OF PIECES	CODE	PART	SIZE	MATERIAL
2	(A)	bottom and top	4 1/2" diam. x 3/4"	walnut, mahogany, or teak
2	(B)	small rattler rods	3 7/8" length	3/4" birch dowel
1	(C)	large rattler rod	3 7/8" length	1" birch dowel
3	(D)	support rods	3 1/2" length	3/8" birch dowels

Fig. 11-2. The completed Rattlin' Roller.

Assembly

☐ Transfer the outline of the clown to 1/4-inch plywood. Birch plywood is best, but fir plywood may be used as the prominent grain will be covered by enamel or acrylics. I used acrylics. Be sure to enlarge the pattern in Fig. 11-3 to 1-inch squares.

☐ Cut out the clown with a jigsaw or coping saw.

☐ Bore the hole for the clown spindle.

Table 11-2. The Spinning Clown Toy Needs These Materials.

NUMBER OF PIECES	PART	SIZE	MATERIAL
1	clown	1/4"x 4 1/4"x 5 3/4"	plywood
2	horizontal bars	1/2"x 3/4"x 12"	hardwood
2	handles	6" length	3/8" birch dowel
1	clown spindle	4" length	1/4" birch dowel

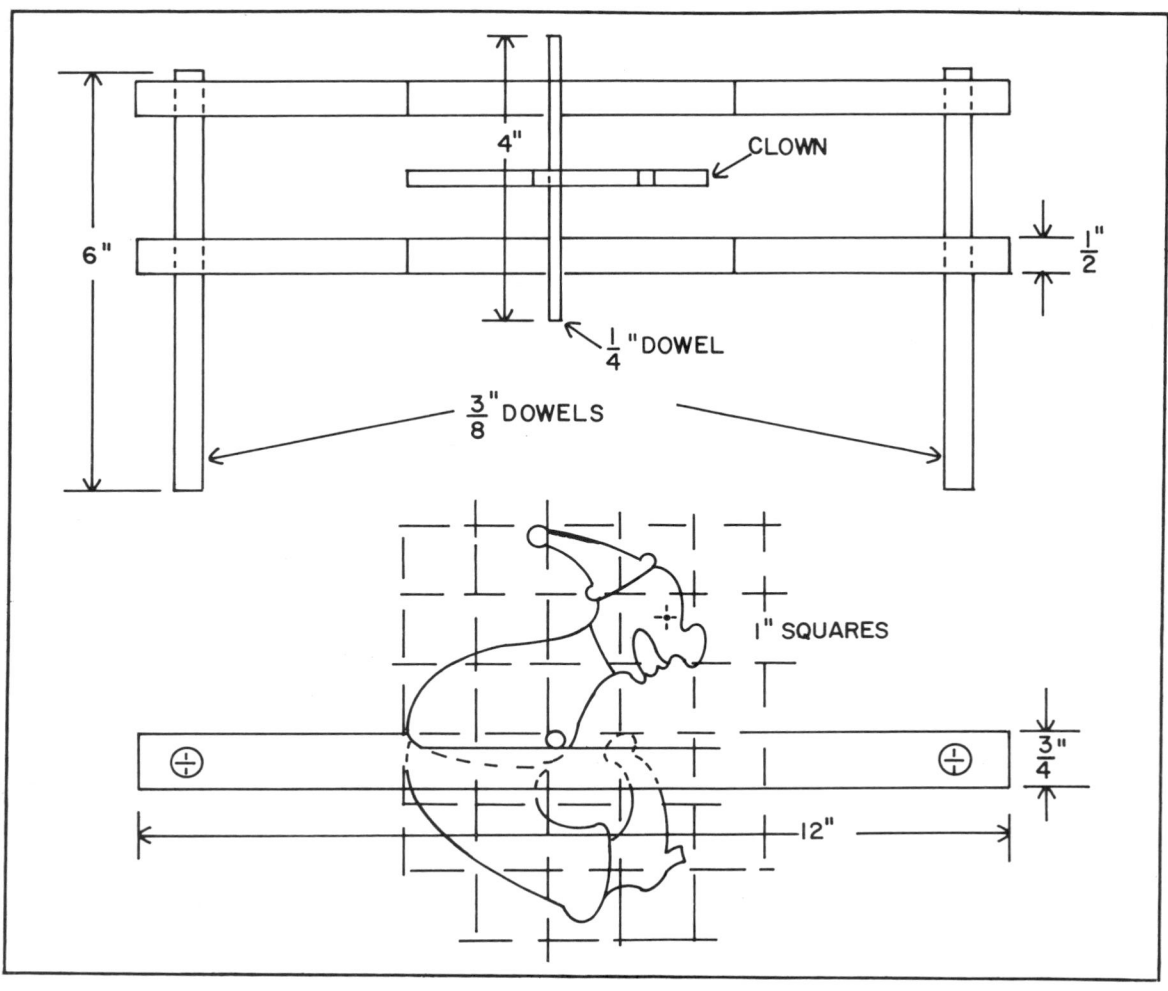

Fig. 11-3. Details of the Spinning Clown.

☐ Balance the clown by inserting a dowel smaller than 1/4 inch through the spindle hole. The clown should be stationary if placed in any position. The heavier side of the clown should be sanded or filed down with a wood rasp until a perfect balance is obtained.

☐ Paint the clown as suggested in Fig. 11-4.

☐ Insert the spindle through the spindle hole. The clown should be centered on the spindle dowel.

☐ Cut the two horizontal bars to size (Table 11-2 and Fig. 11-3).

☐ Saw the recessed portions in the bars about 1/8-inch deep and 4 1/2 inches long in the center of the horizontal bars.

☐ Bore the four 3/8-inch holes, 1/2 inch from the ends of the two bars.

Finishing

☐ Sand the two horizontal bars.

☐ Insert the handle dowels into the holes in the bars. The distance between the bars is 1 3/4 inches.

☐ Spray the horizontal bars and handles with two or three coats of clear Deft.

☐ When dry, rub with #0000 steel wool. Wax and polish. See Fig. 11-5 for the finished project.

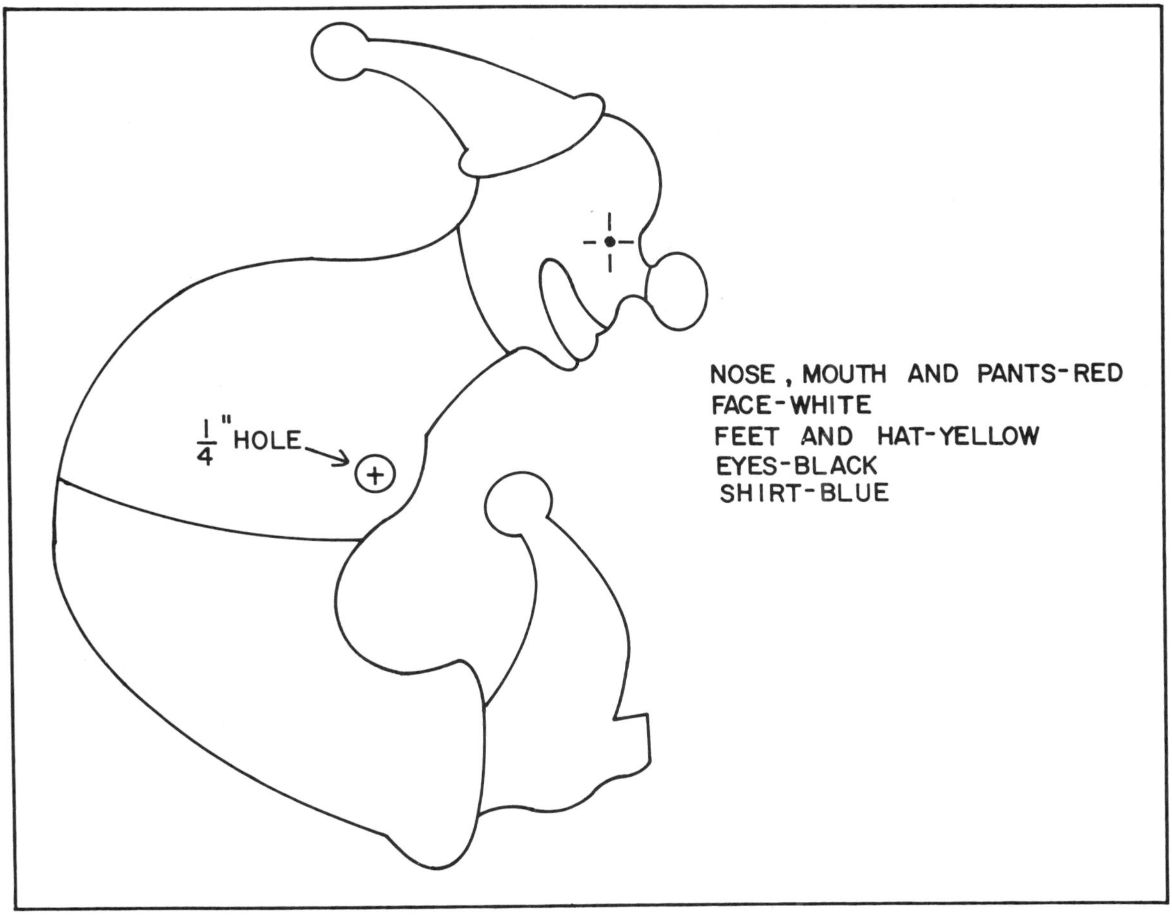

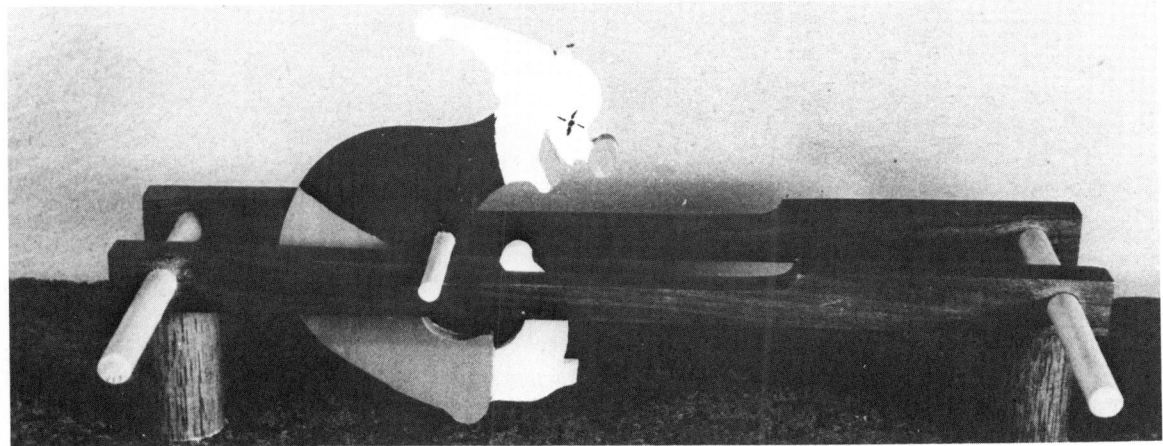

NOSE, MOUTH AND PANTS-RED
FACE-WHITE
FEET AND HAT-YELLOW
EYES-BLACK
SHIRT-BLUE

$\frac{1}{4}$" HOLE →

Fig. 11-4. Pattern for the Spinning Clown body.

Fig. 11-5. The completed Spinning Clown.

Appendix A

Suppliers

Following is a list of suppliers and manufacturers of the products mentioned in this book.

American Handicrafts Co.
Division of Tandy Corp.
Central Office
Fort Worth, TX 76102
Woodburning tool kits

American Machine and Tool Co.
Fourth and Spring Street
Royersford, PA 19468
Power woodworking tools

American Woodcrafters
P.O. Box 919
Piqua, OH 45356
Veneers, hardwoods, carving and turning blocks, hand and power tools, hardware, marquetry supplies, finishing materials, books, and plans

American Wood Working Co.
Montello, WI 53949
Domestic hardwoods and wood parts

Amor Products
P.O. Box 290
Dept. A
Deer Park, NY 11729
Full-size wooden toy plans, toy trucks and trailers, and bulldozers

Atlas Press Co.
2019 N. Pitcher
Kalamazoo, MI 49007
Power and hand tools

Austin Hardwoods, Inc.
2125 Goodrich
Austin, TX 78704
Domestic and imported lumber

Beauty-Wood Industries
339 Lakeshore Road E.
Mississauga, Ontario, Canada
Hardwoods and softwoods

Black and Decker (U.S.) Inc.
701 East Joppa Road
Towson, MD 21204
Tools and holding devices

The Board Store
P.O. Box 205
Bangor, WI 54614
Kiln-dried hardwoods

Brodhead-Garrett
4560 East 71st Street
Cleveland, OH 44105
Woodworking tools, supplies, and lumber to schools, colleges, and universities

Brookside Veneers Ltd.
107 Trumbull Street
Bldg. R-8
Elizabeth, NJ 07206
Exotic hardwood veneers and carving blocks

Brookstone Co.
Vose Farm Road
Peterborough, NH 03458
Hard-to-find tools

Cedar Craft Toys
P.O. Box 22011
Knoxville, TN 37922
Ten wooden toy plans and wooden wheels

Cherry Tree Toys
67131 Mills Road
St. Clairsville, OH 43950
Animated toy plans, hardwood wheels, and toy parts

Chester B. Stern, Inc.
2708 Grant Line Road
New Albany, IN 47150
Foreign and domestic hardwood lumber and veneer

Classic Grain Hardwood Co.
902 E. Hughes Access Road
Tucson, AZ 85706
Hardwoods, wholesale only

Constantine
2050 Eastchester Road
Bronx, NY 10461
Hardwoods, veneers, tools, and books

Craftsman Wood Service Co.
1735 West Cortland Street
Addison, IL 60101
Inlays, veneers, tools, and hardwood

Craft Value Center
Dept. WB-9
P.O. Box 1637
Wayne, NJ 07470
Toy parts

Craftwoods
Div. of O'Shea Lumber Co.
York Road and Beaver Run Lane
Cockeysville, MD 21030
Foreign hardwoods, domestic hardwoods, veneer, and cabinet plywood

The Crane Creek Co.
P.O. Box 5553
Madison, WI 53705
Polyethylene Glycol 1000 wood stabilizer and chemical seasoning agent

Criss-Cross Creations
P.O. Box 324
Wayne, NJ 07470
Wooden toy and craft plans, kits, antique trolley wheels, and parts

D.A. Buckley
R 1
W. Valley, NY 14171
Native American hardwoods

Deft
17451 Von Karman Avenue
Irvine, CA 92714
or
411 East Keystone Avenue
Alliance, OH 44601
Wood finishing materials

223

Design Group
P.O. Box 1052
Dept. B
New York, NY 10034
or
P.O. Box 514
Dept. B
Miller Place, NY 11764
Blueprints for wooden toys and wooden wheels

Dremel
Div. of Emerson Electric Co.
Racine, WI 53406
Small power woodworking tools

Du-er Tools
5448 Edina Ind. Boulevard
Minneapolis, MN 55435
Power woodworking tools

Educational Lumber Co., Inc.
21 Meadow Court
Asheville, NC 28803
Appalachian hardwoods and veneers

F.A.O. Schwarz
Fifth Avenue at 58th Street
New York, NY 10022
Toy retailer

Fox Super Shop, Inc.
6701 W. 110th Street
Bloomington, MN 55438
7-in-1 Super Shop Multi-Purpose Tool

Frog Tool Co. Ltd.
548 North Wells Street
Chicago, IL 60610
*Quality hand woodworking tools and representatives
for Myford Lathe*

General Woodcraft
100 Blinman Street
New London, CT 06320
Hardwood, plywood, and veneers

Green Mountain Cabins (Weird Wood)
P.O. Box 190
Chester, VT 05143
*Hardwood, softwood, boards, slabs, and free-form
cut ovals*

Grofton Ltd.
The Cross Offices
Kingswinford
Brierley Hill
Straffordshire, England
Plastic wheels

Hayes Patterns
6 Willow Street
Dept. W21
Woburn, MA 01801
Wooden toy plans and wooden wheels

Henegan's Wood Shed
7760 Southern Boulevard
West Palm Beach, FL 33411
Lumber

Homecraft Veneer
901 West Way
Latrobe, PA 15650
Veneer

House of Hardwoods
610 Freeman Street
Orange, NJ 07050
*Hardwood, plywood, veneers, carving blocks,
and burls*

Interstate Hardwood Co., Inc.
850 Flora Street
Elizabeth, NJ 07201
Hardwoods

J. Lewman, Toymaker
2918 Campbell
Kansas City, MO 64109
Full-size wooden toy patterns

L.L. Enterprizes
P.O. Box 35203 W.
Phoenix, AZ 85069
Wooden toys, novelties, and children's and outdoor furniture

Love-Built Toys and Crafts
2907 Lake Forest Road
P.O. Box 5459
Tahoe City, CA 95730
Toy patterns, plans, wheels, people, toymaking supplies, and books

Makin' Things
The Family Workshop
P.O. Box 52000
Dept. 48106
Tulsa, OK 74152
Wooden toys, parts, and people

Master Craft Plans
P.O. Box 631
Park Ridge, IL 60068
Wooden toys, jigsaw projects, garden and lawn projects, bird houses, and supplies

Maurice L. Condon Co., Inc.
248 Ferris Avenue
White Plains, NY 10603
Domestic and foreign hardwoods and softwoods

Mayco Sales
P.O. Box 2931
Mesa, AZ 85204
700 furniture, toys, and novelty plans

Rockwell International
400 N. Lexington Avenue
Pittsburgh, PA 15208
Power woodworking tools

The Sawmill
P.O. Box 329
Nazareth, PA 18064
Exotic and precious woods

Sears Roebuck and Co.
Dept. 141
925 S. Homan Avenue
Chicago, IL 60607
Special woodworking tools and supplies catalog

Shopsmith Inc.
750 Center Drive
Vandalia, OH 45377
Five major power tools packaged into one

Sleepy's Toys
1413 Third Avenue
Spencer, IA 51301
Plans for wooden toy trucks, trailers, tractors, tankers, and farm wagons

Small World Toys
1009 Country Hills Road
Santa Maria, CA 93454
Wooden toy plans, wheels, axle stock, reels, turnings, and balls

Sprunger Corp.
P.O. Box 1621
Elkhart, IN 46515
Power woodworking tools

Stanley Tools
P.O. Box 1800
New Britain, CT 06050
12 toy patterns

Toy Designs
Dept. W181
P.O. Box 441
Newton, IA 50208
Wooden toy patterns and kits, people, and parts

Toys by Leroy
24 Cedar Drive
Fairview Heights, IL 62208
Wooden toys and wooden wheels

Uncle Andy's Scrapwood Toys
P.O. Box 574
Franklin, MI 48025
Wooden toy patterns and plans

Unicorn Universal Woods, Ltd.
137 John Street
Toronto, Canada M5V2E4 363 1161
Foreign and domestic hardwoods, softwoods,
and veneer

Watco-Dennis Corp.
Michigan Avenue and 22nd Street
Santa Monica, CA 90404
Danish oil wood finish

Weekend Enterprises
12342 La Barca
San Antonio, TX 78233
Full-size drawings of wooden toy vehicles
from scrapwood

Weird Wood
P.O. Box 190
Chester, VT 05143
Hardwoods and softwoods in boards, slabs, and
free-form cut ovals

Willard Bros. Woodcutters
300 Basin Road
Trenton, NJ 08619
Wood flitches, slabs, mantle clocks, carving boards,
and dimension and unusual wood

Williams and Hussey Machine Corp.
Milford, NH 03055
Combination molder, planer, and edger

Woodcraft Supply Co.
313 Montvale Ave.
Woburn, MA 01801
Wooden toy plans and plastic/rubber wheels

The Wooden Toy
Attn. Harvey Sneidenan
Route 44
Canton, CT 06019

Wood Shed
1807 Elmwood Ave.
Buffalo, NY 14207
Veneers and hardwoods

Woodshop Specialties
P.O. Box 1013
East Middlebury, VT 05740
Woodworking machines and accessories

Woodstream Hardwoods
P.O. Box 11471
Knoxville, TN 37919
Exotic and domestic hardwoods

The Woodworkers Store
21801 Industrial Boulevard
Rogers, MN 55374
3,000 woodworking items

Woodworker's Supply, Inc.
P.O. Box 14117
5604 Alameda, N.E.
Albuquerque, NM 87113
Woodworking tools

Woodworker's Tool Works
222-224 So. Jefferson Street
Chicago, IL 60606
Woodworking tools

Woodworks
P.O. Box 79238
Saginaw, TX 76179
Wooden toy parts, people, and supplies

Wood World
9006 Waukegan Road
Morton Grove, IL 60053
Foreign and domestic hardwood

Zimmerman, Russ
RFD #3
P.O. Box 57A
Putney, VT 05346
Myford Woodturning Lathe

Appendix B

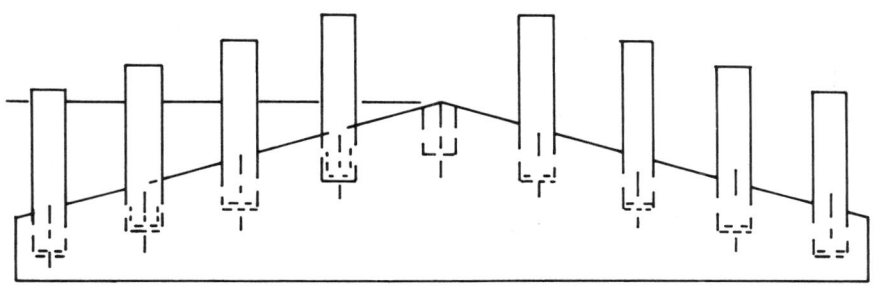

Solution

One Solution to the Up the Hill—Down the Hill Game follows.

- ☐ Number the holes from one to nine. These numbers also apply to the pegs, except there is no number five peg at the start of the game.
- ☐ Move peg 4 to 5 hole.
- ☐ Move peg 6 to 4 hole.
- ☐ Move peg 7 to 6 hole.
- ☐ Move peg 5 to 7 hole.
- ☐ Move peg 3 to 5 hole.
- ☐ Move peg 2 to 3 hole.
- ☐ Move peg 4 to 2 hole.
- ☐ Move peg 6 to 4 hole.
- ☐ Move peg 8 to 6 hole.
- ☐ Move peg 9 to 8 hole.
- ☐ Move peg 7 to 9 hole.
- ☐ Move peg 5 to 7 hole.
- ☐ Move peg 3 to 5 hole.
- ☐ Move peg 1 to 3 hole.
- ☐ Move peg 2 to 1 hole.
- ☐ Move peg 4 to 2 hole.
- ☐ Move peg 6 to 4 hole.
- ☐ Move peg 8 to 6 hole.
- ☐ Move peg 7 to 8 hole.
- ☐ Move peg 5 to 7 hole.
- ☐ Move peg 3 to 5 hole.
- ☐ Move peg 4 to 3 hole.
- ☐ Move peg 6 to 4 hole.
- ☐ Move peg 5 to 6 hole.

Bibliography

Baldwin, Ed. *Makin' Things for Kids*. Boston: Dorison House Pubs., Inc., 1980.

Engler, Nick, ed. Hands On! *The Homeshop Magazine*.

Gilmore, Horace H. *Model Rockets for Beginners*. New York: Harper & Row Pubs., Inc., 1961.

Hayward, Charles H. *Making Toys in Wood*. New York: Sterling Publishing Co., Inc., 1980.

Maginley, C.J. *Toys You Can Build*. New York: Dutton, E. P., 1975.

Mathias, Bob. *Simple Wooden Toy Making*. New York: Hamlyn/American, 1976.

Parker, Xenia L., ed. *Wooden Toys*. New York: Dutton, E. P., 1978.

Ruffner, Robert. Toy Horses and Wagon. *Fine Woodworking*. Nov/Dec 1980, 61.

Ryan, Hugh M. & Ryan, Judith. *101 Quality Wooden Toys You Can Make*. Pennsylvania: TAB Books Inc., 1979

Schnacke, Dick. *American Folk Toys: How to Make Them*. New York: Penguin Books, Inc., 1974.

Schutz, Walter E. *Wooden Toys and Games You Can Make Yourself*. New York: MacMillan Publishing Co., Inc., 1975.

Smith, Mike. *Simple Wooden Toy Designs*. Connecticut: Merrimack Publishing Co., 1975.

Studley, Vance. *The Woodworker's Book of Wooden Toys: How to Make Toys that Whirr, Bob, and Make Musical Sounds*. New York: Van Nostrand Reinhold, 1980.

Swan, Sara K. *Home-Made Baby Toys*. Boston: Houghton Mifflin Co., 1977.

Tangerman, E. J. *Carving Wooden Animals*. New York: Sterling Publishing Co., Inc., 1979.

Zechlin, Katharina. *Making Games in Wood*. New York: Sterling Publishing Co., Inc., 1981.

Index